Occupational Projections and Training Data

2008–09 Edition

U.S. Department of Labor
Elaine L. Chao, Secretary

Bureau of Labor Statistics
Keith Hall, Commissioner

February 2008

Bulletin 2702

Preface

This statistical and research supplement to the 2008–09 Occupational Outlook Handbook (OOH) presents detailed, comprehensive statistics used in preparing the Handbook. In discussing how the data are prepared and other topics, this supplement offers information that is valuable to training officials, education planners, vocational and employment counselors, jobseekers, and others interested in occupational information. This edition of the supplement is the 19th in a series dating back to 1971 and is available on the Internet from www.bls.gov/emp/optd/home.htm.

Chapter I provides an update on the two educational and training classification systems used by the Office of Occupational Statistics and Employment Projections. The first system designates the category that best describes the most significant source of postsecondary education or training for each detailed occupation. The second assigns an education cluster to each occupation, based on the educational attainment distribution of 25– to 44–year-olds as captured by data drawn from the American Community Survey (ACS). Updated results from the two systems are compared and discussed.

Chapter II discusses the structure of the 2006–16 National Employment Matrix–on which the 2006–16 employment projections are based. This chapter also includes the National Employment Matrix occupational and industry directories.

Chapter III presents detailed information about all occupations in the National Employment Matrix. In addition to presenting statistics on employment and employment changes, growth rates, job openings, and self–employed workers, table IIII–1 includes rankings, from very low to very high, for other variables. The table also identifies the most significant source of postsecondary education or training and provides information on the educational attainment distribution of 25– to 44–year olds for each occupation. The table supplies the user with a comprehensive picture of a specific occupation and makes it easier to compare the attributes of different occupations. The data used in preparing the table are available electronically for users who want to arrange them differently for analytical purposes.

Changes in industry employment and in the utilization of an occupation within an industry affect occupational employment. Chapter IV presents information about the factors driving these changes. Table IV–1 provides 2006–16 projections of industry output and employment. Table IV–2 presents factors affecting industry output and employment while table IV–3 presents factors changing occupational utilization.

Chapter V explains the development and uses of data on occupational replacement needs. Projected replacement rates and estimates of replacement needs for 2006–16 are presented in Table V–3.

Finally, data from the National Center for Education Statistics on completions of institutional education and training programs by field of study appear in chapter VI.

In all cases, national data are provided. Data for States and local areas may be obtained from sources identified in the appendix.

Doug Braddock, Olivia Crosby, Arlene Dohm, Eric Figueroa, James Franklin, Samuel L. Greenblatt, Jonathan W. Kelinson, Chester C. Levine, C. Brett Lockard, Kevin M. McCarron, Alice Ramey, Brian Roberts, Lynn Shniper, Kasmira Smarzo, Michael Wolf, Rose Woods, and Ian Wyatt prepared this bulletin. Terry Schau, Supervisory Economist, Division of Occupational Outlook supervised its preparation under the general guidance and direction of Kristina J. Bartsch, Chief, Division of Occupational Outlook. T. Alan Lacey and Dave Terkanian provided layout and table formatting support. Editorial work was provided by Gene Becker. Keith Tapscott designed cover artwork.

For further information about material contained in this bulletin, please call the Chief, Division of Occupational Outlook, at (202) 691–5700, or visit the Office of Occupational Statistics and Employment Projections Web site, **www.bls.gov/emp**. This information is available to sensory–impaired individuals upon request. Voice phone: (202) 691–5200; Federal Relay Service: 1–800–877–8339.

Contents

Chapter *Page*

I. Education and Training Classification Systems 1
Eleven category system 1
Educational attainment cluster system 1
Projecting education and training requirements 2
Results and applications of the two classification systems 4
The educational attainment distribution of occupations: a note on methodology 6

II. The 2006–16 National Employment Matrix Structure 13
2006 base–year employment matrix 13
Change–factor matrix 13
2016 projected–year employment matrix 14
The 2006–16 National Employment Matrix occupational directory 14
The 2006–16 National Employment Matrix industry directory 15

III. Selected Occupational Data, 2006 and Projected 2016 39
Data presented 39
Using ranked information 40

IV. Factors Affecting Industry Employment and Occupational Utilization, 2006–16 79
Industry employment 79
Occupational utilization 79

V. Estimating Occupational Replacement Needs 125
Developing measures of total separations 125
Developing measures of net separations 125
Frequently asked questions about replacement needs 129

VI. Education and Training Statistics: Completions, by field of study 149

Appendix. Sources of State and Local Labor Market and Career Information 188

Tables:

I–1 Employment and total job openings by education and training category, 2006 and projected 2016... 3
I–2 Employment and total job openings, 2006–16 by six education clusters ... 4
I–3. Employment and total job openings by three education clusters, 2006 and projected 2016 ... 4
I–4. Employment by education or training category and education cluster, 2006 and projected 2016....... 5
I–5 Above–average growth and above–average wage occupations, by educational attainment cluster and wages, 2006 and projected 2016 ... 7
II–1. National Employment Matrix occupational directory, 2006 ... 18
II–2. National Employment Matrix industry directory, 2006 ... 30
III–1. Occupational employment and job openings data, 2006–16, and worker characteristics, 2006........ 43
III–2. Employment for occupations not presented in the National Employment Matrix, 2006... 78
IV–1. Employment and output by industry, 1996, 2006, and projected 2016... 80
IV–2. Factors affecting industry output and employment, 2006–16 ... 96
IV–3. Factors changing occupational utilization, 2006–16... 109
V–1. Net separations for registered nurses and for waiters and waitresses, by age group, 2001–2006 ... 150
V–2. Net replacement data for registered nurses, by age group, 2006–16 ... 151
V–3. Total and net replacement rates and annual average projected replacement needs, 2006–16.......... 130
VI–1. Earned awards and degrees, by field of study, 2003–04 ... 150

Figure:

1. Total and net occupational entrants and separations ... 126

Chapter I. Education and Training Classification Systems

The Office of Occupational Statistics and Employment Projections of the Bureau of Labor Statistics (BLS) produces many types of information about education and training requirements. The Occupational Outlook *Handbook*, for example, gives detailed descriptions of the education and training requirements of occupations and occupational groups. Each of the 753 occupations for which the office publishes data are classified by education and training categories. This allows occupations to be grouped and allows for estimates of the education and training needs for the population as a whole and of the outlook for workers with various types of educational and training attainment.

The Bureau uses two classification systems to describe the education and training needs of occupations. This chapter of the Occupational Projections and Training Data bulletin summarizes these two methods of classifying occupations and then analyzes the education and training needs of the future workforce based on the 2006–16 employment projections. The chapter concludes with a list of occupations that have above the median wages and above average employment growth, which are expected to provide good job prospects for workers at each level of educational attainment. (For a full listing of the education or training categories and education cluster assignments for all 753 detailed National Employment Matrix occupations, see table III-1 in chapter III of this bulletin.)

The first system, begun in 1994, assigns occupations to a single education and training category, the one reflecting the most common path into the occupation. This classification is based on analysis by BLS economists.

The second system, introduced in 2004, assigns each occupation to an "educational attainment cluster" based on the educational attainment of current workers in the occupation. These two systems are complimentary and, together, create a more complete picture of occupational education and training requirements.

Eleven category system

BLS identifies 11 education and training categories that describe the most significant education and training pathway to employment for each occupation. A category is defined as the most significant source of education or training needed to become qualified in an occupation. The categories are as follows:

1. First professional degree
2. Doctoral degree
3. Master's degree
4. Bachelor's or higher degree, plus work experience
5. Bachelor's degree
6. Associate degree
7. Postsecondary vocational award
8. Work experience in a related occupation
9. Long-term on-the-job training
10. Moderate-term on-the-job training
11. Short-term on-the-job training

BLS economists assign each occupation to one of these categories based on their knowledge and judgment. Economists analyze data from BLS and other government and private organizations, and interviews with educators, employers, training experts, and experts in professional and trade associations, and unions. For some occupations, such as physician and lawyer, the education and training required is straightforward and established by government laws and regulations. For other occupations, such as computer programmer or industrial machinery repairer, entry requirements vary considerably. When an occupation has more than one path of entry, BLS identifies the path that research suggests is applicable to most current entrants. (For a more detailed discussion of these categories see chapter III page 39 of this bulletin.)

This education and training classification system is simple and includes non-educational paths of entry, such as on-the-job training and work experience. Management occupations, for example, usually require years of experience working in a related job.

However, this classification system does not show the extent to which there are multiple paths of entry into an occupation. It also does not show that there may be multiple entry requirements: an occupation that requires on-the-job training, for example, might also require postsecondary education. In fact, table I-4 shows that in 2006, only 11 percent of jobs in the three on-the-job training categories were mostly filled by workers with a high school degree or less. For jobs requiring moderate or long-term on-the-job training, employers often try to hire individuals with at least some college education, or even a bachelor's degree, before making a large investment in their training.

Educational attainment cluster system

The educational attainment cluster system sorts occupations according to the highest level of educational attainment of current workers. It can be used to study the job outlook for college graduates or the outlook for workers with other levels of education. This system, unlike the first one, allows occupations to fall into multiple educational attainment categories. These are identified as "mixture" occupations.

Occupations are grouped according to the percentage of workers who have a high school diploma or less, some college or an associate degree, or a college diploma (bachelor's degree) or higher. According to the percentage of workers falling into each of these three educational levels, the occupation is assigned to one of six hierarchical education clusters shown in exhibit 1.1

If an education level represents the highest educational attainment of at least 20 percent of workers in an occupation, that education level is included in the education category of the occupation. For example, if more than 60 percent of workers have a high school diploma or less, less than 20 percent have some college or an associate degree, and less than 20 percent have a bachelor's or higher degree, that occupation is considered a high school (HS) occupation. However, if more than 20 percent have

[1]Occupations falling in the high school and college (HS/C) category were included in the HS/SC/C cluster.)

a high school degree or less, more than 20 percent have attended some college or held an associate degree, and less than 20 percent have a bachelor's or higher degree, the occupation is considered to be a high school/some college (HS/SC) occupation.

The key cutoff level for classifying occupations is set at 20 percent to help correct for workers in an occupation who have education levels well outside the norm. (See "The educational attainment distribution of occupations: A note on methodology" on page 6 of this bulletin.)

Exhibit 1. Definitions of education clusters

Education cluster	Percent of employees aged 25 to 44 in the occupation whose highest level of educational attainment is—		
	High school or less	Some college (including associate degree)	Bachelor's or higher degree
High school (HS)	Greater than or equal to 60 percent	Less than 20 percent	Less than 20 percent
High school/some college (HS/SC)	Greater than or equal to 20 percent	Greater than or equal to 20 percent	Less than 20 percent
Some college (SC)	Less than 20 percent	Greater than or equal to 60 percent	Less than 20 percent
High school/some college/ college (HS/SC/C)	Greater than or equal to 20 percent	Greater than or equal to 20 percent	Greater than or equal to 20 percent
Some college/ college (SC/C)	Less than 20 percent	Greater than or equal to 20 percent	Greater than or equal to 20 percent
College (C)	Less than 20 percent	Less than 20 percent	Greater than or equal to 60 percent

When the cluster system was first developed for the 2002–12 projections, the Current Population Survey (CPS) was the source of educational attainment data. For the 2006–16 projections, the CPS was replaced as the source of educational attainment data by the American Community Survey (ACS). (For more information on this change, see the note on methodology later in this chapter.)

The cluster system categorizes occupations on the basis of the educational attainment of 25- to 44-year-olds working in the occupation because these younger workers were assumed to better reflect current hiring practices than information on all workers would.

This system highlights the fact that there are often multiple pathways into an occupation. For example, according to 2005–06 ACS data, 51 percent of electricians aged 25 to 44 years have a high school diploma or less, whereas 42 percent have some college or an associate degree as their highest level of educational attainment. The education cluster system, which assigns electricians to the high school/some college (HS/SC) cluster, has the advantage of being able to capture this split. However, it has the disadvantage of being less able to address the role of training and skills acquired outside of college in career preparation. The 11 category classification system, which puts electricians into the long-term on-the-job training category, better addresses the skill requirements needed for a job.

Projecting education and training requirements

The two classification systems can be used to estimate the number of jobs that will fall into each education and training category. This provides information on the future training needs of the workforce. It can also provide an answer to the frequently asked question: "what is the outlook for college graduates?"

Projections by education and training category. Table I-1 provides the current and projected employment distribution, and the projected numerical and percent change of jobs within the 11 education and training categories. It also lists the total number of job openings by education and training category that are expected over the 2006–16 decade. These openings are due to growth and the need to replace workers who permanently leave the occupation. (A discussion of the calculation of replacement needs can be found in chapter V of this bulletin.)

As table I-1 shows, short-term and moderate-term on-the-job training are by far the largest education and training categories. In 2006, 34.7 percent of all jobs were assigned to the short-term on-the-job training category and 18.1 percent were assigned to the moderate-term on-the-job training category meaning that these jobs can usually be learned in 1 year or less. Over the 2006–16 decade, 54.5 percent of total job openings fall into one of these two on-the-job training categories.

These two categories, however, make up a slightly smaller proportion of projected total jobs. Jobs requiring postsecondary awards and degrees make up a larger proportion of projected jobs, and jobs that primarily require a doctoral degree are expected to increase the fastest—but to generate relatively few new jobs. Most of these new jobs will stem from growth of postsecondary teachers. Occupations for which a bachelor's degree is the most significant source of education or training are expected to gain the largest share of employment over the 2006–16 decade—rising from 12.3 percent in 2006 to 13.0 percent in 2016.

Projections by educational attainment cluster. The cluster classification system also can be used to assess the future education requirements. The number of jobs in each of the six cluster categories can be projected, and these projections can be combined and modified to project the number of jobs to be filled by those with a high school diploma or less, those with some college, and those with a bachelor's or higher degree.

Employment projections by educational attainment cluster are presented in table I-2. As shown only two clusters—some college/college occupations and college occupations—are expected to have an increasing proportion of jobs between 2006 and 2016. These two clusters will rise from 26.7 percent to 28.0 percent of all jobs during the decade, meaning that jobs usually filled by the most highly educated workers are expected to increase fastest over this period. Still, by far the highest proportion of jobs in both 2006 and 2016—47.4 percent and 46.5 percent, respectively—fall into the high school/some college (HS/SC) cluster.

With modification, the six educational attainment clusters can serve as the basis for projecting the number of jobs that fall into three major educational attainment groups: workers with a high school degree or less, those with some college, and those with a bachelor's or higher degree. To arrive at the projection by these three broad educational attainment groups, the proportion of jobs within each of the six clusters that is filled by those with

Table I-1. Employment and total job openings by education and training category, 2006 and projected 2016
(Numbers in thousands)

Most significant source of education and training	Employment				2006–16 change		Total job openings due to growth and net replacement needs, 2006–16[1]	
	Number		Percent distribution					
	2006	2016	2006	2016	Number	Percent	Number	Percent distribution
Total, all occupations	150,620	166,220	100.0	100.0	15,600	10.4	50,732	100.0
First professional degree	1,970	2,247	1.3	1.4	277	14.0	638	1.3
Doctoral degree	2,025	2,462	1.3	1.5	437	21.6	793	1.6
Master's degree	2,167	2,575	1.4	1.5	409	18.9	819	1.6
Bachelor's or higher degree, plus work experience	6,524	7,117	4.3	4.3	592	9.1	2,008	4.0
Bachelor's degree	18,585	21,659	12.3	13.0	3,074	16.5	6,706	13.2
Associate degree	5,812	6,899	3.9	4.2	1,087	18.7	2,240	4.4
Postsecondary vocational award	7,901	8,973	5.2	5.4	1,072	13.6	2,491	4.9
Work experience in a related occupation	14,579	15,889	9.7	9.6	1,310	9.0	4,126	8.1
Long-term on-the-job training	11,489	12,200	7.6	7.3	711	6.2	3,272	6.5
Moderate-term on-the-job training	27,230	29,248	18.1	17.6	2,018	7.4	7,510	14.8
Short-term on-the-job training	52,339	56,951	34.7	34.3	4,613	8.8	20,123	39.7

1 Total job openings represent the sum of employment increases and net replacements. If employment change is negative, job openings due to growth are zero and total job openings equal net replacements.
NOTE: Detail may not equal total or 100 percent due to rounding.

a high school diploma or less, some college, or a bachelor's or higher degree is determined. Projected employment change in an occupation is assigned to the three groups based on the education cluster assigned to the occupation. If the occupation is a high school (HS), some college (SC), or college (C) occupation, all jobs are projected to require this level of educational attainment. If the occupation is a "mixture occupation," that is, it is composed of two or three levels of educational attainment; projected jobs are distributed according to the existing ratio of workers who fall into the educational attainment groups comprising the cluster.

For example, for college (C) occupations (those with 60 percent or more of workers having a bachelor's or higher degree), it is assumed that all jobs in the occupation require a college degree.

Exhibit 2. Projecting jobs by educational attainment group

Education cluster	Proportion of projected jobs assigned to three educational attainment groups
HS	All projected jobs are considered "high school" jobs
HS/SC	Projected jobs are assigned to "high school" or "some college" based on the actual 2006 proportion of workers in the cluster with a high school degree or less and the proportion with some college
SC	All projected jobs are considered "some college" jobs
HS/SC/C	Projected jobs are assigned to all three groups based on the actual 2006 proportion of workers in the cluster with each level of educational attainment
SC/C	Projected jobs are assigned to "some college" or "college" based on the actual 2006 proportion of workers in the cluster with some college and the proportion with a college or higher degree
C	All projected jobs are considered college jobs
HS/C	Projected jobs are treated the same as HS/SC/C jobs

For a mixture occupation, such as some college/college (SC/C), it is assumed that all jobs in the cluster either require some college or a bachelor's or higher degree. To calculate the number of "some college" jobs in the occupation, analysts compute the ratio of the workers in that occupation who have some college to the workers who have some college or a bachelor's or higher degree. The number of "some college" jobs in the occupation is the value of this ratio multiplied by the employment level of the occupation. The procedure is applied to the other mixture occupations.

In this analysis, this technique was applied to data for 2006 and data for the projected 2006–16 decade.

The following tabulation summarizes how employment growth is assigned to the three educational attainment groups of high school or less (high school), some college (some college), and bachelor's or higher degree (college) in the education cluster classification system.

What does this assignment method reveal about the projections of employment by educational attainment over the 2006–16 decade? As Table I-3 shows, the projected change in employment for each of the 753 detailed occupations was assigned to the three educational attainment groups (high school or less, some college, and bachelor's or higher degree). Among these three groups, jobs projected to be filled by workers with a high school degree or less will account for the largest share, 43.0 percent, of all jobs in 2016. However, the jobs expected to be filled by those with a bachelor's or higher degree are expected to grow fastest at 14.8 percent.

Taking growth and replacement needs into consideration, a greater proportion of total job openings are projected to be filled by workers with at least some college rather than by those with a high school degree or less. An estimated 57.3 percent of job openings are expected to be filled by those with some college or a bachelor's or higher degree, whereas 42.7 percent of jobs are expected to be filled by those with only a high school degree or less. This figure is most likely an underestimate because the method for

Table I–2. Employment and total job openings, 2006–16 by six education clusters
(Numbers in thousands)

Education cluster	Employment				Change			Total job openings due to growth and net replacement needs, 2006–16[1]	
	Number		Percent distribution		Number	Percent distribution	Percent	Number	Percent distribution
	2006	2016	2006	2016					
Total	150,620	166,220	100.0	100.0	15,600	100.0	10.4	50,732	100.0
High school occupations	16,959	18,115	11.3	10.9	1,155	7.4	6.8	5,511	10.9
High school/some college occupations	71,343	77,296	47.4	46.5	5,953	38.2	8.3	23,077	45.5
Some college occupations	287	340	.2	.2	53	.3	18.4	97	.2
High school/some college/college occupations	21,883	24,003	14.5	14.4	2,120	13.6	9.7	7,710	15.2
Some college/ college occupations	22,137	25,450	14.7	15.3	3,313	21.2	15.0	7,749	15.3
College occupations	18,011	21,017	12.0	12.6	3,006	19.3	16.7	6,587	13.0

1 Total job openings represent the sum of employment increases and net replacements. If employment change is negative, job openings due to growth are zero and total job openings equal net replacements.

assigning projected employment to educational category assumes no upgrading of educational requirements for occupations over the projection decade.

Results and applications of the two classification systems

Combining the two classification systems—the 11 education and training categories and the 6 educational attainment clusters—uses the strengths of each system to provide further insight into the education and training requirements of jobs. For example, both stonemasons and maids and housekeeping cleaners are high school (HS) occupations under the cluster system. According to the 11 category system, however, stonemasons usually need long-term on-the-job training, whereas maids and housekeeping cleaners usually need short-term on-the-job training. Their respective earnings reflect, in part, the differences in training requirements; stonemasons' median annual wages of $35,960 in May 2006 were more than double the $17,580 median annual wages of maids and housekeeping cleaners. Similar differences exist within each education and training category.

Similarly, both stonemasons and police and sheriff's patrol officers usually need long-term on-the-job training. However, their educational attainment is quite different. Eighty-two percent of stonemasons have a high school diploma or less, whereas 85 percent of police and sheriff's patrol officers have attended some college or have completed college. Compared with stonemasons' median annual wages of $35,960 in May 2006, police and sheriff's patrol officers' median annual wages in May 2006 were $47,460. Again, the respective earnings in each of these two occupations reflect, in part, differences in educational attainment.

Table I-4 shows the distribution of 2006 and projected 2016 employment and percent change by education or training category and by educational attainment cluster. This table shows the increasing importance of education for job seekers in qualifying for future jobs. In fact, the table suggests that the fastest job growth will be in occupations at the higher end of the education spectrum under both classification systems. Although all but one category is expected to gain jobs during the projections decade, high school (HS) and high school/some college (HS/SC) jobs requiring primarily on-the-job training are projected to grow the slowest. However, high school/some college (HS/SC) occupations requiring mostly short-term and moderate term on-the-job training are expected to account for 35 percent of all jobs, even though they are projected to have slower than average growth.

Occupations with above-average growth and above-median wages by education cluster.

Career advisors, students, and job seekers often want to know which jobs offer the best career opportunities and highest wages. Table I-5 sorts occupations by educational cluster and, within each cluster, lists only those occupations that are both growing

Table I–3. Employment and total job openings by three education clusters, 2006 and projected 2016
(Numbers in thousands)

Education cluster	Employment				Change			Total job openings due to growth and net replacements, 2006–16[1]	
	Number		Percent distribution		Number	Percent distribution	Percent	Number	Percent distribution
	2006	2016	2006	2016					
Total	150,620	166,220	100.0	100.0	15,600	100.0	10.4	50,732	100.0
High school graduate or less	66,365	71,484	44.1	43.0	5,119	32.8	7.7	21,656	42.7
Some college	46,229	51,074	30.7	30.7	4,845	31.1	10.5	15,534	30.6
Bachelor's degee or higher	38,026	43,663	25.2	26.3	5,637	36.1	14.8	13,542	26.7

1 Total job openings represent the sum of employment increases and net replacements. If employment change is negative, job openings due to growth are zero and total job openings equal net replacements.

NOTE: Detail may not equal total or 100 percent due to rounding.

faster than the average for total employment–10.4 percent–and have annual wages above the May 2006 median–$30,400. These "above-average" occupations are expected to provide good job opportunities for new entrants into the workforce, although in almost every occupation, some workers earn significantly higher than the occupation's median wages. Moreover, job growth is only one measure of the demand for workers. For specific information on the job outlook for many occupations, see the 2008–09 *Occupational Outlook Handbook.*

Most of the above-average occupations are at the higher end of the educational spectrum, but there are some above-average jobs at every level of education and training. All six of the occupations with above-median wages and above-average growth included in the high school (HS) cluster relate to construction. The 40 above-average occupations in the high school/some college (HS/SC) cluster are varied, but many (such as plumbers) also are construction occupations; many are maintenance and repair occupations (for example, automotive service technicians) or transportation occupations (for instance, bus drivers).

The high school/some college/college (HS/SC/C) cluster contains mostly occupations where a bachelor's degree or work experience in a related occupation are the most significant sources of education or training to become proficient in the occupation. For many occupations in this cluster, a bachelor's degree often substitutes for work experience or is required to work for some employers. Examples of HS/SC/C occupations are property managers, lodging managers, and construction inspectors.

The some college/college (SC/C) occupations on the above-average list include occupations, such as computer support specialists, insurance and real estate sales agents, paralegals, and police officers, that often require some postsecondary education and, increasingly, a college degree.

Not surprisingly, the numerous above-average occupations in the college (C) cluster mostly include professional occupations, such as teachers, engineers, and accountants and auditors.

There are many other criteria that can be used to derive a list of "above-average" or desirable jobs. The data and projections provided in this publication give analysts the ability to sort occupations according to a number of alternative characteristics.

Table I-4. Employment by education or training category and education cluster, 2006 and projected 2016
(Numbers in thousands)

Postsecondary education or training category	Education cluster								
	HS occupations			HS/SC occupations			SC occupations		
	2006	2016	Percent change	2006	2016	Percent change	2006	2016	Percent change
Short-term on-the-job training	10,526	11,280	7.2	34,144	37,384	9.5	8	10	21.9
Moderate-term on-the-job training	4,915	5,198	5.8	17,789	18,763	5.5	–	–	–
Long-term on-the-job training	1,466	1,584	8.1	7,204	7,555	4.9	–	–	–
Work experience in a related occupation	53	52	-0.6	5,496	6,030	9.7	52	58	11.5
Postsecondary vocational award	–	–	–	5,585	6,308	13.0	201	240	19.2
Associate degree	–	–	–	1,126	1,255	11.4	25	31	25.4
Bachelor's degree	–	–	–	–	–	–	–	–	–
Bachelor's or higher degree, plus work experience	–	–	–	–	–	–	–	–	–
Master's degree	–	–	–	–	–	–	–	–	–
Doctoral degree	–	–	–	–	–	–	–	–	–
First professional degree	–	–	–	–	–	–	–	–	–

Postsecondary education or training category	Education cluster								
	HS/SC/C occupations			SC/C occupations			C occupations		
	2006	2016	Percent change	2006	2016	Percent change	2006	2016	Percent change
Short-term on-the-job training	7,498	8,094	8.0	162	183	12.6	–	–	–
Moderate-term on-the-job training	3,451	4,041	17.1	1,076	1,246	15.8	–	–	–
Long-term on-the-job training	821	853	3.8	1,998	2,208	10.5	–	–	–
Work experience in a related occupation	6,887	7,335	6.5	2,091	2,414	15.5	–	–	–
Postsecondary vocational award	1,244	1,461	17.4	871	964	10.7	–	–	–
Associate degree	145	156	7.5	4,515	5,457	20.8	–	–	–
Bachelor's degree	1,330	1,527	14.8	6,983	8,190	17.3	10,272	11,941	16.3
Bachelor's or higher degree, plus work experience	505	537	6.3	4,292	4,609	7.4	1,727	1,970	14.1
Master's degree	–	–	–	124	148	19.3	2,043	2,427	18.8
Doctoral degree	–	–	–	25	31	21.5	1,999	2,431	21.6
First professional degree	–	–	–	–	–	–	1,970	2,247	14.0

The educational attainment distribution of occupations: A note on methodology

Since 2004, the Office of Occupational Statistics and Employment Projections has estimated the educational attainment distribution of employed 25- to 44-year-olds for each of the detailed National Employment Matrix occupations. For the 2002–12 and 2004–14 employment projections, the Current Population Survey (CPS) was the source of these data. Because of the size of the CPS survey, 3 to 5 years of data had to be combined for many of the occupations in order to meet BLS criteria for publication and statistical significance. Other occupations had to be estimated by proxy. For more information on how the CPS was used to derive educational attainment data by occupation see chapter I, Occupational Projections and Training Data, bulletin 2602.

Beginning with the 2006–16 employment projections, the American Community Survey (ACS) replaces the CPS as the source of educational attainment data by occupation. This relatively new Census Bureau survey is designed to replace the long-form version of the decennial census. This survey is based on a much larger sample of workers compared to the CPS, and thus provides greater accuracy in the assignment of educational attainment data to individual occupations. The ACS surveys about 3 million households annually, collecting demographic and employment information. The data developed for educational attainment were based upon the public microdata file, which includes about 1.5 million households or about half of the original sample. Two years of public microdata, 2005 and 2006, were used. With 2 years of data, the total sample includes about 3 million households, a substantially larger sample than was used in prior analyses.[1]

Occupational information in the ACS is classified under a taxonomy that, while consistent with the 2000 Standard Occupational Classification (SOC) system, does not provide the same level of occupational detail as the National Employment Matrix. The ACS occupational classification includes 502 occupations but only publishes data for 465 occupations. The 2006–16 National Employment Matrix published projections for 753 detailed SOC-consistent occupations.

The ACS reduced 502 occupations to 465 occupations to maintain respondent confidentiality; the ACS does not publish microdata for occupations with a weighted estimated employment of less than 10,000. Instead, the ACS merged those occupations with related occupations to create a total of 465 occupations. Details of the occupational coding and of how these merged occupations were created can be found at the U.S. Census Web site: http://www.census.gov/acs/www/Products/PUMS/C2SS/CodeList/2005/Occupation.htm.

Because the ACS includes fewer occupations than the National Employment Matrix, proxy data was used for some Matrix occupations. For example, marketing and sales managers are a single occupation in the ACS, but are two distinct occupations in the Matrix. Since the ACS does not distinguish between the two occupations, the same levels of educational attainment were assigned to both occupations.

Switching to the ACS also led to a change in the methodology for suppressing unreliable data. Previously with the CPS, all data were suppressed for an occupation if the weighted employment in the occupation fell under 10,000. If data were suppressed, they were replaced by one of several substitute data sources.

With the ACS, individual cells (for example, the percent of college graduates in a particular occupation) were suppressed rather than all data for that occupation. Instead of using alternate data sources, cells were simply suppressed. Thus, all of the data for this classification came from a single, uniform data source. Suppression decisions were made based upon the standard error relative to the estimated value of the cell.

As mentioned above, BLS analysts combined ACS data from 2005 and 2006 to create publishable estimates of educational attainment. With a 2-year sample, the standard error of every estimated value was calculated. For the 465 detailed ACS occupations, the standard error was calculated for the percent of workers with a high school degree or less in that occupation (HS), the percent with some college or an associate degree (SC), and the percent with a college or higher degree (C). With 465 occupations having 3 cells each (HS, SC, and C), there were 1,395 (465 x 3=1,395) estimated values. Only 118 of those 1,395 values were not published because the standard error values were too high. In all cases, the suppressed estimated value (the percent of workers in an occupation) was below the 20 percent level of significance for the classification systems.

In the unpublished data, one standard error exceeded 50 percent of the estimated value. For example, if 10 percent of workers in an occupation were estimated to have a college degree, then the data were not published if the standard error was greater than 5 percent.

Another part of the methodology for the education clusters was the determination that if fewer than 20 percent of workers in an occupation had a given level of education, that level should be ignored. Deciding on the 20-percent cutoff point required extensive research. When the education cluster system was first developed and preliminary results were examined, three cutoff points were proposed—15 percent, 20 percent, and 25 percent.

The first step in determining which level of significance to use involved studying the occupations that changed their education cluster when the cutoff point was changed. Of the occupations that changed categories, most did so between the 15 percent and 20 percent cutoff points. Far fewer occupations shifted categories between the 20 percent and 25 percent cutoff points. As the cutoff point increased, the number of occupations in mixture clusters—for example, high school/some college (HS/SC) compared to high school (HS)—decreased.

Moreover, an examination of the data suggested that the 20 percent cutoff level provided the most logical and reasonable cluster assignment for occupations with well-defined training paths. This examination of data also relied on the occupational expertise of analysts who develop employment projections and related information for the *Occupational Outlook Handbook* and other OOSEP publications.

[1] While preparing the educational attainment data for this edition of OPTD, results from the CPS and ACS were compared. The two surveys produced very similar results, and few occupations would have fallen into a different educational attainment category if the CPS had been used instead of the ACS.

Table I–5. Above-average growth and above-average wage occupations, by educational attainment cluster and wages, 2006 and projected 2016
(Numbers in thousands)

2006 National Employment Matrix code and title		Employment		Employment change, 2006–16		2006 Median annual wages	Most significant source of education or training	Educational cluster
		2006	2016	Numeric	Percent			
47-2171	Reinforcing iron and rebar workers	30	34	3	11.5	$38,220	Long-term on-the-job training	HS
47-2044	Tile and marble setters	79	91	12	15.4	36,590	Long-term on-the-job training	HS
47-2051	Cement masons and concrete finishers	222	247	25	11.4	32,650	Moderate-term on-the-job training	HS
47-2181	Roofers	156	179	22	14.3	32,260	Moderate-term on-the-job training	HS
47-2053	Terrazzo workers and finishers	7	8	1	10.9	31,630	Long-term on-the-job training	HS
47-2141	Painters, construction and maintenance	463	517	54	11.8	31,190	Moderate-term on-the-job training	HS
53-5031	Ship engineers	15	17	2	14.1	54,820	Work experience in a related occupation	HS/SC
17-3021	Aerospace engineering and operations technicians	9	9	1	10.4	53,300	Associate degree	HS/SC
53-6051	Transportation inspectors	26	31	4	16.4	50,390	Work experience in a related occupation	HS/SC
53-4041	Subway and streetcar operators	7	8	1	12.1	48,980	Moderate-term on-the-job training	HS/SC
49-3011	Aircraft mechanics and service technicians	122	135	13	10.6	47,740	Postsecondary vocational award	HS/SC
47-2011	Boilermakers	18	20	2	14.0	46,960	Long-term on-the-job training	HS/SC
51-2011	Aircraft structure, surfaces, rigging, and systems assemblers	28	32	4	12.8	45,410	Moderate-term on-the-job training	HS/SC
47-2152	Plumbers, pipefitters, and steamfitters	502	555	53	10.6	42,770	Long-term on-the-job training	HS/SC
33-2011	Fire fighters	293	328	35	12.1	41,190	Long-term on-the-job training	HS/SC
49-9062	Medical equipment repairers	38	46	8	21.7	40,580	Associate degree	HS/SC
17-3025	Environmental engineering technicians	21	26	5	24.8	40,560	Associate degree	HS/SC
49-3042	Mobile heavy equipment mechanics, except engines	131	147	16	12.3	40,440	Long-term on-the-job training	HS/SC
53-1011	Aircraft cargo handling supervisors	6	7	1	23.3	39,840	Work experience in a related occupation	HS/SC
49-9092	Commercial divers	3	4	1	17.7	39,590	Postsecondary vocational award	HS/SC
53-1021	First-line supervisors/managers of helpers, laborers, and material movers, hand	182	205	23	12.5	39,570	Work experience in a related occupation	HS/SC
43-6012	Legal secretaries	275	308	32	11.7	38,190	Associate degree	HS/SC
49-3031	Bus and truck mechanics and diesel engine specialists	275	306	32	11.5	37,660	Postsecondary vocational award	HS/SC
37-1012	First-line supervisors/managers of landscaping, lawn service, and groundskeeping workers	202	237	36	17.6	37,300	Work experience in a related occupation	HS/SC
43-6011	Executive secretaries and administrative assistants	1,618	1,857	239	14.8	37,240	Work experience in a related occupation	HS/SC
43-5011	Cargo and freight agents	86	100	14	16.5	37,110	Moderate-term on-the-job training	HS/SC
29-2061	Licensed practical and licensed vocational nurses	749	854	105	14.0	36,550	Postsecondary vocational award	HS/SC
29-2055	Surgical technologists	86	107	21	24.5	36,080	Postsecondary vocational award	HS/SC
51-8031	Water and liquid waste treatment plant and system operators	111	126	15	13.8	36,070	Long-term on-the-job training	HS/SC
33-3012	Correctional officers and jailers	442	516	75	16.9	35,760	Moderate-term on-the-job training	HS/SC
47-4041	Hazardous materials removal workers	39	44	4	11.2	35,450	Moderate-term on-the-job training	HS/SC
49-3021	Automotive body and related repairers	183	204	21	11.6	35,180	Long-term on-the-job training	HS/SC
53-3032	Truck drivers, heavy and tractor-trailer	1,860	2,053	193	10.4	35,040	Moderate-term on-the-job training	HS/SC
49-2098	Security and fire alarm systems installers	57	68	11	20.2	34,810	Postsecondary vocational award	HS/SC
47-2121	Glaziers	55	62	7	11.9	34,610	Long-term on-the-job training	HS/SC
33-3011	Bailiffs	19	21	2	11.2	34,210	Moderate-term on-the-job training	HS/SC
49-3023	Automotive service technicians and mechanics	773	883	110	14.3	33,780	Postsecondary vocational award	HS/SC

Table I–5. Above-average growth and above-average wage occupations, by educational attainment cluster and wages, 2006 and projected 2016 — Continued
(Numbers in thousands)

2006 National Employment Matrix code and title		Employment		Employment change, 2006–16		2006 Median annual wages	Most significant source of education or training	Educational cluster
		2006	2016	Numeric	Percent			
49-3051	Motorboat mechanics	24	29	5	19.0	33,210	Long-term on-the-job training	HS/SC
17-3031	Surveying and mapping technicians	76	90	15	19.4	32,340	Moderate-term on-the-job training	HS/SC
53-3021	Bus drivers, transit and intercity	198	223	25	12.5	32,090	Moderate-term on-the-job training	HS/SC
49-9094	Locksmiths and safe repairers	26	32	6	22.1	32,020	Moderate-term on-the-job training	HS/SC
39-5091	Makeup artists, theatrical and performance	2	3	1	39.8	31,820	Postsecondary vocational award	HS/SC
49-9011	Mechanical door repairers	15	18	2	14.9	31,610	Moderate-term on-the-job training	HS/SC
49-3092	Recreational vehicle service technicians	14	17	3	18.2	31,510	Long-term on-the-job training	HS/SC
43-5031	Police, fire, and ambulance dispatchers	99	113	13	13.6	31,470	Moderate-term on-the-job training	HS/SC
37-1011	First-line supervisors/managers of housekeeping and janitorial workers	282	318	36	12.7	31,290	Work experience in a related occupation	HS/SC
49-3022	Automotive glass installers and repairers	24	28	4	18.7	30,720	Long-term on-the-job training	HS/SC
53-5011	Sailors and marine oilers	33	38	5	15.7	30,630	Short-term on-the-job training	HS/SC
33-1021	First-line supervisors/managers of fire fighting and prevention workers	52	58	6	11.5	62,900	Work experience in a related occupation	SC
31-2011	Occupational therapist assistants	25	31	6	25.4	42,060	Associate degree	SC
11-9021	Construction managers	487	564	77	15.7	73,700	Bachelor's degree	HS/SC/C
51-8011	Nuclear power reactor operators	4	4	0	10.6	69,370	Long-term on-the-job training	HS/SC/C
11-3011	Administrative services managers	247	276	29	11.7	67,690	Bachelor's or higher, plus work experience	HS/SC/C
41-4011	Sales representatives, wholesale and manufacturing, technical and scientific products	411	462	51	12.4	64,440	Work experience in a related occupation	HS/SC/C
11-9071	Gaming managers	4	5	1	24.4	62,820	Work experience in a related occupation	HS/SC/C
29-2091	Orthotists and prosthetists	6	6	1	11.8	58,980	Bachelor's degree	HS/SC/C
39-6031	Flight attendants	97	107	10	10.6	53,780	Long-term on-the-job training	HS/SC/C
53-5021	Captains, mates, and pilots of water vessels	34	40	6	17.9	53,430	Work experience in a related occupation	HS/SC/C
13-1051	Cost estimators	221	262	41	18.5	52,940	Bachelor's degree	HS/SC/C
33-1011	First-line supervisors/managers of correctional officers	40	45	5	12.5	52,580	Work experience in a related occupation	HS/SC/C
33-2021	Fire inspectors and investigators	14	15	2	11.0	48,050	Work experience in a related occupation	HS/SC/C
47-4011	Construction and building inspectors	110	130	20	18.2	46,570	Work experience in a related occupation	HS/SC/C
23-2091	Court reporters	19	24	5	24.5	45,610	Postsecondary vocational award	HS/SC/C
25-2012	Kindergarten teachers, except special education	170	198	28	16.3	43,580	Bachelor's degree	HS/SC/C
11-9141	Property, real estate, and community association managers	329	379	50	15.1	43,070	Bachelor's degree	HS/SC/C
11-9081	Lodging managers	71	80	9	12.2	42,320	Work experience in a related occupation	HS/SC/C
33-1099	First-line supervisors/managers, protective service workers, all other	48	55	7	14.5	41,570	Work experience in a related occupation	HS/SC/C
39-1011	Gaming supervisors	34	42	8	23.4	41,160	Work experience in a related occupation	HS/SC/C
39-4011	Embalmers	9	10	1	14.3	37,840	Postsecondary vocational award	HS/SC/C
43-4011	Brokerage clerks	73	88	15	20.0	36,390	Moderate-term on-the-job training	HS/SC/C
29-2099	Healthcare technologists and technicians, all other	79	91	12	15.0	35,140	Postsecondary vocational award	HS/SC/C
27-4011	Audio and video equipment technicians	50	62	12	24.2	34,840	Long-term on-the-job training	HS/SC/C
43-4161	Human resources assistants, except payroll and timekeeping	168	187	19	11.3	33,750	Short-term on-the-job training	HS/SC/C

Table I–5. Above-average growth and above-average wage occupations, by educational attainment cluster and wages, 2006 and projected 2016 — Continued
(Numbers in thousands)

2006 National Employment Matrix code	and title	Employment 2006	Employment 2016	Employment change, 2006–16 Numeric	Employment change, 2006–16 Percent	2006 Median annual wages	Most significant source of education or training	Educational cluster
39-1021	First-line supervisors/managers of personal service workers	215	248	33	15.5	32,800	Work experience in a related occupation	HS/SC/C
53-5022	Motorboat operators	3	3	0	10.9	32,350	Moderate-term on-the-job training	HS/SC/C
27-2099	Entertainers and performers, sports and related workers, all other	77	89	12	15.8	N/A	Long-term on-the-job training	HS/SC/C
27-4012	Broadcast technicians	38	42	5	12.1	30,690	Associate degree	HS/SC/C
53-2011	Airline pilots, copilots, and flight engineers	79	90	10	12.9	141,090	Bachelor's degree	SC/C
11-3021	Computer and information systems managers	264	307	43	16.4	101,580	Bachelor's or higher, plus work experience	SC/C
11-2021	Marketing managers	167	192	24	14.4	98,720	Bachelor's or higher, plus work experience	SC/C
15-1011	Computer and information scientists, research	25	31	5	21.5	93,950	Doctoral degree	SC/C
11-3031	Financial managers	506	570	64	12.6	90,970	Bachelor's or higher, plus work experience	SC/C
11-3049	Human resources managers, all other	58	65	7	11.4	88,510	Bachelor's or higher, plus work experience	SC/C
11-3042	Training and development managers	29	33	5	15.6	80,250	Bachelor's or higher, plus work experience	SC/C
29-1071	Physician assistants	66	83	18	27.0	74,980	Master's degree	SC/C
11-3041	Compensation and benefits managers	49	55	6	12.0	74,750	Bachelor's or higher, plus work experience	SC/C
11-9111	Medical and health services managers	262	305	43	16.4	73,340	Bachelor's or higher, plus work experience	SC/C
15-1051	Computer systems analysts	504	650	146	29.0	69,760	Bachelor's degree	SC/C
15-1099	Computer specialists, all other	136	157	21	15.1	68,570	Associate degree	SC/C
41-3031	Securities, commodities, and financial services sales agents	320	399	79	24.8	68,500	Bachelor's degree	SC/C
29-1124	Radiation therapists	15	18	4	24.8	66,170	Associate degree	SC/C
15-1061	Database administrators	119	154	34	28.6	64,670	Bachelor's degree	SC/C
15-2031	Operations research analysts	58	65	6	10.6	64,650	Master's degree	SC/C
15-1081	Network systems and data communications analysts	262	402	140	53.4	64,600	Bachelor's degree	SC/C
13-1081	Logisticians	83	98	14	17.3	63,430	Bachelor's degree	SC/C
29-2021	Dental hygienists	167	217	50	30.1	62,800	Associate degree	SC/C
29-2033	Nuclear medicine technologists	20	23	3	14.8	62,300	Associate degree	SC/C
15-1071	Network and computer systems administrators	309	393	83	27.0	62,130	Bachelor's degree	SC/C
41-9021	Real estate brokers	131	146	15	11.1	60,790	Work experience in a related occupation	SC/C
33-3021	Detectives and criminal investigators	106	125	18	17.3	58,260	Work experience in a related occupation	SC/C
53-2012	Commercial pilots	28	31	4	13.2	57,480	Postsecondary vocational award	SC/C
29-1111	Registered nurses	2,505	3,092	587	23.5	57,280	Associate degree	SC/C
29-2032	Diagnostic medical sonographers	46	54	9	19.1	57,160	Associate degree	SC/C
13-1199	Business operation specialists, all other	1,043	1,261	218	20.9	55,650	Bachelor's degree	SC/C
13-2099	Financial specialists, all other	129	144	15	11.8	53,680	Bachelor's degree	SC/C
13-1079	Human resources, training, and labor relations specialists, all other	214	250	35	16.5	52,270	Bachelor's degree	SC/C
13-2072	Loan officers	373	415	43	11.5	51,760	Bachelor's degree	SC/C
27-1014	Multi-media artists and animators	87	110	23	25.8	51,350	Bachelor's degree	SC/C
13-1072	Compensation, benefits, and job analysis specialists	110	130	20	18.4	50,230	Bachelor's degree	SC/C
29-2011	Medical and clinical laboratory technologists	167	188	21	12.4	49,700	Bachelor's degree	SC/C
11-9061	Funeral directors	29	32	4	12.5	49,620	Associate degree	SC/C
13-1032	Insurance appraisers, auto damage	13	15	2	12.5	49,180	Postsecondary vocational award	SC/C

Table I–5. Above-average growth and above-average wage occupations, by educational attainment cluster and wages, 2006 and projected 2016 — Continued
(Numbers in thousands)

2006 National Employment Matrix code and title		Employment		Employment change, 2006–16		2006 Median annual wages	Most significant source of education or training	Educational cluster
		2006	2016	Numeric	Percent			
29-2034	Radiologic technologists and technicians	196	226	30	15.1	48,170	Associate degree	SC/C
41-3099	Sales representatives, services, all other	540	690	151	27.9	48,100	Work experience in a related occupation	SC/C
13-1073	Training and development specialists	210	249	38	18.3	47,830	Bachelor's or higher, plus work experience	SC/C
33-3051	Police and sheriff's patrol officers	648	719	70	10.8	47,460	Long-term on-the-job training	SC/C
29-1126	Respiratory therapists	102	126	23	22.6	47,420	Associate degree	SC/C
13-1061	Emergency management specialists	12	13	1	12.3	47,410	Work experience in a related occupation	SC/C
27-4032	Film and video editors	21	23	3	12.7	46,670	Bachelor's degree	SC/C
19-4092	Forensic science technicians	13	17	4	30.7	45,330	Bachelor's degree	SC/C
13-2021	Appraisers and assessors of real estate	101	118	17	16.9	44,460	Bachelor's degree	SC/C
25-3011	Adult literacy, remedial education, and GED teachers and instructors	76	87	11	14.2	43,910	Bachelor's degree	SC/C
27-1029	Designers, all other	16	18	2	11.8	43,870	Bachelor's degree	SC/C
41-3021	Insurance sales agents	436	492	56	12.9	43,870	Bachelor's degree	SC/C
17-3019	Drafters, all other	25	27	3	11.0	43,060	Postsecondary vocational award	SC/C
23-2011	Paralegals and legal assistants	238	291	53	22.2	43,040	Associate degree	SC/C
41-3011	Advertising sales agents	170	205	35	20.3	42,750	Moderate-term on-the-job training	SC/C
27-3099	Media and communication workers, all other	36	40	4	11.7	42,570	Long-term on-the-job training	SC/C
21-1092	Probation officers and correctional treatment specialists	94	105	10	10.9	42,500	Bachelor's degree	SC/C
13-1071	Employment, recruitment, and placement specialists	197	233	36	18.4	42,420	Bachelor's degree	SC/C
29-2031	Cardiovascular technologists and technicians	45	57	12	25.5	42,300	Associate degree	SC/C
27-1025	Interior designers	72	86	14	19.5	42,260	Associate degree	SC/C
13-1121	Meeting and convention planners	51	61	10	19.9	42,180	Bachelor's degree	SC/C
27-1027	Set and exhibit designers	12	14	2	17.8	41,820	Bachelor's degree	SC/C
15-1041	Computer support specialists	552	624	71	12.9	41,470	Associate degree	SC/C
31-2021	Physical therapist assistants	60	80	20	32.4	41,360	Associate degree	SC/C
21-1091	Health educators	62	78	16	26.2	41,330	Bachelor's degree	SC/C
27-2021	Athletes and sports competitors	18	21	3	19.2	41,060	Long-term on-the-job training	SC/C
27-4031	Camera operators, television, video, and motion picture	27	30	3	11.5	40,060	Postsecondary vocational award	SC/C
41-9022	Real estate sales agents	432	478	46	10.6	39,760	Postsecondary vocational award	SC/C
27-2041	Music directors and composers	68	77	9	12.9	39,750	Bachelor's or higher, plus work experience	SC/C
19-4091	Environmental science and protection technicians, including health	36	47	10	28.0	38,090	Associate degree	SC/C
53-2022	Airfield operations specialists	5	5	1	11.8	37,630	Long-term on-the-job training	SC/C
19-4021	Biological technicians	79	91	13	16.0	35,710	Bachelor's degree	SC/C
27-3091	Interpreters and translators	41	51	10	23.6	35,560	Long-term on-the-job training	SC/C
21-1099	Community and social service specialists, all other	118	148	30	25.1	35,210	Bachelor's degree	SC/C
21-2021	Directors, religious activities and education	99	119	20	19.7	34,260	Bachelor's degree	SC/C
41-9099	Sales and related workers, all other	180	205	25	14.0	34,250	Moderate-term on-the-job training	SC/C
19-4061	Social science research assistants	18	20	2	12.4	33,860	Associate degree	SC/C
33-9021	Private detectives and investigators	52	61	9	18.2	33,750	Work experience in a related occupation	SC/C
25-3021	Self-enrichment education teachers	261	322	60	23.1	33,440	Work experience in a related occupation	SC/C
31-9011	Massage therapists	118	142	24	20.3	33,400	Postsecondary vocational award	SC/C

Table I–5. Above-average growth and above-average wage occupations, by educational attainment cluster and wages, 2006 and projected 2016 — Continued
(Numbers in thousands)

2006 National Employment Matrix code and title		Employment		Employment change, 2006–16		2006 Median annual wages	Most significant source of education or training	Educational cluster
		2006	2016	Numeric	Percent			
29-2012	Medical and clinical laboratory technicians	151	174	23	15.0	32,840	Associate degree	SC/C
29-1024	Prosthodontists	1	1	0	10.7	N/A	First professional degree	C
29-1060	Physicians and surgeons	633	723	90	14.2	N/A	First professional degree	C
23-1011	Lawyers	761	844	84	11.0	102,470	First professional degree	C
11-9121	Natural sciences managers	41	45	5	11.4	100,080	Bachelor's or higher, plus work experience	C
29-1051	Pharmacists	243	296	53	21.7	94,520	First professional degree	C
29-1041	Optometrists	33	36	4	11.3	91,040	First professional degree	C
19-3032	Industrial-organizational psychologists	2	2	0	21.3	86,420	Master's degree	C
15-1032	Computer software engineers, systems software	350	449	99	28.2	85,370	Bachelor's degree	C
15-2011	Actuaries	18	22	4	23.7	82,800	Bachelor's or higher, plus work experience	C
11-2031	Public relations managers	50	58	8	16.9	82,180	Bachelor's or higher, plus work experience	C
15-1031	Computer software engineers, applications	507	733	226	44.6	79,780	Bachelor's degree	C
19-2021	Atmospheric and space scientists	9	10	1	10.6	77,150	Bachelor's degree	C
19-1021	Biochemists and biophysicists	20	23	3	15.9	76,320	Doctoral degree	C
11-9033	Education administrators, postsecondary	131	150	19	14.2	73,990	Bachelor's or higher, plus work experience	C
17-2031	Biomedical engineers	14	17	3	21.1	73,930	Bachelor's degree	C
17-2121	Marine engineers and naval architects	9	10	1	10.9	72,990	Bachelor's degree	C
19-2042	Geoscientists, except hydrologists and geographers	31	38	7	21.9	72,660	Master's degree	C
29-1131	Veterinarians	62	84	22	35.0	71,990	First professional degree	C
17-2081	Environmental engineers	54	68	14	25.4	69,940	Bachelor's degree	C
17-2112	Industrial engineers	201	242	41	20.3	68,620	Bachelor's degree	C
17-2051	Civil engineers	256	302	46	18.0	68,600	Bachelor's degree	C
13-1111	Management analysts	678	827	149	21.9	68,050	Bachelor's or higher, plus work experience	C
11-9039	Education administrators, all other	30	33	4	12.6	66,620	Bachelor's or higher, plus work experience	C
13-2051	Financial analysts	221	295	75	33.8	66,590	Bachelor's degree	C
19-2043	Hydrologists	8	10	2	24.3	66,260	Master's degree	C
29-1123	Physical therapists	173	220	47	27.1	66,200	Master's degree	C
13-2052	Personal financial advisors	176	248	72	41.0	66,120	Bachelor's degree	C
13-2061	Financial examiners	26	28	3	10.7	65,370	Bachelor's degree	C
29-1011	Chiropractors	53	60	8	14.4	65,220	First professional degree	C
17-1011	Architects, except landscape and naval	132	155	23	17.7	64,150	Bachelor's degree	C
15-2099	Mathematical scientists, all other	10	13	2	21.3	63,570	Master's degree	C
19-1042	Medical scientists, except epidemiologists	87	105	18	20.2	61,680	Doctoral degree	C
29-1199	Health diagnosing and treating practitioners, all other	65	73	8	11.8	61,570	Bachelor's degree	C
29-1122	Occupational therapists	99	122	23	23.1	60,470	Master's degree	C
19-3031	Clinical, counseling, and school psychologists	152	176	24	15.8	59,440	Doctoral degree	C
19-3021	Market research analysts	234	281	47	20.1	58,820	Bachelor's degree	C
27-3042	Technical writers	49	59	10	19.5	58,050	Bachelor's degree	C
19-1022	Microbiologists	17	19	2	11.2	57,980	Doctoral degree	C
29-1127	Speech-language pathologists	110	121	12	10.6	57,710	Master's degree	C
19-1099	Life scientists, all other	14	16	2	15.3	56,970	Bachelor's degree	C
19-1041	Epidemiologists	5	5	1	13.6	56,670	Master's degree	C
19-3051	Urban and regional planners	34	39	5	14.5	56,630	Master's degree	C
27-2012	Producers and directors	93	103	10	11.1	56,310	Bachelor's or higher, plus work experience	C
25-1000	Postsecondary teachers	1,672	2,054	382	22.9	56,120	Doctoral degree	C

Table I–5. Above-average growth and above-average wage occupations, by educational attainment cluster and wages, 2006 and projected 2016 — Continued
(Numbers in thousands)

2006 National Employment Matrix code and title		Employment		Employment change, 2006–16		2006 Median annual wages	Most significant source of education or training	Educational cluster
		2006	2016	Numeric	Percent			
19-2041	Environmental scientists and specialists, including health	83	104	21	25.1	56,100	Master's degree	C
17-1012	Landscape architects	28	32	5	16.4	55,140	Bachelor's degree	C
13-2011	Accountants and auditors............	1,274	1,500	226	17.7	54,630	Bachelor's degree	C
25-9031	Instructional coordinators	129	159	29	22.5	52,790	Master's degree	C
11-9151	Social and community service managers	130	162	32	24.7	52,070	Bachelor's degree	C
19-3091	Anthropologists and archeologists	6	6	1	15.0	49,930	Master's degree	C
23-1022	Arbitrators, mediators, and conciliators	8	9	1	10.6	49,490	Bachelor's or higher, plus work experience	C
27-3043	Writers and authors	135	153	17	12.8	48,640	Bachelor's degree	C
17-1022	Surveyors	60	74	14	23.7	48,290	Bachelor's degree	C
17-1021	Cartographers and photogrammetrists	12	15	2	20.3	48,240	Bachelor's degree	C
25-2042	Special education teachers, middle school	102	118	16	15.8	47,650	Bachelor's degree	C
21-1012	Educational, vocational, and school counselors	260	292	33	12.6	47,530	Master's degree	C
27-3031	Public relations specialists	243	286	43	17.6	47,350	Bachelor's degree	C
25-2041	Special education teachers, preschool, kindergarten, and elementary school..................	219	262	43	19.6	46,360	Bachelor's degree	C
25-2022	Middle school teachers, except special and vocational education	658	732	74	11.2	46,300	Bachelor's degree	C
25-4012	Curators	10	13	2	23.3	46,300	Master's degree	C
25-2021	Elementary school teachers, except special education	1,540	1,749	209	13.6	45,570	Bachelor's degree	C
21-1029	Social workers, all other	66	78	12	17.8	43,580	Bachelor's degree	C
21-1013	Marriage and family therapists.....	25	32	7	29.8	43,210	Master's degree	C
21-1022	Medical and public health social workers	124	154	30	24.2	43,040	Bachelor's degree	C
29-9012	Occupational health and safety technicians..............................	10	12	2	14.6	42,160	Bachelor's degree	C
25-4011	Archivists.....................................	6	7	1	14.4	40,730	Master's degree	C
21-2011	Clergy..	404	481	76	18.9	39,680	Master's degree	C
21-1019	Counselors, all other	27	32	5	16.6	38,210	Master's degree	C
11-9031	Education administrators, preschool and child care center/ program...................................	56	69	13	23.5	37,740	Bachelor's or higher, plus work experience	C
21-1021	Child, family, and school social workers	282	336	54	19.1	37,480	Bachelor's degree	C
29-9099	Healthcare practitioners and technical workers, all other	53	61	8	14.8	37,200	Bachelor's degree	C
29-9091	Athletic trainers	17	21	4	24.3	36,560	Bachelor's degree	C
21-1023	Mental health and substance abuse social workers	122	159	37	29.9	35,410	Master's degree	C
21-1014	Mental health counselors	100	130	30	30.0	34,380	Master's degree	C
25-4013	Museum Technicians and Conservators............................	11	12	2	15.9	34,340	Bachelor's degree	C
21-1011	Substance abuse and behavioral disorder counselors.................	83	112	29	34.3	34,040	Bachelor's degree	C
19-3022	Survey researchers	27	31	4	15.9	33,360	Bachelor's degree	C
25-9099	Education, training, and library workers, all other	99	110	10	10.5	32,160	Bachelor's degree	C

Chapter II. The 2006–16 National Employment Matrix Structure

The Bureau of Labor Statistics (BLS) develops occupational projections biennially as part of its Employment Projections program. These projections, to 2016, along with 2006 base-year employment data, are presented in the National Employment Matrix. The National Employment Matrix incorporates data from multiple BLS surveys in order to present a comprehensive measure of both base- and projected-year employment. The Matrix measures total employment as a count of jobs, not individual workers. This concept is different from that used by another BLS measure familiar to many readers, the Current Population Survey's total employment as a count of the number of workers. The Matrix total employment concept is also different from the BLS Current Employment Statistics total employment measure which, while a count of jobs, includes nonfarm payroll jobs while the Matrix includes all jobs. The Matrix is constructed using three separate employment matrices consisting of a 2006 base-year employment matrix, a change factor matrix, and a 2016 projected-year employment matrix. These matrices are used as tools for analyzing the utilization of occupations within industries and for projecting occupational employment. There are numerous iterations of these three matrices that incorporate analyst review. Because all matrices share the same configuration, an early step in each projection cycle is defining their occupation and industry employment structure. Occupations define matrix rows, while industries define matrix columns. Wage and salary industries account for the vast majority of columns. Separate columns encompass the other two classes of worker categories—the self-employed and unpaid family workers—which are treated as individual industries. Once defined, the three matrices use the same structure.

As mentioned, the National Employment Matrix was developed to provide the most comprehensive measure possible of base- and projected-year employment. The availability of data for constructing the 2006 base-year employment matrix generally is the limiting factor. Data on current employment for wage and salary industries, the self-employed, and unpaid family workers come from a few different sources.

This chapter first discusses the base-year employment, change factor, and projected-year employment matrices. Afterwards, the occupational and industry structures for the matrices are described in detail, including any adjustments made to data sources to fit the structure. A brief historical overview of the National Employment Matrix can be found in the box at the end of the chapter.

2006 base-year employment matrix

Calculating employment for each cell in the 2006 base-year matrix establishes the initial employment levels on which occupational projections are based.

For most industries, Occupational Employment Statistics (OES) survey data identify the occupational staffing pattern—the detailed occupations that comprise each wage and salary industry—and Current Employment Statistics (CES) data provide information on total wage and salary employment in each industry.[1] Estimates of wage and salary employment for each occupation in each industry are derived by multiplying each occupation's proportion–or ratio–of employment in each industry, based on OES survey data, by CES industry employment.

Other sources provide information on industries not included in the scope of the OES survey. The OES program obtains Federal Government and U.S. Postal Service (USPS) occupational wage and salary employment data from the U.S. Office of Personnel Management (OPM) and the USPS, respectively. The Current Population Survey (CPS) furnishes wage and salary employment data for agriculture; forestry, fishing, and hunting; support activities for agriculture and forestry; and private households.[2]

Data on self-employed and unpaid family worker employment also come from the CPS. Information on second jobs is collected for one-quarter of the sample each month and is combined with primary-job occupational employment estimates to yield a broader employment measure of the self-employed and unpaid family workers. Employment figures for these two categories of workers are available only at the total, all-industries level.

Total base-year employment for an occupation is the sum of employment in a row across all columns—the combination of wage and salary, self-employed, and unpaid family workers. Occupational employment within each industry, divided by total wage and salary employment in each industry, yields the occupational distribution ratios used in developing the change factor matrix and the projected-year employment matrix.

Over the numerous iterations of the National Employment Matrix, only a few changes are made to the base-year employment matrix to resolve known data issues. These issues are discussed later in the occupational directory section.

Change-factor matrix

A second matrix, the change-factor matrix, estimates changes in the utilization of occupations within wage and salary industries. For example, computer systems analysts would be expected to become a greater proportion of each industry's employment as the number of computer applications continues to increase. The

[1] Since November 2002, the OES survey has been a semiannual mail survey of approximately 200,000 establishments collected in May and November of each year. Over the course of a 3-year cycle, approximately 1.2 million establishments are sampled. For the May 2006 OES survey estimates, data collected in May 2006 were combined with data collected in November 2005, May 2005, November 2004, May 2004, and November 2003. Detailed information about the May 2006 OES survey is available at the OES web site (**http://www.bls.gov/oes/home.htm**). CES wage and salary employment data come from a monthly sample that includes about 160,000 businesses and government agencies, which cover approximately 400,000 individual worksites. The base-year employment matrix uses CES annual average data for 2006. For more information, visit: **http://www.bls.gov/ces/home.htm**

[2] The CPS is a monthly household survey on labor force characteristics. Each month, personal and telephone interviews are conducted at about 60,000 households. The base-year employment matrix uses CPS annual average data for 2006. Detailed information is available at the CPS Web site (**http://www.bls.gov/cps/home.htm**).

change factor multiplied by the occupation's base-year ratio of wage and salary industry employment determines the occupation's projected-year ratio of industry employment. Occupational change factors are prepared only for wage and salary employment in detailed industries. (See chapter IV and table IV-3.)

Over the numerous iterations of the National Employment Matrix, many changes occurred to the change factor matrix to incorporate analyst research and review. However, a change factor matrix was not needed for the final iteration of the projected-year employment matrix, as is discussed in the following section.

2016 projected-year employment matrix

Preparing the projected-year employment matrix is the last step in the projections process. For each wage and salary industry, projected-year industry wage and salary employment is multiplied by the projected-year occupational distribution ratio to yield projected-year wage and salary occupational employment for the industry.[3] Occupational employment data for the self-employed and unpaid family workers are projected separately with the help of time-series analysis and literature review. Total projected-year occupational employment is the sum of employment in a row across all columns—the sum of the employment figures for wage and salary, self-employed, and unpaid family workers.

With each iteration of the National Employment Matrix, numerous changes to the projected-year employment matrix occurred. Usually, changes were due to revisions in the change factor matrix or the industry projections. However, the final iteration of the projected-year employment matrix was adjusted primarily based on analyst recommendations.

The 2006–16 National Employment Matrix occupational directory

The occupational structure of the Matrix is based on the same structure used by the May 2006 OES employment estimates, which includes 801 detailed occupations from the 2000 Standard Occupational Classification (SOC) system. Occupational data for industries not surveyed by the OES were distributed across the full 2000 SOC.

This section will discuss the three types of occupations in the matrix, any adjustments made to the May 2006 OES employment estimates, and any adjustments made to 2006 CPS employment estimates. The occupation structure for the 2006–16 Matrix is shown in table II-1.

Occupation types. Occupations define the rows in the matrix, and three types of occupations exist in the final structure of the matrix:

1) Line-item occupations (753 published in total) possess the greatest level of published occupation employment detail in the matrix and display 2006 and projected 2016 employment estimates.

2) Summary occupations (268) combine employment information on line-item occupations and display 2006 and projected 2016 employment estimates.

3) Excluded occupations (52) were suppressed because of insufficient information to prepare projections. For example, in the 2006–16 National Employment Matrix occupational directory, separate projections were not released for three detailed rail transportation occupations: 53-4011, "locomotive engineers"; 53-4012, "locomotive firers"; and 53-4013, "railyard engineers, dinkey operators, and hostlers." Base-year Matrix employment and projected-year Matrix employment for these three occupations were each summed into the corresponding line item occupation 53-4010, "locomotive engineers and operators." (See table III-2.)

Adjusting May 2006 OES employment data. Some alterations to the May 2006 OES survey data were needed to improve the coverage of information in the National Employment Matrix. These adjustments took place primarily in NAICS industry 8131 "religious organizations" and in the OES-designated (non-NAICS) Federal Government sector.

Religious organizations. The OES survey generated May 2006 occupational employment estimates by applying industry employment data from the Quarterly Census of Employment and Wages (QCEW) program to OES survey occupation patterns in each industry. The QCEW program measures the employment of workers covered by unemployment insurance programs. QCEW employment for NAICS industry 8131, "religious organizations," however, does not reflect all workers because unemployment insurance coverage for this industry is incomplete.

In preparing occupation projections, the matrix staff uses industry employment from the Current Employment Statistics (CES) program for most industries, including religious organizations. The CES employment figure for religious organizations is almost 10 times greater than the figure derived from the QCEW; consequently, there is concern that some occupations in this industry may not be represented adequately by the OES survey. In particular, occupation 21-2011, "clergy," the most significant occupation in religious organizations, is considerably undercounted by using QCEW employment to select the OES sampling frame. Employment for clergy in the 2006 CPS industry-occupation matrix was significantly higher than the QCEW-based OES estimate. Accordingly, the occupational distribution for religious organizations was altered by increasing employment estimates for clergy to match the CPS estimate. This forced a decrease in the ratios for every other occupation within the industry before applying the distribution to 2006 CES employment.

Federal Government. Payroll data from the U.S. Office of Personnel Management on Federal occupational employment provided to OES staff use occupational codes and titles unique to the Federal Government. On the basis of information provided by OPM, Federal occupational data are recoded to the appropriate SOC occupations and are used to develop OES staffing patterns. Because of limited information provided for information technology occupations, the OES survey assigns OPM data on computer specialists to two non-residual SOC occupations, with the remainder going

[3] Industry sector employment projections prepared in the Division of Industry Employment Projections use a comprehensive modeling technique that estimates output as well as employment. More detailed industry employment projections produced using historical time series information are included in the Matrix and are consistent with their parent industry sector (See chapter IV and table IV-1).

to the residual occupation 15-1099, "All other computer specialists." The matrix staff developed a methodology for redistributing the OES occupation data over all SOC-based computer specialist occupations for matrix industry 919999, "Federal Government, excluding Postal Service." The distribution of computer specialists in this industry is adjusted to better reflect the distribution found across nearly all industries covered by oes outside of matrix industry 919999. However, the ratio for computer programmers in Federal Government is assumed to be less than other industries because computer programming is expected to be increasingly outsourced. The adjustment by matrix staff increases the number of information technology occupations from 3 to 10 as follows:

oes-coded Federal Government information technology occupations in matrix industry 919999

1) 15-1011 Computer and information scientist, research
2) 15-1041 Computer support specialists
3) 15-1099 All other computer specialists

Matrix-coded Federal Government information technology occupations in matrix industry 919999

1) 15-1011 Computer and information scientist, research
2) 15-1021 Computer programmers
3) 15-1031 Computer software engineers, applications
4) 15-1032 Computer software engineers, systems software
5) 15-1041 Computer support specialists
6) 15-1051 Computer systems analysts
7) 15-1061 Database administrators
8) 15-1071 Network and computer systems administrators
9) 15-1081 Network systems and data communications analyst
10) 15-1099 All other computer specialists

Adjusting 2006 CPS employment. The 2006–16 National Employment Matrix uses 2006 CPS employment data for estimates of the numbers of self-employed and unpaid family workers, as well as wage and salary workers in agriculture and private household industries. The 2006 CPS data were coded using the 2000 Census of Population occupation classification system, which closely resembles the 2000 SOC system. Of the 502 CPS occupations, 373 were exact matches to National Employment Matrix occupations. The remaining CPS occupations were distributed over two or more SOC occupations. When one CPS occupation had the coverage of multiple matrix occupations, CPS self-employed and unpaid family worker employment were distributed over the detailed matrix occupations on the basis of total occupation employment in the 2004 matrix. Occupational analysts then reviewed and recommended changes to the distributed employment.

The 2006–16 National Employment Matrix industry directory

In order to develop the matrix industry structure, bls staff made judgments to reconcile data from the ces, oes, and cps. This section covers the class of worker categories; cps coverage; ces and oes treatment of educational services, hospitals, and government; and a note on 5-digit naics industries covered by oes. The Matrix industry directory can be found in table II-2.

Class-of-worker categories. The class-of-worker categories—wage and salary jobs, by industry; self-employed workers; and unpaid family workers—define the columns of the 2006–16 Matrix. Detailed employment by NAICS industry or government sector is presented only for wage and salary jobs. There are two general types found in the industry directory:

1) Rollups and line items (311 published in total) show the greatest level of published employment detail in the Matrix.

2) Summaries (164) show combined employment for rollups and line-items.

As the following tabulation shows, the CES survey contributes industry employment for wage and salary jobs in 299 of the 311 most detailed matrix columns and is by far the largest source of industry data.

Class-of-worker category	*Number of columns*	*Data Source*
Total, rollups and line items	*311*	*CES/CPS*
Nonfarm wage and salary jobs	*299*	*CES*
Wage and salary workers, primary job, agriculture, forestry, fishing, and private households	*6*	*CPS*
Wage and salary workers with secondary job, agriculture, forestry, fishing, and private households	*2*	*CPS*
Self-employed workers, primary job	*1*	*CPS*
Self-employed workers, secondary job	*1*	*CPS*
Unpaid family workers, primary job	*1*	*CPS*
Unpaid family workers, secondary job	*1*	*CPS*

In comparison, the BLS Division of Industry Employment Projections (DIEP) uses the same employment data, but has less detail in their industry structure—about 200 line item columns.

For industries using CES employment, OES occupational distribution information—or industry staffing patterns—for wage and salary jobs is multiplied by CES industry control totals to find occupational employment within each industry. When CPS data are used for wage and salary industry control totals, as in agriculture or private households, industry staffing patterns are based on CPS data. Occupational distribution information for self-employed or unpaid family workers is based on CPS data.

The CPS provides data on industries and classes of worker outside of the scope of the CES and OES surveys. As seen in the table above, CPS data are primarily used for wage and salary workers in agriculture or private households, self-employment, and unpaid family workers.

The only industry group within NAICS sector 11, "Agriculture, forestry, fishing and hunting," fully surveyed by both the CES and OES programs is NAICS 113300, "Logging." For the remainder of NAICS 11, data from the CPS are used because the CES and OES surveys have limited or no coverage.

ces and oes treatment of educational services, hospitals, and government. The ces program publishes industry employment data for private educational services and private hospitals separately from State or local government education and hospitals. Conversely, the oes program develops occupational distribution information for education and hospitals by combining public and private ownership. In order to identify differences between public and private ownership and match the structure used by DIEP, the 2002–12 and the 2004–14 versions of the National Employment Matrix presented employment data in the configuration used by the ces program. However, the 2006–16 projections return to presenting employment data in education and hospitals for public and private ownership combined, to be consistent with the oes program. Correspondingly, employment data for State and local government exclude education and hospitals.

The CES and OES programs have special designations for government sectors that are not part of the 2002 NAICS structure, except for NAICS 491100, "Postal Service." The National Employment Matrix uses the following non-NAICS codes and titles for these government sectors:

919999 Federal Government, excluding Postal Service
929200 State government, excluding education and hospitals
939300 Local government, excluding education and hospitals

When CES industry employment detail was unavailable, industry control totals were estimated by distributing CES employment with information from the Quarterly Census of Employment and Wages (QCEW). The summaries NAICS 611000, "Educational services, public and private," and NAICS 622000, "Hospitals, public and private," used only CES data for industry control totals. However, employment data for 4-digit NAICS detail under these summaries was only available for the private sector. To determine employment estimates for 4-digit NAICS detail in State and local government, CES employment data were distributed using ratios calculated from QCEW employment data. As mentioned above, the OES program currently publishes occupational distribution information for all of the published detailed levels of education and hospitals for public and private ownership combined.

The industry control totals for the following industries partly used CES data that were distributed with information from QCEW data:

Code	*Title*	*Type*
611100	*Elementary and secondary schools, public and private*	*Line item*
6112-3	*Junior colleges, colleges, universities, and professional schools, public and private*	*Summary*
611200	*Junior colleges, public and private*	*Line item*
611300	*Colleges, universities, and professional schools, public and private*	*Line item*
6114-7	*Other educational services, public and private*	*Summary*
611400	*Business schools and computer and management training, public and private*	*Line item*
611500	*Technical and trade schools, public and private*	*Line item*
611600	*Other schools and instruction, public and private*	*Line item*
611700	*Educational support services, public and private*	*Line item*
622100	*General medical and surgical hospitals, public and private*	*Line item*
622200	*Psychiatric and substance abuse hospitals, public and private*	*Line item*
622300	*Specialty (except psychiatric and substance abuse) hospitals, public and private*	*Line item*
721100	*Traveler accommodation, including hotels and motels*	*Summary*

Example of distributing ces employment using information from qcew. For 2006 annual average employment data, the ces program combines naics 721100, "traveler accommodation," with naics 721300, "rooming and boarding houses." This happens because a part of the traveler accommodation industry group, namely naics 721190, "other traveler accommodation," is combined with rooming and boarding houses. To determine employment in other traveler accommodation separately from rooming and boarding houses, employment ratios are calculated with qcew data and these ratios are applied to ces employment estimates.

At the time of developing the 2006 base-year matrix, the most recent annual average QCEW employment data available were for 2005. The following tabulation summarizes the results.

NAICS	2005 QCEW employment	2006 CES employment
721190, 721300	37,075	34,800
721190	26,316	24,701 *
721300	10,759	10,099 *

* Estimated by Matrix staff.

The formula to determine 2006 CES employment in NAICS 721300 would be:

34,800*(10,759/37,075) =10,099

While NAICS 721190 and NAICS 721300 were both excluded industries, the summary NAICS 721100 published in the National Employment Matrix no longer includes rooming and boarding houses.

Note on 5-digit NAICS industries covered by OES. While the matrix provides 4- and 5-digit NAICS industry detail whenever possible, the 2006–16 Matrix has less 5-digit detail than the 2004–14 matrix. Because of confidentiality or reliability concerns, industries that were a combination of more than one 5-digit NAICS industry are suppressed in the 2006–16 Matrix. For example, 2004–14 matrix industry code 2371RR, "Water and sewer system and all other utility system construction" is a combination of NAICS 237110 and NAICS 237120. There were 22 such industries published in the 2004–14 National Employment Matrix that are excluded from the 2006–16 Matrix. However, single 5-digit NAICS industries, such as NAICS 237130, "Power and communication line and related structures constructions," continue to be included in the 2006–16 National Employment Matrix.

History of National Employment Matrix data sources and changes to classification systems

Since its inception, the National Employment Matrix has incorporated industry-by-occupation wage and salary employment information from two different data sources. Data from the Census Bureau's decennial Census of Population initially yielded industry-by-occupation employment patterns based on individuals' responses coded to that Agency's industry and occupation classification systems.

The OES survey-based industry-by-occupation employment data, first adopted for use with the 1980-90 projections, became the primary data source used in preparing the National Employment Matrix. OES survey data were preferred because the data were collected from establishments that were given occupational definitions for reporting employment and because the OES data were collected more frequently than the Census was conducted. The BLS National Employment Matrix used OES data based on a structure consistent with the 1980 Standard Occupational Classification (SOC) through its 1998-2008 set of occupational employment projections.

Occupational projections for 2000-10 incorporated the newly available 2000 SOC system for the first time.[1] This revised classification system resulted in major changes to the occupational definitions and taxonomy used in the projections. These differences between the 2000 SOC-structured OES survey data and earlier 1980 SOC-system-based OES survey occupational data resulted in a break in the historical occupational employment time series. In this case, the differences resulted not from a change in a data source, but from the change in the classification system.

The OES survey's industry classification system—based first on the 1977 Standard Industrial Classification (SIC) system and later on the 1987 revision to the SIC system—underwent relatively few changes until the creation of the 2002 North American Industry Classification System (NAICS), which was first used with the 2002–12 employment projections, replacing the 1987 SIC.[2]

The CPS began collecting 2000 SOC- and 2002 NAICS-based data in the January 2003 survey.

The 2006–16 BLS National Employment Matrix uses May 2006 OES data coded to the 2000 SOC system and CES data coded to the 2002 NAICS. CPS industry and occupational data used to construct the 2006–16 National Employment Matrix also are consistent with the 2000 SOC system and 2002 NAICS.

[1] See "Chapter I. 2000-10 Occupational Projections Incorporate the 2000 Standard Occupational Classification System," *Occupational Projections and Training Data*, Bulletin 2542 (Bureau of Labor Statistics, January 2002).

[2] See "Chapter II. 2002–12 National Employment Matrix Structure," *Occupational Projections and Training Data*, Bulletin 2572 (Bureau of Labor Statistics, March 2004).

Table II-1. National Employment Matrix occupational directory, 2006

Matrix code	Matrix occupation title	Occupation type
00-00001	Total, all occupations	Summary
11-13001	Management, business, and financial occupations	Summary
11-0000	Management occupations	Summary
11-1000	Top executives	Summary
11-1011	Chief executives	Line item
11-1021	General and operations managers	Line item
11-1031	Legislators	Line item
11-2000	Advertising, marketing, promotions, public relations, and sales managers	Summary
11-2011	Advertising and promotions managers	Line item
11-2020	Marketing and sales managers	Summary
11-2021	Marketing managers	Line item
11-2022	Sales managers	Line item
11-2031	Public relations managers	Line item
11-3000	Operations specialties managers	Summary
11-3011	Administrative services managers	Line item
11-3021	Computer and information systems managers	Line item
11-3031	Financial managers	Line item
11-3040	Human resources managers	Summary
11-3041	Compensation and benefits managers	Line item
11-3042	Training and development managers	Line item
11-3049	Human resources managers, all other	Line item
11-3051	Industrial production managers	Line item
11-3061	Purchasing managers	Line item
11-3071	Transportation, storage, and distribution managers	Line item
11-9000	Other management occupations	Summary
11-9010	Agricultural managers	Summary
11-9011	Farm, ranch, and other agricultural managers	Line item
11-9012	Farmers and ranchers	Line item
11-9021	Construction managers	Line item
11-9030	Education administrators	Summary
11-9031	Education administrators, preschool and child care center/program	Line item
11-9032	Education administrators, elementary and secondary school	Line item
11-9033	Education administrators, postsecondary	Line item
11-9039	Education administrators, all other	Line item
11-9041	Engineering managers	Line item
11-9051	Food service managers	Line item
11-9061	Funeral directors	Line item
11-9071	Gaming managers	Line item
11-9081	Lodging managers	Line item
11-9111	Medical and health services managers	Line item
11-9121	Natural sciences managers	Line item
11-9131	Postmasters and mail superintendents	Line item
11-9141	Property, real estate, and community association managers	Line item
11-9151	Social and community service managers	Line item
11-9199	Managers, all other	Line item
13-0000	Business and financial operations occupations	Summary
13-1000	Business operations specialists	Summary
13-1011	Agents and business managers of artists, performers, and athletes	Line item
13-1020	Buyers and purchasing agents	Summary
13-1021	Purchasing agents and buyers, farm products	Line item
13-1022	Wholesale and retail buyers, except farm products	Line item
13-1023	Purchasing agents, except wholesale, retail, and farm products	Line item
13-1030	Claims adjusters, appraisers, examiners, and investigators	Summary
13-1031	Claims adjusters, examiners, and investigators	Line item
13-1032	Insurance appraisers, auto damage	Line item
13-1041	Compliance officers, except agriculture, construction, health and safety, and transportation	Line item
13-1051	Cost estimators	Line item
13-1061	Emergency management specialists	Line item
13-1070	Human resources, training, and labor relations specialists	Summary
13-1071	Employment, recruitment, and placement specialists	Line item
13-1072	Compensation, benefits, and job analysis specialists	Line item
13-1073	Training and development specialists	Line item
13-1079	Human resources, training, and labor relations specialists, all other	Line item
13-1081	Logisticians	Line item
13-1111	Management analysts	Line item
13-1121	Meeting and convention planners	Line item
13-1199	Business operation specialists, all other	Line item
13-2000	Financial specialists	Summary
13-2011	Accountants and auditors	Line item
13-2021	Appraisers and assessors of real estate	Line item
13-2031	Budget analysts	Line item
13-2041	Credit analysts	Line item
13-2050	Financial analysts and advisors	Summary
13-2051	Financial analysts	Line item
13-2052	Personal financial advisors	Line item
13-2053	Insurance underwriters	Line item
13-2061	Financial examiners	Line item
13-2070	Loan counselors and officers	Summary
13-2071	Loan counselors	Line item
13-2072	Loan officers	Line item
13-2080	Tax examiners, collectors, preparers, and revenue agents	Summary
13-2081	Tax examiners, collectors, and revenue agents	Line item
13-2082	Tax preparers	Line item
13-2099	Financial specialists, all other	Line item
15-29001	Professional and related occupations	Summary
15-0000	Computer and mathematical science occupations	Summary
15-1000	Computer specialists	Summary
15-1011	Computer and information scientists, research	Line item
15-1021	Computer programmers	Line item
15-1030	Computer software engineers	Summary
15-1031	Computer software engineers, applications	Line item
15-1032	Computer software engineers, systems software	Line item
15-1041	Computer support specialists	Line item

Table II-1. National Employment Matrix occupational directory, 2006 — Continued

Matrix code	Matrix occupation title	Occupation type
15-1051	Computer systems analysts	Line item
15-1061	Database administrators	Line item
15-1071	Network and computer systems administrators	Line item
15-1081	Network systems and data communications analysts	Line item
15-1099	Computer specialists, all other	Line item
15-2000	Mathematical science occupations	Summary
15-2011	Actuaries	Line item
15-2021	Mathematicians	Line item
15-2031	Operations research analysts	Line item
15-2041	Statisticians	Line item
15-2090	Miscellaneous mathematical science occupations	Summary
15-2091	Mathematical technicians	Line item
15-2099	Mathematical scientists, all other	Line item
17-0000	Architecture and engineering occupations	Summary
17-1000	Architects, surveyors, and cartographers	Summary
17-1010	Architects, except naval	Summary
17-1011	Architects, except landscape and naval	Line item
17-1012	Landscape architects	Line item
17-1020	Surveyors, cartographers, and photogrammetrists	Summary
17-1021	Cartographers and photogrammetrists	Line item
17-1022	Surveyors	Line item
17-2000	Engineers	Summary
17-2011	Aerospace engineers	Line item
17-2021	Agricultural engineers	Line item
17-2031	Biomedical engineers	Line item
17-2041	Chemical engineers	Line item
17-2051	Civil engineers	Line item
17-2061	Computer hardware engineers	Line item
17-2070	Electrical and electronics engineers	Summary
17-2071	Electrical engineers	Line item
17-2072	Electronics engineers, except computer	Line item
17-2081	Environmental engineers	Line item
17-2110	Industrial engineers, including health and safety	Summary
17-2111	Health and safety engineers, except mining safety engineers and inspectors	Line item
17-2112	Industrial engineers	Line item
17-2121	Marine engineers and naval architects	Line item
17-2131	Materials engineers	Line item
17-2141	Mechanical engineers	Line item
17-2151	Mining and geological engineers, including mining safety engineers	Line item
17-2161	Nuclear engineers	Line item
17-2171	Petroleum engineers	Line item
17-2199	Engineers, all other	Line item
17-3000	Drafters, engineering, and mapping technicians	Summary
17-3010	Drafters	Summary
17-3011	Architectural and civil drafters	Line item
17-3012	Electrical and electronics drafters	Line item
17-3013	Mechanical drafters	Line item
17-3019	Drafters, all other	Line item
17-3020	Engineering technicians, except drafters	Summary
17-3021	Aerospace engineering and operations technicians	Line item
17-3022	Civil engineering technicians	Line item
17-3023	Electrical and electronic engineering technicians	Line item
17-3024	Electro-mechanical technicians	Line item
17-3025	Environmental engineering technicians	Line item
17-3026	Industrial engineering technicians	Line item
17-3027	Mechanical engineering technicians	Line item
17-3029	Engineering technicians, except drafters, all other	Line item
17-3031	Surveying and mapping technicians	Line item
19-0000	Life, physical, and social science occupations	Summary
19-1000	Life scientists	Summary
19-1010	Agricultural and food scientists	Summary
19-1011	Animal scientists	Line item
19-1012	Food scientists and technologists	Line item
19-1013	Soil and plant Scientists	Line item
19-1020	Biological scientists	Summary
19-1021	Biochemists and biophysicists	Line item
19-1022	Microbiologists	Line item
19-1023	Zoologists and wildlife biologists	Line item
19-1029	Biological scientists, all other	Line item
19-1030	Conservation scientists and foresters	Summary
19-1031	Conservation scientists	Line item
19-1032	Foresters	Line item
19-1040	Medical scientists	Summary
19-1041	Epidemiologists	Line item
19-1042	Medical scientists, except epidemiologists	Line item
19-1099	Life scientists, all other	Line item
19-2000	Physical scientists	Summary
19-2010	Astronomers and physicists	Summary
19-2011	Astronomers	Line item
19-2012	Physicists	Line item
19-2021	Atmospheric and space scientists	Line item
19-2030	Chemists and materials scientists	Summary
19-2031	Chemists	Line item
19-2032	Materials scientists	Line item
19-2040	Environmental scientists and geoscientists	Summary
19-2041	Environmental scientists and specialists, including health	Line item
19-2042	Geoscientists, except hydrologists and geographers	Line item
19-2043	Hydrologists	Line item
19-2099	Physical scientists, all other	Line item
19-3000	Social scientists and related occupations	Summary
19-3011	Economists	Line item
19-3020	Market and survey researchers	Summary
19-3021	Market research analysts	Line item
19-3022	Survey researchers	Line item
19-3030	Psychologists	Summary
19-3031	Clinical, counseling, and school psychologists	Line item
19-3032	Industrial-organizational psychologists	Line item
19-3039	Psychologists, all other	Line item

Table II-1. National Employment Matrix occupational directory, 2006 — Continued

Matrix code	Matrix occupation title	Occupation type
19-3041	Sociologists	Line item
19-3051	Urban and regional planners	Line item
19-3090	Miscellaneous social scientists and related workers	Summary
19-3091	Anthropologists and archeologists	Line item
19-3092	Geographers	Line item
19-3093	Historians	Line item
19-3094	Political scientists	Line item
19-3099	Social scientists and related workers, all other	Line item
19-4000	Life, physical, and social science technicians	Summary
19-4011	Agricultural and food science technicians	Line item
19-4021	Biological technicians	Line item
19-4031	Chemical technicians	Line item
19-4041	Geological and petroleum technicians	Line item
19-4051	Nuclear technicians	Line item
19-4061	Social science research assistants	Line item
19-4090	Other life, physical, and social science technicians	Summary
19-4091	Environmental science and protection technicians, including health	Line item
19-4092	Forensic science technicians	Line item
19-4093	Forest and conservation technicians	Line item
19-4099	Life, physical, and social science technicians, all other	Line item
21-0000	Community and social services occupations	Summary
21-1000	Counselors, social workers, and other community and social service specialists	Summary
21-1010	Counselors	Summary
21-1011	Substance abuse and behavioral disorder counselors	Line item
21-1012	Educational, vocational, and school counselors	Line item
21-1013	Marriage and family therapists	Line item
21-1014	Mental health counselors	Line item
21-1015	Rehabilitation counselors	Line item
21-1019	Counselors, all other	Line item
21-1020	Social workers	Summary
21-1021	Child, family, and school social workers	Line item
21-1022	Medical and public health social workers	Line item
21-1023	Mental health and substance abuse social workers	Line item
21-1029	Social workers, all other	Line item
21-1090	Miscellaneous community and social service specialists	Summary
21-1091	Health educators	Line item
21-1092	Probation officers and correctional treatment specialists	Line item
21-1093	Social and human service assistants	Line item
21-1099	Community and social service specialists, all other	Line item
21-2000	Religious workers	Summary
21-2011	Clergy	Line item
21-2021	Directors, religious activities and education	Line item
21-2099	Religious workers, all other	Line item
23-0000	Legal occupations	Summary
23-1000	Lawyers, judges, and related workers	Summary
23-1011	Lawyers	Line item
23-1020	Judges, magistrates, and other judicial workers	Summary
23-1021	Administrative law judges, adjudicators, and hearing officers	Line item
23-1022	Arbitrators, mediators, and conciliators	Line item
23-1023	Judges, magistrate judges, and magistrates	Line item
23-2000	Legal support workers	Summary
23-2011	Paralegals and legal assistants	Line item
23-2090	Miscellaneous legal support workers	Summary
23-2091	Court reporters	Line item
23-2092	Law clerks	Line item
23-2093	Title examiners, abstractors, and searchers	Line item
23-2099	Legal support workers, all other	Line item
25-0000	Education, training, and library occupations	Summary
25-1000	Postsecondary teachers	Line item
25-1011	Business teachers, postsecondary	Exclude
25-1021	Computer science teachers, postsecondary	Exclude
25-1022	Mathematical science teachers, postsecondary	Exclude
25-1031	Architecture teachers, postsecondary	Exclude
25-1032	Engineering teachers, postsecondary	Exclude
25-1041	Agricultural sciences teachers, postsecondary	Exclude
25-1042	Biological science teachers, postsecondary	Exclude
25-1043	Forestry and conservation science teachers, postsecondary	Exclude
25-1051	Atmospheric, earth, marine, and space sciences teachers, postsecondary	Exclude
25-1052	Chemistry teachers, postsecondary	Exclude
25-1053	Environmental science teachers, postsecondary	Exclude
25-1054	Physics teachers, postsecondary	Exclude
25-1061	Anthropology and archeology teachers, postsecondary	Exclude
25-1062	Area, ethnic, and cultural studies teachers, postsecondary	Exclude
25-1063	Economics teachers, postsecondary	Exclude
25-1064	Geography teachers, postsecondary	Exclude
25-1065	Political science teachers, postsecondary	Exclude
25-1066	Psychology teachers, postsecondary	Exclude
25-1067	Sociology teachers, postsecondary	Exclude
25-1069	Social sciences teachers, postsecondary, all other	Exclude
25-1071	Health specialties teachers, postsecondary	Exclude
25-1072	Nursing instructors and teachers, postsecondary	Exclude
25-1081	Education teachers, postsecondary	Exclude
25-1082	Library science teachers, postsecondary	Exclude
25-1111	Criminal justice and law enforcement teachers, postsecondary	Exclude
25-1112	Law teachers, postsecondary	Exclude
25-1113	Social work teachers, postsecondary	Exclude
25-1121	Art, drama, and music teachers, postsecondary	Exclude
25-1122	Communications teachers, postsecondary	Exclude
25-1123	English language and literature teachers, postsecondary	Exclude
25-1124	Foreign language and literature teachers, postsecondary	Exclude
25-1125	History teachers, postsecondary	Exclude

Table II-1. National Employment Matrix occupational directory, 2006 — Continued

Matrix code	Matrix occupation title	Occupation type
25-1126	Philosophy and religion teachers, postsecondary	Exclude
25-1191	Graduate teaching assistants	Exclude
25-1192	Home economics teachers, postsecondary	Exclude
25-1193	Recreation and fitness studies teachers, postsecondary	Exclude
25-1194	Vocational education teachers, postsecondary	Exclude
25-1199	Postsecondary teachers, all other	Exclude
25-2000	Primary, secondary, and special education teachers	Summary
25-2010	Preschool and kindergarten teachers	Summary
25-2011	Preschool teachers, except special education	Line item
25-2012	Kindergarten teachers, except special education	Line item
25-2020	Elementary and middle school teachers	Summary
25-2021	Elementary school teachers, except special education	Line item
25-2022	Middle school teachers, except special and vocational education	Line item
25-2023	Vocational education teachers, middle school	Line item
25-2030	Secondary school teachers	Summary
25-2031	Secondary school teachers, except special and vocational education	Line item
25-2032	Vocational education teachers, secondary school	Line item
25-2040	Special education teachers	Summary
25-2041	Special education teachers, preschool, kindergarten, and elementary school	Line item
25-2042	Special education teachers, middle school	Line item
25-2043	Special education teachers, secondary school	Line item
25-3000	Other teachers and instructors	Summary
25-3011	Adult literacy, remedial education, and GED teachers and instructors	Line item
25-3021	Self-enrichment education teachers	Line item
25-3099	Teachers and instructors, all other	Line item
25-4000	Librarians, curators, and archivists	Summary
25-4010	Archivists, curators, and museum technicians	Summary
25-4011	Archivists	Line item
25-4012	Curators	Line item
25-4013	Museum Technicians and Conservators	Line item
25-4021	Librarians	Line item
25-4031	Library technicians	Line item
25-9000	Other education, training, and library occupations	Summary
25-9011	Audio-visual collections specialists	Line item
25-9021	Farm and home management advisors	Line item
25-9031	Instructional coordinators	Line item
25-9041	Teacher assistants	Line item
25-9099	Education, training, and library workers, all other	Line item
27-0000	Arts, design, entertainment, sports, and media occupations	Summary
27-1000	Art and design occupations	Summary
27-1010	Artists and related workers	Summary
27-1011	Art directors	Line item
27-1012	Craft artists	Line item
27-1013	Fine artists, including painters, sculptors, and illustrators	Line item
27-1014	Multi-media artists and animators	Line item
27-1019	Artists and related workers, all other	Line item
27-1020	Designers	Summary
27-1021	Commercial and industrial designers	Line item
27-1022	Fashion designers	Line item
27-1023	Floral designers	Line item
27-1024	Graphic designers	Line item
27-1025	Interior designers	Line item
27-1026	Merchandise displayers and window trimmers	Line item
27-1027	Set and exhibit designers	Line item
27-1029	Designers, all other	Line item
27-2000	Entertainers and performers, sports and related occupations	Summary
27-2010	Actors, producers, and directors	Summary
27-2011	Actors	Line item
27-2012	Producers and directors	Line item
27-2020	Athletes, coaches, umpires, and related workers	Summary
27-2021	Athletes and sports competitors	Line item
27-2022	Coaches and scouts	Line item
27-2023	Umpires, referees, and other sports officials	Line item
27-2030	Dancers and choreographers	Summary
27-2031	Dancers	Line item
27-2032	Choreographers	Line item
27-2040	Musicians, singers, and related workers	Summary
27-2041	Music directors and composers	Line item
27-2042	Musicians and singers	Line item
27-2099	Entertainers and performers, sports and related workers, all other	Line item
27-3000	Media and communication occupations	Summary
27-3010	Announcers	Summary
27-3011	Radio and television announcers	Line item
27-3012	Public address system and other announcers	Line item
27-3020	News analysts, reporters and correspondents	Summary
27-3021	Broadcast news analysts	Line item
27-3022	Reporters and correspondents	Line item
27-3031	Public relations specialists	Line item
27-3040	Writers and editors	Summary
27-3041	Editors	Line item
27-3042	Technical writers	Line item
27-3043	Writers and authors	Line item
27-3090	Miscellaneous media and communications workers	Summary
27-3091	Interpreters and translators	Line item
27-3099	Media and communication workers, all other	Line item
27-4000	Media and communication equipment occupations	Summary
27-4010	Broadcast and sound engineering technicians and radio operators	Summary
27-4011	Audio and video equipment technicians	Line item
27-4012	Broadcast technicians	Line item
27-4013	Radio operators	Line item
27-4014	Sound engineering technicians	Line item
27-4021	Photographers	Line item

Table II-1. National Employment Matrix occupational directory, 2006 — Continued

Matrix code	Matrix occupation title	Occupation type
27-4030	Television, video, and motion picture camera operators and editors	Summary
27-4031	Camera operators, television, video, and motion picture	Line item
27-4032	Film and video editors	Line item
27-4099	Media and communication equipment workers, all other	Line item
29-0000	Healthcare practitioners and technical occupations	Summary
29-1000	Health diagnosing and treating practitioners	Summary
29-1011	Chiropractors	Line item
29-1020	Dentists	Summary
29-1021	Dentists, general	Line item
29-1022	Oral and maxillofacial surgeons	Line item
29-1023	Orthodontists	Line item
29-1024	Prosthodontists	Line item
29-1029	Dentists, all other specialists	Line item
29-1031	Dietitians and nutritionists	Line item
29-1041	Optometrists	Line item
29-1051	Pharmacists	Line item
29-1060	Physicians and surgeons	Line item
29-1061	Anesthesiologists	Exclude
29-1062	Family and general practitioners	Exclude
29-1063	Internists, general	Exclude
29-1064	Obstetricians and gynecologists	Exclude
29-1065	Pediatricians, general	Exclude
29-1066	Psychiatrists	Exclude
29-1067	Surgeons	Exclude
29-1069	Physicians and surgeons, all other	Exclude
29-1071	Physician assistants	Line item
29-1081	Podiatrists	Line item
29-1111	Registered nurses	Line item
29-1120	Therapists	Summary
29-1121	Audiologists	Line item
29-1122	Occupational therapists	Line item
29-1123	Physical therapists	Line item
29-1124	Radiation therapists	Line item
29-1125	Recreational therapists	Line item
29-1126	Respiratory therapists	Line item
29-1127	Speech-language pathologists	Line item
29-1129	Therapists, all other	Line item
29-1131	Veterinarians	Line item
29-1199	Health diagnosing and treating practitioners, all other	Line item
29-2000	Health technologists and technicians	Summary
29-2010	Clinical laboratory technologists and technicians	Summary
29-2011	Medical and clinical laboratory technologists	Line item
29-2012	Medical and clinical laboratory technicians	Line item
29-2021	Dental hygienists	Line item
29-2030	Diagnostic related technologists and technicians	Summary
29-2031	Cardiovascular technologists and technicians	Line item
29-2032	Diagnostic medical sonographers	Line item
29-2033	Nuclear medicine technologists	Line item
29-2034	Radiologic technologists and technicians	Line item
29-2041	Emergency medical technicians and paramedics	Line item
29-2050	Health diagnosing and treating practitioner support technicians	Summary
29-2051	Dietetic technicians	Line item
29-2052	Pharmacy technicians	Line item
29-2053	Psychiatric technicians	Line item
29-2054	Respiratory therapy technicians	Line item
29-2055	Surgical technologists	Line item
29-2056	Veterinary technologists and technicians	Line item
29-2061	Licensed practical and licensed vocational nurses	Line item
29-2071	Medical records and health information technicians	Line item
29-2081	Opticians, dispensing	Line item
29-2090	Miscellaneous health technologists and technicians	Summary
29-2091	Orthotists and prosthetists	Line item
29-2099	Healthcare technologists and technicians, all other	Line item
29-9000	Other healthcare practitioners and technical occupations	Summary
29-9010	Occupational health and safety specialists and technicians	Summary
29-9011	Occupational health and safety specialists	Line item
29-9012	Occupational health and safety technicians	Line item
29-9090	Miscellaneous health practitioners and technical workers	Summary
29-9091	Athletic trainers	Line item
29-9099	Healthcare practitioners and technical workers, all other	Line item
31-39001	Service occupations	Summary
31-0000	Healthcare support occupations	Summary
31-1000	Nursing, psychiatric, and home health aides	Summary
31-1011	Home health aides	Line item
31-1012	Nursing aides, orderlies, and attendants	Line item
31-1013	Psychiatric aides	Line item
31-2000	Occupational and physical therapist assistants and aides	Summary
31-2010	Occupational therapist assistants and aides	Summary
31-2011	Occupational therapist assistants	Line item
31-2012	Occupational therapist aides	Line item
31-2020	Physical therapist assistants and aides	Summary
31-2021	Physical therapist assistants	Line item
31-2022	Physical therapist aides	Line item
31-9000	Other healthcare support occupations	Summary
31-9011	Massage therapists	Line item
31-9090	Miscellaneous healthcare support occupations	Summary
31-9091	Dental assistants	Line item
31-9092	Medical assistants	Line item
31-9093	Medical equipment preparers	Line item
31-9094	Medical transcriptionists	Line item
31-9095	Pharmacy aides	Line item
31-9096	Veterinary assistants and laboratory animal caretakers	Line item
31-9099	Healthcare support workers, all other	Line item
33-0000	Protective service occupations	Summary

Table II-1. National Employment Matrix occupational directory, 2006 — Continued

Matrix code	Matrix occupation title	Occupation type
33-1000	First-line supervisors/managers, protective service workers	Summary
33-1010	First-line supervisors/managers, law enforcement workers	Summary
33-1011	First-line supervisors/managers of correctional officers	Line item
33-1012	First-line supervisors/managers of police and detectives	Line item
33-1021	First-line supervisors/managers of fire fighting and prevention workers	Line item
33-1099	First-line supervisors/managers, protective service workers, all other	Line item
33-2000	Fire fighting and prevention workers	Summary
33-2011	Fire fighters	Line item
33-2020	Fire inspectors	Summary
33-2021	Fire inspectors and investigators	Line item
33-2022	Forest fire inspectors and prevention specialists	Line item
33-3000	Law enforcement workers	Summary
33-3010	Bailiffs, correctional officers, and jailers	Summary
33-3011	Bailiffs	Line item
33-3012	Correctional officers and jailers	Line item
33-3021	Detectives and criminal investigators	Line item
33-3031	Fish and game wardens	Line item
33-3041	Parking enforcement workers	Line item
33-3050	Police officers	Summary
33-3051	Police and sheriff's patrol officers	Line item
33-3052	Transit and railroad police	Line item
33-9000	Other protective service workers	Summary
33-9011	Animal control workers	Line item
33-9021	Private detectives and investigators	Line item
33-9030	Security guards and gaming surveillance officers	Summary
33-9031	Gaming surveillance officers and gaming investigators	Line item
33-9032	Security guards	Line item
33-9090	Miscellaneous protective service workers	Summary
33-9091	Crossing guards	Line item
33-9092	Lifeguards, ski patrol, and other recreational protective service workers	Line item
33-9099	Protective service workers, all other	Line item
35-0000	Food preparation and serving related occupations	Summary
35-1000	Supervisors, food preparation and serving workers	Summary
35-1011	Chefs and head cooks	Line item
35-1012	First-line supervisors/managers of food preparation and serving workers	Line item
35-2000	Cooks and food preparation workers	Summary
35-2010	Cooks	Summary
35-2011	Cooks, fast food	Line item
35-2012	Cooks, institution and cafeteria	Line item
35-2013	Cooks, private household	Line item
35-2014	Cooks, restaurant	Line item
35-2015	Cooks, short order	Line item
35-2019	Cooks, all other	Line item
35-2021	Food preparation workers	Line item
35-3000	Food and beverage serving workers	Summary
35-3011	Bartenders	Line item
35-3020	Fast food and counter workers	Summary
35-3021	Combined food preparation and serving workers, including fast food	Line item
35-3022	Counter attendants, cafeteria, food concession, and coffee shop	Line item
35-3031	Waiters and waitresses	Line item
35-3041	Food servers, nonrestaurant	Line item
35-9000	Other food preparation and serving related workers	Summary
35-9011	Dining room and cafeteria attendants and bartender helpers	Line item
35-9021	Dishwashers	Line item
35-9031	Hosts and hostesses, restaurant, lounge, and coffee shop	Line item
35-9099	Food preparation and serving related workers, all other	Line item
37-0000	Building and grounds cleaning and maintenance occupations	Summary
37-1000	Supervisors, building and grounds cleaning and maintenance workers	Summary
37-1011	First-line supervisors/managers of housekeeping and janitorial workers	Line item
37-1012	First-line supervisors/managers of landscaping, lawn service, and groundskeeping workers	Line item
37-2000	Building cleaning and pest control workers	Summary
37-2010	Building cleaning workers	Summary
37-2011	Janitors and cleaners, except maids and housekeeping cleaners	Line item
37-2012	Maids and housekeeping cleaners	Line item
37-2019	Building cleaning workers, all other	Line item
37-2021	Pest control workers	Line item
37-3000	Grounds maintenance workers	Summary
37-3010	Grounds maintenance workers	Summary
37-3011	Landscaping and groundskeeping workers	Line item
37-3012	Pesticide handlers, sprayers, and applicators, vegetation	Line item
37-3013	Tree trimmers and pruners	Line item
37-3019	Grounds maintenance workers, all other	Line item
39-0000	Personal care and service occupations	Summary
39-1000	Supervisors, personal care and service workers	Summary
39-1010	First-line supervisors/managers of gaming workers	Summary
39-1011	Gaming supervisors	Line item
39-1012	Slot key persons	Line item
39-1021	First-line supervisors/managers of personal service workers	Line item
39-2000	Animal care and service workers	Summary
39-2011	Animal trainers	Line item
39-2021	Nonfarm animal caretakers	Line item
39-3000	Entertainment attendants and related workers	Summary
39-3010	Gaming services workers	Summary
39-3011	Gaming dealers	Line item
39-3012	Gaming and sports book writers and runners	Line item
39-3019	Gaming service workers, all other	Line item
39-3021	Motion picture projectionists	Line item
39-3031	Ushers, lobby attendants, and ticket takers	Line item

Table II-1. National Employment Matrix occupational directory, 2006 — Continued

Matrix code	Matrix occupation title	Occupation type
39-3090	Miscellaneous entertainment attendants and related workers	Summary
39-3091	Amusement and recreation attendants	Line item
39-3092	Costume attendants	Line item
39-3093	Locker room, coatroom, and dressing room attendants	Line item
39-3099	Entertainment attendants and related workers, all other	Exclude
39-4000	Funeral service workers	Summary
39-4011	Embalmers	Line item
39-4021	Funeral attendants	Line item
39-5000	Personal appearance workers	Summary
39-5010	Barbers and cosmetologists	Summary
39-5011	Barbers	Line item
39-5012	Hairdressers, hairstylists, and cosmetologists	Line item
39-5090	Miscellaneous personal appearance workers	Summary
39-5091	Makeup artists, theatrical and performance	Line item
39-5092	Manicurists and pedicurists	Line item
39-5093	Shampooers	Line item
39-5094	Skin care specialists	Line item
39-6000	Transportation, tourism, and lodging attendants	Summary
39-6010	Baggage porters, bellhops, and concierges	Summary
39-6011	Baggage porters and bellhops	Line item
39-6012	Concierges	Line item
39-6020	Tour and travel guides	Summary
39-6021	Tour guides and escorts	Line item
39-6022	Travel guides	Line item
39-6030	Transportation attendants	Summary
39-6031	Flight attendants	Line item
39-6032	Transportation attendants, except flight attendants and baggage porters	Line item
39-9000	Other personal care and service workers	Summary
39-9011	Child care workers	Line item
39-9021	Personal and home care aides	Line item
39-9030	Recreation and fitness workers	Summary
39-9031	Fitness trainers and aerobics instructors	Line item
39-9032	Recreation workers	Line item
39-9041	Residential advisors	Line item
39-9099	Personal care and service workers, all other	Line item
41-0000	Sales and related occupations	Summary
41-1000	Supervisors, sales workers	Summary
41-1011	First-line supervisors/managers of retail sales workers	Line item
41-1012	First-line supervisors/managers of non-retail sales workers	Line item
41-2000	Retail sales workers	Summary
41-2010	Cashiers	Summary
41-2011	Cashiers, except gaming	Line item
41-2012	Gaming change persons and booth cashiers	Line item
41-2020	Counter and rental clerks and parts salespersons	Summary
41-2021	Counter and rental clerks	Line item
41-2022	Parts salespersons	Line item
41-2031	Retail salespersons	Line item
41-3000	Sales representatives, services	Summary
41-3011	Advertising sales agents	Line item
41-3021	Insurance sales agents	Line item
41-3031	Securities, commodities, and financial services sales agents	Line item
41-3041	Travel agents	Line item
41-3099	Sales representatives, services, all other	Line item
41-4000	Sales representatives, wholesale and manufacturing	Summary
41-4011	Sales representatives, wholesale and manufacturing, technical and scientific products	Line item
41-4012	Sales representatives, wholesale and manufacturing, except technical and scientific products	Line item
41-9000	Other sales and related workers	Summary
41-9010	Models, demonstrators, and product promoters	Summary
41-9011	Demonstrators and product promoters	Line item
41-9012	Models	Line item
41-9020	Real estate brokers and sales agents	Summary
41-9021	Real estate brokers	Line item
41-9022	Real estate sales agents	Line item
41-9031	Sales engineers	Line item
41-9041	Telemarketers	Line item
41-9090	Miscellaneous sales and related workers	Summary
41-9091	Door-to-door sales workers, news and street vendors, and related workers	Line item
41-9099	Sales and related workers, all other	Line item
43-0000	Office and administrative support occupations	Summary
43-1000	Supervisors, office and administrative support workers	Summary
43-1011	First-line supervisors/managers of office and administrative support workers	Line item
43-2000	Communications equipment operators	Summary
43-2011	Switchboard operators, including answering service	Line item
43-2021	Telephone operators	Line item
43-2099	Communications equipment operators, all other	Line item
43-3000	Financial clerks	Summary
43-3011	Bill and account collectors	Line item
43-3021	Billing and posting clerks and machine operators	Line item
43-3031	Bookkeeping, accounting, and auditing clerks	Line item
43-3041	Gaming cage workers	Line item
43-3051	Payroll and timekeeping clerks	Line item
43-3061	Procurement clerks	Line item
43-3071	Tellers	Line item
43-4000	Information and record clerks	Summary
43-4011	Brokerage clerks	Line item
43-4021	Correspondence clerks	Line item
43-4031	Court, municipal, and license clerks	Line item
43-4041	Credit authorizers, checkers, and clerks	Line item
43-4051	Customer service representatives	Line item
43-4061	Eligibility interviewers, government programs	Line item
43-4071	File clerks	Line item
43-4081	Hotel, motel, and resort desk clerks	Line item
43-4111	Interviewers, except eligibility and loan	Line item
43-4121	Library assistants, clerical	Line item

Table II-1. National Employment Matrix occupational directory, 2006 — Continued

Matrix code	Matrix occupation title	Occupation type
43-4131	Loan interviewers and clerks	Line item
43-4141	New accounts clerks	Line item
43-4151	Order clerks	Line item
43-4161	Human resources assistants, except payroll and timekeeping	Line item
43-4171	Receptionists and information clerks	Line item
43-4181	Reservation and transportation ticket agents and travel clerks	Line item
43-4199	Information and record clerks, all other	Line item
43-5000	Material recording, scheduling, dispatching, and distributing occupations	Summary
43-5011	Cargo and freight agents	Line item
43-5021	Couriers and messengers	Line item
43-5030	Dispatchers	Summary
43-5031	Police, fire, and ambulance dispatchers	Line item
43-5032	Dispatchers, except police, fire, and ambulance	Line item
43-5041	Meter readers, utilities	Line item
43-5050	Postal service workers	Summary
43-5051	Postal service clerks	Line item
43-5052	Postal service mail carriers	Line item
43-5053	Postal service mail sorters, processors, and processing machine operators	Line item
43-5061	Production, planning, and expediting clerks	Line item
43-5071	Shipping, receiving, and traffic clerks	Line item
43-5081	Stock clerks and order fillers	Line item
43-5111	Weighers, measurers, checkers, and samplers, recordkeeping	Line item
43-6000	Secretaries and administrative assistants	Summary
43-6011	Executive secretaries and administrative assistants	Line item
43-6012	Legal secretaries	Line item
43-6013	Medical secretaries	Line item
43-6014	Secretaries, except legal, medical, and executive	Line item
43-9000	Other office and administrative support workers	Summary
43-9011	Computer operators	Line item
43-9020	Data entry and information processing workers	Summary
43-9021	Data entry keyers	Line item
43-9022	Word processors and typists	Line item
43-9031	Desktop publishers	Line item
43-9041	Insurance claims and policy processing clerks	Line item
43-9051	Mail clerks and mail machine operators, except postal service	Line item
43-9061	Office clerks, general	Line item
43-9071	Office machine operators, except computer	Line item
43-9081	Proofreaders and copy markers	Line item
43-9111	Statistical assistants	Line item
43-9199	Office and administrative support workers, all other	Line item
45-0000	Farming, fishing, and forestry occupations	Summary
45-1000	Supervisors, farming, fishing, and forestry workers	Line item
45-1011	First-line supervisors/managers of farming, fishing, and forestry workers	Exclude
45-1012	Farm labor contractors	Exclude
45-2000	Agricultural workers	Summary
45-2011	Agricultural inspectors	Line item
45-2021	Animal breeders	Line item
45-2041	Graders and sorters, agricultural products	Line item
45-2090	Miscellaneous agricultural workers	Summary
45-2091	Agricultural equipment operators	Line item
45-2092	Farmworkers and laborers, crop, nursery, and greenhouse	Line item
45-2093	Farmworkers, farm and ranch animals	Line item
45-2099	Agricultural workers, all other	Line item
45-3000	Fishing and hunting workers	Summary
45-3011	Fishers and related fishing workers	Line item
45-3021	Hunters and trappers	Line item
45-4000	Forest, conservation, and logging workers	Summary
45-4011	Forest and conservation workers	Line item
45-4020	Logging workers	Summary
45-4021	Fallers	Line item
45-4022	Logging equipment operators	Line item
45-4023	Log graders and scalers	Line item
45-4029	Logging workers, all other	Line item
47-0000	Construction and extraction occupations	Summary
47-1000	Supervisors, construction and extraction workers	Summary
47-1011	First-line supervisors/managers of construction trades and extraction workers	Line item
47-2000	Construction trades and related workers	Summary
47-2011	Boilermakers	Line item
47-2020	Brickmasons, blockmasons, and stonemasons	Summary
47-2021	Brickmasons and blockmasons	Line item
47-2022	Stonemasons	Line item
47-2031	Carpenters	Line item
47-2040	Carpet, floor, and tile installers and finishers	Summary
47-2041	Carpet installers	Line item
47-2042	Floor layers, except carpet, wood, and hard tiles	Line item
47-2043	Floor sanders and finishers	Line item
47-2044	Tile and marble setters	Line item
47-2050	Cement masons, concrete finishers, and terrazzo workers	Summary
47-2051	Cement masons and concrete finishers	Line item
47-2053	Terrazzo workers and finishers	Line item
47-2061	Construction laborers	Line item
47-2070	Construction equipment operators	Summary
47-2071	Paving, surfacing, and tamping equipment operators	Line item
47-2072	Pile-driver operators	Line item
47-2073	Operating engineers and other construction equipment operators	Line item
47-2080	Drywall installers, ceiling tile installers, and tapers	Summary
47-2081	Drywall and ceiling tile installers	Line item
47-2082	Tapers	Line item
47-2111	Electricians	Line item
47-2121	Glaziers	Line item
47-2130	Insulation workers	Summary
47-2131	Insulation workers, floor, ceiling, and wall	Line item
47-2132	Insulation workers, mechanical	Line item
47-2140	Painters and paperhangers	Summary
47-2141	Painters, construction and maintenance	Line item

Table II-1. National Employment Matrix occupational directory, 2006 — Continued

Matrix code	Matrix occupation title	Occupation type
47-2142	Paperhangers	Line item
47-2150	Pipelayers, plumbers, pipefitters, and steamfitters	Summary
47-2151	Pipelayers	Line item
47-2152	Plumbers, pipefitters, and steamfitters	Line item
47-2161	Plasterers and stucco masons	Line item
47-2171	Reinforcing iron and rebar workers	Line item
47-2181	Roofers	Line item
47-2211	Sheet metal workers	Line item
47-2221	Structural iron and steel workers	Line item
47-3000	Helpers, construction trades	Summary
47-3010	Helpers, construction trades	Summary
47-3011	Helpers—Brickmasons, blockmasons, stonemasons, and tile and marble setters	Line item
47-3012	Helpers—Carpenters	Line item
47-3013	Helpers—Electricians	Line item
47-3014	Helpers—Painters, paperhangers, plasterers, and stucco masons	Line item
47-3015	Helpers—Pipelayers, plumbers, pipefitters, and steamfitters	Line item
47-3016	Helpers—Roofers	Line item
47-3019	Helpers, construction trades, all other	Line item
47-4000	Other construction and related workers	Summary
47-4011	Construction and building inspectors	Line item
47-4021	Elevator installers and repairers	Line item
47-4031	Fence erectors	Line item
47-4041	Hazardous materials removal workers	Line item
47-4051	Highway maintenance workers	Line item
47-4061	Rail-track laying and maintenance equipment operators	Line item
47-4071	Septic tank servicers and sewer pipe cleaners	Line item
47-4090	Miscellaneous construction and related workers	Summary
47-4091	Segmental pavers	Line item
47-4099	Construction and related workers, all other	Line item
47-5000	Extraction workers	Summary
47-5010	Derrick, rotary drill, and service unit operators, oil, gas, and mining	Summary
47-5011	Derrick operators, oil and gas	Line item
47-5012	Rotary drill operators, oil and gas	Line item
47-5013	Service unit operators, oil, gas, and mining	Line item
47-5021	Earth drillers, except oil and gas	Line item
47-5031	Explosives workers, ordnance handling experts, and blasters	Line item
47-5040	Mining machine operators	Summary
47-5041	Continuous mining machine operators	Line item
47-5042	Mine cutting and channeling machine operators	Line item
47-5049	Mining machine operators, all other	Line item
47-5051	Rock splitters, quarry	Line item
47-5061	Roof bolters, mining	Line item
47-5071	Roustabouts, oil and gas	Line item
47-5081	Helpers—Extraction workers	Line item
47-5099	Extraction workers, all other	Line item
49-0000	Installation, maintenance, and repair occupations	Summary
49-1000	Supervisors of installation, maintenance, and repair workers	Summary
49-1011	First-line supervisors/managers of mechanics, installers, and repairers	Line item
49-2000	Electrical and electronic equipment mechanics, installers, and repairers	Summary
49-2011	Computer, automated teller, and office machine repairers	Line item
49-2020	Radio and telecommunications equipment installers and repairers	Summary
49-2021	Radio mechanics	Line item
49-2022	Telecommunications equipment installers and repairers, except line installers	Line item
49-2090	Miscellaneous electrical and electronic equipment mechanics, installers, and repairers	Summary
49-2091	Avionics technicians	Line item
49-2092	Electric motor, power tool, and related repairers	Line item
49-2093	Electrical and electronics installers and repairers, transportation equipment	Line item
49-2094	Electrical and electronics repairers, commercial and industrial equipment	Line item
49-2095	Electrical and electronics repairers, powerhouse, substation, and relay	Line item
49-2096	Electronic equipment installers and repairers, motor vehicles	Line item
49-2097	Electronic home entertainment equipment installers and repairers	Line item
49-2098	Security and fire alarm systems installers	Line item
49-3000	Vehicle and mobile equipment mechanics, installers, and repairers	Summary
49-3011	Aircraft mechanics and service technicians	Line item
49-3020	Automotive technicians and repairers	Summary
49-3021	Automotive body and related repairers	Line item
49-3022	Automotive glass installers and repairers	Line item
49-3023	Automotive service technicians and mechanics	Line item
49-3031	Bus and truck mechanics and diesel engine specialists	Line item
49-3040	Heavy vehicle and mobile equipment service technicians and mechanics	Summary
49-3041	Farm equipment mechanics	Line item
49-3042	Mobile heavy equipment mechanics, except engines	Line item
49-3043	Rail car repairers	Line item
49-3050	Small engine mechanics	Summary
49-3051	Motorboat mechanics	Line item
49-3052	Motorcycle mechanics	Line item
49-3053	Outdoor power equipment and other small engine mechanics	Line item
49-3090	Miscellaneous vehicle and mobile equipment mechanics, installers, and repairers	Summary
49-3091	Bicycle repairers	Line item
49-3092	Recreational vehicle service technicians	Line item
49-3093	Tire repairers and changers	Line item
49-9000	Other installation, maintenance, and repair occupations	Summary
49-9010	Control and valve installers and repairers	Summary
49-9011	Mechanical door repairers	Line item
49-9012	Control and valve installers and repairers, except mechanical door	Line item
49-9021	Heating, air conditioning, and refrigeration mechanics and installers	Line item

Table II-1. National Employment Matrix occupational directory, 2006 — Continued

Matrix code	Matrix occupation title	Occupation type
49-9031	Home appliance repairers	Line item
49-9040	Industrial machinery installation, repair, and maintenance workers	Summary
49-9041	Industrial machinery mechanics	Line item
49-9042	Maintenance and repair workers, general	Line item
49-9043	Maintenance workers, machinery	Line item
49-9044	Millwrights	Line item
49-9045	Refractory materials repairers, except brickmasons	Line item
49-9050	Line installers and repairers	Summary
49-9051	Electrical power-line installers and repairers	Line item
49-9052	Telecommunications line installers and repairers	Line item
49-9060	Precision instrument and equipment repairers	Summary
49-9061	Camera and photographic equipment repairers	Line item
49-9062	Medical equipment repairers	Line item
49-9063	Musical instrument repairers and tuners	Line item
49-9064	Watch repairers	Line item
49-9069	Precision instrument and equipment repairers, all other	Line item
49-9090	Miscellaneous installation, maintenance, and repair workers	Summary
49-9091	Coin, vending, and amusement machine servicers and repairers	Line item
49-9092	Commercial divers	Line item
49-9093	Fabric menders, except garment	Line item
49-9094	Locksmiths and safe repairers	Line item
49-9095	Manufactured building and mobile home installers	Line item
49-9096	Riggers	Line item
49-9097	Signal and track switch repairers	Line item
49-9098	Helpers--Installation, maintenance, and repair workers	Line item
49-9099	Installation, maintenance, and repair workers, all other	Line item
51-0000	Production occupations	Summary
51-1000	Supervisors, production workers	Summary
51-1011	First-line supervisors/managers of production and operating workers	Line item
51-2000	Assemblers and fabricators	Summary
51-2011	Aircraft structure, surfaces, rigging, and systems assemblers	Line item
51-2020	Electrical, electronics, and electromechanical assemblers	Summary
51-2021	Coil winders, tapers, and finishers	Line item
51-2022	Electrical and electronic equipment assemblers	Line item
51-2023	Electromechanical equipment assemblers	Line item
51-2031	Engine and other machine assemblers	Line item
51-2041	Structural metal fabricators and fitters	Line item
51-2090	Miscellaneous assemblers and fabricators	Summary
51-2091	Fiberglass laminators and fabricators	Line item
51-2092	Team assemblers	Line item
51-2093	Timing device assemblers, adjusters, and calibrators	Line item
51-2099	Assemblers and fabricators, all other	Line item
51-3000	Food processing occupations	Summary
51-3011	Bakers	Line item
51-3020	Butchers and other meat, poultry, and fish processing workers	Summary
51-3021	Butchers and meat cutters	Line item
51-3022	Meat, poultry, and fish cutters and trimmers	Line item
51-3023	Slaughterers and meat packers	Line item
51-3090	Miscellaneous food processing workers	Summary
51-3091	Food and tobacco roasting, baking, and drying machine operators and tenders	Line item
51-3092	Food batchmakers	Line item
51-3093	Food cooking machine operators and tenders	Line item
51-4000	Metal workers and plastic workers	Summary
51-4010	Computer control programmers and operators	Summary
51-4011	Computer-controlled machine tool operators, metal and plastic	Line item
51-4012	Numerical tool and process control programmers	Line item
51-4020	Forming machine setters, operators, and tenders, metal and plastic	Summary
51-4021	Extruding and drawing machine setters, operators, and tenders, metal and plastic	Line item
51-4022	Forging machine setters, operators, and tenders, metal and plastic	Line item
51-4023	Rolling machine setters, operators, and tenders, metal and plastic	Line item
51-4030	Machine tool cutting setters, operators, and tenders, metal and plastic	Summary
51-4031	Cutting, punching, and press machine setters, operators, and tenders, metal and plastic	Line item
51-4032	Drilling and boring machine tool setters, operators, and tenders, metal and plastic	Line item
51-4033	Grinding, lapping, polishing, and buffing machine tool setters, operators, and tenders, metal and plastic	Line item
51-4034	Lathe and turning machine tool setters, operators, and tenders, metal and plastic	Line item
51-4035	Milling and planing machine setters, operators, and tenders, metal and plastic	Line item
51-4041	Machinists	Line item
51-4050	Metal furnace and kiln operators and tenders	Summary
51-4051	Metal-refining furnace operators and tenders	Line item
51-4052	Pourers and casters, metal	Line item
51-4060	Model makers and patternmakers, metal and plastic	Summary
51-4061	Model makers, metal and plastic	Line item
51-4062	Patternmakers, metal and plastic	Line item
51-4070	Molders and molding machine setters, operators, and tenders, metal and plastic	Summary
51-4071	Foundry mold and coremakers	Line item
51-4072	Molding, coremaking, and casting machine setters, operators, and tenders, metal and plastic	Line item
51-4081	Multiple machine tool setters, operators, and tenders, metal and plastic	Line item
51-4111	Tool and die makers	Line item
51-4120	Welding, soldering, and brazing workers	Summary
51-4121	Welders, cutters, solderers, and brazers	Line item

Table II-1. National Employment Matrix occupational directory, 2006 — Continued

Matrix code	Matrix occupation title	Occupation type
51-4122	Welding, soldering, and brazing machine setters, operators, and tenders	Line item
51-4190	Miscellaneous metalworkers and plastic workers	Summary
51-4191	Heat treating equipment setters, operators, and tenders, metal and plastic	Line item
51-4192	Lay-out workers, metal and plastic	Line item
51-4193	Plating and coating machine setters, operators, and tenders, metal and plastic	Line item
51-4194	Tool grinders, filers, and sharpeners	Line item
51-4199	Metal workers and plastic workers, all other	Line item
51-5000	Printing occupations	Summary
51-5010	Bookbinders and bindery workers	Summary
51-5011	Bindery workers	Line item
51-5012	Bookbinders	Line item
51-5020	Printers	Summary
51-5021	Job printers	Line item
51-5022	Prepress technicians and workers	Line item
51-5023	Printing machine operators	Line item
51-6000	Textile, apparel, and furnishings occupations	Summary
51-6011	Laundry and dry-cleaning workers	Line item
51-6021	Pressers, textile, garment, and related materials	Line item
51-6031	Sewing machine operators	Line item
51-6040	Shoe and leather workers	Summary
51-6041	Shoe and leather workers and repairers	Line item
51-6042	Shoe machine operators and tenders	Line item
51-6050	Tailors, dressmakers, and sewers	Summary
51-6051	Sewers, hand	Line item
51-6052	Tailors, dressmakers, and custom sewers	Line item
51-6060	Textile machine setters, operators, and tenders	Summary
51-6061	Textile bleaching and dyeing machine operators and tenders	Line item
51-6062	Textile cutting machine setters, operators, and tenders	Line item
51-6063	Textile knitting and weaving machine setters, operators, and tenders	Line item
51-6064	Textile winding, twisting, and drawing out machine setters, operators, and tenders	Line item
51-6090	Miscellaneous textile, apparel, and furnishings workers	Summary
51-6091	Extruding and forming machine setters, operators, and tenders, synthetic and glass fibers	Line item
51-6092	Fabric and apparel patternmakers	Line item
51-6093	Upholsterers	Line item
51-6099	Textile, apparel, and furnishings workers, all other	Line item
51-7000	Woodworkers	Summary
51-7011	Cabinetmakers and bench carpenters	Line item
51-7021	Furniture finishers	Line item
51-7030	Model makers and patternmakers, wood	Summary
51-7031	Model makers, wood	Line item
51-7032	Patternmakers, wood	Line item
51-7040	Woodworking machine setters, operators, and tenders	Summary
51-7041	Sawing machine setters, operators, and tenders, wood	Line item
51-7042	Woodworking machine setters, operators, and tenders, except sawing	Line item
51-7099	Woodworkers, all other	Line item
51-8000	Plant and system operators	Summary
51-8010	Power plant operators, distributors, and dispatchers	Summary
51-8011	Nuclear power reactor operators	Line item
51-8012	Power distributors and dispatchers	Line item
51-8013	Power plant operators	Line item
51-8021	Stationary engineers and boiler operators	Line item
51-8031	Water and liquid waste treatment plant and system operators	Line item
51-8090	Miscellaneous plant and system operators	Summary
51-8091	Chemical plant and system operators	Line item
51-8092	Gas plant operators	Line item
51-8093	Petroleum pump system operators, refinery operators, and gaugers	Line item
51-8099	Plant and system operators, all other	Line item
51-9000	Other production occupations	Summary
51-9010	Chemical processing machine setters, operators, and tenders	Summary
51-9011	Chemical equipment operators and tenders	Line item
51-9012	Separating, filtering, clarifying, precipitating, and still machine setters, operators, and tenders	Line item
51-9020	Crushing, grinding, polishing, mixing, and blending workers	Summary
51-9021	Crushing, grinding, and polishing machine setters, operators, and tenders	Line item
51-9022	Grinding and polishing workers, hand	Line item
51-9023	Mixing and blending machine setters, operators, and tenders	Line item
51-9030	Cutting workers	Summary
51-9031	Cutters and trimmers, hand	Line item
51-9032	Cutting and slicing machine setters, operators, and tenders	Line item
51-9041	Extruding, forming, pressing, and compacting machine setters, operators, and tenders	Line item
51-9051	Furnace, kiln, oven, drier, and kettle operators and tenders	Line item
51-9061	Inspectors, testers, sorters, samplers, and weighers	Line item
51-9071	Jewelers and precious stone and metal workers	Line item
51-9080	Medical, dental, and ophthalmic laboratory technicians	Summary
51-9081	Dental laboratory technicians	Line item
51-9082	Medical appliance technicians	Line item
51-9083	Ophthalmic laboratory technicians	Line item
51-9111	Packaging and filling machine operators and tenders	Line item
51-9120	Painting workers	Summary
51-9121	Coating, painting, and spraying machine setters, operators, and tenders	Line item
51-9122	Painters, transportation equipment	Line item
51-9123	Painting, coating, and decorating workers	Line item
51-9130	Photographic process workers and processing machine operators	Summary
51-9131	Photographic process workers	Line item
51-9132	Photographic processing machine operators	Line item

Table II-1. National Employment Matrix occupational directory, 2006 — Continued

Matrix code	Matrix occupation title	Occupation type
51-9141	Semiconductor processors	Line item
51-9190	Miscellaneous production workers	Summary
51-9191	Cementing and gluing machine operators and tenders	Line item
51-9192	Cleaning, washing, and metal pickling equipment operators and tenders	Line item
51-9193	Cooling and freezing equipment operators and tenders	Line item
51-9194	Etchers and engravers	Line item
51-9195	Molders, shapers, and casters, except metal and plastic	Line item
51-9196	Paper goods machine setters, operators, and tenders	Line item
51-9197	Tire builders	Line item
51-9198	Helpers--Production workers	Line item
51-9199	Production workers, all other	Line item
53-0000	Transportation and material moving occupations	Summary
53-1000	Supervisors, transportation and material moving workers	Summary
53-1011	Aircraft cargo handling supervisors	Line item
53-1021	First-line supervisors/managers of helpers, laborers, and material movers, hand	Line item
53-1031	First-line supervisors/managers of transportation and material-moving machine and vehicle operators	Line item
53-2000	Air transportation occupations	Summary
53-2010	Aircraft pilots and flight engineers	Summary
53-2011	Airline pilots, copilots, and flight engineers	Line item
53-2012	Commercial pilots	Line item
53-2020	Air traffic controllers and airfield operations specialists	Summary
53-2021	Air traffic controllers	Line item
53-2022	Airfield operations specialists	Line item
53-3000	Motor vehicle operators	Summary
53-3011	Ambulance drivers and attendants, except emergency medical technicians	Line item
53-3020	Bus drivers	Summary
53-3021	Bus drivers, transit and intercity	Line item
53-3022	Bus drivers, school	Line item
53-3030	Driver/sales workers and truck drivers	Summary
53-3031	Driver/sales workers	Line item
53-3032	Truck drivers, heavy and tractor-trailer	Line item
53-3033	Truck drivers, light or delivery services	Line item
53-3041	Taxi drivers and chauffeurs	Line item
53-3099	Motor vehicle operators, all other	Line item
53-4000	Rail transportation occupations	Summary
53-4010	Locomotive engineers and operators	Line item
53-4011	Locomotive engineers	Exclude
53-4012	Locomotive firers	Exclude
53-4013	Rail yard engineers, dinkey operators, and hostlers	Exclude
53-4021	Railroad brake, signal, and switch operators	Line item
53-4031	Railroad conductors and yardmasters	Line item
53-4041	Subway and streetcar operators	Line item
53-4099	Rail transportation workers, all other	Line item
53-5000	Water transportation occupations	Summary
53-5011	Sailors and marine oilers	Line item
53-5020	Ship and boat captains and operators	Summary
53-5021	Captains, mates, and pilots of water vessels	Line item
53-5022	Motorboat operators	Line item
53-5031	Ship engineers	Line item
53-6000	Other transportation workers	Summary
53-6011	Bridge and lock tenders	Line item
53-6021	Parking lot attendants	Line item
53-6031	Service station attendants	Line item
53-6041	Traffic technicians	Line item
53-6051	Transportation inspectors	Line item
53-6099	Transportation workers, all other	Line item
53-7000	Material moving occupations	Summary
53-7011	Conveyor operators and tenders	Line item
53-7021	Crane and tower operators	Line item
53-7030	Dredge, excavating, and loading machine operators	Summary
53-7031	Dredge operators	Line item
53-7032	Excavating and loading machine and dragline operators	Line item
53-7033	Loading machine operators, underground mining	Line item
53-7041	Hoist and winch operators	Line item
53-7051	Industrial truck and tractor operators	Line item
53-7060	Laborers and material movers, hand	Summary
53-7061	Cleaners of vehicles and equipment	Line item
53-7062	Laborers and freight, stock, and material movers, hand	Line item
53-7063	Machine feeders and offbearers	Line item
53-7064	Packers and packagers, hand	Line item
53-7070	Pumping station operators	Summary
53-7071	Gas compressor and gas pumping station operators	Line item
53-7072	Pump operators, except wellhead pumpers	Line item
53-7073	Wellhead pumpers	Line item
53-7081	Refuse and recyclable material collectors	Line item
53-7111	Shuttle car operators	Line item
53-7121	Tank car, truck, and ship loaders	Line item
53-7199	Material moving workers, all other	Line item

[1] Non-SOC codes used for these combinations of major occupational groups.

Table II-2. National Employment Matrix industry directory, 2006–16

Matrix code	2002 NAICS coverage	Matrix/NAICS match?	Matrix industry title	Industry type
000001	N.A.	NO	Total employment, all workers	Summary
000500	N.A.	NO	Total wage and salary employment	Summary
000520	N.A.	NO	Wage and salary employment, except agriculture, forestry, fishing, hunting, and private households	Summary
113300	113300	YES	Logging	Summary
113310	113310	YES	Logging	Line item
210000	210000	YES	Mining	Summary
211000	211000	YES	Oil and gas extraction	Summary
211100	211100	YES	Oil and gas extraction	Line item
212000	212000	YES	Mining (except oil and gas)	Summary
212100	212100	YES	Coal mining	Line item
212200	212200	YES	Metal ore mining	Line item
212300	212300	YES	Nonmetallic mineral mining and quarrying	Line item
213000	213000	YES	Support activities for mining	Summary
213100	213100	YES	Support activities for mining	Line item
220000	220000	YES	Utilities	Summary
221000	221000	YES	Utilities	Summary
221100	221100	YES	Electric power generation, transmission and distribution	Line item
221200	221200	YES	Natural gas distribution	Line item
221300	221300	YES	Water, sewage and other systems	Line item
230000	230000	YES	Construction	Summary
236000	236000	YES	Construction of buildings	Summary
236100	236100	YES	Residential building construction	Line item
236200	236200	YES	Nonresidential building construction	Line item
237000	237000	YES	Heavy and civil engineering construction	Summary
237100	237100	YES	Utility system construction	Summary
237130	237130	YES	Power and communication line and related structures construction	Line item
237200	237200	YES	Land subdivision	Line item
237300	237300	YES	Highway, street, and bridge construction	Line item
237900	237900	YES	Other heavy and civil engineering construction	Line item
238000	238000	YES	Specialty trade contractors	Summary
238100	238100	YES	Foundation, structure, and building exterior contractors	Summary
238110	238110	YES	Poured concrete foundation and structure contractors	Line item
238140	238140	YES	Masonry contractors	Line item
238160	238160	YES	Roofing contractors	Line item
238200	238200	YES	Building equipment contractors	Summary
238210	238210	YES	Electrical contractors	Line item
238220	238220	YES	Plumbing, heating, and air-conditioning contractors	Line item
238290	238290	YES	Other building equipment contractors	Line item
238300	238300	YES	Building finishing contractors	Summary
238310	238310	YES	Drywall and insulation contractors	Line item
238320	238320	YES	Painting and wall covering contractors	Line item
238900	238900	YES	Other specialty trade contractors	Line item
31-33	310000-330000	YES	Manufacturing	Summary
311000	311000	YES	Food manufacturing	Summary
311100	311100	YES	Animal food manufacturing	Line item
311200	311200	YES	Grain and oilseed milling	Line item
311300	311300	YES	Sugar and confectionery product manufacturing	Line item
311400	311400	YES	Fruit and vegetable preserving and specialty food manufacturing	Line item
311500	311500	YES	Dairy product manufacturing	Line item
311600	311600	YES	Animal slaughtering and processing	Line item
311700	311700	YES	Seafood product preparation and packaging	Line item
311800	311800	YES	Bakeries and tortilla manufacturing	Line item
311900	311900	YES	Other food manufacturing	Line item
312000	312000	YES	Beverage and tobacco product manufacturing	Summary
312100	312100	YES	Beverage manufacturing	Line item
312200	312200	YES	Tobacco manufacturing	Line item
313000	313000	YES	Textile mills	Summary
313100	313100	YES	Fiber, yarn, and thread mills	Line item
313200	313200	YES	Fabric mills	Line item

Table II-2. National Employment Matrix industry directory, 2006–16 — Continued

Matrix code	2002 NAICS coverage	Matrix/NAICS match?	Matrix industry title	Industry type
313300	313300	YES	Textile and fabric finishing and fabric coating mills	Line item
314000	314000	YES	Textile product mills	Summary
314100	314100	YES	Textile furnishings mills	Line item
314900	314900	YES	Other textile product mills	Line item
315000	315000	YES	Apparel manufacturing	Summary
315100	315100	YES	Apparel knitting mills	Line item
315200	315200	YES	Cut and sew apparel manufacturing	Line item
315900	315900	YES	Apparel accessories and other apparel manufacturing	Line item
316000	316000	YES	Leather and allied product manufacturing	Summary
316200	316200	YES	Footwear manufacturing	Line item
321000	321000	YES	Wood product manufacturing	Summary
321100	321100	YES	Sawmills and wood preservation	Line item
321200	321200	YES	Veneer, plywood, and engineered wood product manufacturing	Line item
321900	321900	YES	Other wood product manufacturing	Line item
322000	322000	YES	Paper manufacturing	Summary
322100	322100	YES	Pulp, paper, and paperboard mills	Line item
322200	322200	YES	Converted paper product manufacturing	Line item
323000	323000	YES	Printing and related support activities	Summary
323100	323100	YES	Printing and related support activities	Line item
324000	324000	YES	Petroleum and coal products manufacturing	Summary
324100	324100	YES	Petroleum and coal products manufacturing	Line item
325000	325000	YES	Chemical manufacturing	Summary
325100	325100	YES	Basic chemical manufacturing	Line item
325200	325200	YES	Resin, synthetic rubber, and artificial synthetic fibers and filaments manufacturing	Line item
325300	325300	YES	Pesticide, fertilizer, and other agricultural chemical manufacturing	Line item
325400	325400	YES	Pharmaceutical and medicine manufacturing	Line item
325500	325500	YES	Paint, coating, and adhesive manufacturing	Line item
325600	325600	YES	Soap, cleaning compound, and toilet preparation manufacturing	Line item
325900	325900	YES	Other chemical product and preparation manufacturing	Line item
326000	326000	YES	Plastics and rubber products manufacturing	Summary
326100	326100	YES	Plastics product manufacturing	Line item
326200	326200	YES	Rubber product manufacturing	Line item
327000	327000	YES	Nonmetallic mineral product manufacturing	Summary
327100	327100	YES	Clay product and refractory manufacturing	Line item
327200	327200	YES	Glass and glass product manufacturing	Line item
327300	327300	YES	Cement and concrete product manufacturing	Line item
331000	331000	YES	Primary metal manufacturing	Summary
331100	331100	YES	Iron and steel mills and ferroalloy manufacturing	Line item
331200	331200	YES	Steel product manufacturing from purchased steel	Line item
331300	331300	YES	Alumina and aluminum production and processing	Line item
331400	331400	YES	Nonferrous metal (except aluminum) production and processing	Line item
331500	331500	YES	Foundries	Line item
332000	332000	YES	Fabricated metal product manufacturing	Summary
332100	332100	YES	Forging and stamping	Line item
332200	332200	YES	Cutlery and handtool manufacturing	Line item
332300	332300	YES	Architectural and structural metals manufacturing	Line item
332400	332400	YES	Boiler, tank, and shipping container manufacturing	Line item
332500	332500	YES	Hardware manufacturing	Line item
332600	332600	YES	Spring and wire product manufacturing	Line item
332700	332700	YES	Machine shops; turned product; and screw, nut, and bolt manufacturing	Summary
332710	332710	YES	Machine shops	Line item
332720	332720	YES	Turned product and screw, nut, and bolt manufacturing	Line item
332800	332800	YES	Coating, engraving, heat treating, and allied activities	Line item
332900	332900	YES	Other fabricated metal product manufacturing	Line item
333000	333000	YES	Machinery manufacturing	Summary
333100	333100	YES	Agriculture, construction, and mining machinery manufacturing	Line item
333200	333200	YES	Industrial machinery manufacturing	Line item
333300	333300	YES	Commercial and service industry machinery manufacturing	Line item
333400	333400	YES	Ventilation, heating, air-conditioning, and commercial refrigeration equipment manufacturing	Line item

Table II-2. National Employment Matrix industry directory, 2006–16 — Continued

Matrix code	2002 NAICS coverage	Matrix/NAICS match?	Matrix industry title	Industry type
333500	333500	YES	Metalworking machinery manufacturing	Line item
333600	333600	YES	Engine, turbine, and power transmission equipment manufacturing	Line item
333900	333900	YES	Other general purpose machinery manufacturing	Line item
334000	334000	YES	Computer and electronic product manufacturing	Summary
334100	334100	YES	Computer and peripheral equipment manufacturing	Line item
334200	334200	YES	Communications equipment manufacturing	Line item
334300	334300	YES	Audio and video equipment manufacturing	Line item
334400	334400	YES	Semiconductor and other electronic component manufacturing	Line item
334500	334500	YES	Navigational, measuring, electromedical, and control instruments manufacturing	Line item
334600	334600	YES	Manufacturing and reproducing magnetic and optical media	Line item
335000	335000	YES	Electrical equipment, appliance, and component manufacturing	Summary
335100	335100	YES	Electric lighting equipment manufacturing	Line item
335200	335200	YES	Household appliance manufacturing	Line item
335300	335300	YES	Electrical equipment manufacturing	Line item
335900	335900	YES	Other electrical equipment and component manufacturing	Line item
336000	336000	YES	Transportation equipment manufacturing	Summary
336100	336100	YES	Motor vehicle manufacturing	Line item
336200	336200	YES	Motor vehicle body and trailer manufacturing	Line item
336300	336300	YES	Motor vehicle parts manufacturing	Line item
336400	336400	YES	Aerospace product and parts manufacturing	Line item
336500	336500	YES	Railroad rolling stock manufacturing	Line item
336600	336600	YES	Ship and boat building	Line item
336900	336900	YES	Other transportation equipment manufacturing	Line item
337000	337000	YES	Furniture and related product manufacturing	Summary
337100	337100	YES	Household and institutional furniture and kitchen cabinet manufacturing	Summary
337110	337110	YES	Wood kitchen cabinet and countertop manufacturing	Line item
337120	337120	YES	Household and institutional furniture manufacturing	Line item
337200	337200	YES	Office furniture (including fixtures) manufacturing	Line item
337900	337900	YES	Other furniture related product manufacturing	Line item
339000	339000	YES	Miscellaneous manufacturing	Summary
339100	339100	YES	Medical equipment and supplies manufacturing	Line item
339900	339900	YES	Other miscellaneous manufacturing	Summary
339910	339910	YES	Jewelry and silverware manufacturing	Line item
420000	420000	YES	Wholesale trade	Summary
423000	423000	YES	Merchant wholesalers, durable goods	Summary
423100	423100	YES	Motor vehicle and motor vehicle parts and supplies merchant wholesalers	Line item
423200	423200	YES	Furniture and home furnishing merchant wholesalers	Line item
423300	423300	YES	Lumber and other construction materials merchant wholesalers	Line item
423400	423400	YES	Professional and commercial equipment and supplies merchant wholesalers	Line item
423500	423500	YES	Metal and mineral (except petroleum) merchant wholesalers	Line item
423600	423600	YES	Electrical and electronic goods merchant wholesalers	Line item
423700	423700	YES	Hardware, and plumbing and heating equipment and supplies merchant wholesalers	Line item
423800	423800	YES	Machinery, equipment, and supplies merchant wholesalers	Summary
423820	423820	YES	Farm and garden machinery and equipment merchant wholesalers	Line item
423900	423900	YES	Miscellaneous durable goods merchant wholesalers	Line item
424000	424000	YES	Merchant wholesalers, nondurable goods	Summary
424100	424100	YES	Paper and paper product merchant wholesalers	Line item
424200	424200	YES	Drugs and druggists' sundries merchant wholesalers	Line item
424300	424300	YES	Apparel, piece goods, and notions merchant wholesalers	Line item
424400	424400	YES	Grocery and related product wholesalers	Line item
424500	424500	YES	Farm product raw material merchant wholesalers	Line item
424600	424600	YES	Chemical and allied products merchant wholesalers	Line item
424700	424700	YES	Petroleum and petroleum products merchant wholesalers	Line item
424800	424800	YES	Beer, wine, and distilled alcoholic beverage merchant wholesalers	Line item
424900	424900	YES	Miscellaneous nondurable goods merchant wholesalers	Line item
425000	425000	YES	Wholesale electronic markets and agents and brokers	Summary
425100	425100	YES	Wholesale electronic markets and agents and brokers	Line item
44-45	440000-450000	YES	Retail trade	Summary
441000	441000	YES	Motor vehicle and parts dealers	Summary

Table II-2. National Employment Matrix industry directory, 2006–16 — Continued

Matrix code	2002 NAICS coverage	Matrix/NAICS match?	Matrix industry title	Industry type
441100	441100	YES	Automobile dealers	Line item
441200	441200	YES	Other motor vehicle dealers	Line item
441300	441300	YES	Automotive parts, accessories, and tire stores	Line item
442000	442000	YES	Furniture and home furnishings stores	Summary
442100	442100	YES	Furniture stores	Line item
442200	442200	YES	Home furnishings stores	Line item
443000	443000	YES	Electronics and appliance stores	Summary
443100	443100	YES	Electronics and appliance stores	Rollup
444000	444000	YES	Building material and garden equipment and supplies dealers	Summary
444100	444100	YES	Building material and supplies dealers	Line item
444200	444200	YES	Lawn and garden equipment and supplies stores	Line item
445000	445000	YES	Food and beverage stores	Summary
445100	445100	YES	Grocery stores	Line item
445200	445200	YES	Specialty food stores	Line item
445300	445300	YES	Beer, wine, and liquor stores	Line item
446000	446000	YES	Health and personal care stores	Summary
446100	446100	YES	Health and personal care stores	Summary
446110	446110	YES	Pharmacies and drug stores	Line item
447000	447000	YES	Gasoline stations	Summary
447100	447100	YES	Gasoline stations	Line item
448000	448000	YES	Clothing and clothing accessories stores	Summary
448100	448100	YES	Clothing stores	Line item
448200	448200	YES	Shoe stores	Line item
448300	448300	YES	Jewelry, luggage, and leather goods stores	Line item
451000	451000	YES	Sporting goods, hobby, book, and music stores	Summary
451100	451100	YES	Sporting goods, hobby, and musical instrument stores	Summary
451110	451110	YES	Sporting goods stores	Line item
451200	451200	YES	Book, periodical, and music stores	Line item
452000	452000	YES	General merchandise stores	Summary
452100	452100	YES	Department stores	Line item
452900	452900	YES	Other general merchandise stores	Line item
453000	453000	YES	Miscellaneous store retailers	Summary
453100	453100	YES	Florists	Line item
453200	453200	YES	Office supplies, stationery, and gift stores	Line item
453300	453300	YES	Used merchandise stores	Line item
453900	453900	YES	Other miscellaneous store retailers	Line item
454000	454000	YES	Nonstore retailers	Summary
454100	454100	YES	Electronic shopping and mail-order houses	Line item
454200	454200	YES	Vending machine operators	Line item
454300	454300	YES	Direct selling establishments	Line item
48-49	480000-490000	YES	Transportation and warehousing	Summary
481000	481000	YES	Air transportation	Summary
481100	481100	YES	Scheduled air transportation	Line item
481200	481200	YES	Nonscheduled air transportation	Line item
482000	482000	YES	Rail transportation	Summary
482100	482100	YES	Rail transportation	Line item
483000	483000	YES	Water transportation	Summary
483100	483100	YES	Deep sea, coastal, and great lakes water transportation	Line item
483200	483200	YES	Inland water transportation	Line item
484000	484000	YES	Truck transportation	Summary
484100	484100	YES	General freight trucking	Line item
484200	484200	YES	Specialized freight trucking	Line item
485000	485000	YES	Transit and ground passenger transportation	Summary
485100	485100	YES	Urban transit systems	Line item
485200	485200	YES	Interurban and rural bus transportation	Line item
485300	485300	YES	Taxi and limousine service	Line item
485400	485400	YES	School and employee bus transportation	Line item
485500	485500	YES	Charter bus industry	Line item
485900	485900	YES	Other transit and ground passenger transportation	Line item

Table II-2. National Employment Matrix industry directory, 2006–16 — Continued

Matrix code	2002 NAICS coverage	Matrix/NAICS match?	Matrix industry title	Industry type
486000	486000	YES	Pipeline transportation	Rollup
487000	487000	YES	Scenic and sightseeing transportation	Rollup
488000	488000	YES	Support activities for transportation	Summary
488100	488100	YES	Support activities for air transportation	Line item
488300	488300	YES	Support activities for water transportation	Line item
488400	488400	YES	Support activities for road transportation	Line item
488500	488500	YES	Freight transportation arrangement	Line item
492000	492000	YES	Couriers and messengers	Summary
492100	492100	YES	Couriers	Line item
492200	492200	YES	Local messengers and local delivery	Line item
493000	493000	YES	Warehousing and storage	Summary
493100	493100	YES	Warehousing and storage	Line item
510000	510000	YES	Information	Summary
511000	511000	YES	Publishing industries (except Internet)	Summary
511100	511100	YES	Newspaper, periodical, book, and directory publishers	Summary
511110	511110	YES	Newspaper publishers	Line item
511200	511200	YES	Software publishers	Line item
512000	512000	YES	Motion picture, video, and sound recording industries	Summary
512100	512100	YES	Motion picture and video industries	Summary
512130	512130	YES	Motion picture and video exhibition	Line item
512200	512200	YES	Sound recording industries	Line item
515000	515000	YES	Broadcasting (except Internet)	Summary
515100	515100	YES	Radio and television broadcasting	Summary
515110	515110	YES	Radio broadcasting	Line item
515120	515120	YES	Television broadcasting	Line item
515200	515200	YES	Cable and other subscription programming	Line item
517000	517000	YES	Telecommunications	Summary
517100	517100	YES	Wired telecommunications carriers	Line item
517200	517200	YES	Wireless telecommunications carriers (except satellite)	Line item
517300	517300	YES	Telecommunications resellers	Line item
517500	517500	YES	Cable and other program distribution	Line item
516890	516000, 518000, 519000	NO	Internet and other information services	Summary
516000	516000	YES	Internet publishing and broadcasting	Summary
516100	516100	YES	Internet publishing and broadcasting	Line item
518000	518000	YES	Internet service providers, Web search portals, and data processing services	Summary
518100	518100	YES	Internet service providers and Web search portals	Line item
518200	518200	YES	Data processing, hosting, and related services	Line item
519000	519000	YES	Other information services	Summary
519100	519100	YES	Other information services	Line item
520000	520000	YES	Finance and insurance	Summary
521-2	521000-2000	YES	Monetary authorities, credit intermediation, and related activities	Summary
521000	521000	YES	Monetary authorities - central bank	Summary
521100	521100	YES	Monetary authorities - central bank	Line item
522000	522000	YES	Credit intermediation and related activities	Summary
522100	522100	YES	Depository credit intermediation	Line item
522200	522200	YES	Nondepository credit intermediation	Summary
522290	522290	YES	Other nondepository credit intermediation, including real estate credit and consumer lending	Line item
522300	522300	YES	Activities related to credit intermediation	Line item
523000	523000	YES	Securities, commodity contracts, and other financial investments and related activities	Summary
5231-2	523100-200	YES	Securities and commodity contracts, brokerages, and exchanges	Rollup
523900	523900	YES	Other financial investment activities	Line item
524000	524000	YES	Insurance carriers and related activities	Summary
524100	524100	YES	Insurance carriers	Summary
524120	524120	YES	Direct insurance (except life, health, and medical) carriers	Line item
524200	524200	YES	Agencies, brokerages, and other insurance related activities	Summary
524210	524210	YES	Insurance agencies and brokerages	Line item
524290	524290	YES	Other insurance related activities	Line item
525000	525000	YES	Funds, trusts, and other financial vehicles	Summary

Table II-2. National Employment Matrix industry directory, 2006–16 — Continued

Matrix code	2002 NAICS coverage	Matrix/NAICS match?	Matrix industry title	Industry type
525100	525100	YES	Insurance and employee benefit funds	Line item
525900	525900	YES	Other investment pools and funds	Line item
530000	530000	YES	Real estate and rental and leasing	Summary
531000	531000	YES	Real estate	Summary
531100	531100	YES	Lessors of real estate	Line item
531200	531200	YES	Offices of real estate agents and brokers	Line item
531300	531300	YES	Activities related to real estate	Line item
532000	532000	YES	Rental and leasing services	Summary
532100	532100	YES	Automotive equipment rental and leasing	Line item
5322-3	532200-300	YES	Consumer goods rental and general rental centers	Summary
532200	532200	YES	Consumer goods rental	Line item
532300	532300	YES	General rental centers	Line item
532400	532400	YES	Commercial and industrial machinery and equipment rental and leasing	Line item
533000	533000	YES	Lessors of nonfinancial intangible assets (except copyrighted works)	Summary
533100	533100	YES	Lessors of nonfinancial intangible assets (except copyrighted works)	Line item
540000	540000	YES	Professional, scientific, and technical services	Summary
541000	541000	YES	Professional, scientific, and technical services	Summary
541100	541100	YES	Legal services	Line item
541200	541200	YES	Accounting, tax preparation, bookkeeping, and payroll services	Line item
541300	541300	YES	Architectural, engineering, and related services	Summary
541380	541380	YES	Testing laboratories	Line item
541400	541400	YES	Specialized design services	Line item
541500	541500	YES	Computer systems design and related services	Line item
541600	541600	YES	Management, scientific, and technical consulting services	Line item
541700	541700	YES	Scientific research and development services	Summary
541710	541710	YES	Research and development in the physical, engineering, and life sciences	Line item
541720	541720	YES	Research and development in the social sciences and humanities	Line item
541800	541800	YES	Advertising and related services	Line item
541900	541900	YES	Other professional, scientific, and technical services	Summary
541920	541920	YES	Photographic services	Line item
541940	541940	YES	Veterinary services	Line item
550000	550000	YES	Management of companies and enterprises	Summary
551000	551000	YES	Management of companies and enterprises	Summary
551100	551100	YES	Management of companies and enterprises	Line item
560000	560000	YES	Administrative and support and waste management and remediation services	Summary
561000	561000	YES	Administrative and support services	Summary
561100	561100	YES	Office administrative services	Line item
561200	561200	YES	Facilities support services	Line item
561300	561300	YES	Employment services	Line item
561400	561400	YES	Business support services	Summary
561420	561420	YES	Telephone call centers	Line item
561500	561500	YES	Travel arrangement and reservation services	Summary
561510	561510	YES	Travel agencies	Line item
561600	561600	YES	Investigation and security services	Summary
561610	561610	YES	Investigation, guard, and armored car services	Line item
561620	561620	YES	Security systems services	Line item
561700	561700	YES	Services to buildings and dwellings	Summary
561710	561710	YES	Exterminating and pest control services	Line item
561730	561730	YES	Landscaping services	Line item
561900	561900	YES	Other support services	Line item
562000	562000	YES	Waste management and remediation services	Summary
562100	562100	YES	Waste collection	Line item
5622-9	562200-900	YES	Waste treatment and disposal and waste management services	Summary
562200	562200	YES	Waste treatment and disposal	Line item
562900	562900	YES	Remediation and other waste management services	Line item
610000	610000	YES	Educational services, public and private	Summary
611000	611000	YES	Educational services, public and private	Summary
611100	611100	YES	Elementary and secondary schools, public and private	Line item
6112-3	611200-300	YES	Junior colleges, colleges, universities, and professional schools, public and private	Summary

Table II-2. National Employment Matrix industry directory, 2006–16 — Continued

Matrix code	2002 NAICS coverage	Matrix/NAICS match?	Matrix industry title	Industry type
611200	611200	YES	Junior colleges, public and private	Line item
611300	611300	YES	Colleges, universities, and professional schools, public and private	Line item
6114-7	611400-700	YES	Other educational services, public and private	Summary
611400	611400	YES	Business schools and computer and management training, public and private	Line item
611500	611500	YES	Technical and trade schools, public and private	Line item
611600	611600	YES	Other schools and instruction, public and private	Line item
611700	611700	YES	Educational support services, public and private	Line item
620000	620000	YES	Health care and social assistance	Summary
621-3	621000-3000	YES	Health care	Summary
621000	621000	YES	Ambulatory health care services	Summary
6211-3	621100-300	YES	Offices of health practitioners	Summary
621100	621100	YES	Offices of physicians	Line item
621200	621200	YES	Offices of dentists	Line item
621300	621300	YES	Offices of other health practitioners	Summary
621310	621310	YES	Offices of chiropractors	Line item
621320	621320	YES	Offices of optometrists	Line item
621330	621330	YES	Offices of mental health practitioners (except physicians)	Line item
621340	621340	YES	Offices of physical, occupational and speech therapists, and audiologists	Line item
621390	621390	YES	Offices of all other health practitioners	Line item
621600	621600	YES	Home health care services	Line item
621459	621400, 500, 900	NO	Outpatient, laboratory, and other ambulatory care services	Summary
621400	621400	YES	Outpatient care centers	Summary
621420	621420	YES	Outpatient mental health and substance abuse centers	Line item
621500	621500	YES	Medical and diagnostic laboratories	Line item
621900	621900	YES	Other ambulatory health care services	Summary
621910	621910	YES	Ambulance services	Line item
621990	621990	YES	All other ambulatory health care services	Line item
622000	622000	YES	Hospitals, public and private	Summary
622100	622100	YES	General medical and surgical hospitals, public and private	Line item
622200	622200	YES	Psychiatric and substance abuse hospitals, public and private	Line item
622300	622300	YES	Specialty (except psychiatric and substance abuse) hospitals, public and private	Line item
623000	623000	YES	Nursing and residential care facilities	Summary
623100	623100	YES	Nursing care facilities	Line item
6232-9	623200-900	YES	Residential care facilities	Summary
623200	623200	YES	Residential mental retardation, mental health and substance abuse facilities	Summary
623210	623210	YES	Residential mental retardation facilities	Line item
623220	623220	YES	Residential mental health and substance abuse facilities	Line item
623300	623300	YES	Community care facilities for the elderly	Line item
623900	623900	YES	Other residential care facilities	Line item
624000	624000	YES	Social assistance	Summary
6241-3	624100-300	YES	Individual, family, community, and vocational rehabilitation services	Summary
624100	624100	YES	Individual and family services	Summary
624120	624120	YES	Services for the elderly and persons with disabilities	Line item
624200	624200	YES	Community food and housing, and emergency and other relief services	Line item
624300	624300	YES	Vocational rehabilitation services	Line item
624400	624400	YES	Child day care services	Line item
710000	710000	YES	Arts, entertainment, and recreation	Summary
711000	711000	YES	Performing arts, spectator sports, and related industries	Summary
711100	711100	YES	Performing arts companies	Rollup
711200	711200	YES	Spectator sports	Line item
7113-4	711300-400	YES	Promoters of events, and agents and managers	Rollup
711500	711500	YES	Independent artists, writers, and performers	Line item
712000	712000	YES	Museums, historical sites, and similar institutions	Summary
712100	712100	YES	Museums, historical sites, and similar institutions	Line item
713000	713000	YES	Amusement, gambling, and recreation industries	Summary
713100	713100	YES	Amusement parks and arcades	Line item
713200	713200	YES	Gambling industries	Line item
713900	713900	YES	Other amusement and recreation industries	Summary
713940	713940	YES	Fitness and recreational sports centers	Line item

Table II-2. National Employment Matrix industry directory, 2006–16 — Continued

Matrix code	2002 NAICS coverage	Matrix/NAICS match?	Matrix industry title	Industry type
720000	720000	YES	Accommodation and food services	Summary
721000	721000	YES	Accommodation, including hotels and motels	Summary
721100	721100	YES	Traveler accommodation, including hotels and motels	Summary
721120	721120	YES	Casino hotels	Line item
721200	721200	YES	RV (recreational vehicle) parks and recreational camps	Line item
722000	722000	YES	Food services and drinking places	Summary
722100	722100	YES	Full-service restaurants	Line item
722200	722200	YES	Limited-service eating places	Line item
722300	722300	YES	Special food services	Line item
722400	722400	YES	Drinking places (alcoholic beverages)	Line item
810000	810000	YES	Other services (except government and private households)	Summary
811000	811000	YES	Repair and maintenance	Summary
811100	811100	YES	Automotive repair and maintenance	Summary
811110	811110	YES	Automotive mechanical and electrical repair and maintenance	Line item
811120	811120	YES	Automotive body, paint, interior, and glass repair	Line item
811190	811190	YES	Other automotive repair and maintenance	Line item
811200	811200	YES	Electronic and precision equipment repair and maintenance	Line item
811300	811300	YES	Commercial and industrial machinery and equipment (except automotive and electronic) repair and maintenance	Line item
811400	811400	YES	Personal and household goods repair and maintenance	Line item
812000	812000	YES	Personal and laundry services	Summary
812100	812100	YES	Personal care services	Line item
812200	812200	YES	Death care services	Line item
812300	812300	YES	Drycleaning and laundry services	Line item
812900	812900	YES	Other personal services	Line item
813000	813000	YES	Religious, grantmaking, civic, professional, and similar organizations	Summary
813100	813100	YES	Religious organizations	Line item
8132-3	813200-300	YES	Grantmaking services and social advocacy organizations	Summary
813200	813200	YES	Grantmaking and giving services	Line item
813300	813300	YES	Social advocacy organizations	Line item
8134-9	813400-900	YES	Civic, social, professional, and similar organizations	Summary
813400	813400	YES	Civic and social organizations	Line item
813900	813900	YES	Business, professional, labor, political, and similar organizations	Summary
813930	813930	YES	Labor unions and similar labor organizations	Line item
990000	N.A.	NO	Government	Summary
910000	N.A.	NO	Federal government	Summary
491100	491100	YES	Postal service	Line item
919999	N.A.	NO	Federal government, excluding postal service	Line item
940000	N.A.	NO	State and local government	Summary
949400	N.A.	NO	State and local government, excluding education and hospitals	Summary
920000	N.A.	NO	State government	Summary
929200	N.A.	NO	State government, excluding education and hospitals	Rollup
930000	N.A.	NO	Local government	Summary
939300	N.A.	NO	Local government, excluding education and hospitals	Rollup
000530	N.A.	NO	Wage and salary employment in agriculture, forestry, fishing, hunting, and private households	Summary
110000	110000	YES	Agriculture, forestry, fishing and hunting; primary job	Summary
111000	111000	YES	Crop production; primary job	Line item
112000	112000	YES	Animal production; primary job	Line item
113132	113100-3200	NO	Forestry; primary job	Line item
114000	114000	YES	Fishing, hunting and trapping; primary job	Line item
115000	115000	YES	Support activities for agriculture and forestry; primary job	Line item
814000	814000	YES	Private households; primary and secondary jobs	Summary
814100	814100	YES	Private households, primary jobs	Line item
814102	N.A.	NO	Private households, secondary jobs	Line item
000510	N.A.	NO	Wage and salary workers with secondary jobs in agriculture, forestry, fishing, and hunting	Rollup
006700	N.A.	NO	Self-employed and unpaid family workers, all jobs	Summary
006701	N.A.	NO	Total self-employed and unpaid family workers, primary job	Summary
006702	N.A.	NO	Total self-employed and unpaid family workers, secondary job	Summary
000600	N.A.	NO	Self-employed workers, all jobs	Summary

Table II-2. National Employment Matrix industry directory, 2006–16 — Continued

Matrix code	2002 NAICS coverage	Matrix/NAICS match?	Matrix industry title	Industry type
000601	N.A.	NO	Self-employed workers, primary job	Rollup
000602	N.A.	NO	Self-employed workers, secondary job	Rollup
000700	N.A.	NO	Unpaid family workers, all jobs	Summary
000701	N.A.	NO	Unpaid family workers, primary job	Rollup
000702	N.A.	NO	Unpaid family workers, secondary job	Rollup

Chapter III. Selected Occupational Data, 2006 and Projected 2016

This chapter presents data on current and projected employment, annual average job openings, and other information for each National Employment Matrix occupation. Every other year, the Bureau of Labor Statistics updates the occupational employment projections. The 2006–16 projections—the most current—are shown in the job outlook section of the 2008–09 edition of the *Occupational Outlook Handbook*. Additionally, the *Monthly Labor Review* (November 2007) has tables and a detailed discussion of these projections while the *Occupational Outlook Quarterly* (fall edition, 2007) includes the data in brief textual and graphic presentations. The information in this chapter also is available on the Internet via two searchable databases: the National Employment Matrix **http://data.bls.gov/oep/nioem/empiohm.jsp** and the Occupational Employment, Training, and Earnings site **http://data.bls.gov/oep/noeted/empoptd.jsp**.

Table III–1 displays data on 2006 and projected 2016 employment, employment change, self-employment, annual average job openings, and other characteristics for each National Employment Matrix occupation. As a result, readers using table III–1 can obtain specific data about several variables for any occupation in the Matrix and compare the result against data for another detailed occupation or a group of occupations.

Table III–2 displays 2006 employment for the detailed occupations that are excluded from table III–1. These approximately 50 occupations are excluded because of reliability concerns or because the research required to prepare a projection from them could not be completed. Since current employment provides a measure of an excluded occupation's significance in the labor market, table III–2 can be used as a supplement to table III–1. Except for "entertainment attendants and related workers, all other," each of the excluded occupations falls under a line item occupation included in table III–1. For example, the line item "physicians and surgeons" includes employment data from eight excluded physician specialties, such as pediatricians.

Data presented

Information about each variable's data source and potential use is presented in this section.

The Occupational Employment Statistics (OES) survey and the Current Population Survey (CPS) provide almost all of the employment data used in developing the 2006–16 projections.[1] (See chapter II for more details on the structure of the 2006–16 National Employment Matrices.) These surveys also are the sources of most other statistical information contained in table III–1.

Occupational data from the OES survey are not entirely comparable with those from the CPS, because of differences in occupational classification systems and in concepts and methods used in the two surveys[2].

Data from CPS proxy occupations are substituted for CPS occupations with a small number of workers or were otherwise considered unreliable. Where possible, larger, closely related CPS occupations were chosen as proxies for the excluded occupations. When a detailed occupation could not be identified, a summary occupational group was used. (See chapter V for more discussion.)

The following sections describe the variables presented in table III–1.

Employment, 2006 and 2016. (Source: Bureau of Labor Statistics, National Employment Matrices for 2006 and 2016.) Employment information is a useful starting point for assessing opportunities, because large occupations usually have more openings than small ones have, regardless of growth or replacement needs. Employment for wage and salary jobs, the self-employed, and unpaid family workers are included.

Employment change, 2006–16, numeric. (Source: Bureau of Labor Statistics, National Employment Matrices for 2006 and 2016.) The numerical change in employment measures the projected number of job gains or losses.

Employment change, 2006–16, percent. (Source: Bureau of Labor Statistics, National Employment Matrices for 2006 and 2016.) The percent change in employment measures the rate of change of an occupation. A rapidly growing occupation usually indicates favorable prospects for employment. Moreover, the high demand for workers in a rapidly growing occupation improves their chances for advancement and mobility. Even modest employment growth in a large occupation can result in many more job openings due to growth than rapid employment growth in a small occupation.

Job openings due to growth and total replacement needs, 2006–16. (Source: Bureau of Labor Statistics, see chapter V.) These data provide the broadest measure of job opportunities and identify the total additional employees needed annually in an occupation. The number of openings due to growth is calculated from data on increases in employment of detailed occupations from the National

[1] Since November 2002, the OES survey has been a semiannual mail survey of approximately 200,000 establishments collected in May and November of each year. Over the course of a 3-year cycle, approximately 1.2 million establishments are sampled. For the May 2006 OES survey estimates, data collected in May 2006 were combined with data collected in November 2005, May 2005, November 2004, May 2004, and November 2003. Detailed information about the May 2006 OES survey is available at the OES web site (**http://www.bls.gov/oes/home.htm**). The CPS is a monthly household survey on labor force characteristics. Each month, personal and telephone interviews are conducted at about 60,000 households. Detailed information is available at the CPS Web site (**http://www.bls.gov/cps/home.htm**).

[2] For example, the OES program provides employment estimates for more than 800 detailed occupations in the 2000 Standard Occupational Classification (SOC) system. However, the CPS program provides employment estimates based on the 2000 Census of Population occupation system, which combines 2000 SOC occupations into 502 detailed occupations. Of the 502 CPS occupations, 373 were exact matches to OES occupations. The remaining CPS occupations were distributed over two or more SOC occupations. Information about worker characteristics from the CPS is applied to matrix occupations on the basis of the relationship between the 2000 Census of Population occupational classification system and the 2000 SOC system used by the OES survey.

Employment Matrices for 2006–16. If employment declines, job openings due to growth are zero. Estimates of total replacement needs encompass the replacement of workers at all experience levels who leave their jobs to work in another occupation or who stop working because of retirement or other reasons. Total replacement needs reflect the normal movements in the labor force, are calculated from 2005–06 CPS data, and are described in chapter V. Data from CPS proxy occupations are used to estimate replacement needs for some matrix occupations, as indicated.

Job openings due to growth and net replacement needs, 2006–16. (Source: Bureau of Labor Statistics, see chapter V.) These data indicate the number of new workers needed annually in an occupation and, if training is required, measure minimum training needs. The number of openings due to growth is calculated from data on increases in employment of detailed occupations in the 2006–16 National Employment Matrices. If employment declines, job openings due to growth are zero. Job openings due to net replacement needs typically arise because experienced workers permanently leave the occupation or the labor force. Net replacement needs are calculated from monthly CPS data between 1997 and 2006, and are described in chapter V. Data from CPS proxy occupations are used to estimate replacement needs for some matrix occupations.

Median annual wages, 2006. (Source: May 2006 OES survey.) Table III–1 presents median annual wages for employees in each occupation.

Percent self-employed, 2006. (Source: Bureau of Labor Statistics, National Employment Matrix for 2006.) Individuals who are interested in creating and managing their own businesses may find it important to know the percentage of self-employed workers in an occupation. This percentage shows how many jobs in a matrix occupation come from CPS data on unincorporated self-employed persons in their primary or secondary job. The unincorporated self-employed work for earnings or fees in their own businesses, while the incorporated self-employed receive a wage or salary from their business.

Unemployment rate. (Source: Average of 2004–06 CPS monthly data.) Some occupations are more susceptible to factors that result in unemployment, including seasonality, fluctuations in economic conditions, and individual business failures. A high unemployment rate indicates that individuals in a given occupation are more likely to become unemployed than are those in occupations with a low rate. Data from CPS proxy occupations are used to estimate unemployment rates for some matrix occupations.

Percent part time. (Source: Average of 2004–06 CPS monthly data.) Persons who prefer part-time work may want to know the proportion of workers in an occupation who usually work fewer than 35 hours per week, that is, part time. The data on usual weekly hours were chosen for a respondent's primary job, although they may hold more than one job. Data from CPS proxy occupations are used to estimate the proportion of part-time workers for some matrix occupations.

Most significant source of postsecondary education or training. (Source: Bureau of Labor Statistics, see chapter I.) BLS uses 11 categories to describe all types of postsecondary education or training (see figure at the end of this chapter for detailed category descriptions.) Occupational analysts assign a single category that best describes the education or training needed by most workers to become fully qualified in a given occupation.

These categories can be used as an initial reference for assessing what postsecondary education or training may be preferable. However, these categories should not be viewed as an absolute standard because multiple paths of entry are available for many occupations. Reviewing the material on "Training, other qualifications, and advancement" in the *Occupational Outlook Handbook* and the educational attainment cluster data in table III–1 can help determine whether alternatives exist. In most occupations, alternatives do exist. For example, a significant number of computer systems analysts have acquired the qualifying skills, but do not have a bachelor's degree—the postsecondary education category designated for the occupation. Insights such as this are available from the *Handbook*.

The categories identify the postsecondary education or training used by most individuals in an occupation to become fully qualified in that occupation. The categories cannot and do not describe all paths and are not intended to indicate the level of education and training required for a person to be hired.

Educational attainment cluster. (Source: Bureau of Labor Statistics, see chapter I.) Six clusters are defined on the basis of the distribution of the highest level of educational attainment of workers age 25-44 across nearly 500 occupations. The clusters are as follows:

- HS = High school occupations
- HS/SC = High school/Some college occupations
- HS/SC/C = High school/Some college/College occupations
- SC = Some college
- SC/C = Some college/College occupations
- C = College occupations.

Percent distribution of educational attainment for workers aged 25-44. (Source: 2005–06 American Community Survey (ACS) annual average data, see chapter I.) These data show the percentage of employees in each occupation who are 25-44 years old and who have a high school degree or less, some college (including, but not limited to, recipients of associate degrees), or at least a bachelor's degree. Individuals in surveyed households self-report their occupation and highest educational attainment.

Note that the highest level of educational attainment for a worker is not necessarily the level of education needed for their job. Also, care must be taken in comparing educational attainment for workers age 25-44 with workers of other age groups, because educational attainment may vary by group.

Using occupational information in this chapter

Table III–1 consolidates 2006 and 2016 projected employment data and provides comparisons of occupational data. The table displays information about current and projected employment, projected job openings, wages, percent self-employed, the proportion of part-time workers, and common paths of entry.

The data in table III–1 have many uses. At times, users may want to know how a particular occupation—for example, "tellers", matrix code 43-3071—compares with others. The first row in the table is for "Total, all occupations." The data in this row can be used as a benchmark against the data in subsequent rows. For example, the percent growth for all occupations from 2006–16 is about 10 percent, while the percent growth for tellers is 13 percent. This shows that the teller occupation is growing slightly faster than all occupations. Also, the percent self-employed for all occupations in 2006 is 8 percent, while tellers did not show any self-employment at all. This indicates that self-employment is more common in other occupations besides tellers. Alternatively, a detailed occupation can be compared to a major occupation group. The percent self-employed for 43-0000 "Office and administrative support occupations" is 1.7 percent, which indicates that occupations in the same major group as tellers also have little or no self-employment.

When evaluating the education attainment data in table III–1 it is important for users to consider both the education and training category along with the educational attainment cluster. For example, the table shows that the registered nurses occupation generally requires an associate degree; however the majority of workers age 25-44 have a college (bachelor's) or higher degree. While seemingly contradictory, this information taken in context implies that while the most significant source of education is an associate degree, younger workers entering the occupation increasingly have bachelor's or higher degrees. Thus, it could be concluded that an associate degree will help a jobseeker prepare for this occupation, but a bachelor's degree will help them be more competitive for the best jobs.

Jobseekers may use their own judgment to determine what characteristics are most appealing. For example, an occupation with an above-average proportion of part time workers may be desirable to some jobseekers with considerable school or family responsibilities. However, recent college graduates may prefer a career with more opportunities for full-time work.

Some readers might wish to identify occupations with favorable characteristics that jobseekers can pursue through a specific type of training. For example, a student might be interested in a technical occupation, but might not care to obtain a 4-year college degree. In another instance, a planner might wish to ensure that training programs provided by junior colleges in the area are consistent with the needs of the national labor market. To obtain appropriate information, both the student and the planner could examine information on occupations for which the associate degree is the most significant source of education or training.

Although table III–1 contains a great deal of information that is useful for career guidance, information about occupational comparisons should be used as an aid, not as a sole source of information for making career choices. After using the table to identify occupations with favorable prospects, the reader should obtain additional information from other sources, such as the *Occupational Outlook Handbook*, the *Occupational Outlook Quarterly*, and local sources, if available. Consideration should be given to individual aptitudes and preferences, and alternative sources of training available in the local area should be investigated. The appendix to this publication identifies State and local sources of information.

An electronic version of table III–1 is available on the Internet at: **ftp://ftp.bls.gov/pub/special.requests/ep/optddata/**

Classification of occupations by most significant source of education or training

Occupations are classified into 1 of the 11 categories according to the following principles:

- An occupation is placed into the category that best describes the education or training that most workers need to become fully qualified in that occupation.
- Postsecondary awards, if generally needed for entry into the occupation, take precedence over work-related training, even though additional skills or experience may be needed for a worker to become fully qualified.
- The length of time that an average worker generally needs to become fully qualified through a combination of on-the-job training and experience is used to categorize occupations in which a postsecondary award generally is not needed for entry.

Postsecondary awards

First professional degree. Completion of this degree usually requires at least 3 years of full-time academic study beyond a bachelor's degree. The first professional degree is the minimum preparation required for entry into several professions, including lawyer, physician and surgeon, and dentist.

Doctoral degree. Completion of a Ph.D. or other doctoral degree usually requires at least 3 years of full-time academic work beyond the bachelor's degree: for example, postsecondary teachers or medical scientists, except epidemiologists.

Master's degree. Completion of this degree usually requires 1 or 2 years of full-time academic study beyond a bachelor's degree: for example, clergy or educational, vocational, and school counselors.

Bachelor's or higher degree, plus work experience. Most occupations in this category are management occupations. All require experience in a related nonmanagement position for which a bachelor's or higher degree is usually required. Jobs usually are filled with experienced staff who are promoted into a management position, such as engineers who advance to engineering manager.

Bachelor's degree. Completion of this degree generally requires at least 4 years, but not more than 5 years, of full-time academic study beyond high school: for example, accountants and auditors or elementary school teachers, except special education.

Associate degree. Completion of this degree usually requires at least 2 years of full-time academic study beyond high school for example, paralegals and legal assistants or medical record and health information technicians.

Postsecondary vocational awards. These programs lead to a certificate or other award, but not a degree. Some such programs last only a few weeks, while others may last more than a year. Occupations in this category include some that require only the completion of a training program and some that require individuals to pass a licensing exam after completion of the program before they can work. Examples include nursing aides, orderlies, and attendants or hairdressers, hairstylists, and cosmetologists.

Work-related training

Work experience in a related occupation. Many occupations requiring work experience are first-line supervisors/managers of service, sales and related, production, or other occupations, or are other types of managers.

Long-term on-the-job training. More than 12 months of on-the-job training or combined work experience and formal classroom instruction are needed for workers to develop the skills to become fully qualified. This category includes formal or informal apprenticeships that may last up to 5 years. Long-term on-the-job training also includes intensive occupation-specific, employer-sponsored programs that workers must successfully complete. These programs include fire and police academies and schools for air traffic controllers and flight attendants. In other occupations—insurance sales and securities sales, for example—trainees take formal courses, often provided at the jobsite, to prepare for the required licensing exams. Individuals undergoing training usually are considered to be employed in the occupation. Also included in this category is the development of natural ability—such as that possessed by musicians, athletes, actors, and other entertainers—that must be cultivated over several years, frequently in a nonwork setting.

Moderate-term on-the-job training. Skills needed for a worker to become fully qualified can be acquired during 1 to 12 months of combined on-the-job experience and informal training. For example, heavy and tractor-trailer truck drivers or secretaries, except legal, medical, and executive.

Short-term on-the-job training. Skills needed for a worker to become fully qualified can be acquired during a short demonstration of job duties or during 1 month or less of on-the-job experience or instruction. For example, retail salespersons or waiters and waitresses.

Table III–1. Occupational employment and job openings data, 2006–16, and worker characteristics, 2006
(Numbers in thousands)

Code	2006 National Employment Matrix occupation and code	Employment 2006	Employment 2016	Employment change, 2006–16 Numeric	Employment change, 2006–16 Percent	Annual average job openings due to growth and total replacement needs, 2006–16	Annual average job openings due to growth and net replacement needs, 2006–16	2006 median annual wages Dollars	2006 median annual wages Rank	Percent self-employed, 2006	Unemployment rate	Percent part-time	Most significant source of postsecondary education or training[2]	Educational attainment cluster[3]	Percent of workers aged 25 to 44, by educational attainment[4] High school or less	Some college	College or higher
00-0000	**Total, all occupations**	**150,620**	**166,220**	**15,600**	**10.4**	**26,923**	**5,073**	**$30,400**	—	**8.1**	—	—	—	—	**37.8**	**29.9**	**32.3**
11-1300	**Management, business, and financial occupations**	**15,397**	**16,993**	**1,596**	**10.4**	**1,749**	**458**	—	—	**19.2**	—	—	—	—	—	—	—
11-0000	Management occupations	8,789	9,322	533	6.1	896	237	—	—	27.6	—	—	—	—	—	—	—
11-1000	Top executives	2,187	2,222	35	1.6	137	57	—	—	4.7	—	—	—	—	—	—	—
11-1011	Chief executives	402	410	8	2.0	21	12	NA	—	22.0	VL	VL	Bachelor's or higher, plus work experience	SC/C	13.0	21.8	65.2
11-1021	General and operations managers	1,720	1,746	26	1.5	112	44	85,230	VH	.9	L	VL	Bachelor's or higher, plus work experience	SC/C	19.6	32.5	48.0
11-1031	Legislators[1]	65	65	1	1.0	3	1	15,660	VL	0.0	VL	VL	Bachelor's or higher, plus work experience	SC/C	13.0	21.8	65.2
11-2000	Advertising, marketing, promotions, public relations, and sales managers	583	651	68	11.7	65	20	—	—	3.1	—	—	—	—	—	—	—
11-2011	Advertising and promotions managers[1]	47	50	3	6.2	3	1	73,060	VH	13.4	L	VL	Bachelor's or higher, plus work experience	C	7.1	17.5	75.5
11-2020	Marketing and sales managers	486	542	57	11.6	57	16	—	—	2.2	—	—	—	—	—	—	—
11-2021	Marketing managers	167	192	24	14.4	20	6	98,720	VH	2.3	VL	VL	Bachelor's or higher, plus work experience	SC/C	9.2	22.1	68.7
11-2022	Sales managers	318	351	33	10.2	36	10	91,560	VH	2.2	VL	VL	Bachelor's or higher, plus work experience	SC/C	9.2	22.1	68.7
11-2031	Public relations managers[1]	50	58	8	16.9	6	2	82,180	VH	1.7	L	VL	Bachelor's or higher, plus work experience	C	8.7	16.3	75.0
11-3000	Operations specialties managers	1,474	1,628	154	10.5	154	47	—	—	2.6	—	—	—	—	—	—	—
11-3011	Administrative services managers	247	276	29	11.7	20	9	67,690	VH	.6	VL	VL	Bachelor's or higher, plus work experience	HS/SC/C	21.4	38.8	39.9
11-3021	Computer and information systems managers	264	307	43	16.4	31	9	101,580	VH	1.4	L	VL	Bachelor's or higher, plus work experience	SC/C	4.6	23.0	72.5
11-3031	Financial managers	506	570	64	12.6	58	14	90,970	VH	4.6	VL	VL	Bachelor's or higher, plus work experience	SC/C	12.9	27.2	59.9
11-3040	Human resources managers	136	153	17	12.5	17	4	—	—	1.4	—	—	—	—	—	—	—
11-3041	Compensation and benefits managers	49	55	6	12.0	6	2	74,750	VH	1.4	L	VL	Bachelor's or higher, plus work experience	SC/C	14.8	27.8	57.5
11-3042	Training and development managers	29	33	5	15.6	4	1	80,250	VH	1.6	L	VL	Bachelor's or higher, plus work experience	SC/C	14.8	27.8	57.5
11-3049	Human resources managers, all other	58	65	7	11.4	7	2	88,510	VH	1.3	L	VL	Bachelor's or higher, plus work experience	SC/C	14.8	27.8	57.5
11-3051	Industrial production managers	157	148	-9	-5.9	15	5	77,670	VH	2.0	L	VL	Work experience in a related occupation	HS/SC/C	25.4	31.6	43.0
11-3061	Purchasing managers	70	72	2	3.4	7	2	81,570	VH	2.7	VL	VL	Bachelor's or higher, plus work experience	SC/C	14.9	28.1	57.0
11-3071	Transportation, storage, and distribution managers	94	102	8	8.3	7	4	73,080	VH	2.6	L	VL	Work experience in a related occupation	HS/SC/C	38.5	36.4	25.1
11-9000	Other management occupations	4,545	4,821	276	6.1	539	113	—	—	49.9	—	—	—	—	—	—	—
11-9010	Agricultural managers	1,317	1,230	-87	-6.6	148	12	—	—	80.4	—	—	—	—	—	—	—
11-9011	Farm, ranch, and other agricultural managers	258	261	3	1.1	18	2	52,070	VH	0.0	VL	L	Bachelor's or higher, plus work experience	HS/SC/C	44.6	29.4	26.0
11-9012	Farmers and ranchers	1,058	969	-90	-8.5	130	10	37,130	H	100.0	VL	H	Long-term on-the-job training	HS/SC	53.6	30.4	16.0
11-9021	Construction managers	487	564	77	15.7	44	15	73,700	VH	56.3	VL	VL	Bachelor's degree	HS/SC/C	39.5	31.1	29.4
11-9030	Education administrators	443	496	53	11.9	56	18	—	—	3.3	—	—	—	—	—	—	—
11-9031	Education administrators, preschool and child care center/program	56	69	13	23.5	8	3	37,740	H	3.4	VL	L	Bachelor's or higher, plus work experience	C	6.4	15.2	78.4
11-9032	Education administrators, elementary and secondary school	226	243	17	7.6	27	8	77,740	VH	3.3	VL	L	Bachelor's or higher, plus work experience	C	6.4	15.2	78.4

See footnotes at end of table.

Table III-1. Occupational employment and job openings data, 2006–16, and worker characteristics, 2006 — Continued
(Numbers in thousands)

Code	2006 National Employment Matrix occupation and code	Employment		Employment change, 2006–16		Annual average job openings due to growth and total replacement needs, 2006–16	Annual average job openings due to growth and net replacement needs, 2006–16	2006 median annual wages		Percent self-employed, 2006	Unemployment rate	Percent part-time	Most significant source of postsecondary education or training[2]	Educational attainment cluster[3]	Percent of workers aged 25 to 44, by educational attainment[4]		
		2006	2016	Numeric	Percent			Dollars	Rank						High school or less	Some college	College or higher
11-9033	Education administrators, postsecondary	131	150	19	14.2	17	6	73,990	VH	3.3	VL	L	Bachelor's or higher, plus work experience	C	6.4	15.2	78.4
11-9039	Education administrators, all other	30	33	4	12.6	4	1	66,620	VH	2.9	VL	L	Bachelor's or higher, plus work experience	C	6.4	15.2	78.4
11-9041	Engineering managers	187	201	14	7.3	7	5	105,430	VH	0.0	VL	VL	Bachelor's or higher, plus work experience	C	4.4	11.9	83.7
11-9051	Food service managers	350	368	18	5.0	59	10	43,020	H	44.8	L	L	Work experience in a related occupation	HS/SC/C	40.0	35.8	24.2
11-9061	Funeral directors	29	32	4	12.5	4	1	49,620	VH	19.7	VL	L	Associate degree	SC/C	8.7	50.7	40.6
11-9071	Gaming managers[1]	4	5	1	24.4	1	0	62,820	VH	16.3	H	VL	Work experience in a related occupation	HS/SC/C	33.6	42.4	24.0
11-9081	Lodging managers	71	80	9	12.2	6	2	42,320	H	53.0	VL	L	Work experience in a related occupation	HS/SC/C	23.2	32.2	44.6
11-9111	Medical and health services managers	262	305	43	16.4	32	9	73,340	VH	8.2	VL	VL	Bachelor's or higher, plus work experience	SC/C	11.4	32.0	56.6
11-9121	Natural sciences managers[1]	41	45	5	11.4	4	1	100,080	VH	.6	VL	VL	Bachelor's or higher, plus work experience	C	0.0	0.0	92.8
11-9131	Postmasters and mail superintendents[1]	26	26	0	-.8	2	1	55,790	VH	0.0	L	VL	Work experience in a related occupation	SC/C	17.3	27.3	55.4
11-9141	Property, real estate, and community association managers	329	379	50	15.1	50	10	43,070	H	50.9	VL	H	Bachelor's degree	HS/SC/C	27.3	36.5	36.2
11-9151	Social and community service managers	130	162	32	24.7	24	6	52,070	VH	5.9	L	L	Bachelor's degree	C	8.9	19.6	71.5
11-9199	Managers, all other	870	930	60	6.9	104	23	82,490	VH	60.0	VL	L	Work experience in a related occupation	SC/C	17.3	27.3	55.4
13-0000	Business and financial operations occupations	6,608	7,671	1,063	16.1	853	220	—	—	8.1	—	—	—	—	—	—	—
13-1000	Business operations specialists	3,860	4,466	606	15.7	545	128	—	—	6.6	—	—	—	—	—	—	—
13-1011	Agents and business managers of artists, performers, and athletes	25	27	2	9.6	4	1	64,500	VH	55.8	H	H	Bachelor's or higher, plus work experience	SC/C	17.6	23.0	59.4
13-1020	Buyers and purchasing agents	460	459	-1	-.3	44	10	—	—	5.3	—	—	—	—	—	—	—
13-1021	Purchasing agents and buyers, farm products[1]	16	15	-1	-8.6	2	0	46,770	VH	5.1	L	VL	Long-term on-the-job training	HS/SC/C	35.5	42.5	0.0
13-1022	Wholesale and retail buyers, except farm products	157	156	0	-.1	20	4	44,640	H	12.0	L	H	Long-term on-the-job training	HS/SC/C	27.8	36.2	36.0
13-1023	Purchasing agents, except wholesale, retail, and farm products	287	288	0	.1	22	6	50,730	VH	1.6	L	VL	Long-term on-the-job training	HS/SC/C	21.8	35.8	42.4
13-1030	Claims adjusters, appraisers, examiners, and investigators	319	347	29	9.1	23	11	—	—	3.5	—	—	—	—	—	—	—
13-1031	Claims adjusters, examiners, and investigators	305	332	27	8.9	22	10	50,660	VH	3.5	VL	VL	Long-term on-the-job training	SC/C	18.3	35.1	46.7
13-1032	Insurance appraisers, auto damage	13	15	2	12.5	1	1	49,180	VH	4.1	VL	VL	Postsecondary vocational award	SC/C	18.3	35.1	46.7
13-1041	Compliance officers, except agriculture, construction, health and safety, and transportation	237	249	12	4.9	16	4	47,050	VH	.4	VL	VL	Long-term on-the-job training	SC/C	14.0	27.9	58.0
13-1051	Cost estimators	221	262	41	18.5	38	9	52,940	VH	1.1	L	VL	Bachelor's degree	HS/SC/C	27.5	40.2	32.3
13-1061	Emergency management specialists	12	13	1	12.3	2	0	47,410	VH	.1	L	L	Work experience in a related occupation	SC/C	18.2	33.2	48.7
13-1070	Human resources, training, and labor relations specialists	732	862	130	17.8	124	29	—	—	2.1	—	—	—	—	—	—	—
13-1071	Employment, recruitment, and placement specialists	197	233	36	18.4	34	8	42,420	H	2.1	L	L	Bachelor's degree	SC/C	14.1	30.4	55.5

See footnotes at end of table.

Table III–1. Occupational employment and job openings data, 2006–16, and worker characteristics, 2006 — Continued
(Numbers in thousands)

Code	2006 National Employment Matrix occupation and code	Employment		Employment change, 2006–16		Annual average job openings due to growth and total replacement needs, 2006–16	Annual average job openings due to growth and net replacement needs, 2006–16	2006 median annual wages		Percent self-employed, 2006	Unemployment rate	Percent part-time	Most significant source of postsecondary education or training[2]	Educational attainment cluster[3]	Percent of workers aged 25 to 44, by educational attainment[4]		
		2006	2016	Numeric	Percent			Dollars	Rank						High school or less	Some college	College or higher
13-1072	Compensation, benefits, and job analysis specialists	110	130	20	18.4	19	4	50,230	VH	2.1	L	L	Bachelor's degree	SC/C	14.1	30.4	55.5
13-1073	Training and development specialists	210	249	38	18.3	36	8	47,830	VH	2.3	L	L	Bachelor's or higher, plus work experience	SC/C	14.1	30.4	55.5
13-1079	Human resources, training, and labor relations specialists, all other	214	250	35	16.5	36	8	52,270	VH	1.8	L	L	Bachelor's degree	SC/C	14.1	30.4	55.5
13-1081	Logisticians	83	98	14	17.3	10	3	63,430	VH	1.5	VL	VL	Bachelor's degree	SC/C	19.2	37.9	42.9
13-1111	Management analysts	678	827	149	21.9	126	26	68,050	VH	27.0	VL	L	Bachelor's or higher, plus work experience	C	6.6	15.9	77.5
13-1121	Meeting and convention planners[1]	51	61	10	19.9	8	2	42,180	H	5.6	L	L	Bachelor's degree	SC/C	10.6	22.0	67.4
13-1199	Business operation specialists, all other	1,043	1,261	218	20.9	151	33	55,650	VH	.1	L	L	Bachelor's degree	SC/C	18.2	33.2	48.7
13-2000	Financial specialists	2,748	3,204	457	16.6	308	93	—	—	10.0	—	—	—	—	—	—	—
13-2011	Accountants and auditors	1,274	1,500	226	17.7	134	45	54,630	VH	9.5	VL	L	Bachelor's degree	C	3.7	17.1	79.1
13-2021	Appraisers and assessors of real estate	101	118	17	16.9	6	4	44,460	H	32.7	VL	L	Bachelor's degree	SC/C	17.0	39.2	43.8
13-2031	Budget analysts[1]	62	66	4	7.1	6	2	61,430	VH	0.0	VL	VL	Bachelor's degree	C	4.2	17.8	78.1
13-2041	Credit analysts[1]	67	68	1	1.9	3	3	52,350	VH	0.0	VL	VL	Bachelor's degree	SC/C	14.9	25.4	59.7
13-2050	Financial analysts and advisors	501	655	153	30.6	53	21	—	—	14.5	—	—	—	—	—	—	—
13-2051	Financial analysts	221	295	75	33.8	29	9	66,590	VH	8.3	VL	L	Bachelor's degree	C	3.1	9.6	87.3
13-2052	Personal financial advisors	176	248	72	41.0	17	9	66,120	VH	30.9	VL	L	Bachelor's degree	C	4.2	15.2	80.5
13-2053	Insurance underwriters	104	111	7	6.3	7	3	52,350	VH	0.0	VL	VL	Bachelor's degree	SC/C	15.7	31.6	52.8
13-2061	Financial examiners[1]	26	28	3	10.7	2	1	65,370	VH	0.0	VL	L	Bachelor's degree	C	0.0	15.0	76.1
13-2070	Loan counselors and officers	406	450	44	10.8	59	9	—	—	3.0	—	—	—	—	—	—	—
13-2071	Loan counselors	33	35	1	4.0	4	0	35,790	H	3.8	L	VL	Bachelor's degree	SC/C	16.4	34.8	48.8
13-2072	Loan officers	373	415	43	11.5	54	8	51,760	VH	2.9	L	VL	Bachelor's degree	SC/C	16.4	34.8	48.8
13-2080	Tax examiners, collectors, preparers, and revenue agents	181	174	-7	-3.7	31	4	—	—	18.2	—	—	—	—	—	—	—
13-2081	Tax examiners, collectors, and revenue agents	81	82	2	2.1	4	2	45,620	H	0.0	VL	VL	Bachelor's degree	HS/SC/C	23.1	34.2	42.7
13-2082	Tax preparers	100	92	-8	-8.4	26	2	27,360	L	32.8	VH	H	Moderate-term on-the-job training	SC/C	14.9	30.9	54.2
13-2099	Financial specialists, all other	129	144	15	11.6	12	5	53,680	VH	2.5	L	L	Bachelor's degree	SC/C	16.8	33.8	49.5
15-2900	**Professional and related occupations**	**29,819**	**34,790**	**4,970**	**16.7**	**3,612**	**1,107**	—	—	**6.6**	—	—	—	—	—	—	—
15-0000	Computer and mathematical science occupations	3,313	4,135	822	24.8	393	157	—	—	3.9	—	—	—	—	—	—	—
15-1000	Computer specialists	3,200	4,006	807	25.2	378	152	—	—	4.0	—	—	—	—	—	—	—
15-1011	Computer and information scientists, research	25	31	5	21.5	3	1	93,950	VH	5.3	L	VL	Doctoral degree	SC/C	7.0	24.6	68.4
15-1021	Computer programmers	435	417	-18	-4.1	28	9	65,510	VH	3.9	L	VL	Bachelor's degree	SC/C	5.5	21.8	72.7
15-1030	Computer software engineers	857	1,181	324	37.9	92	45	—	—	2.0	—	—	—	—	—	—	—
15-1031	Computer software engineers, applications	507	733	226	44.6	59	30	79,780	VH	2.0	VL	VL	Bachelor's degree	C	2.2	13.0	84.8
15-1032	Computer software engineers, systems software	350	449	99	28.2	33	15	85,370	VH	2.1	VL	VL	Bachelor's degree	C	2.2	13.0	84.8

See footnotes at end of table.

Table III-1. Occupational employment and job openings data, 2006–16, and worker characteristics, 2006 — Continued
(Numbers in thousands)

Code	2006 National Employment Matrix occupation and code	Employment 2006	Employment 2016	Employment change, 2006–16 Numeric	Employment change, 2006–16 Percent	Annual average job openings due to growth and total replacement needs, 2006–16	Annual average job openings due to growth and net replacement needs, 2006–16	2006 median annual wages Dollars	2006 median annual wages Rank	Percent self-employed, 2006	Unemployment rate	Percent part-time	Most significant source of postsecondary education or training[2]	Educational attainment cluster[3]	Percent of workers aged 25 to 44, by educational attainment[4]: High school or less	Some college	College or higher
15-1041	Computer support specialists	552	624	71	12.9	97	24	41,470	H	1.3	L	L	Associate degree	SC/C	13.4	44.0	42.6
15-1051	Computer systems analysts	504	650	146	29.0	63	28	69,760	VH	5.8	L	VL	Bachelor's degree	SC/C	7.0	24.6	68.4
15-1061	Database administrators	119	154	34	28.6	8	5	64,670	VH	1.3	VL	VL	Bachelor's degree	SC/C	4.6	23.9	71.5
15-1071	Network and computer systems administrators	309	393	83	27.0	37	15	62,130	VH	.4	L	VL	Bachelor's degree	SC/C	8.3	41.5	50.2
15-1081	Network systems and data communications analysts	262	402	140	53.4	35	19	64,600	VH	17.5	L	L	Bachelor's degree	SC/C	8.1	34.8	57.1
15-1099	Computer specialists, all other	136	157	21	15.1	14	6	68,570	VH	6.6	L	VL	Associate degree	SC/C	7.0	24.6	68.4
15-2000	Mathematical science occupations	114	129	15	13.2	15	4	—	—	1.3	—	—	—	—	—	—	—
15-2011	Actuaries[1]	18	22	4	23.7	3	1	82,800	VH	0.0	VL	VL	Bachelor's or higher, plus work experience	C	0.0	0.0	98.9
15-2021	Mathematicians[1]	3	3	0	10.2	0	0	86,930	VH	0.0	VL	VL	Doctoral degree	C	0.0	6.1	93.3
15-2031	Operations research analysts	58	65	6	10.6	6	2	64,650	VH	.2	VL	VL	Master's degree	SC/C	6.6	22.7	70.7
15-2041	Statisticians[1]	22	24	2	8.5	3	1	65,720	VH	6.0	VL	L	Master's degree	C	0.0	6.1	93.3
15-2090	Miscellaneous mathematical science occupations	12	14	2	19.8	2	1	—	—	0.0	—	—	—	—	—	—	—
15-2091	Mathematical technicians[1]	1	1	0	7.9	0	0	37,880	H	0.0	VL	VL	Master's degree	C	0.0	6.1	93.3
15-2099	Mathematical scientists, all other[1]	10	13	2	21.3	2	0	63,570	VH	0.0	VL	VL	Master's degree	C	0.0	6.1	93.3
17-0000	Architecture and engineering occupations	2,583	2,852	268	10.4	207	85	—	—	3.9	—	—	—	—	—	—	—
17-1000	Architects, surveyors, and cartographers	232	277	45	19.2	31	10	—	—	14.9	—	—	—	—	—	—	—
17-1010	Architects, except naval	160	188	28	17.5	14	6	—	—	20.0	—	—	—	—	—	—	—
17-1011	Architects, except landscape and naval	132	155	23	17.7	11	5	64,150	VH	20.3	VL	VL	Bachelor's degree	C	1.6	10.1	88.3
17-1012	Landscape architects	28	32	5	16.4	2	1	55,140	VH	18.5	VL	VL	Bachelor's degree	C	1.6	10.1	88.3
17-1020	Surveyors, cartographers, and photogrammetrists	72	89	17	23.1	17	4	—	—	3.6	—	—	—	—	—	—	—
17-1021	Cartographers and photogrammetrists	12	15	2	20.3	3	1	48,240	VH	3.4	VL	VL	Bachelor's degree	C	0.0	17.8	81.6
17-1022	Surveyors	60	74	14	23.7	14	3	48,290	VH	3.7	VL	VL	Bachelor's degree	C	0.0	17.8	81.6
17-2000	Engineers	1,512	1,671	160	10.6	93	51	—	—	3.0	—	—	—	—	—	—	—
17-2011	Aerospace engineers[1]	90	99	9	10.2	6	3	87,610	VH	1.4	VL	VL	Bachelor's degree	C	3.3	9.9	86.8
17-2021	Agricultural engineers[1]	3	3	0	8.6	0	0	66,030	VH	0.0	L	L	Bachelor's degree	C	0.0	18.0	75.7
17-2031	Biomedical engineers[1]	14	17	3	21.1	2	1	73,930	VH	0.0	L	VL	Bachelor's degree	C	0.0	18.0	75.7
17-2041	Chemical engineers[1]	30	33	2	7.9	2	1	78,860	VH	1.9	L	VL	Bachelor's degree	C	0.0	5.9	91.4
17-2051	Civil engineers	256	302	46	18.0	16	11	68,600	VH	4.9	VL	VL	Bachelor's degree	C	2.7	10.0	87.3
17-2061	Computer hardware engineers	79	82	4	4.6	4	3	88,470	VH	3.6	VL	VL	Bachelor's degree	SC/C	7.2	22.8	70.0
17-2070	Electrical and electronics engineers	291	306	15	5.0	13	8	—	—	2.1	—	—	—	—	—	—	—
17-2071	Electrical engineers	153	163	10	6.3	7	5	75,930	VH	2.1	VL	VL	Bachelor's degree	C	2.9	16.5	80.5
17-2072	Electronics engineers, except computer	138	143	5	3.7	6	4	81,050	VH	2.2	VL	VL	Bachelor's degree	C	2.9	16.5	80.5
17-2081	Environmental engineers[1]	54	68	14	25.4	5	3	69,940	VH	2.7	VL	VL	Bachelor's degree	C	0.0	9.9	86.4

See footnotes at end of table.

Table III–1. Occupational employment and job openings data, 2006–16, and worker characteristics, 2006 — Continued
(Numbers in thousands)

Code	2006 National Employment Matrix occupation and code	Employment		Employment change, 2006–16		Annual average job openings due to growth and total replacement needs, 2006–16	Annual average job openings due to growth and net replacement needs, 2006–16	2006 median annual wages		Percent self-employed, 2006	Unemployment rate	Percent part-time	Most significant source of postsecondary education or training[2]	Educational attainment cluster[3]	Percent of workers aged 25 to 44, by educational attainment[4]		
		2006	2016	Numeric	Percent			Dollars	Rank						High school or less	Some college	College or higher
17-2110	Industrial engineers, including health and safety	227	270	43	19.1	12	10	—	—	.9	—	—	—	—	—	—	—
17-2111	Health and safety engineers, except mining safety engineers and inspectors	25	28	2	9.6	1	1	66,290	VH	1.1	VL	VL	Bachelor's degree	C	7.6	18.5	73.9
17-2112	Industrial engineers	201	242	41	20.3	11	9	68,620	VH	.9	VL	VL	Bachelor's degree	C	7.6	18.5	73.9
17-2121	Marine engineers and naval architects[1]	9	10	1	10.9	0	0	72,990	VH	12.4	VL	VL	Bachelor's degree	C	0.0	18.1	78.1
17-2131	Materials engineers[1]	22	22	1	4.0	1	1	73,990	VH	0.0	L	VL	Bachelor's degree	C	0.0	19.1	77.0
17-2141	Mechanical engineers	226	235	9	4.2	12	6	69,850	VH	2.2	VL	VL	Bachelor's degree	C	3.5	18.3	78.2
17-2151	Mining and geological engineers, including mining safety engineers[1]	7	8	1	10.0	0	0	72,160	VH	0.0	VL	VL	Bachelor's degree	C	0.0	17.6	79.6
17-2161	Nuclear engineers[1]	15	16	1	7.2	1	0	90,220	VH	0.0	VL	VL	Bachelor's degree	C	3.0	14.7	82.4
17-2171	Petroleum engineers[1]	17	18	1	5.2	1	1	98,380	VH	9.2	VL	VL	Bachelor's degree	C	0.0	17.6	79.6
17-2199	Engineers, all other	170	180	9	5.5	16	3	81,660	VH	6.4	VL	VL	Bachelor's degree	C	3.0	14.7	82.4
17-3000	Drafters, engineering, and mapping technicians	840	904	64	7.6	84	25	—	—	2.5	—	—	—	—	—	—	—
17-3010	Drafters	253	268	15	6.0	36	9	—	—	5.3	—	—	—	—	—	—	—
17-3011	Architectural and civil drafters	116	123	7	6.1	16	4	41,960	H	5.0	L	VL	Postsecondary vocational award	SC/C	13.0	62.4	24.6
17-3012	Electrical and electronics drafters	35	36	1	4.1	5	1	46,830	VH	5.7	L	VL	Postsecondary vocational award	SC/C	13.0	62.4	24.6
17-3013	Mechanical drafters	78	82	4	5.2	11	3	43,700	H	5.5	L	VL	Postsecondary vocational award	SC/C	13.0	62.4	24.6
17-3019	Drafters, all other	25	27	3	11.0	4	1	43,060	H	5.1	L	VL	Postsecondary vocational award	SC/C	13.0	62.4	24.6
17-3020	Engineering technicians, except drafters	511	545	34	6.7	40	13	—	—	.9	—	—	—	—	—	—	—
17-3021	Aerospace engineering and operations technicians	9	9	1	10.4	1	0	53,300	VH	.9	L	VL	Associate degree	HS/SC	27.2	54.4	18.4
17-3022	Civil engineering technicians	91	100	9	10.2	7	3	40,560	H	.9	L	VL	Associate degree	HS/SC	27.2	54.4	18.4
17-3023	Electrical and electronic engineering technicians	170	177	6	3.6	13	4	50,660	VH	.9	L	VL	Associate degree	HS/SC	27.2	54.4	18.4
17-3024	Electro-mechanical technicians	16	16	0	2.6	1	0	44,720	H	1.0	L	VL	Associate degree	HS/SC	27.2	54.4	18.4
17-3025	Environmental engineering technicians	21	26	5	24.8	2	1	40,560	H	.8	L	VL	Associate degree	HS/SC	27.2	54.4	18.4
17-3026	Industrial engineering technicians	75	82	7	9.9	6	2	46,810	VH	.8	L	VL	Associate degree	HS/SC	27.2	54.4	18.4
17-3027	Mechanical engineering technicians	48	51	3	6.4	4	1	45,850	H	.8	L	VL	Associate degree	HS/SC	27.2	54.4	18.4
17-3029	Engineering technicians, except drafters, all other	82	83	2	2.0	6	2	54,250	VH	.9	L	VL	Associate degree	HS/SC	27.2	54.4	18.4
17-3031	Surveying and mapping technicians	76	90	15	19.4	8	3	32,340	H	4.2	H	VL	Moderate-term on-the-job training	HS/SC	42.2	51.0	6.8
19-0000	Life, physical, and social science occupations	1,407	1,610	203	14.4	173	54	—	—	6.9	—	—	—	—	—	—	—
19-1000	Life scientists	258	292	33	12.8	23	10	—	—	4.5	—	—	—	—	—	—	—
19-1010	Agricultural and food scientists	33	36	3	9.3	2	1	—	—	16.7	—	—	—	—	—	—	—
19-1011	Animal scientists	5	6	1	9.8	0	0	47,800	VH	9.0	L	L	Bachelor's degree	C	0.0	17.7	82.0
19-1012	Food scientists and technologists	12	13	1	10.3	1	0	53,810	VH	16.3	L	L	Bachelor's degree	C	0.0	17.7	82.0

See footnotes at end of table.

Table III–1. Occupational employment and job openings data, 2006–16, and worker characteristics, 2006 — Continued
(Numbers in thousands)

Code	2006 National Employment Matrix occupation and code	Employment 2006	Employment 2016	Employment change, 2006–16 Numeric	Employment change, 2006–16 Percent	Annual average job openings due to growth and total replacement needs, 2006–16	Annual average job openings due to growth and net replacement needs, 2006–16	2006 median annual wages Dollars	2006 median annual wages Rank	Percent self-employed, 2006	Unemployment rate	Percent part-time	Most significant source of postsecondary education or training[2]	Educational attainment cluster[3]	Percent of workers aged 25 to 44, by educational attainment[4]: High school or less	Some college	College or higher
19-1013	Soil and plant Scientists	16	17	1	8.4	1	1	56,080	VH	19.5	L	L	Bachelor's degree	C	0.0	17.7	82.0
19-1020	Biological scientists	87	95	8	9.2	6	3	—	—	2.8	—	—	—	—	—	—	—
19-1021	Biochemists and biophysicists	20	23	3	15.9	2	1	76,320	VH	2.5	L	L	Doctoral degree	C	0.0	5.3	94.6
19-1022	Microbiologists	17	19	2	11.2	1	1	57,980	VH	2.7	L	L	Doctoral degree	C	0.0	5.3	94.6
19-1023	Zoologists and wildlife biologists	20	22	2	8.7	1	1	53,300	VH	2.6	L	L	Bachelor's degree	C	0.0	5.3	94.6
19-1029	Biological scientists, all other	29	30	1	3.7	2	1	60,940	VH	3.2	L	L	Doctoral degree	C	0.0	5.3	94.6
19-1030	Conservation scientists and foresters	33	35	2	5.3	2	1	—	—	4.0	—	—	—	—	—	—	—
19-1031	Conservation scientists[1]	20	21	1	5.3	1	1	54,970	VH	3.9	VL	VL	Bachelor's degree	C	0.0	14.0	85.7
19-1032	Foresters[1]	13	14	1	5.1	1	0	51,190	VH	4.2	VL	VL	Bachelor's degree	C	0.0	14.0	85.7
19-1040	Medical scientists	92	110	18	19.9	11	5	—	—	2.1	—	—	—	—	—	—	—
19-1041	Epidemiologists	5	5	1	13.6	1	0	56,670	VH	2.6	VL	VL	Master's degree	C	0.0	0.0	99.3
19-1042	Medical scientists, except epidemiologists	87	105	18	20.2	11	4	61,680	VH	2.0	VL	VL	Doctoral degree	C	0.0	0.0	99.3
19-1099	Life scientists, all other	14	16	2	15.3	2	1	56,970	VH	2.7	VL	VL	Bachelor's degree	C	0.0	0.0	99.3
19-2000	Physical scientists	267	309	42	15.7	23	11	—	—	1.8	—	—	—	—	—	—	—
19-2010	Astronomers and physicists	18	19	1	6.7	1	1	—	—	.8	—	—	—	—	—	—	—
19-2011	Astronomers[1]	2	2	0	5.6	0	0	95,740	VH	.4	VL	VL	Doctoral degree	C	0.0	0.0	95.2
19-2012	Physicists[1]	17	18	1	6.8	1	1	94,240	VH	.8	VL	VL	Doctoral degree	C	0.0	0.0	95.2
19-2021	Atmospheric and space scientists[1]	9	10	1	10.6	1	0	77,150	VH	0.0	VL	VL	Bachelor's degree	C	0.0	0.0	85.4
19-2030	Chemists and materials scientists	93	102	8	9.1	10	3	—	—	1.2	—	—	—	—	—	—	—
19-2031	Chemists	84	91	8	9.1	9	3	59,870	VH	1.2	VL	VL	Bachelor's degree	C	0.0	6.5	93.2
19-2032	Materials scientists	10	11	1	8.7	1	0	74,610	VH	1.0	VL	VL	Bachelor's degree	C	0.0	6.5	93.2
19-2040	Environmental scientists and geoscientists	123	152	30	24.2	10	6	—	—	2.2	—	—	—	—	—	—	—
19-2041	Environmental scientists and specialists, including health	83	104	21	25.1	7	4	56,100	VH	2.1	VL	VL	Master's degree	C	0.0	6.9	93.0
19-2042	Geoscientists, except hydrologists and geographers	31	38	7	21.9	2	1	72,660	VH	2.2	VL	VL	Master's degree	C	0.0	6.9	93.0
19-2043	Hydrologists	8	10	2	24.3	1	0	66,260	VH	2.4	VL	VL	Master's degree	C	0.0	6.9	93.0
19-2099	Physical scientists, all other	24	25	1	6.2	1	1	83,450	VH	3.4	VL	VL	Bachelor's degree	C	0.0	1.5	98.4
19-3000	Social scientists and related occupations	530	616	86	16.3	66	16	—	—	14.7	—	—	—	—	—	—	—
19-3011	Economists[1]	15	16	1	7.5	2	1	77,010	VH	6.5	L	VL	Master's degree	C	0.0	0.0	99.7
19-3020	Market and survey researchers	261	313	51	19.6	50	7	—	—	6.6	—	—	—	—	—	—	—
19-3021	Market research analysts	234	281	47	20.1	45	6	58,820	VH	6.6	L	L	Bachelor's degree	C	4.4	13.5	82.2
19-3022	Survey researchers	27	31	4	15.9	5	1	33,360	H	6.8	L	L	Bachelor's degree	C	4.4	13.5	82.2
19-3030	Psychologists	166	191	25	15.3	9	5	—	—	33.7	—	—	—	—	—	—	—
19-3031	Clinical, counseling, and school psychologists	152	176	24	15.8	8	5	59,440	VH	34.2	VL	H	Doctoral degree	C	0.0	0.0	99.3
19-3032	Industrial-organizational psychologists	2	2	0	21.3	0	0	86,420	VH	39.3	VL	H	Master's degree	C	0.0	0.0	99.3
19-3039	Psychologists, all other	12	13	1	7.9	1	0	76,310	VH	26.5	VL	H	Master's degree	C	0.0	0.0	99.3

See footnotes at end of table.

Table III-1. Occupational employment and job openings data, 2006–16, and worker characteristics, 2006 — Continued
(Numbers in thousands)

Code	2006 National Employment Matrix occupation and code	Employment 2006	Employment 2016	Employment change, 2006–16 Numeric	Employment change, 2006–16 Percent	Annual average job openings due to growth and total replacement needs, 2006–16	Annual average job openings due to growth and net replacement needs, 2006–16	2006 median annual wages Dollars	2006 median annual wages Rank	Percent self-employed, 2006	Unemployment rate	Percent part-time	Most significant source of postsecondary education or training[2]	Educational attainment cluster[3]	Percent of workers aged 25 to 44, by educational attainment[4] High school or less	Some college	College or higher
19-3041	Sociologists[1]	4	4	0	10.0	0	0	60,290	VH	0.0	VL	H	Master's degree	C	0.0	10.2	89.8
19-3051	Urban and regional planners[1]	34	39	5	14.5	2	1	56,630	VH	.2	VL	VL	Master's degree	C	0.0	0.0	92.2
19-3090	Miscellaneous social scientists and related workers	51	54	3	6.1	3	2	—	—	7.0	—	—	—	—	—	—	—
19-3091	Anthropologists and archeologists	6	6	1	15.0	0	0	49,930	VH	6.1	L	H	Master's degree	C	0.0	10.2	89.8
19-3092	Geographers	1	1	0	6.1	0	0	62,990	VH	5.3	L	H	Master's degree	C	0.0	10.2	89.8
19-3093	Historians	3	4	0	7.8	0	0	48,520	VH	5.2	L	H	Master's degree	C	0.0	10.2	89.8
19-3094	Political scientists	5	5	0	5.3	0	0	90,140	VH	7.5	L	H	Master's degree	C	0.0	10.2	89.8
19-3099	Social scientists and related workers, all other	36	38	2	4.7	2	1	64,920	VH	7.2	L	H	Master's degree	C	0.0	10.2	89.8
19-4000	Life, physical, and social science technicians	351	393	42	11.8	60	17	—	—	1.0	—	—	—	—	—	—	—
19-4011	Agricultural and food science technicians[1]	26	28	2	6.6	4	1	31,730	H	.7	H	L	Associate degree	HS/SC/C	42.7	25.6	31.6
19-4021	Biological technicians	79	91	13	16.0	15	4	35,710	H	0.0	H	VL	Bachelor's degree	SC/C	13.7	25.9	60.4
19-4031	Chemical technicians	61	65	4	5.8	4	2	39,240	H	.4	VL	VL	Associate degree	HS/SC/C	30.3	32.5	37.2
19-4041	Geological and petroleum technicians[1]	12	13	1	8.6	2	1	46,160	H	0.0	H	VL	Associate degree	HS/SC/C	33.6	34.6	31.7
19-4051	Nuclear technicians[1]	7	7	0	6.7	1	0	65,500	VH	0.0	VL	VL	Associate degree	SC/C	19.4	34.9	45.7
19-4061	Social science research assistants	18	20	2	12.4	4	1	33,860	H	1.7	L	H	Associate degree	SC/C	19.4	34.9	45.7
19-4090	Other life, physical, and social science technicians	150	170	20	13.4	30	8	—	—	1.8	—	—	—	—	—	—	—
19-4091	Environmental science and protection technicians, including health	36	47	10	28.0	8	2	38,090	H	1.5	L	H	Associate degree	SC/C	19.4	34.9	45.7
19-4092	Forensic science technicians	13	17	4	30.7	3	1	45,330	H	1.3	L	H	Bachelor's degree	SC/C	19.4	34.9	45.7
19-4093	Forest and conservation technicians	34	33	-1	-2.0	6	1	30,880	H	1.7	L	H	Associate degree	SC/C	19.4	34.9	45.7
19-4099	Life, physical, and social science technicians, all other	66	73	7	9.8	13	3	37,920	H	2.2	L	H	Associate degree	SC/C	19.4	34.9	45.7
21-0000	Community and social services occupations	2,386	2,927	541	22.7	413	94	—	—	2.3	—	—	—	—	—	—	—
21-1000	Counselors, social workers, and other community and social service specialists	1,843	2,280	438	23.8	358	76	—	—	3.0	—	—	—	—	—	—	—
21-1010	Counselors	635	771	136	21.3	143	26	—	—	6.0	—	—	—	—	—	—	—
21-1011	Substance abuse and behavioral disorder counselors	83	112	29	34.3	21	5	34,040	H	5.8	L	H	Bachelor's degree	C	8.9	18.3	72.8
21-1012	Educational, vocational, and school counselors	260	292	33	12.6	54	8	47,530	VH	6.1	L	H	Master's degree	C	8.9	18.3	72.8
21-1013	Marriage and family therapists	25	32	7	29.8	6	1	43,210	H	6.2	L	H	Master's degree	C	8.9	18.3	72.8
21-1014	Mental health counselors	100	130	30	30.0	24	5	34,380	H	6.1	L	H	Master's degree	C	8.9	18.3	72.8
21-1015	Rehabilitation counselors	141	173	32	23.0	32	6	29,200	L	5.9	L	H	Master's degree	C	8.9	18.3	72.8
21-1019	Counselors, all other	27	32	5	16.6	6	1	38,210	H	5.8	L	H	Master's degree	C	8.9	18.3	72.8
21-1020	Social workers	595	727	132	22.2	77	26	—	—	2.8	—	—	—	—	—	—	—

See footnotes at end of table.

Table III–1. Occupational employment and job openings data, 2006–16, and worker characteristics, 2006 — Continued
(Numbers in thousands)

Code	2006 National Employment Matrix occupation and code	Employment 2006	Employment 2016	Employment change, 2006–16 Numeric	Employment change, 2006–16 Percent	Annual average job openings due to growth and total replacement needs, 2006–16	Annual average job openings due to growth and net replacement needs, 2006–16	2006 median annual wages Dollars	2006 median annual wages Rank	Percent self-employed, 2006	Unemployment rate	Percent part-time	Most significant source of postsecondary education or training[2]	Educational attainment cluster[3]	Percent of workers aged 25 to 44, by educational attainment[4]: High school or less	Some college	College or higher
21-1021	Child, family, and school social workers	282	336	54	19.1	35	11	37,480	H	2.8	VL	L	Bachelor's degree	C	7.1	15.7	77.2
21-1022	Medical and public health social workers	124	154	30	24.2	16	6	43,040	H	2.6	VL	L	Bachelor's degree	C	7.1	15.7	77.2
21-1023	Mental health and substance abuse social workers	122	159	37	29.9	17	6	35,410	H	2.8	VL	L	Master's degree	C	7.1	15.7	77.2
21-1029	Social workers, all other	66	78	12	17.8	8	3	43,580	H	2.9	VL	L	Bachelor's degree	C	7.1	15.7	77.2
21-1090	Miscellaneous community and social service specialists	613	783	170	27.7	138	24	—	—	.1	—	—	—	—	—	—	—
21-1091	Health educators	62	78	16	26.2	14	2	41,330	H	.1	L	L	Bachelor's degree	SC/C	15.6	26.3	58.1
21-1092	Probation officers and correctional treatment specialists	94	105	10	10.9	18	2	42,500	H	.1	L	L	Bachelor's degree	SC/C	15.6	26.3	58.1
21-1093	Social and human service assistants	339	453	114	33.6	80	15	25,580	L	.1	L	L	Moderate-term on-the-job training	SC/C	15.6	26.3	58.1
21-1099	Community and social service specialists, all other	118	148	30	25.1	26	4	35,210	H	.1	L	L	Bachelor's degree	SC/C	15.6	26.3	58.1
21-2000	Religious workers	543	646	104	19.1	54	18	—	—	.1	—	—	—	—	—	—	—
21-2011	Clergy	404	481	76	18.9	35	13	39,680	H	.1	VL	L	Master's degree	C	8.5	16.9	74.6
21-2021	Directors, religious activities and education	99	119	20	19.7	11	4	34,260	H	0.0	VL	H	Bachelor's degree	SC/C	9.7	26.0	64.4
21-2099	Religious workers, all other	39	47	8	19.7	8	1	24,330	L	.4	VL	VH	Bachelor's degree	SC/C	15.6	28.6	55.8
23-0000	Legal occupations	1,222	1,367	145	11.8	93	36	—	—	18.5	—	—	—	—	—	—	—
23-1000	Lawyers, judges, and related workers	812	898	86	10.6	52	24	—	—	25.0	—	—	—	—	—	—	—
23-1011	Lawyers	761	844	84	11.0	49	23	102,470	VH	26.7	VL	VL	First professional degree	C	.2	.7	99.1
23-1020	Judges, magistrates, and other judicial workers	51	53	2	4.5	3	1	—	—	0.0	—	—	—	—	—	—	—
23-1021	Administrative law judges, adjudicators, and hearing officers[1]	15	15	0	.1	1	0	72,600	VH	0.0	VL	VL	Bachelor's or higher, plus work experience	C	.2	.7	99.1
23-1022	Arbitrators, mediators, and conciliators[1]	8	9	1	10.6	1	0	49,490	VH	0.0	VL	VL	Bachelor's or higher, plus work experience	C	.2	.7	99.1
23-1023	Judges, magistrate judges, and magistrates[1]	27	29	1	5.1	2	1	101,690	VH	0.0	VL	VL	Bachelor's or higher, plus work experience	C	.2	.7	99.1
23-2000	Legal support workers	410	469	59	14.3	41	12	—	—	5.5	—	—	—	—	—	—	—
23-2011	Paralegals and legal assistants	238	291	53	22.2	23	8	43,040	H	2.2	VL	L	Associate degree	SC/C	12.7	42.7	44.6
23-2090	Miscellaneous legal support workers	173	179	6	3.4	18	4	—	—	10.2	—	—	—	—	—	—	—
23-2091	Court reporters	19	24	5	24.5	3	1	45,610	H	7.9	L	L	Postsecondary vocational award	HS/SC/C	22.5	39.3	38.1
23-2092	Law clerks	37	36	0	-1.2	4	1	36,360	H	11.5	L	L	Bachelor's degree	HS/SC/C	22.5	39.3	38.1
23-2093	Title examiners, abstractors, and searchers	69	68	-1	-1.2	7	1	36,020	H	7.4	L	L	Moderate-term on-the-job training	HS/SC/C	22.5	39.3	38.1
23-2099	Legal support workers, all other	48	50	2	5.1	5	1	45,140	H	14.2	L	L	Moderate-term on-the-job training	HS/SC/C	22.5	39.3	38.1
25-0000	Education, training, and library occupations	9,034	10,298	1,265	14.0	1,269	305	—	—	2.4	—	—	—	—	—	—	—
25-1000	Postsecondary teachers	1,672	2,054	382	22.9	237	66	56,120	VH	.4	VL	VH	Doctoral degree	C	.2	5.2	94.6
25-2000	Primary, secondary, and special education teachers	4,413	4,963	550	12.5	504	158	—	—	.2	—	—	—	—	—	—	—
25-2010	Preschool and kindergarten teachers	607	750	143	23.5	106	24	—	—	1.1	—	—	—	—	—	—	—

See footnotes at end of table.

Table III–1. Occupational employment and job openings data, 2006–16, and worker characteristics, 2006 — Continued
(Numbers in thousands)

2006 National Employment Matrix occupation and code		Employment		Employment change, 2006–16		Annual average job openings due to growth and total replacement needs, 2006–16	Annual average job openings due to growth and net replacement needs, 2006–16	2006 median annual wages		Percent self-employed, 2006	Unemployment rate	Percent part-time	Most significant source of postsecondary education or training[2]	Educational attainment cluster[3]	Percent of workers aged 25 to 44, by educational attainment[4]		
		2006	2016	Numeric	Percent			Dollars	Rank						High school or less	Some college	College or higher
25-2011	Preschool teachers, except special education	437	552	115	26.3	78	19	22,680	L	1.1	L	H	Postsecondary vocational award	HS/SC/C	20.0	37.5	42.5
25-2012	Kindergarten teachers, except special education	170	198	28	16.3	28	6	43,580	H	1.1	L	H	Bachelor's degree	HS/SC/C	20.0	37.5	42.5
25-2020	Elementary and middle school teachers	2,214	2,496	282	12.7	258	77	—	—	0.0	—	—	—	—	—	—	—
25-2021	Elementary school teachers, except special education	1,540	1,749	209	13.6	182	55	45,570	H	0.0	VL	L	Bachelor's degree	C	.3	5.2	94.5
25-2022	Middle school teachers, except special and vocational education	658	732	74	11.2	75	22	46,300	H	0.0	VL	L	Bachelor's degree	C	.3	5.2	94.5
25-2023	Vocational education teachers, middle school	16	15	-1	-5.1	2	0	44,240	H	0.0	VL	L	Bachelor's or higher, plus work experience	C	.3	5.2	94.5
25-2030	Secondary school teachers	1,133	1,187	54	4.8	101	40	—	—	0.0	—	—	—	—	—	—	—
25-2031	Secondary school teachers, except special and vocational education	1,038	1,096	59	5.6	93	37	47,740	VH	0.0	VL	L	Bachelor's degree	C	.6	3.5	95.9
25-2032	Vocational education teachers, secondary school	96	91	-4	-4.6	8	3	48,690	VH	0.0	VL	L	Bachelor's or higher, plus work experience	C	.6	3.5	95.9
25-2040	Special education teachers	459	530	71	15.4	39	17	—	—	.3	—	—	—	—	—	—	—
25-2041	Special education teachers, preschool, kindergarten, and elementary school	219	262	43	19.6	20	9	46,360	VH	.3	VL	L	Bachelor's degree	C	4.5	8.3	87.2
25-2042	Special education teachers, middle school	102	118	16	15.8	9	4	47,650	VH	.3	VL	L	Bachelor's degree	C	4.5	8.3	87.2
25-2043	Special education teachers, secondary school	138	150	12	8.5	11	4	48,330	VH	.3	VL	L	Bachelor's degree	C	4.5	8.3	87.2
25-3000	Other teachers and instructors	1,078	1,214	136	12.6	243	25	—	—	18.1	—	—	—	—	—	—	—
25-3011	Adult literacy, remedial education, and GED teachers and instructors	76	87	11	14.2	17	2	43,910	H	0.0	L	VH	Bachelor's degree	SC/C	16.7	29.4	53.9
25-3021	Self-enrichment education teachers	261	322	60	23.1	64	9	33,440	H	21.5	L	VH	Work experience in a related occupation	SC/C	16.7	29.4	53.9
25-3099	Teachers and instructors, all other	741	805	64	8.7	161	14	28,660	L	18.8	L	VH	Bachelor's degree	SC/C	16.7	29.4	53.9
25-4000	Librarians, curators, and archivists	307	328	21	6.9	52	13	—	—	.4	—	—	—	—	—	—	—
25-4010	Archivists, curators, and museum technicians	27	33	5	18.3	4	2	—	—	1.3	—	—	—	—	—	—	—
25-4011	Archivists	6	7	1	14.4	1	0	40,730	H	1.3	L	H	Master's degree	C	5.4	8.7	85.9
25-4012	Curators	10	13	2	23.3	1	1	46,300	H	1.3	L	H	Master's degree	C	5.4	8.7	85.9
25-4013	Museum Technicians and Conservators	11	12	2	15.9	1	1	34,340	H	1.3	L	H	Bachelor's degree	C	5.4	8.7	85.9
25-4021	Librarians	158	164	6	3.6	19	5	49,060	VH	.6	VL	H	Master's degree	C	0.0	15.3	84.5
25-4031	Library technicians	121	132	10	8.5	29	7	26,560	L	0.0	H	VH	Postsecondary vocational award	HS/SC/C	45.9	27.6	26.5
25-9000	Other education, training, and library occupations	1,563	1,739	176	11.2	233	42	—	—	.6	—	—	—	—	—	—	—
25-9011	Audio-visual collections specialists	7	6	-1	-13.8	1	0	40,530	H	4.3	VL	H	Bachelor's degree	C	4.3	16.7	79.0
25-9021	Farm and home management advisors	15	16	1	5.1	2	0	41,710	H	3.6	VL	H	Bachelor's degree	C	4.3	16.7	79.0
25-9031	Instructional coordinators	129	159	29	22.5	21	5	52,790	VH	3.1	VL	H	Master's degree	C	4.3	16.7	79.0

See footnotes at end of table.

Table III–1. Occupational employment and job openings data, 2006–16, and worker characteristics, 2006 — Continued
(Numbers in thousands)

Code	2006 National Employment Matrix occupation and code	Employment		Employment change, 2006–16		Annual average job openings due to growth and total replacement needs, 2006–16	Annual average job openings due to growth and net replacement needs, 2006–16	2006 median annual wages		Percent self-employed, 2006	Unemployment rate	Percent part-time	Most significant source of postsecondary education or training[2]	Educational attainment cluster[3]	Percent of workers aged 25 to 44, by educational attainment[4]		
		2006	2016	Numeric	Percent			Dollars	Rank						High school or less	Some college	College or higher
25-9041	Teacher assistants	1,312	1,449	137	10.4	194	35	20,740	VL	.2	L	VH	Short-term on-the-job training	HS/SC	37.4	44.7	17.9
25-9099	Education, training, and library workers, all other	99	110	10	10.5	14	2	32,160	H	2.6	VL	H	Bachelor's degree	C	4.3	16.7	79.0
27-0000	Arts, design, entertainment, sports, and media occupations	2,677	2,982	305	11.4	394	97	—	—	30.3	—	—	—	—	—	—	—
27-1000	Art and design occupations	821	905	84	10.2	91	30	—	—	36.6	—	—	—	—	—	—	—
27-1010	Artists and related workers	218	253	34	15.8	30	9	—	—	62.0	—	—	—	—	—	—	—
27-1011	Art directors	78	85	7	9.0	10	3	68,100	VH	59.0	L	H	Bachelor's or higher, plus work experience	SC/C	13.6	28.5	58.0
27-1012	Craft artists	9	10	1	8.0	1	0	24,090	L	44.9	L	H	Long-term on-the-job training	SC/C	13.6	28.5	58.0
27-1013	Fine artists, including painters, sculptors, and illustrators	30	33	3	9.9	4	1	41,970	H	62.6	L	H	Long-term on-the-job training	SC/C	13.6	28.5	58.0
27-1014	Multi-media artists and animators	87	110	23	25.8	13	4	51,350	VH	69.7	L	H	Bachelor's degree	SC/C	13.6	28.5	58.0
27-1019	Artists and related workers, all other	14	15	1	8.4	2	0	41,990	H	40.1	L	H	Long-term on-the-job training	SC/C	13.6	28.5	58.0
27-1020	Designers	603	653	50	8.2	62	22	—	—	27.4	—	—	—	—	—	—	—
27-1021	Commercial and industrial designers	48	51	3	7.2	5	2	54,560	VH	29.8	L	H	Bachelor's degree	SC/C	13.9	31.4	54.6
27-1022	Fashion designers	20	21	1	5.0	2	1	62,610	VH	23.6	L	H	Associate degree	SC/C	13.9	31.4	54.6
27-1023	Floral designers	87	79	-8	-8.9	7	2	21,700	L	32.7	L	H	Moderate-term on-the-job training	SC/C	13.9	31.4	54.6
27-1024	Graphic designers	261	286	26	9.8	27	9	39,900	H	25.3	L	H	Bachelor's degree	SC/C	13.9	31.4	54.6
27-1025	Interior designers	72	86	14	19.5	8	3	42,260	H	26.3	L	H	Associate degree	SC/C	13.9	31.4	54.6
27-1026	Merchandise displayers and window trimmers	87	96	9	10.7	9	3	23,820	L	28.6	L	H	Moderate-term on-the-job training	SC/C	13.9	31.4	54.6
27-1027	Set and exhibit designers	12	14	2	17.8	1	1	41,820	H	29.8	L	H	Bachelor's degree	SC/C	13.9	31.4	54.6
27-1029	Designers, all other	16	18	2	11.8	2	1	43,870	H	28.3	L	H	Bachelor's degree	SC/C	13.9	31.4	54.6
27-2000	Entertainers and performers, sports and related occupations	798	897	100	12.5	134	31	—	—	31.9	—	—	—	—	—	—	—
27-2010	Actors, producers, and directors	163	182	18	11.3	30	6	—	—	27.7	—	—	—	—	—	—	—
27-2011	Actors	70	78	8	11.6	21	2	NA	—	25.3	VH	H	Long-term on-the-job training	SC/C	15.6	22.3	62.1
27-2012	Producers and directors	93	103	10	11.1	9	4	56,310	VH	29.5	H	L	Bachelor's or higher, plus work experience	C	6.1	19.4	74.5
27-2020	Athletes, coaches, umpires, and related workers	253	291	38	15.1	60	10	—	—	23.1	—	—	—	—	—	—	—
27-2021	Athletes and sports competitors	18	21	3	19.2	4	1	41,060	H	27.0	H	VH	Long-term on-the-job training	SC/C	13.7	26.4	59.9
27-2022	Coaches and scouts	217	249	32	14.6	51	9	26,950	L	22.7	H	VH	Long-term on-the-job training	SC/C	13.7	26.4	59.9
27-2023	Umpires, referees, and other sports officials	19	22	3	16.0	4	1	22,880	L	24.0	H	VH	Long-term on-the-job training	SC/C	13.7	26.4	59.9
27-2030	Dancers and choreographers	40	43	2	5.9	3	2	—	—	17.1	—	—	—	—	—	—	—
27-2031	Dancers	20	22	2	9.5	1	1	NA	—	17.5	VH	VH	Long-term on-the-job training	HS/SC/C	41.2	36.4	22.4
27-2032	Choreographers	20	21	0	2.4	1	1	34,660	H	16.8	VH	VH	Work experience in a related occupation	HS/SC/C	41.2	36.4	22.4
27-2040	Musicians, singers, and related workers	264	293	29	10.8	33	8	—	—	47.8	—	—	—	—	—	—	—
27-2041	Music directors and composers	68	77	9	12.9	9	2	39,750	H	44.7	H	VH	Bachelor's or higher, plus work experience	SC/C	19.3	28.2	52.5

See footnotes at end of table.

Table III–1. Occupational employment and job openings data, 2006–16, and worker characteristics, 2006 — Continued
(Numbers in thousands)

2006 National Employment Matrix occupation and code		Employment		Employment change, 2006–16		Annual average job openings due to growth and total replacement needs, 2006–16	Annual average job openings due to growth and net replacement needs, 2006–16	2006 median annual wages		Percent self-employed, 2006	Unemployment rate	Percent part-time	Most significant source of postsecondary education or training[2]	Educational attainment cluster[3]	Percent of workers aged 25 to 44, by educational attainment[4]		
		2006	2016	Numeric	Percent			Dollars	Rank						High school or less	Some college	College or higher
27-2042	Musicians and singers	196	216	20	10.1	24	6	NA	—	48.9	H	VH	Long-term on-the-job training	SC/C	19.3	28.2	52.5
27-2099	Entertainers and performers, sports and related workers, all other	77	89	12	15.8	9	4	NA	—	23.3	L	H	Long-term on-the-job training	HS/SC/C	31.4	33.4	30.2
27-3000	Media and communication occupations	764	847	83	10.8	134	24	—	—	22.2	—	—	—	—	—	—	—
27-3010	Announcers	71	66	-5	-6.9	8	2	—	—	30.1	—	—	—	—	—	—	—
27-3011	Radio and television announcers	59	54	-5	-8.3	6	2	24,310	L	30.2	H	VH	Long-term on-the-job training	HS/SC/C	26.2	35.7	38.1
27-3012	Public address system and other announcers	12	12	0	-.2	1	0	24,990	L	30.0	H	VH	Long-term on-the-job training	HS/SC/C	26.2	35.7	38.1
27-3020	News analysts, reporters and correspondents	67	68	1	1.7	12	2	—	—	10.7	—	—	—	—	—	—	—
27-3021	Broadcast news analysts	8	8	0	6.0	1	0	46,710	VH	11.1	L	H	Bachelor's or higher, plus work experience	C	1.3	13.6	85.1
27-3022	Reporters and correspondents	59	60	1	1.2	11	2	33,470	H	10.7	L	H	Bachelor's degree	C	1.3	13.6	85.1
27-3031	Public relations specialists	243	286	43	17.6	51	6	47,350	VH	4.9	VL	L	Bachelor's degree	C	5.3	13.9	80.8
27-3040	Writers and editors	306	336	30	9.7	52	10	—	—	35.4	—	—	—	—	—	—	—
27-3041	Editors	122	124	3	2.3	20	4	46,990	VH	13.4	H	L	Bachelor's degree	C	4.0	14.7	81.4
27-3042	Technical writers	49	59	10	19.5	7	2	58,050	VH	6.0	VH	VL	Bachelor's degree	C	7.2	18.4	74.4
27-3043	Writers and authors	135	153	17	12.8	24	4	48,640	VH	65.9	H	H	Bachelor's degree	C	3.5	12.4	84.1
27-3090	Miscellaneous media and communications workers	77	91	14	18.1	12	3	—	—	26.4	—	—	—	—	—	—	—
27-3091	Interpreters and translators	41	51	10	23.6	7	2	35,560	H	21.6	H	VH	Long-term on-the-job training	SC/C	15.9	36.3	47.8
27-3099	Media and communication workers, all other	36	40	4	11.7	5	1	42,570	H	32.1	H	VH	Long-term on-the-job training	SC/C	15.9	36.3	47.8
27-4000	Media and communication equipment occupations	294	332	38	13.0	34	11	—	—	29.7	—	—	—	—	—	—	—
27-4010	Broadcast and sound engineering technicians and radio operators	105	123	18	17.0	9	5	—	—	12.5	—	—	—	—	—	—	—
27-4011	Audio and video equipment technicians	50	62	12	24.2	5	3	34,840	H	12.8	L	L	Long-term on-the-job training	HS/SC/C	21.2	43.9	35.0
27-4012	Broadcast technicians	38	42	5	12.1	3	2	30,690	H	12.4	L	L	Associate degree	HS/SC/C	21.2	43.9	35.0
27-4013	Radio operators	2	1	0	-16.3	0	0	37,890	H	17.6	L	L	Moderate-term on-the-job training	HS/SC/C	21.2	43.9	35.0
27-4014	Sound engineering technicians	16	18	1	9.1	1	1	43,010	H	11.3	L	L	Postsecondary vocational award	HS/SC/C	21.2	43.9	35.0
27-4021	Photographers	122	135	13	10.3	16	4	26,170	L	54.3	H	H	Long-term on-the-job training	SC/C	18.7	35.6	45.7
27-4030	Television, video, and motion picture camera operators and editors	47	53	6	12.0	6	1	—	—	16.5	—	—	—	—	—	—	—
27-4031	Camera operators, television, video, and motion picture	27	30	3	11.5	3	1	40,060	H	16.9	H	H	Postsecondary vocational award	SC/C	12.8	28.7	58.4
27-4032	Film and video editors	21	23	3	12.7	3	1	46,670	VH	15.9	H	H	Bachelor's degree	SC/C	12.8	28.7	58.4
27-4099	Media and communication equipment workers, all other[1]	19	21	2	10.2	3	1	52,070	VH	0.0	H	H	Moderate-term on-the-job training	HS/SC/C	21.2	43.9	35.0
29-0000	Healthcare practitioners and technical occupations	7,198	8,620	1,423	19.8	671	279	—	—	4.5	—	—	—	—	—	—	—

See footnotes at end of table.

Table III–1. Occupational employment and job openings data, 2006–16, and worker characteristics, 2006 — Continued
(Numbers in thousands)

Code	2006 National Employment Matrix occupation and code	Employment 2006	Employment 2016	Employment change, 2006–16 Numeric	Employment change, 2006–16 Percent	Annual average job openings due to growth and total replacement needs, 2006–16	Annual average job openings due to growth and net replacement needs, 2006–16	2006 median annual wages Dollars	2006 median annual wages Rank	Percent self-employed, 2006	Unemployment rate	Percent part-time	Most significant source of postsecondary education or training[2]	Educational attainment cluster[3]	Percent of workers aged 25 to 44, by educational attainment[4] High school or less	Some college	College or higher
29-1000	Health diagnosing and treating practitioners	4,460	5,383	923	20.7	370	167	—	—	6.6	—	—	—	—	—	—	—
29-1011	Chiropractors[1]	53	60	8	14.4	3	1	65,220	VH	51.7	VL	H	First professional degree	C	0.0	0.0	97.5
29-1020	Dentists	161	176	15	9.1	8	5	—	—	36.5	—	—	—	—	—	—	—
29-1021	Dentists, general[1]	136	149	13	9.2	7	4	132,140	VH	36.6	VL	H	First professional degree	C	0.0	0.0	99.5
29-1022	Oral and maxillofacial surgeons[1]	8	8	1	9.1	0	0	NA	—	30.6	VL	H	First professional degree	C	0.0	0.0	99.5
29-1023	Orthodontists[1]	9	10	1	9.2	0	0	NA	—	43.3	VL	H	First professional degree	C	0.0	0.0	99.5
29-1024	Prosthodontists[1]	1	1	0	10.7	0	0	NA	—	51.3	VL	H	First professional degree	C	0.0	0.0	99.5
29-1029	Dentists, all other specialists[1]	7	7	0	6.8	0	0	91,200	VH	29.1	VL	H	First professional degree	C	0.0	0.0	99.5
29-1031	Dietitians and nutritionists	57	62	5	8.6	5	2	46,980	VH	7.9	VL	VH	Bachelor's degree	C	14.7	13.6	71.7
29-1041	Optometrists[1]	33	36	4	11.3	2	1	91,040	VH	25.5	VL	H	First professional degree	C	0.0	0.0	100.0
29-1051	Pharmacists	243	296	53	21.7	16	10	94,520	VH	.5	VL	H	First professional degree	C	0.0	2.9	97.0
29-1060	Physicians and surgeons	633	723	90	14.2	38	20	NA	—	14.7	VL	L	First professional degree	C	0.0	0.0	100.0
29-1071	Physician assistants	66	83	18	27.0	7	3	74,980	VH	1.8	VL	H	Master's degree	SC/C	7.6	25.5	66.9
29-1081	Podiatrists[1]	12	13	1	9.5	1	1	108,220	VH	23.9	VL	H	First professional degree	C	0.0	0.0	99.2
29-1111	Registered nurses	2,505	3,092	587	23.5	233	100	57,280	VH	.8	VL	H	Associate degree	SC/C	1.0	42.7	56.2
29-1120	Therapists	570	684	114	19.9	47	20	—	—	10.0	—	—	—	—	—	—	—
29-1121	Audiologists[1]	12	13	1	9.8	1	0	57,120	VH	10.2	VL	VH	First professional degree	C	0.0	0.0	91.2
29-1122	Occupational therapists	99	122	23	23.1	8	4	60,470	VH	8.6	VL	VH	Master's degree	C	0.0	9.0	90.3
29-1123	Physical therapists	173	220	47	27.1	12	7	66,200	VH	8.4	VL	H	Master's degree	C	1.8	8.8	89.3
29-1124	Radiation therapists[1]	15	18	4	24.8	1	1	66,170	VH	0.0	VL	L	Associate degree	SC/C	0.0	55.4	42.1
29-1125	Recreational therapists[1]	25	26	1	3.7	2	0	34,990	H	0.0	VL	H	Bachelor's degree	C	0.0	13.6	76.5
29-1126	Respiratory therapists	102	126	23	22.6	6	4	47,420	VH	1.1	VL	H	Associate degree	SC/C	1.1	71.2	27.7
29-1127	Speech-language pathologists	110	121	12	10.6	11	3	57,710	VH	8.8	VL	H	Master's degree	C	0.0	0.0	97.9
29-1129	Therapists, all other	35	38	3	10.0	6	1	42,250	H	64.5	VL	VH	Bachelor's degree	C	3.2	14.2	82.6
29-1131	Veterinarians[1]	62	84	22	35.0	5	3	71,990	VH	17.1	VL	L	First professional degree	C	0.0	0.0	99.9
29-1199	Health diagnosing and treating practitioners, all other[1]	65	73	8	11.8	3	2	61,570	VH	14.3	VL	VH	Bachelor's degree	C	0.0	0.0	93.6
29-2000	Health technologists and technicians	2,612	3,094	482	18.5	290	107	—	—	1.0	—	—	—	—	—	—	—
29-2010	Clinical laboratory technologists and technicians	319	362	43	13.6	22	9	—	—	.7	—	—	—	—	—	—	—
29-2011	Medical and clinical laboratory technologists	167	188	21	12.4	11	5	49,700	VH	.7	VL	L	Bachelor's degree	SC/C	14.2	35.3	50.5
29-2012	Medical and clinical laboratory technicians	151	174	23	15.0	11	5	32,840	H	.7	VL	L	Associate degree	SC/C	14.2	35.3	50.5
29-2021	Dental hygienists	167	217	50	30.1	10	8	62,800	VH	.1	VL	VH	Associate degree	SC/C	2.9	63.8	33.3
29-2030	Diagnostic related technologists and technicians	307	360	53	17.2	21	9	—	—	1.1	—	—	—	—	—	—	—

See footnotes at end of table.

Table III-1. Occupational employment and job openings data, 2006–16, and worker characteristics, 2006 — Continued
(Numbers in thousands)

Code	2006 National Employment Matrix occupation and code	Employment		Employment change, 2006–16		Annual average job openings due to growth and total replacement needs, 2006–16	Annual average job openings due to growth and net replacement needs, 2006–16	2006 median annual wages		Percent self-employed, 2006	Unemployment rate	Percent part-time	Most significant source of postsecondary education or training[2]	Educational attainment cluster[3]	Percent of workers aged 25 to 44, by educational attainment[4]		
		2006	2016	Numeric	Percent			Dollars	Rank						High school or less	Some college	College or higher
29-2031	Cardiovascular technologists and technicians	45	57	12	25.5	4	2	42,300	H	1.1	VL	H	Associate degree	SC/C	7.2	67.9	24.9
29-2032	Diagnostic medical sonographers	46	54	9	19.1	3	1	57,160	VH	1.1	VL	H	Associate degree	SC/C	7.2	67.9	24.9
29-2033	**Nuclear medicine technologists**	**20**	**23**	**3**	**14.8**	**1**	**1**	**62,300**	**VH**	**1.0**	**VL**	**H**	**Associate degree**	**SC/C**	**7.2**	**67.9**	**24.9**
29-2034	Radiologic technologists and technicians	196	226	30	15.1	13	6	48,170	VH	1.1	VL	H	Associate degree	SC/C	7.2	67.9	24.9
29-2041	Emergency medical technicians and paramedics	201	240	39	19.2	20	6	27,070	L	.2	VL	L	Postsecondary vocational award	SC	18.0	68.1	13.9
29-2050	Health diagnosing and treating practitioner support technicians	549	692	143	26.1	100	31	—	—	.2	—	—	—	—	—	—	—
29-2051	Dietetic technicians	25	29	4	14.8	4	1	24,040	L	.2	VL	H	Postsecondary vocational award	HS/SC	27.0	57.0	16.0
29-2052	Pharmacy technicians	285	376	91	32.0	54	18	25,630	L	.2	VL	H	Moderate-term on-the-job training	HS/SC	27.0	57.0	16.0
29-2053	Psychiatric technicians	62	60	-2	-3.3	8	2	27,780	L	.2	VL	H	Postsecondary vocational award	HS/SC	27.0	57.0	16.0
29-2054	Respiratory therapy technicians	19	19	0	.9	3	1	39,120	H	.3	VL	H	Associate degree	HS/SC	27.0	57.0	16.0
29-2055	**Surgical technologists**	**86**	**107**	**21**	**24.5**	**15**	**5**	**36,080**	**H**	**.2**	**VL**	**H**	**Postsecondary vocational award**	**HS/SC**	**27.0**	**57.0**	**16.0**
29-2056	Veterinary technologists and technicians	71	100	29	41.0	15	5	26,780	L	.2	VL	H	Associate degree	HS/SC	27.0	57.0	16.0
29-2061	Licensed practical and licensed vocational nurses	749	854	105	14.0	71	31	36,550	H	1.5	L	H	Postsecondary vocational award	HS/SC	20.6	72.4	7.0
29-2071	Medical records and health information technicians[1]	170	200	30	17.8	39	8	28,030	L	.2	L	L	Associate degree	HS/SC	36.8	51.4	11.8
29-2081	Opticians, dispensing	66	72	6	8.7	3	3	30,300	L	2.4	VL	H	Long-term on-the-job training	HS/SC	28.7	56.1	15.2
29-2090	Miscellaneous health technologists and technicians	85	98	13	14.7	5	2	—	—	6.6	—	—	—	—	—	—	—
29-2091	Orthotists and prosthetists	6	6	1	11.8	0	0	58,980	VH	6.5	VL	H	Bachelor's degree	HS/SC/C	28.3	44.6	27.0
29-2099	Healthcare technologists and technicians, all other	79	91	12	15.0	4	2	35,140	H	6.6	VL	H	Postsecondary vocational award	HS/SC/C	28.3	44.6	27.0
29-9000	**Other healthcare practitioners and technical occupations**	**126**	**143**	**17**	**13.7**	**10**	**4**	**—**	**—**	**1.2**	**—**	**—**	**—**	**—**	**—**	**—**	**—**
29-9010	Occupational health and safety specialists and technicians	56	61	5	9.3	4	2	—	—	1.9	—	—	—	—	—	—	—
29-9011	Occupational health and safety specialists[1]	45	49	4	8.1	3	1	58,030	VH	2.4	VL	L	Bachelor's degree	C	9.4	18.3	72.4
29-9012	Occupational health and safety technicians[1]	10	12	2	14.6	1	0	42,160	H	0.0	VL	L	Bachelor's degree	C	9.4	18.3	72.4
29-9090	Miscellaneous health practitioners and technical workers	70	82	12	17.1	6	3	—	—	.6	—	—	—	—	—	—	—
29-9091	Athletic trainers[1]	17	21	4	24.3	2	1	36,560	H	2.4	VL	L	Bachelor's degree	C	9.4	18.3	72.4
29-9099	Healthcare practitioners and technical workers, all other[1]	53	61	8	14.8	4	2	37,200	H	0.0	VL	L	Bachelor's degree	C	9.4	18.3	72.4
31-3900	**Service occupations**	**28,950**	**33,780**	**4,830**	**16.7**	**7,556**	**1,222**	**—**	**—**	**7.3**	**—**	**—**	**—**	**—**	**—**	**—**	**—**
31-0000	Healthcare support occupations	3,723	4,721	997	26.8	785	140	—	—	4.2	—	—	—	—	—	—	—
31-1000	Nursing, psychiatric, and home health aides	2,296	2,944	647	28.2	554	85	—	—	2.3	—	—	—	—	—	—	—

See footnotes at end of table.

Table III–1. Occupational employment and job openings data, 2006–16, and worker characteristics, 2006 — Continued
(Numbers in thousands)

Code	2006 National Employment Matrix occupation and code	Employment 2006	Employment 2016	Employment change, 2006–16 Numeric	Employment change, 2006–16 Percent	Annual average job openings due to growth and total replacement needs, 2006–16	Annual average job openings due to growth and net replacement needs, 2006–16	2006 median annual wages Dollars	2006 median annual wages Rank	Percent self-employed, 2006	Unemployment rate	Percent part-time	Most significant source of postsecondary education or training[2]	Educational attainment cluster[3]	Percent of workers aged 25 to 44, by educational attainment[4] High school or less	Some college	College or higher
31-1011	Home health aides	787	1,171	384	48.7	221	45	19,420	VL	1.9	H	H	Short-term on-the-job training	HS/SC	55.3	37.3	7.4
31-1012	Nursing aides, orderlies, and attendants	1,447	1,711	264	18.2	321	39	22,180	L	2.4	H	H	Postsecondary vocational award	HS/SC	55.3	37.3	7.4
31-1013	Psychiatric aides	62	62	0	-.1	12	1	23,900	L	2.3	H	H	Short-term on-the-job training	HS/SC	55.3	37.3	7.4
31-2000	Occupational and physical therapist assistants and aides	140	179	39	27.9	14	6	—	—	.9	—	—	—	—	—	—	—
31-2010	Occupational therapist assistants and aides	33	41	8	24.5	3	1	—	—	3.3	—	—	—	—	—	—	—
31-2011	Occupational therapist assistants[1]	25	31	6	25.4	3	1	42,060	H	3.5	VL	H	Associate degree	SC	0.0	85.6	13.3
31-2012	Occupational therapist aides[1]	8	10	2	21.9	1	0	25,020	L	2.7	VL	H	Short-term on-the-job training	SC	0.0	85.6	13.3
31-2020	Physical therapist assistants and aides	107	137	31	28.9	10	4	—	—	.2	—	—	—	—	—	—	—
31-2021	Physical therapist assistants	60	80	20	32.4	6	3	41,360	H	.2	VL	VH	Associate degree	SC/C	11.7	65.4	22.9
31-2022	Physical therapist aides	46	58	11	24.4	4	2	22,060	L	.2	VL	VH	Short-term on-the-job training	SC/C	11.7	65.4	22.9
31-9000	Other healthcare support occupations	1,287	1,598	311	24.2	218	49	—	—	8.1	—	—	—	—	—	—	—
31-9011	Massage therapists	118	142	24	20.3	9	4	33,400	H	64.0	VL	VH	Postsecondary vocational award	SC/C	18.7	49.1	32.2
31-9090	Miscellaneous healthcare support occupations	1,170	1,457	287	24.5	209	45	—	—	2.4	—	—	—	—	—	—	—
31-9091	Dental assistants	280	362	82	29.2	29	13	30,220	L	0.0	VL	VH	Moderate-term on-the-job training	HS/SC	33.6	57.5	8.9
31-9092	Medical assistants	417	565	148	35.4	93	20	26,290	L	0.0	L	H	Moderate-term on-the-job training	HS/SC	30.6	58.9	10.4
31-9093	Medical equipment preparers	45	52	6	14.2	8	1	25,950	L	2.8	L	H	Short-term on-the-job training	HS/SC	30.6	58.9	10.4
31-9094	Medical transcriptionists	98	112	13	13.5	18	3	29,950	L	9.7	L	H	Postsecondary vocational award	HS/SC	30.6	58.9	10.4
31-9095	Pharmacy aides	50	45	-6	-11.1	8	1	19,440	VL	4.2	L	H	Short-term on-the-job training	HS/SC	30.6	58.9	10.4
31-9096	Veterinary assistants and laboratory animal caretakers	75	86	12	15.7	14	2	19,960	VL	2.9	L	H	Short-term on-the-job training	HS/SC	30.6	58.9	10.4
31-9099	Healthcare support workers, all other	204	236	32	15.6	38	6	26,990	L	6.6	L	H	Short-term on-the-job training	HS/SC	30.6	58.9	10.4
33-0000	Protective service occupations	3,163	3,616	453	14.3	466	133	—	—	.8	—	—	—	—	—	—	—
33-1000	First-line supervisors/managers, protective service workers	233	260	26	11.3	22	9	—	—	.6	—	—	—	—	—	—	—
33-1010	First-line supervisors/managers, law enforcement workers	133	146	13	10.2	14	5	—	—	0.0	—	—	—	—	—	—	—
33-1011	First-line supervisors/managers of correctional officers	40	45	5	12.5	4	2	52,580	VH	0.0	VL	VL	Work experience in a related occupation	HS/SC/C	25.9	49.2	24.9
33-1012	First-line supervisors/managers of police and detectives[1]	93	102	9	9.2	9	4	69,310	VH	0.0	VL	VL	Work experience in a related occupation	SC/C	17.5	49.4	33.0
33-1021	First-line supervisors/managers of fire fighting and prevention workers[1]	52	58	6	11.5	4	2	62,900	VH	0.0	VL	VL	Work experience in a related occupation	SC	18.4	64.3	17.3
33-1099	First-line supervisors/managers, protective service workers, all other	48	55	7	14.5	5	1	41,570	H	2.9	L	VL	Work experience in a related occupation	HS/SC/C	25.5	46.9	27.5
33-2000	Fire fighting and prevention workers	308	345	37	12.0	20	15	—	—	0.0	—	—	—	—	—	—	—
33-2011	Fire fighters	293	328	35	12.1	19	14	41,190	H	0.0	VL	VL	Long-term on-the-job training	HS/SC	22.9	58.8	18.3
33-2020	Fire inspectors	16	17	2	10.0	1	1	—	—	0.0	—	—	—	—	—	—	—

See footnotes at end of table.

Table III-1. Occupational employment and job openings data, 2006–16, and worker characteristics, 2006 — Continued
(Numbers in thousands)

Code	2006 National Employment Matrix occupation and code	Employment		Employment change, 2006–16		Annual average job openings due to growth and total replacement needs, 2006–16	Annual average job openings due to growth and net replacement needs, 2006–16	2006 median annual wages		Percent self-employed, 2006	Unemployment rate	Percent part-time	Most significant source of postsecondary education or training[2]	Educational attainment cluster[3]	Percent of workers aged 25 to 44, by educational attainment[4]		
		2006	2016	Numeric	Percent			Dollars	Rank						High school or less	Some college	College or higher
33-2021	Fire inspectors and investigators	14	15	2	11.0	1	0	48,050	VH	0.0	VL	VL	Work experience in a related occupation	HS/SC/C	20.9	51.7	27.4
33-2022	Forest fire inspectors and prevention specialists	2	2	0	2.1	0	0	32,940	H	0.0	VL	VL	Work experience in a related occupation	HS/SC/C	20.9	51.7	27.4
33-3000	Law enforcement workers	1,239	1,406	167	13.5	113	47	—	—	0.0	—	—	—	—	—	—	—
33-3010	Bailiffs, correctional officers, and jailers	460	537	77	16.6	59	18	—	—	0.0	—	—	—	—	—	—	—
33-3011	Bailiffs	19	21	2	11.2	2	1	34,210	H	0.0	VL	VL	Moderate-term on-the-job training	HS/SC	40.1	49.2	10.6
33-3012	Correctional officers and jailers	442	516	75	16.9	57	18	35,760	H	0.0	VL	VL	Moderate-term on-the-job training	HS/SC	40.1	49.2	10.6
33-3021	Detectives and criminal investigators	106	125	18	17.3	15	4	58,260	VH	.3	VL	VL	Work experience in a related occupation	SC/C	10.2	35.4	54.4
33-3031	Fish and game wardens[1]	8	8	0	-.2	1	0	43,700	H	0.0	VL	VL	Associate degree	HS/SC/C	31.8	26.1	42.1
33-3041	Parking enforcement workers[1]	11	12	1	12.3	1	0	30,160	L	0.0	VL	VL	Short-term on-the-job training	HS/SC/C	31.8	26.1	42.1
33-3050	Police officers	654	724	70	10.8	38	25	—	—	0.0	—	—	—	—	—	—	—
33-3051	Police and sheriff's patrol officers	648	719	70	10.8	38	24	47,460	VH	0.0	VL	VL	Long-term on-the-job training	SC/C	15.5	51.7	32.8
33-3052	Transit and railroad police[1]	6	6	0	6.4	0	0	47,080	VH	0.0	VL	VL	Long-term on-the-job training	SC/C	15.5	51.7	32.8
33-9000	Other protective service workers	1,382	1,605	223	16.1	311	61	—	—	1.6	—	—	—	—	—	—	—
33-9011	Animal control workers[1]	15	17	2	12.5	3	1	27,910	L	.1	H	H	Moderate-term on-the-job training	HS/SC	32.9	54.9	12.2
33-9021	Private detectives and investigators	52	61	9	18.2	7	2	33,750	H	29.7	H	L	Work experience in a related occupation	SC/C	17.7	30.2	52.0
33-9030	Security guards and gaming surveillance officers	1,049	1,227	178	17.0	224	39	—	—	.7	—	—	—	—	—	—	—
33-9031	Gaming surveillance officers and gaming investigators	9	12	3	33.6	2	0	27,130	L	.7	VH	H	Moderate-term on-the-job training	HS/SC	45.9	41.6	12.5
33-9032	Security guards	1,040	1,216	175	16.9	222	39	21,530	L	.7	VH	H	Short-term on-the-job training	HS/SC	45.9	41.6	12.5
33-9090	Miscellaneous protective service workers	266	299	33	12.4	76	20	—	—	0.0	—	—	—	—	—	—	—
33-9091	Crossing guards	69	71	1	1.9	4	2	21,060	VL	0.0	VH	VH	Short-term on-the-job training	HS/SC	67.1	27.9	5.0
33-9092	Lifeguards, ski patrol, and other recreational protective service workers	114	136	21	18.7	42	11	17,160	VL	0.0	VH	VH	Short-term on-the-job training	HS/SC/C	34.5	34.2	31.2
33-9099	Protective service workers, all other	83	93	10	12.6	29	7	26,920	L	0.0	VH	VH	Short-term on-the-job training	HS/SC/C	34.5	34.2	31.2
35-0000	Food preparation and serving related occupations	11,352	12,789	1,436	12.7	3,775	538	—	—	.9	—	—	—	—	—	—	—
35-1000	Supervisors, food preparation and serving workers	932	1,033	101	10.8	164	18	—	—	4.5	—	—	—	—	—	—	—
35-1011	Chefs and head cooks	115	124	9	7.6	9	2	34,370	H	7.2	H	L	Work experience in a related occupation	HS/SC	47.7	38.8	13.5
35-1012	First-line supervisors/managers of food preparation and serving workers	817	909	92	11.3	154	15	26,980	L	4.1	L	L	Work experience in a related occupation	HS/SC	51.3	35.2	13.5
35-2000	Cooks and food preparation workers	2,998	3,340	342	11.4	878	122	—	—	1.1	—	—	—	—	—	—	—
35-2010	Cooks	2,097	2,301	204	9.7	580	77	—	—	1.3	—	—	—	—	—	—	—
35-2011	Cooks, fast food	629	681	52	8.3	172	22	15,410	VL	1.3	VH	VH	Short-term on-the-job training	HS	76.5	18.7	4.8
35-2012	Cooks, institution and cafeteria	401	445	43	10.8	112	15	20,410	VL	1.4	VH	VH	Moderate-term on-the-job training	HS	76.5	18.7	4.8
35-2013	Cooks, private household	5	5	0	8.8	1	0	22,870	L	0.0	VH	VH	Long-term on-the-job training	HS	76.5	18.7	4.8
35-2014	Cooks, restaurant	850	948	98	11.5	239	33	20,340	VL	1.2	VH	VH	Long-term on-the-job training	HS	76.5	18.7	4.8

See footnotes at end of table.

Table III–1. Occupational employment and job openings data, 2006–16, and worker characteristics, 2006 — Continued
(Numbers in thousands)

2006 National Employment Matrix occupation and code		Employment		Employment change, 2006–16		Annual average job openings due to growth and total replacement needs, 2006–16	Annual average job openings due to growth and net replacement needs, 2006–16	2006 median annual wages		Percent self-employed, 2006	Unemployment rate	Percent part-time	Most significant source of postsecondary education or training[2]	Educational attainment cluster[3]	Percent of workers aged 25 to 44, by educational attainment[4]		
		2006	2016	Numeric	Percent			Dollars	Rank						High school or less	Some college	College or higher
35-2015	Cooks, short order	195	205	9	4.8	52	6	17,880	VL	1.5	VH	VH	Short-term on-the-job training	HS	76.5	18.7	4.8
35-2019	Cooks, all other	16	16	1	3.4	4	0	21,610	L	1.1	VH	VH	Moderate-term on-the-job training	HS	76.5	18.7	4.8
35-2021	Food preparation workers	902	1,040	138	15.3	298	45	17,410	VL	.8	VH	VH	Short-term on-the-job training	HS	74.1	18.5	7.4
35-3000	Food and beverage serving workers	6,081	6,927	846	13.9	2,210	318	—	—	.3	—	—	—	—	—	—	—
35-3011	Bartenders	495	551	56	11.2	88	24	16,350	VL	.6	H	VH	Short-term on-the-job training	HS/SC	41.9	40.9	17.3
35-3020	Fast food and counter workers	3,036	3,542	506	16.7	1,298	135	—	—	.3	—	—	—	—	—	—	—
35-3021	Combined food preparation and serving workers, including fast food	2,503	2,955	452	18.1	1,043	93	15,050	VL	.2	VH	VH	Short-term on-the-job training	HS/SC	71.0	23.8	5.2
35-3022	Counter attendants, cafeteria, food concession, and coffee shop	533	587	54	10.2	255	42	16,130	VL	.3	VH	VH	Short-term on-the-job training	HS	72.9	19.1	8.0
35-3031	Waiters and waitresses	2,361	2,615	255	10.8	768	154	14,850	VL	.3	VH	VH	Short-term on-the-job training	HS/SC	50.8	35.1	14.1
35-3041	Food servers, nonrestaurant	189	219	30	15.8	56	6	18,090	VL	1.1	H	VH	Short-term on-the-job training	HS/SC	63.8	27.3	8.9
35-9000	Other food preparation and serving related workers	1,341	1,488	147	11.0	524	80	—	—	.3	—	—	—	—	—	—	—
35-9011	Dining room and cafeteria attendants and bartender helpers	416	466	49	11.8	154	22	15,310	VL	.3	VH	VH	Short-term on-the-job training	HS	75.9	18.2	5.9
35-9021	Dishwashers	517	571	54	10.4	201	27	15,750	VL	.2	VH	VH	Short-term on-the-job training	HS	86.6	10.2	3.2
35-9031	Hosts and hostesses, restaurant, lounge, and coffee shop	351	388	37	10.4	146	28	16,170	VL	.3	VH	VH	Short-term on-the-job training	HS/SC	50.7	32.7	16.6
35-9099	Food preparation and serving related workers, all other[1]	56	64	7	13.0	23	3	17,780	VL	0.0	VH	VH	Short-term on-the-job training	HS	75.9	18.2	5.9
37-0000	Building and grounds cleaning and maintenance occupations	5,745	6,595	850	14.8	1,245	183	—	—	11.7	—	—	—	—	—	—	—
37-1000	Supervisors, building and grounds cleaning and maintenance workers	484	555	71	14.7	50	13	—	—	36.3	—	—	—	—	—	—	—
37-1011	First-line supervisors/managers of housekeeping and janitorial workers	282	318	36	12.7	31	8	31,290	H	30.7	L	L	Work experience in a related occupation	HS/SC	58.0	31.5	10.5
37-1012	First-line supervisors/managers of landscaping, lawn service, and groundskeeping workers	202	237	36	17.6	19	5	37,300	H	44.1	VL	VL	Work experience in a related occupation	HS/SC	53.7	31.3	15.0
37-2000	Building cleaning and pest control workers	3,941	4,486	544	13.8	864	130	—	—	5.7	—	—	—	—	—	—	—
37-2010	Building cleaning workers	3,872	4,405	533	13.8	858	127	—	—	5.6	—	—	—	—	—	—	—
37-2011	Janitors and cleaners, except maids and housekeeping cleaners	2,387	2,732	345	14.5	533	80	19,930	VL	4.9	H	H	Short-term on-the-job training	HS/SC	75.3	20.4	4.3
37-2012	Maids and housekeeping cleaners	1,470	1,656	186	12.7	322	46	17,580	VL	6.8	VH	VH	Short-term on-the-job training	HS	80.5	14.8	4.7
37-2019	Building cleaning workers, all other	16	18	2	15.1	4	1	25,090	L	4.7	H	H	Short-term on-the-job training	HS/SC	75.3	20.4	4.3
37-2021	Pest control workers	70	80	11	15.5	6	3	27,880	L	8.7	H	VL	Moderate-term on-the-job training	HS/SC	58.0	32.8	9.2
37-3000	Grounds maintenance workers	1,319	1,554	235	17.8	331	41	—	—	20.7	—	—	—	—	—	—	—
37-3010	Grounds maintenance workers	1,319	1,554	235	17.8	331	41	—	—	20.7	—	—	—	—	—	—	—
37-3011	Landscaping and groundskeeping workers	1,220	1,441	221	18.1	307	38	21,260	L	20.5	VH	L	Short-term on-the-job training	HS	77.5	16.7	5.8

See footnotes at end of table.

Table III–1. Occupational employment and job openings data, 2006–16, and worker characteristics, 2006 — Continued
(Numbers in thousands)

Code	2006 National Employment Matrix occupation and code	Employment 2006	Employment 2016	Employment change, 2006–16 Numeric	Employment change, 2006–16 Percent	Annual average job openings due to growth and total replacement needs, 2006–16	Annual average job openings due to growth and net replacement needs, 2006–16	2006 median annual wages Dollars	2006 median annual wages Rank	Percent self-employed, 2006	Unemployment rate	Percent part-time	Most significant source of postsecondary education or training[2]	Educational attainment cluster[3]	Percent of workers aged 25 to 44, by educational attainment[4]: High school or less	Some college	College or higher
37-3012	Pesticide handlers, sprayers, and applicators, vegetation	31	35	4	14.0	7	1	26,700	L	20.5	VH	L	Moderate-term on-the-job training	HS	77.5	16.7	5.8
37-3013	Tree trimmers and pruners	41	45	5	11.1	10	1	28,250	L	28.9	VH	L	Short-term on-the-job training	HS	77.5	16.7	5.8
37-3019	Grounds maintenance workers, all other	28	33	5	16.6	7	1	20,420	VL	16.3	VH	L	Short-term on-the-job training	HS	77.5	16.7	5.8
39-0000	Personal care and service occupations	4,966	6,060	1,094	22.0	1,285	228	—	—	23.3	—	—	—	—	—	—	—
39-1000	Supervisors, personal care and service workers	268	312	43	16.2	44	10	—	—	36.8	—	—	—	—	—	—	—
39-1010	First-line supervisors/managers of gaming workers	54	64	10	18.9	7	2	—	—	29.8	—	—	—	—	—	—	—
39-1011	Gaming supervisors	34	42	8	23.4	5	1	41,160	H	29.2	L	L	Work experience in a related occupation	HS/SC/C	33.7	36.1	30.2
39-1012	Slot key persons	20	22	2	11.1	2	1	22,720	L	30.8	L	L	Postsecondary vocational award	HS/SC/C	33.7	36.1	30.2
39-1021	First-line supervisors/managers of personal service workers	215	248	33	15.5	38	8	32,800	H	38.6	VL	H	Work experience in a related occupation	HS/SC/C	37.4	36.3	26.4
39-2000	Animal care and service workers	200	238	39	19.3	43	7	—	—	32.8	—	—	—	—	—	—	—
39-2011	Animal trainers	43	53	10	22.7	7	2	26,310	L	56.9	VL	H	Moderate-term on-the-job training	HS/SC/C	48.5	27.7	23.9
39-2021	Nonfarm animal caretakers	157	185	29	18.4	36	5	18,140	VL	26.2	L	VH	Short-term on-the-job training	HS/SC	46.8	37.2	16.0
39-3000	Entertainment attendants and related workers	546	667	120	22.1	188	38	—	—	.8	—	—	—	—	—	—	—
39-3010	Gaming services workers	117	146	29	25.0	17	5	—	—	.5	—	—	—	—	—	—	—
39-3011	Gaming dealers	84	104	20	24.1	12	4	14,730	VL	.5	H	H	Postsecondary vocational award	HS/SC	45.4	43.6	11.0
39-3012	Gaming and sports book writers and runners	18	24	5	28.0	3	1	18,800	VL	.5	H	H	Short-term on-the-job training	HS/SC	45.4	43.6	11.0
39-3019	Gaming service workers, all other	15	18	4	26.2	2	1	21,890	L	.5	H	H	Moderate-term on-the-job training	HS/SC	45.4	43.6	11.0
39-3021	Motion picture projectionists[1]	11	11	-1	-8.4	3	1	17,450	VL	7.7	VH	VH	Short-term on-the-job training	HS/SC/C	24.2	46.8	29.0
39-3031	Ushers, lobby attendants, and ticket takers[1]	103	121	17	16.9	36	9	15,880	VL	0.0	VH	VH	Short-term on-the-job training	HS/SC	52.5	30.0	17.5
39-3090	Miscellaneous entertainment attendants and related workers	315	390	75	23.8	132	23	—	—	1.0	—	—	—	—	—	—	—
39-3091	Amusement and recreation attendants	247	308	60	24.3	104	18	16,290	VL	1.0	VH	VH	Short-term on-the-job training	HS/SC/C	46.4	31.5	22.2
39-3092	Costume attendants	4	5	1	14.1	2	0	25,740	L	.8	VH	VH	Short-term on-the-job training	HS/SC/C	46.4	31.5	22.2
39-3093	Locker room, coatroom, and dressing room attendants	19	24	4	21.6	8	1	18,610	VL	1.3	VH	VH	Short-term on-the-job training	HS/SC/C	46.4	31.5	22.2
39-4000	Funeral service workers	42	48	6	14.3	8	2	—	—	.7	—	—	—	—	—	—	—
39-4011	Embalmers	9	10	1	14.3	2	0	37,840	H	.7	H	H	Postsecondary vocational award	HS/SC/C	37.3	33.3	29.4
39-4021	Funeral attendants	33	37	5	14.3	6	1	20,350	VL	.6	H	H	Short-term on-the-job training	HS/SC/C	37.3	33.3	29.4
39-5000	Personal appearance workers	825	942	117	14.2	100	22	—	—	46.2	—	—	—	—	—	—	—
39-5010	Barbers and cosmetologists	677	755	77	11.4	76	16	—	—	47.7	—	—	—	—	—	—	—
39-5011	Barbers	60	61	1	1.1	3	1	23,150	L	80.9	L	H	Postsecondary vocational award	HS/SC	62.0	33.9	4.1
39-5012	Hairdressers, hairstylists, and cosmetologists	617	694	77	12.4	73	15	21,320	L	44.5	VL	VH	Postsecondary vocational award	HS/SC	51.3	42.3	6.4

See footnotes at end of table.

Table III–1. Occupational employment and job openings data, 2006–16, and worker characteristics, 2006 — Continued
(Numbers in thousands)

Code	2006 National Employment Matrix occupation and code	Employment		Employment change, 2006–16		Annual average job openings due to growth and total replacement needs, 2006–16	Annual average job openings due to growth and net replacement needs, 2006–16	2006 median annual wages		Percent self-employed, 2006	Unemployment rate	Percent part-time	Most significant source of postsecondary education or training[2]	Educational attainment cluster[3]	Percent of workers aged 25 to 44, by educational attainment[4]		
		2006	2016	Numeric	Percent			Dollars	Rank						High school or less	Some college	College or higher
39-5090	Miscellaneous personal appearance workers	148	187	39	26.6	24	5	—	—	39.5	—	—	—	—	—	—	—
39-5091	Makeup artists, theatrical and performance	2	3	1	39.8	0	0	31,820	H	39.7	VL	VH	Postsecondary vocational award	HS/SC	59.6	30.5	9.9
39-5092	Manicurists and pedicurists	78	100	22	27.6	13	3	19,190	VL	37.6	VL	VH	Postsecondary vocational award	HS/SC	59.6	30.5	9.9
39-5093	Shampooers	29	33	4	13.3	4	1	16,170	VL	45.0	VL	VH	Short-term on-the-job training	HS/SC	59.6	30.5	9.9
39-5094	Skin care specialists	38	51	13	34.3	7	2	26,170	L	38.9	VL	VH	Postsecondary vocational award	HS/SC	59.6	30.5	9.9
39-6000	Transportation, tourism, and lodging attendants	232	261	29	12.7	46	8	—	—	4.1	—	—	—	—	—	—	—
39-6010	Baggage porters, bellhops, and concierges	69	76	7	10.4	17	2	—	—	.3	—	—	—	—	—	—	—
39-6011	Baggage porters and bellhops	49	54	4	9.0	12	1	18,360	VL	.3	VL	H	Short-term on-the-job training	HS/SC	50.5	32.9	16.6
39-6012	Concierges	20	23	3	14.1	5	1	24,600	L	.3	VL	H	Moderate-term on-the-job training	HS/SC	50.5	32.9	16.6
39-6020	Tour and travel guides	45	54	9	20.1	17	3	—	—	20.8	—	—	—	—	—	—	—
39-6021	Tour guides and escorts	40	49	9	21.2	15	2	20,420	VL	20.1	VH	VH	Moderate-term on-the-job training	HS/SC/C	35.7	35.9	28.5
39-6022	Travel guides	5	5	0	10.5	2	0	28,460	L	26.3	VH	VH	Moderate-term on-the-job training	HS/SC/C	35.7	35.9	28.5
39-6030	Transportation attendants	118	131	13	11.2	13	3	—	—	0.0	—	—	—	—	—	—	—
39-6031	Flight attendants	97	107	10	10.6	11	3	53,780	VH	0.0	H	H	Long-term on-the-job training	HS/SC/C	24.7	44.4	30.8
39-6032	Transportation attendants, except flight attendants and baggage porters	21	24	3	14.0	2	1	20,070	VL	0.0	H	H	Short-term on-the-job training	HS/SC/C	24.7	44.4	30.8
39-9000	Other personal care and service workers	2,853	3,593	739	25.9	856	142	—	—	21.0	—	—	—	—	—	—	—
39-9011	Child care workers	1,388	1,636	248	17.8	472	65	17,630	VL	34.3	H	VH	Short-term on-the-job training	HS/SC	47.7	37.8	14.5
39-9021	Personal and home care aides	767	1,156	389	50.6	255	52	17,770	VL	7.6	VH	VH	Short-term on-the-job training	HS/SC	58.5	31.9	9.6
39-9030	Recreation and fitness workers	555	658	104	18.7	113	21	—	—	8.1	—	—	—	—	—	—	—
39-9031	Fitness trainers and aerobics instructors	235	298	63	26.8	51	11	25,910	L	7.6	H	VH	Postsecondary vocational award	HS/SC/C	21.0	31.7	47.3
39-9032	Recreation workers	320	360	41	12.7	61	10	20,470	VL	8.5	H	VH	Short-term on-the-job training	HS/SC/C	21.0	31.7	47.3
39-9041	Residential advisors	57	67	11	18.5	8	3	22,670	L	4.9	H	H	Short-term on-the-job training	HS/SC/C	25.6	46.1	28.3
39-9099	Personal care and service workers, all other[1]	86	75	-11	-12.9	8	2	18,970	VL	18.8	H	VH	Short-term on-the-job training	HS/SC/C	45.6	33.2	21.2
41-0000	**Sales and related occupations**	**15,985**	**17,203**	**1,218**	**7.6**	**3,855**	**617**	—	—	**11.8**	—	—	—	—	—	—	—
41-1000	Supervisors, sales workers	2,206	2,296	91	4.1	270	52	—	—	36.9	—	—	—	—	—	—	—
41-1011	First-line supervisors/managers of retail sales workers	1,676	1,747	71	4.2	221	42	33,960	H	34.2	L	L	Work experience in a related occupation	HS/SC/C	38.8	36.7	24.6
41-1012	First-line supervisors/managers of non-retail sales workers	530	549	19	3.7	49	10	65,510	VH	45.4	VL	VL	Work experience in a related occupation	HS/SC/C	30.8	30.9	38.3
41-2000	Retail sales workers	8,719	9,263	544	6.2	2,740	393	—	—	2.4	—	—	—	—	—	—	—
41-2010	Cashiers	3,527	3,411	-116	-3.3	1,197	168	—	—	1.0	—	—	—	—	—	—	—
41-2011	Cashiers, except gaming	3,500	3,382	-118	-3.4	1,187	166	16,810	VL	1.0	VH	VH	Short-term on-the-job training	HS/SC	62.8	27.7	9.5
41-2012	Gaming change persons and booth cashiers	27	29	2	6.7	10	1	20,680	VL	1.0	VH	VH	Short-term on-the-job training	HS/SC	62.8	27.7	9.5

See footnotes at end of table.

Table III–1. Occupational employment and job openings data, 2006–16, and worker characteristics, 2006 — Continued
(Numbers in thousands)

Code	2006 National Employment Matrix occupation and code	Employment 2006	Employment 2016	Employment change, 2006–16 Numeric	Employment change, 2006–16 Percent	Annual average job openings due to growth and total replacement needs, 2006–16	Annual average job openings due to growth and net replacement needs, 2006–16	2006 median annual wages Dollars	2006 median annual wages Rank	Percent self-employed, 2006	Unemployment rate	Percent part-time	Most significant source of postsecondary education or training[2]	Educational attainment cluster[3]	Percent of workers aged 25 to 44, by educational attainment[4]: High school or less	Some college	College or higher
41-2020	Counter and rental clerks and parts salespersons	715	819	104	14.6	176	32	—	—	1.2	—	—	—	—	—	—	—
41-2021	Counter and rental clerks	477	586	109	22.9	124	29	19,570	VL	1.0	H	VH	Short-term on-the-job training	HS/SC	53.4	30.3	16.3
41-2022	Parts salespersons	238	233	-5	-2.2	52	3	27,430	L	1.6	H	L	Moderate-term on-the-job training	HS/SC	59.0	35.1	5.9
41-2031	Retail salespersons	4,477	5,034	557	12.4	1,367	194	19,760	VL	3.6	H	VH	Short-term on-the-job training	HS/SC/C	38.4	36.5	25.2
41-3000	Sales representatives, services	1,567	1,889	322	20.5	230	66	—	—	14.2	—	—	—	—	—	—	—
41-3011	Advertising sales agents	170	205	35	20.3	29	6	42,750	H	5.6	L	L	Moderate-term on-the-job training	SC/C	14.3	30.1	55.7
41-3021	Insurance sales agents	436	492	56	12.9	64	15	43,870	H	25.5	VL	L	Bachelor's degree	SC/C	18.4	36.4	45.2
41-3031	Securities, commodities, and financial services sales agents	320	399	79	24.8	48	16	68,500	VH	17.7	L	L	Bachelor's degree	SC/C	10.3	23.1	66.6
41-3041	Travel agents	101	102	1	1.0	13	1	29,210	L	13.4	L	H	Postsecondary vocational award	HS/SC/C	25.2	48.7	26.1
41-3099	Sales representatives, services, all other	540	690	151	27.9	76	28	48,100	VH	5.8	H	L	Work experience in a related occupation	SC/C	19.4	32.3	48.3
41-4000	Sales representatives, wholesale and manufacturing	1,973	2,155	182	9.2	200	62	—	—	4.0	—	—	—	—	—	—	—
41-4011	Sales representatives, wholesale and manufacturing, technical and scientific products	411	462	51	12.4	43	14	64,440	VH	4.2	VL	L	Work experience in a related occupation	HS/SC/C	20.6	28.0	51.4
41-4012	Sales representatives, wholesale and manufacturing, except technical and scientific products	1,562	1,693	131	8.4	156	48	49,610	VH	4.0	VL	L	Work experience in a related occupation	HS/SC/C	20.6	28.0	51.4
41-9000	Other sales and related workers	1,520	1,599	79	5.2	414	44	—	—	37.4	—	—	—	—	—	—	—
41-9010	Models, demonstrators, and product promoters	107	126	19	17.9	33	5	—	—	20.8	—	—	—	—	—	—	—
41-9011	Demonstrators and product promoters	105	124	19	18.0	33	5	22,150	L	20.8	VH	VH	Moderate-term on-the-job training	HS/SC/C	38.3	35.9	25.8
41-9012	Models	2	2	0	9.8	1	0	23,340	L	20.3	VH	VH	Moderate-term on-the-job training	HS/SC/C	38.3	35.9	25.8
41-9020	Real estate brokers and sales agents	564	624	60	10.7	80	15	—	—	61.0	—	—	—	—	—	—	—
41-9021	Real estate brokers	131	146	15	11.1	19	4	60,790	VH	63.5	VL	H	Work experience in a related occupation	SC/C	17.9	37.4	44.7
41-9022	Real estate sales agents	432	478	46	10.6	61	11	39,760	H	60.2	VL	H	Postsecondary vocational award	SC/C	17.9	37.4	44.7
41-9031	Sales engineers[1]	76	82	6	8.5	7	3	77,720	VH	0.0	VL	VL	Bachelor's degree	C	0.0	16.4	78.9
41-9041	Telemarketers	395	356	-39	-9.9	211	14	20,990	VL	1.1	VH	VH	Short-term on-the-job training	HS/SC	50.1	35.7	14.2
41-9090	Miscellaneous sales and related workers	379	412	33	8.6	83	8	—	—	52.3	—	—	—	—	—	—	—
41-9091	Door-to-door sales workers, news and street vendors, and related workers	200	207	7	3.7	49	3	20,190	VL	93.5	H	VH	Short-term on-the-job training	HS/SC/C	47.2	31.5	21.3
41-9099	Sales and related workers, all other	180	205	25	14.0	34	4	34,250	H	6.6	H	H	Moderate-term on-the-job training	SC/C	14.6	23.8	61.6
43-0000	**Office and administrative support occupations**	**24,344**	**26,089**	**1,745**	**7.2**	**4,563**	**742**	—	—	**1.7**	—	—	—	—	—	—	—
43-1000	Supervisors, office and administrative support workers	1,418	1,500	82	5.8	138	37	—	—	1.6	—	—	—	—	—	—	—
43-1011	First-line supervisors/managers of office and administrative support workers	1,418	1,500	82	5.8	138	37	43,510	H	1.6	L	L	Work experience in a related occupation	HS/SC/C	28.1	43.1	28.9
43-2000	Communications equipment operators	209	183	-25	-12.1	45	4	—	—	.2	—	—	—	—	—	—	—

See footnotes at end of table.

Table III–1. Occupational employment and job openings data, 2006–16, and worker characteristics, 2006 — Continued
(Numbers in thousands)

Code	2006 National Employment Matrix occupation and code	Employment 2006	Employment 2016	Employment change, 2006–16 Numeric	Employment change, 2006–16 Percent	Annual average job openings due to growth and total replacement needs, 2006–16	Annual average job openings due to growth and net replacement needs, 2006–16	2006 median annual wages Dollars	2006 median annual wages Rank	Percent self-employed, 2006	Unemployment rate	Percent part-time	Most significant source of postsecondary education or training[2]	Educational attainment cluster[3]	High school or less	Some college	College or higher
															Percent of workers aged 25 to 44, by educational attainment[4]		
43-2011	Switchboard operators, including answering service	177	163	-15	-8.4	40	4	22,640	L	0.0	H	H	Short-term on-the-job training	HS/SC	39.2	50.7	10.1
43-2021	Telephone operators	27	16	-11	-39.5	4	0	34,140	H	1.5	VH	H	Short-term on-the-job training	HS/SC	40.3	48.6	11.1
43-2099	Communications equipment operators, all other[1]	4	5	0	7.4	1	0	31,680	H	0.0	H	H	Short-term on-the-job training	HS/SC/C	20.8	50.3	28.9
43-3000	Financial clerks	4,007	4,482	476	11.9	663	128	—	—	3.9	—	—	—	—	—	—	—
43-3011	Bill and account collectors	434	534	99	22.9	119	17	29,050	L	1.0	H	L	Short-term on-the-job training	HS/SC	38.4	48.2	13.3
43-3021	Billing and posting clerks and machine operators	542	566	24	4.4	82	9	28,850	L	1.6	L	L	Moderate-term on-the-job training	HS/SC	36.1	48.5	15.4
43-3031	Bookkeeping, accounting, and auditing clerks	2,114	2,377	264	12.5	287	59	30,560	L	6.6	L	H	Moderate-term on-the-job training	HS/SC	33.7	50.3	16.0
43-3041	Gaming cage workers[1]	18	20	2	11.3	4	1	23,150	L	0.0	L	H	Short-term on-the-job training	HS/SC	47.0	39.9	0.0
43-3051	Payroll and timekeeping clerks	214	220	7	3.1	19	6	32,400	H	1.2	L	H	Moderate-term on-the-job training	HS/SC	32.9	49.6	17.5
43-3061	Procurement clerks[1]	78	76	-2	-2.1	7	2	33,100	H	1.1	VL	VL	Moderate-term on-the-job training	HS/SC/C	28.4	47.8	23.8
43-3071	Tellers	608	689	82	13.5	146	35	22,140	L	0.0	L	VH	Short-term on-the-job training	HS/SC	38.9	44.8	16.4
43-4000	Information and record clerks	5,738	6,389	651	11.3	1,356	232	—	—	1.0	—	—	—	—	—	—	—
43-4011	Brokerage clerks[1]	73	88	15	20.0	11	4	36,390	H	0.0	L	H	Moderate-term on-the-job training	HS/SC/C	24.4	44.6	31.0
43-4021	Correspondence clerks[1]	17	20	2	12.0	4	1	28,700	L	0.0	L	L	Short-term on-the-job training	HS/SC	46.8	36.7	16.4
43-4031	Court, municipal, and license clerks	115	125	10	8.8	16	4	30,980	H	2.7	VL	L	Short-term on-the-job training	HS/SC/C	27.2	49.1	23.6
43-4041	Credit authorizers, checkers, and clerks	69	63	-6	-8.4	9	2	29,970	L	1.6	H	L	Short-term on-the-job training	HS/SC/C	35.3	36.8	27.9
43-4051	Customer service representatives	2,202	2,747	545	24.8	601	116	28,330	L	.4	H	H	Moderate-term on-the-job training	HS/SC/C	33.8	44.2	22.0
43-4061	Eligibility interviewers, government programs	112	116	3	3.1	11	2	37,540	H	0.0	L	VL	Moderate-term on-the-job training	SC/C	16.8	44.9	38.3
43-4071	File clerks	234	137	-97	-41.3	50	6	22,090	L	1.7	H	VH	Short-term on-the-job training	HS/SC/C	36.4	43.3	20.3
43-4081	Hotel, motel, and resort desk clerks	219	257	38	17.4	76	13	18,460	VL	.1	VH	H	Short-term on-the-job training	HS/SC	43.5	42.2	14.2
43-4111	Interviewers, except eligibility and loan	221	242	21	9.5	54	8	26,290	L	.8	VH	H	Short-term on-the-job training	HS/SC/C	28.0	48.0	24.0
43-4121	Library assistants, clerical	116	125	9	7.9	19	5	21,640	L	.3	H	VH	Short-term on-the-job training	SC/C	19.4	43.8	36.8
43-4131	Loan interviewers and clerks	256	254	-2	-.9	40	4	30,970	H	2.5	H	VL	Short-term on-the-job training	HS/SC/C	31.6	44.9	23.5
43-4141	New accounts clerks[1]	81	68	-13	-16.3	17	2	28,390	L	0.0	VL	L	Work experience in a related occupation	HS/SC/C	36.9	35.4	27.7
43-4151	Order clerks	271	205	-66	-24.3	47	6	26,340	L	1.9	H	H	Short-term on-the-job training	HS/SC	46.8	36.7	16.4
43-4161	Human resources assistants, except payroll and timekeeping	168	187	19	11.3	19	3	33,750	H	0.0	H	L	Short-term on-the-job training	HS/SC/C	25.0	46.0	29.0
43-4171	Receptionists and information clerks	1,173	1,375	202	17.2	334	49	22,900	L	1.4	H	VH	Short-term on-the-job training	HS/SC	41.8	45.5	12.7
43-4181	Reservation and transportation ticket agents and travel clerks	165	167	2	1.1	31	4	28,540	L	3.7	L	H	Short-term on-the-job training	HS/SC/C	28.9	42.6	28.5
43-4199	Information and record clerks, all other	245	213	-32	-12.9	18	4	31,150	H	.7	L	L	Short-term on-the-job training	HS/SC/C	26.8	52.3	20.9
43-5000	Material recording, scheduling, dispatching, and distributing occupations	4,016	3,931	-86	-2.1	758	105	—	—	1.0	—	—	—	—	—	—	—
43-5011	Cargo and freight agents	86	100	14	16.5	10	4	37,110	H	1.1	VL	VL	Moderate-term on-the-job training	HS/SC	42.8	41.7	15.5

See footnotes at end of table.

Table III-1. Occupational employment and job openings data, 2006–16, and worker characteristics, 2006 — Continued
(Numbers in thousands)

2006 National Employment Matrix occupation and code		Employment		Employment change, 2006–16		Annual average job openings due to growth and total replacement needs, 2006–16	Annual average job openings due to growth and net replacement needs, 2006–16	2006 median annual wages		Percent self-employed, 2006	Unemployment rate	Percent part-time	Most significant source of postsecondary education or training[2]	Educational attainment cluster[3]	Percent of workers aged 25 to 44, by educational attainment[4]		
		2006	2016	Numeric	Percent			Dollars	Rank						High school or less	Some college	College or higher
43-5021	Couriers and messengers[1]	134	134	0	-.2	22	4	21,540	L	19.3	L	H	Short-term on-the-job training	HS/SC	46.3	41.8	11.8
43-5030	Dispatchers	289	306	16	5.7	47	9		—	1.2	—	—					
43-5031	Police, fire, and ambulance dispatchers	99	113	13	13.6	18	4	31,470	H	1.2	L	VL	Moderate-term on-the-job training	HS/SC	44.0	45.1	10.9
43-5032	Dispatchers, except police, fire, and ambulance	190	193	3	1.5	30	5	32,190	H	1.1	L	VL	Moderate-term on-the-job training	HS/SC	44.0	45.1	10.9
43-5041	Meter readers, utilities	47	42	-5	-10.3	7	1	30,330	L	0.0	VL	VL	Short-term on-the-job training	HS/SC	49.5	44.7	5.9
43-5050	Postal service workers	615	603	-12	-2.0	27	14	—	—	0.0	—	—	—	—	—	—	—
43-5051	Postal service clerks	80	80	1	1.2	4	2	44,800	H	0.0	VL	VL	Short-term on-the-job training	HS/SC	42.6	46.0	11.3
43-5052	Postal service mail carriers	338	341	4	1.0	17	10	44,350	H	0.0	VL	L	Short-term on-the-job training	HS/SC	41.8	47.7	10.6
43-5053	Postal service mail sorters, processors, and processing machine operators	198	181	-17	-8.4	7	2	43,900	H	0.0	L	VL	Short-term on-the-job training	HS/SC	40.7	47.2	12.1
43-5061	Production, planning, and expediting clerks	293	305	12	4.2	53	9	38,620	H	1.4	L	VL	Moderate-term on-the-job training	HS/SC/C	30.0	39.7	30.3
43-5071	Shipping, receiving, and traffic clerks	769	797	28	3.7	139	21	26,070	L	.2	H	L	Short-term on-the-job training	HS/SC	64.3	29.6	6.1
43-5081	Stock clerks and order fillers	1,705	1,574	-131	-7.7	439	40	20,440	VL	.2	VH	VH	Short-term on-the-job training	HS/SC	63.2	29.1	7.7
43-5111	Weighers, measurers, checkers, and samplers, recordkeeping	79	70	-9	-11.3	14	2	25,370	L	.8	H	L	Short-term on-the-job training	HS/SC	54.9	32.6	12.5
43-6000	Secretaries and administrative assistants	4,241	4,603	362	8.5	574	104	—	—	1.4	—	—	—	—	—	—	—
43-6011	Executive secretaries and administrative assistants	1,618	1,857	239	14.8	235	50	37,240	H	1.4	L	H	Work experience in a related occupation	HS/SC	33.0	48.7	18.3
43-6012	Legal secretaries	275	308	32	11.7	39	8	38,190	H	1.4	L	H	Associate degree	HS/SC	33.0	48.7	18.3
43-6013	Medical secretaries	408	477	68	16.7	61	13	28,090	L	1.3	L	H	Moderate-term on-the-job training	HS/SC	33.0	48.7	18.3
43-6014	Secretaries, except legal, medical, and executive	1,940	1,962	22	1.2	240	33	27,450	L	1.4	L	H	Moderate-term on-the-job training	HS/SC	33.0	48.7	18.3
43-9000	Other office and administrative support workers	4,715	5,001	286	6.1	1,027	132	—	—	1.6	—	—	—	—	—	—	—
43-9011	Computer operators	130	98	-32	-24.7	18	2	33,560	H	1.8	L	L	Moderate-term on-the-job training	HS/SC/C	26.8	46.4	26.8
43-9020	Data entry and information processing workers	492	457	-35	-7.2	111	11	—	—	4.4	—	—	—	—	—	—	—
43-9021	Data entry keyers	313	299	-15	-4.7	79	8	24,690	L	1.7	VH	H	Moderate-term on-the-job training	HS/SC	35.2	47.0	17.7
43-9022	Word processors and typists	179	158	-21	-11.6	32	3	29,430	L	9.2	H	H	Moderate-term on-the-job training	HS/SC	29.0	51.9	19.1
43-9031	Desktop publishers[1]	32	32	0	1.0	6	1	34,130	H	2.2	L	L	Postsecondary vocational award	HS/SC/C	24.7	43.3	31.9
43-9041	Insurance claims and policy processing clerks	254	251	-3	-1.3	42	3	31,120	H	.4	L	L	Moderate-term on-the-job training	HS/SC/C	30.5	47.5	22.0
43-9051	Mail clerks and mail machine operators, except postal service	152	134	-18	-11.6	28	4	23,810	L	.8	H	H	Short-term on-the-job training	HS/SC	56.2	34.6	9.2
43-9061	Office clerks, general	3,200	3,604	404	12.6	766	99	23,710	L	.7	H	H	Short-term on-the-job training	HS/SC	36.0	45.3	18.7
43-9071	Office machine operators, except computer	94	91	-3	-2.7	8	3	24,540	L	0.0	H	H	Short-term on-the-job training	HS/SC	48.9	37.4	13.7
43-9081	Proofreaders and copy markers[1]	18	19	1	6.4	4	0	27,450	L	1.7	H	H	Short-term on-the-job training	HS/SC/C	21.5	31.3	47.2
43-9111	Statistical assistants[1]	23	24	2	7.6	5	1	31,250	H	6.6	VL	L	Moderate-term on-the-job training	HS/SC/C	23.7	46.5	29.8

See footnotes at end of table.

Table III-1. Occupational employment and job openings data, 2006–16, and worker characteristics, 2006 — Continued
(Numbers in thousands)

Code	2006 National Employment Matrix occupation and code	Employment 2006	Employment 2016	Employment change, 2006–16 Numeric	Employment change, 2006–16 Percent	Annual average job openings due to growth and total replacement needs, 2006–16	Annual average job openings due to growth and net replacement needs, 2006–16	2006 median annual wages Dollars	2006 median annual wages Rank	Percent self-employed, 2006	Unemployment rate	Percent part-time	Most significant source of postsecondary education or training[2]	Educational attainment cluster[3]	Percent of workers aged 25 to 44, by educational attainment[4]: High school or less	Some college	College or higher
43-9199	Office and administrative support workers, all other	320	290	-30	-9.3	39	7	27,200	L	7.4	L	L	Short-term on-the-job training	HS/SC/C	24.7	43.3	31.9
45-0000	**Farming, fishing, and forestry occupations**	**1,039**	**1,010**	**-29**	**-2.8**	**231**	**25**	—	—	**6.5**	—	—	—	—	—	—	—
45-1000	Supervisors, farming, fishing, and forestry workers	53	53	0	-.4	12	1	36,470	H	24.8	H	L	Work experience in a related occupation	HS/SC	63.0	24.5	12.5
45-2000	Agricultural workers	858	838	-21	-2.4	205	21	—	—	.8	—	—	—	—	—	—	—
45-2011	Agricultural inspectors[1]	16	16	0	-1.1	4	0	38,100	H	0.0	H	VL	Work experience in a related occupation	HS/SC/C	37.6	36.5	25.9
45-2021	Animal breeders[1]	11	11	0	4.4	3	0	27,090	L	50.2	L	VH	Work experience in a related occupation	HS	86.3	9.7	4.0
45-2041	Graders and sorters, agricultural products	42	41	-1	-1.8	9	1	17,200	VL	0.0	VH	VL	Work experience in a related occupation	HS	85.2	9.7	0.0
45-2090	Miscellaneous agricultural workers	790	769	-20	-2.6	190	20	—	—	.2	—	—	—	—	—	—	—
45-2091	Agricultural equipment operators	59	56	-3	-5.0	14	1	20,230	VL	.2	VH	H	Moderate-term on-the-job training	HS	86.3	9.7	4.0
45-2092	Farmworkers and laborers, crop, nursery, and greenhouse	603	583	-20	-3.4	145	15	16,540	VL	.2	VH	H	Short-term on-the-job training	HS	86.3	9.7	4.0
45-2093	Farmworkers, farm and ranch animals	107	110	3	2.7	27	3	19,060	VL	.2	VH	H	Short-term on-the-job training	HS	86.3	9.7	4.0
45-2099	Agricultural workers, all other	20	20	0	0.0	5	1	22,470	L	.2	VH	H	Short-term on-the-job training	HS	86.3	9.7	4.0
45-3000	Fishing and hunting workers	39	33	-6	-16.2	7	1	—	—	64.7	—	—	—	—	—	—	—
45-3011	Fishers and related fishing workers	38	32	-6	-16.1	7	1	27,250	L	65.5	VH	L	Moderate-term on-the-job training	HS/SC	66.7	22.6	10.7
45-3021	Hunters and trappers[1]	0	0	0	-19.0	0	0	26,460	L	0.0	VH	H	Moderate-term on-the-job training	HS/SC	66.7	22.6	10.7
45-4000	Forest, conservation, and logging workers	88	87	-1	-1.4	6	2	—	—	25.1	—	—	—	—	—	—	—
45-4011	Forest and conservation workers	20	21	1	5.5	2	1	20,810	VL	13.9	VH	H	Moderate-term on-the-job training	HS/SC/C	63.1	14.7	22.2
45-4020	Logging workers	69	66	-2	-3.4	5	1	—	—	28.3	—	—	—	—	—	—	—
45-4021	Fallers	13	12	-1	-7.4	1	0	28,710	L	30.6	H	VL	Moderate-term on-the-job training	HS	83.5	14.2	2.2
45-4022	Logging equipment operators	40	40	-1	-1.3	3	1	29,700	L	28.0	H	VL	Moderate-term on-the-job training	HS	83.5	14.2	2.2
45-4023	Log graders and scalers	7	7	0	-5.3	0	0	29,240	L	31.6	H	VL	Moderate-term on-the-job training	HS	83.5	14.2	2.2
45-4029	Logging workers, all other	8	7	0	-5.9	1	0	31,870	H	23.5	H	VL	Moderate-term on-the-job training	HS	83.5	14.2	2.2
47-0000	**Construction and extraction occupations**	**8,295**	**9,079**	**785**	**9.5**	**1,340**	**225**	—	—	**18.3**	—	—	—	—	—	—	—
47-1000	Supervisors, construction and extraction workers	772	842	70	9.1	83	18	—	—	24.4	—	—	—	—	—	—	—
47-1011	First-line supervisors/managers of construction trades and extraction workers	772	842	70	9.1	83	18	53,850	VH	24.4	L	VL	Work experience in a related occupation	HS/SC	59.5	30.1	10.3
47-2000	Construction trades and related workers	6,422	7,044	622	9.7	1,022	172	—	—	20.0	—	—	—	—	—	—	—
47-2011	Boilermakers	18	20	2	14.0	2	1	46,960	VH	.2	VH	VL	Long-term on-the-job training	HS/SC	75.0	25.0	0.0
47-2020	Brickmasons, blockmasons, and stonemasons	182	200	18	9.7	20	6	—	—	24.3	—	—	—	—	—	—	—
47-2021	Brickmasons and blockmasons	158	174	15	9.7	18	5	42,980	H	24.5	VH	L	Long-term on-the-job training	HS	81.7	15.0	3.3
47-2022	Stonemasons	24	26	2	10.0	3	1	35,960	H	22.8	VH	L	Long-term on-the-job training	HS	81.7	15.0	3.3
47-2031	Carpenters	1,462	1,612	150	10.3	223	35	36,550	H	31.8	VH	VL	Long-term on-the-job training	HS/SC	72.8	21.6	5.5
47-2040	Carpet, floor, and tile installers and finishers	196	203	8	3.9	20	4	—	—	42.5	—	—	—	—	—	—	—

See footnotes at end of table.

Table III–1. Occupational employment and job openings data, 2006–16, and worker characteristics, 2006 — Continued
(Numbers in thousands)

2006 National Employment Matrix occupation and code		Employment		Employment change, 2006–16		Annual average job openings due to growth and total replacement needs, 2006–16	Annual average job openings due to growth and net replacement needs, 2006–16	2006 median annual wages		Percent self-employed, 2006	Unemployment rate	Percent part-time	Most significant source of postsecondary education or training[2]	Educational attainment cluster[3]	Percent of workers aged 25 to 44, by educational attainment[4]		
		2006	2016	Numeric	Percent			Dollars	Rank						High school or less	Some college	College or higher
47-2041	Carpet installers	73	72	-1	-1.2	7	1	34,560	H	49.0	H	L	Moderate-term on-the-job training	HS	79.7	17.0	3.3
47-2042	Floor layers, except carpet, wood, and hard tiles	29	25	-4	-12.2	3	0	34,190	H	47.7	H	L	Moderate-term on-the-job training	HS	79.7	17.0	3.3
47-2043	Floor sanders and finishers	14	14	0	-1.8	1	0	28,890	L	46.6	H	L	Moderate-term on-the-job training	HS	79.7	17.0	3.3
47-2044	Tile and marble setters	79	91	12	15.4	9	2	36,590	H	33.8	H	L	Long-term on-the-job training	HS	79.7	17.0	3.3
47-2050	Cement masons, concrete finishers, and terrazzo workers	228	254	26	11.4	36	9	—	—	2.0	—	—	—	—	—	—	—
47-2051	Cement masons and concrete finishers	222	247	25	11.4	35	9	32,650	H	2.0	VH	VL	Moderate-term on-the-job training	HS	85.6	12.3	2.0
47-2053	Terrazzo workers and finishers	7	8	1	10.9	1	0	31,630	H	2.3	VH	VL	Long-term on-the-job training	HS	85.6	12.3	2.0
47-2061	Construction laborers	1,232	1,366	134	10.9	257	23	26,320	L	16.4	VH	L	Moderate-term on-the-job training	HS	78.5	16.8	4.7
47-2070	Construction equipment operators	494	536	42	8.5	60	14	—	—	5.2	—	—	—	—	—	—	—
47-2071	Paving, surfacing, and tamping equipment operators	64	70	6	9.0	3	2	31,300	H	1.8	VH	VL	Moderate-term on-the-job training	HS	83.6	15.0	0.0
47-2072	Pile-driver operators[1]	6	6	0	8.3	1	0	46,180	H	5.0	VH	VL	Moderate-term on-the-job training	HS	77.8	19.6	2.6
47-2073	Operating engineers and other construction equipment operators	424	460	35	8.4	55	12	36,890	H	5.7	VH	VL	Moderate-term on-the-job training	HS	77.8	19.6	2.6
47-2080	Drywall installers, ceiling tile installers, and tapers	240	258	17	7.2	40	5	—	—	23.4	—	—	—	—	—	—	—
47-2081	Drywall and ceiling tile installers	186	199	14	7.3	31	4	36,140	H	23.0	VH	VL	Moderate-term on-the-job training	HS	85.1	12.9	2.0
47-2082	Tapers	54	58	4	7.1	9	1	41,280	H	24.9	VH	VL	Moderate-term on-the-job training	HS	85.1	12.9	2.0
47-2111	Electricians	705	757	52	7.4	79	23	43,610	H	10.7	H	VL	Long-term on-the-job training	HS/SC	50.7	42.4	6.8
47-2121	Glaziers[1]	55	62	7	11.9	6	2	34,610	H	5.3	H	VL	Long-term on-the-job training	HS/SC	71.8	25.3	0.0
47-2130	Insulation workers	61	66	5	8.5	12	2	—	—	1.0	—	—	—	—	—	—	—
47-2131	Insulation workers, floor, ceiling, and wall	32	35	3	8.4	7	1	30,510	L	1.3	H	VL	Moderate-term on-the-job training	HS	79.7	15.9	0.0
47-2132	Insulation workers, mechanical	28	31	2	8.6	6	1	36,900	H	.7	H	VL	Moderate-term on-the-job training	HS	79.7	15.9	0.0
47-2140	Painters and paperhangers	473	526	53	11.3	103	14	—	—	42.1	—	—	—	—	—	—	—
47-2141	Painters, construction and maintenance	463	517	54	11.8	101	14	31,190	H	42.2	VH	L	Moderate-term on-the-job training	HS	76.4	17.3	6.3
47-2142	Paperhangers[1]	10	9	-1	-12.2	2	0	33,710	H	37.6	VH	L	Moderate-term on-the-job training	HS/SC	65.9	32.4	0.0
47-2150	Pipelayers, plumbers, pipefitters, and steamfitters	569	628	59	10.4	78	18	—	—	12.3	—	—	—	—	—	—	—
47-2151	Pipelayers	67	72	6	8.7	9	2	30,330	L	11.6	H	VL	Moderate-term on-the-job training	HS/SC	67.6	28.5	3.9
47-2152	Plumbers, pipefitters, and steamfitters	502	555	53	10.6	69	16	42,770	H	12.3	H	VL	Long-term on-the-job training	HS/SC	67.6	28.5	3.9
47-2161	Plasterers and stucco masons	61	66	5	8.1	5	2	34,700	H	15.7	VH	VL	Long-term on-the-job training	HS	87.3	10.0	0.0
47-2171	Reinforcing iron and rebar workers[1]	30	34	3	11.5	5	1	38,220	H	0.0	VH	VL	Long-term on-the-job training	HS	82.6	14.7	0.0
47-2181	Roofers	156	179	22	14.3	38	6	32,260	H	20.1	VH	L	Moderate-term on-the-job training	HS	85.7	11.4	2.8
47-2211	Sheet metal workers	189	201	13	6.7	32	6	37,360	H	4.7	VH	VL	Long-term on-the-job training	HS/SC	63.4	32.4	4.2
47-2221	Structural iron and steel workers	72	76	4	6.0	7	3	40,480	H	5.3	VH	VL	Long-term on-the-job training	HS/SC	67.6	28.6	3.8
47-3000	Helpers, construction trades	448	491	43	9.6	153	16	—	—	3.1	—	—	—	—	—	—	—
47-3010	Helpers, construction trades	448	491	43	9.6	153	16	—	—	3.1	—	—	—	—	—	—	—

See footnotes at end of table.

Table III–1. Occupational employment and job openings data, 2006–16, and worker characteristics, 2006 — Continued
(Numbers in thousands)

Code	2006 National Employment Matrix occupation and code	Employment 2006	Employment 2016	Employment change, 2006–16 Numeric	Employment change, 2006–16 Percent	Annual average job openings due to growth and total replacement needs, 2006–16	Annual average job openings due to growth and net replacement needs, 2006–16	2006 median annual wages Dollars	2006 median annual wages Rank	Percent self-employed, 2006	Unemployment rate	Percent part-time	Most significant source of postsecondary education or training[2]	Educational attainment cluster[3]	Percent of workers aged 25 to 44, by educational attainment[4]: High school or less	Some college	College or higher
47-3011	Helpers—Brickmasons, blockmasons, stonemasons, and tile and marble setters	65	73	7	11.0	22	2	25,350	L	3.0	VH	L	Short-term on-the-job training	HS	84.0	12.9	3.1
47-3012	Helpers—Carpenters	109	122	13	11.7	38	4	23,060	L	3.2	VH	L	Short-term on-the-job training	HS	84.0	12.9	3.1
47-3013	Helpers—Electricians	105	112	7	6.8	35	3	23,760	L	2.9	VH	L	Short-term on-the-job training	HS	84.0	12.9	3.1
47-3014	Helpers—Painters, paperhangers, plasterers, and stucco masons	24	24	0	-.7	8	1	21,330	L	3.5	VH	L	Short-term on-the-job training	HS	84.0	12.9	3.1
47-3015	Helpers—Pipelayers, plumbers, pipefitters, and steamfitters	85	95	10	11.9	29	3	23,910	L	2.9	VH	L	Short-term on-the-job training	HS	84.0	12.9	3.1
47-3016	Helpers—Roofers	22	23	1	6.7	7	1	21,760	L	3.2	VH	L	Short-term on-the-job training	HS	84.0	12.9	3.1
47-3019	Helpers, construction trades, all other	38	42	5	12.6	13	1	22,760	L	3.3	VH	L	Short-term on-the-job training	HS	84.0	12.9	3.1
47-4000	Other construction and related workers	451	502	51	11.4	60	14	—	—	6.0	—	—	—	—	—	—	—
47-4011	Construction and building inspectors	110	130	20	18.2	13	4	46,570	VH	9.4	VL	VL	Work experience in a related occupation	HS/SC/C	30.5	46.4	23.0
47-4021	Elevator installers and repairers[1]	22	24	2	8.8	3	1	63,620	VH	0.0	VL	VL	Long-term on-the-job training	HS/SC	48.0	42.2	9.8
47-4031	Fence erectors[1]	32	36	3	10.6	3	1	26,400	L	23.2	VH	L	Moderate-term on-the-job training	HS	79.0	17.7	3.3
47-4041	Hazardous materials removal workers	39	44	4	11.2	2	1	35,450	H	1.6	VH	VL	Moderate-term on-the-job training	HS/SC	63.2	27.3	9.4
47-4051	Highway maintenance workers	145	158	13	8.9	25	4	31,540	H	.9	H	VL	Moderate-term on-the-job training	HS/SC	69.0	26.0	5.0
47-4061	Rail-track laying and maintenance equipment operators[1]	15	15	1	4.8	2	0	40,000	H	0.0	H	VL	Moderate-term on-the-job training	HS/SC	60.9	32.2	0.0
47-4071	Septic tank servicers and sewer pipe cleaners[1]	24	26	2	10.2	3	1	31,430	H	6.4	H	L	Moderate-term on-the-job training	HS/SC	75.1	21.1	3.8
47-4090	Miscellaneous construction and related workers	63	69	6	8.9	10	2	—	—	8.7	—	—	—	—	—	—	—
47-4091	Segmental pavers	1	1	0	10.2	0	0	28,700	L	7.8	H	L	Moderate-term on-the-job training	HS/SC	75.1	21.1	3.8
47-4099	Construction and related workers, all other	62	68	6	8.8	10	2	30,470	L	8.7	H	L	Moderate-term on-the-job training	HS/SC	75.1	21.1	3.8
47-5000	Extraction workers	202	200	-2	-.8	22	5	—	—	2.3	—	—	—	—	—	—	—
47-5010	Derrick, rotary drill, and service unit operators, oil, gas, and mining	67	63	-4	-5.5	7	1	—	—	2.4	—	—	—	—	—	—	—
47-5011	Derrick operators, oil and gas[1]	19	18	-1	-5.8	2	0	36,240	H	2.7	VL	VL	Moderate-term on-the-job training	HS	77.1	18.9	0.0
47-5012	Rotary drill operators, oil and gas[1]	20	19	-1	-5.4	2	0	38,460	H	2.5	VL	VL	Moderate-term on-the-job training	HS	77.1	18.9	0.0
47-5013	Service unit operators, oil, gas, and mining[1]	28	26	-2	-5.4	3	0	32,910	H	2.1	VL	VL	Moderate-term on-the-job training	HS	77.1	18.9	0.0
47-5021	Earth drillers, except oil and gas	22	23	1	6.5	3	1	34,500	H	9.6	H	VL	Moderate-term on-the-job training	HS	77.8	17.6	0.0
47-5031	Explosives workers, ordnance handling experts, and blasters[1]	5	5	0	1.4	1	0	39,890	H	0.0	H	VL	Moderate-term on-the-job training	HS/SC	62.9	33.9	0.0
47-5040	Mining machine operators	21	22	1	4.3	2	1	—	—	1.6	—	—	—	—	—	—	—
47-5041	Continuous mining machine operators	10	11	0	4.6	1	0	40,430	H	1.9	H	VL	Moderate-term on-the-job training	HS/SC	70.5	26.6	0.0
47-5042	Mine cutting and channeling machine operators	8	8	0	3.8	1	0	39,990	H	1.1	H	VL	Moderate-term on-the-job training	HS/SC	70.5	26.6	0.0
47-5049	Mining machine operators, all other	3	3	0	4.9	0	0	37,370	H	2.1	H	VL	Moderate-term on-the-job training	HS/SC	70.5	26.6	0.0

See footnotes at end of table.

Table III–1. Occupational employment and job openings data, 2006–16, and worker characteristics, 2006 — Continued
(Numbers in thousands)

Code	2006 National Employment Matrix occupation and code	Employment 2006	Employment 2016	Employment change, 2006–16 Numeric	Employment change, 2006–16 Percent	Annual average job openings due to growth and total replacement needs, 2006–16	Annual average job openings due to growth and net replacement needs, 2006–16	2006 median annual wages Dollars	2006 median annual wages Rank	Percent self-employed, 2006	Unemployment rate	Percent part-time	Most significant source of postsecondary education or training[2]	Educational attainment cluster[3]	Percent of workers aged 25 to 44, by educational attainment[4]: High school or less	Some college	College or higher
47-5051	Rock splitters, quarry	4	5	1	25.1	1	0	27,130	L	3.4	H	VL	Moderate-term on-the-job training	HS/SC	74.4	23.6	0.0
47-5061	Roof bolters, mining[1]	4	4	0	1.2	0	0	41,250	H	0.0	H	VL	Moderate-term on-the-job training	HS/SC	74.4	23.6	0.0
47-5071	Roustabouts, oil and gas[1]	44	43	-1	-3.2	5	1	25,700	L	.2	H	VL	Moderate-term on-the-job training	HS	77.1	18.9	0.0
47-5081	Helpers—Extraction workers[1]	25	25	0	-.2	3	1	28,680	L	0.0	H	VL	Short-term on-the-job training	HS/SC	74.4	23.6	0.0
47-5099	Extraction workers, all other	10	10	0	.3	1	0	35,450	H	4.6	H	VL	Moderate-term on-the-job training	HS/SC	74.4	23.6	0.0
49-0000	**Installation, maintenance, and repair occupations**	**5,883**	**6,433**	**550**	**9.3**	**657**	**150**	—	—	**7.3**	—	—	—	—	—	—	—
49-1000	Supervisors of installation, maintenance, and repair workers	465	499	34	7.3	24	14	—	—	1.5	—	—	—	—	—	—	—
49-1011	First-line supervisors/managers of mechanics, installers, and repairers	465	499	34	7.3	24	14	53,890	VH	1.5	VL	VL	Work experience in a related occupation	HS/SC	43.2	43.6	13.2
49-2000	Electrical and electronic equipment mechanics, installers, and repairers	661	690	29	4.4	60	17	—	—	8.5	—	—	—	—	—	—	—
49-2011	Computer, automated teller, and office machine repairers	175	180	5	3.0	22	3	36,480	H	19.7	H	L	Postsecondary vocational award	HS/SC/C	22.5	52.7	24.7
49-2020	Radio and telecommunications equipment installers and repairers	205	209	5	2.3	14	6	—	—	4.1	—	—	—	—	—	—	—
49-2021	Radio mechanics	7	6	0	-4.1	0	0	37,690	H	3.9	H	VL	Long-term on-the-job training	HS/SC	36.4	50.7	12.9
49-2022	Telecommunications equipment installers and repairers, except line installers	198	203	5	2.5	14	5	52,430	VH	4.1	H	VL	Postsecondary vocational award	HS/SC	36.4	50.7	12.9
49-2090	Miscellaneous electrical and electronic equipment mechanics, installers, and repairers	281	301	19	6.8	24	9	—	—	4.7	—	—	—	—	—	—	—
49-2091	Avionics technicians[1]	16	17	1	8.1	1	0	46,950	VH	0.0	H	VL	Postsecondary vocational award	HS/SC	30.9	64.5	0.0
49-2092	Electric motor, power tool, and related repairers	25	24	-1	-4.2	3	1	32,860	H	12.5	H	L	Postsecondary vocational award	HS/SC	44.5	43.4	0.0
49-2093	Electrical and electronics installers and repairers, transportation equipment[1]	21	22	1	4.3	2	1	43,110	H	0.0	H	VL	Postsecondary vocational award	HS/SC	46.4	46.0	0.0
49-2094	Electrical and electronics repairers, commercial and industrial equipment[1]	80	86	5	6.8	7	3	45,180	H	0.0	L	VL	Postsecondary vocational award	HS/SC	46.4	46.0	0.0
49-2095	Electrical and electronics repairers, powerhouse, substation, and relay[1]	22	21	-1	-4.7	2	1	57,400	VH	0.0	L	VL	Postsecondary vocational award	HS/SC	46.4	46.0	0.0
49-2096	Electronic equipment installers and repairers, motor vehicles[1]	20	21	1	4.6	2	1	28,220	L	4.5	H	VL	Postsecondary vocational award	HS/SC	54.2	38.6	7.1
49-2097	Electronic home entertainment equipment installers and repairers[1]	40	41	1	3.0	3	0	29,980	L	12.3	H	VL	Postsecondary vocational award	HS/SC	44.9	44.0	11.1
49-2098	Security and fire alarm systems installers[1]	57	68	11	20.2	6	2	34,810	H	7.2	H	VL	Postsecondary vocational award	HS/SC	48.3	44.0	7.7
49-3000	Vehicle and mobile equipment mechanics, installers, and repairers	1,771	2,003	232	13.1	224	59	—	—	11.8	—	—	—	—	—	—	—
49-3011	Aircraft mechanics and service technicians	122	135	13	10.6	10	3	47,740	VH	.4	VL	VL	Postsecondary vocational award	HS/SC	32.9	56.6	10.5
49-3020	Automotive technicians and repairers	979	1,115	136	13.9	138	34	—	—	16.4	—	—	—	—	—	—	—

See footnotes at end of table.

Table III-1. Occupational employment and job openings data, 2006–16, and worker characteristics, 2006 — Continued
(Numbers in thousands)

Code	2006 National Employment Matrix occupation and code	Employment 2006	Employment 2016	Employment change, 2006–16 Numeric	Employment change, 2006–16 Percent	Annual average job openings due to growth and total replacement needs, 2006–16	Annual average job openings due to growth and net replacement needs, 2006–16	2006 median annual wages Dollars	2006 median annual wages Rank	Percent self-employed, 2006	Unemployment rate	Percent part-time	Most significant source of postsecondary education or training[2]	Educational attainment cluster[3]	Percent of workers aged 25 to 44, by educational attainment[4]: High school or less	Some college	College or higher
49-3021	Automotive body and related repairers....	183	204	21	11.6	37	6	35,180	H	14.1	H	VL	Long-term on-the-job training	HS/SC	74.3	22.5	3.1
49-3022	Automotive glass installers and repairers[1]	24	28	4	18.7	3	1	30,720	H	20.7	L	VL	Long-term on-the-job training	HS/SC	75.7	22.4	0.0
49-3023	Automotive service technicians and mechanics	773	883	110	14.3	97	27	33,780	H	16.8	H	VL	Postsecondary vocational award	HS/SC	62.4	33.7	3.9
49-3031	Bus and truck mechanics and diesel engine specialists	275	306	32	11.5	25	9	37,660	H	5.8	L	VL	Postsecondary vocational award	HS/SC	65.7	31.2	3.1
49-3040	Heavy vehicle and mobile equipment service technicians and mechanics....	188	206	18	9.5	15	5	—	—	4.9	—	—	—	—	—	—	—
49-3041	Farm equipment mechanics	31	31	0	1.4	2	1	29,460	L	5.6	L	VL	Long-term on-the-job training	HS/SC	61.8	35.0	3.2
49-3042	Mobile heavy equipment mechanics, except engines	131	147	16	12.3	11	4	40,440	H	5.0	L	VL	Long-term on-the-job training	HS/SC	61.8	35.0	3.2
49-3043	Rail car repairers	27	28	1	5.1	2	1	43,320	H	4.0	L	VL	Long-term on-the-job training	HS/SC	61.8	35.0	3.2
49-3050	Small engine mechanics..........	78	87	9	11.6	13	2	—	—	22.6	—	—	—	—	—	—	—
49-3051	Motorboat mechanics	24	29	5	19.0	4	1	33,210	H	22.6	H	L	Long-term on-the-job training	HS/SC	63.5	32.0	4.5
49-3052	Motorcycle mechanics..........	21	24	3	12.5	4	1	30,050	L	21.9	H	L	Long-term on-the-job training	HS/SC	63.5	32.0	4.5
49-3053	Outdoor power equipment and other small engine mechanics..........	33	35	2	5.5	5	1	26,910	L	23.0	H	L	Moderate-term on-the-job training	HS/SC	63.5	32.0	4.5
49-3090	Miscellaneous vehicle and mobile equipment mechanics, installers, and repairers	128	153	25	19.1	23	5		—	3.4	—	—					
49-3091	Bicycle repairers..........	9	9	1	7.2	1	0	21,790	L	3.6	VH	L	Moderate-term on-the-job training	HS/SC	73.7	20.4	5.9
49-3092	Recreational vehicle service technicians.	14	17	3	18.2	2	1	31,510	H	3.5	VH	L	Long-term on-the-job training	HS/SC	73.7	20.4	5.9
49-3093	Tire repairers and changers..........	106	127	21	20.2	19	4	21,340	L	3.3	VH	L	Short-term on-the-job training	HS/SC	73.7	20.4	5.9
49-9000	Other installation, maintenance, and repair occupations	2,987	3,241	254	8.5	348	60	—	—	5.2	—	—	—	—	—	—	—
49-9010	Control and valve installers and repairers .	58	61	2	4.2	6	1	—	—	.3	—	—	—	—	—	—	—
49-9011	Mechanical door repairers[1]..........	15	18	2	14.9	2	0	31,610	H	.3	VL	VL	Moderate-term on-the-job training	HS/SC	55.1	38.0	6.9
49-9012	Control and valve installers and repairers, except mechanical door[1]	43	43	0	.3	4	1	45,440	H	.3	VL	VL	Moderate-term on-the-job training	HS/SC	55.1	38.0	6.9
49-9021	Heating, air conditioning, and refrigeration mechanics and installers	292	317	25	8.7	30	8	37,660	H	12.7	L	VL	Long-term on-the-job training	HS/SC	57.6	39.0	3.4
49-9031	Home appliance repairers	57	58	1	1.5	4	1	33,860	H	26.7	VL	L	Long-term on-the-job training	HS/SC	50.3	42.5	7.2
49-9040	Industrial machinery installation, repair, and maintenance workers	1,794	1,960	165	9.2	209	27	—	—	1.7	—	—	—	—	—	—	—
49-9041	Industrial machinery mechanics	261	284	24	9.0	23	7	41,050	H	2.5	L	VL	Long-term on-the-job training	HS/SC	55.9	38.8	5.3
49-9042	Maintenance and repair workers, general	1,391	1,531	140	10.1	166	17	31,910	H	1.5	L	VL	Moderate-term on-the-job training	HS/SC	58.3	35.6	6.1
49-9043	Maintenance workers, machinery..........	84	83	-1	-1.1	15	1	34,550	H	0.0	H	VL	Moderate-term on-the-job training	HS/SC	56.6	39.3	0.0
49-9044	Millwrights..........	55	58	3	5.8	5	1	45,630	H	3.2	H	VL	Long-term on-the-job training	HS/SC	53.9	43.3	0.0
49-9045	Refractory materials repairers, except brickmasons	3	3	0	-11.5	0	0	40,780	H	3.1	L	VL	Moderate-term on-the-job training	HS/SC	55.9	38.8	5.3

See footnotes at end of table.

Table III–1. Occupational employment and job openings data, 2006–16, and worker characteristics, 2006 — Continued
(Numbers in thousands)

2006 National Employment Matrix occupation and code		Employment		Employment change, 2006–16		Annual average job openings due to growth and total replacement needs, 2006–16	Annual average job openings due to growth and net replacement needs, 2006–16	2006 median annual wages		Percent self-employed, 2006	Unemployment rate	Percent part-time	Most significant source of postsecondary education or training[2]	Educational attainment cluster[3]	Percent of workers aged 25 to 44, by educational attainment[4]		
		2006	2016	Numeric	Percent			Dollars	Rank						High school or less	Some college	College or higher
49-9050	Line installers and repairers	275	290	16	5.7	21	9	—	—	2.2	—	—	—	—	—	—	—
49-9051	Electrical power-line installers and repairers	112	120	8	7.2	6	4	50,780	VH	.6	H	VL	Long-term on-the-job training	HS/SC	55.9	38.2	6.0
49-9052	Telecommunications line installers and repairers	162	170	7	4.6	15	5	46,280	H	3.3	H	VL	Long-term on-the-job training	HS/SC	47.9	44.2	7.9
49-9060	Precision instrument and equipment repairers	68	77	9	12.8	4	3	—	—	16.3	—	—	—	—	—	—	—
49-9061	Camera and photographic equipment repairers[1]	4	4	0	-2.1	0	0	34,850	H	20.9	VL	L	Moderate-term on-the-job training	HS/SC	28.3	57.0	14.7
49-9062	Medical equipment repairers[1]	38	46	8	21.7	2	2	40,580	H	14.0	VL	L	Associate degree	HS/SC	28.3	57.0	14.7
49-9063	Musical instrument repairers and tuners[1]	6	6	0	2.8	0	0	29,200	L	18.4	VL	L	Long-term on-the-job training	HS/SC	28.3	57.0	14.7
49-9064	Watch repairers[1]	4	4	0	-5.1	0	0	30,900	H	20.3	VL	L	Long-term on-the-job training	HS/SC	28.3	57.0	14.7
49-9069	Precision instrument and equipment repairers, all other[1]	16	17	1	4.3	1	1	46,250	H	18.5	VL	L	Moderate-term on-the-job training	HS/SC	28.3	57.0	14.7
49-9090	Miscellaneous installation, maintenance, and repair workers	442	478	36	8.2	74	11	—	—	12.7	—	—	—	—	—	—	—
49-9091	Coin, vending, and amusement machine servicers and repairers	48	46	-1	-3.0	5	1	28,710	L	17.9	H	L	Moderate-term on-the-job training	HS/SC	62.6	29.2	8.3
49-9092	Commercial divers[1]	3	4	1	17.7	0	0	39,590	H	12.7	H	L	Postsecondary vocational award	HS/SC	61.1	30.1	8.8
49-9093	Fabric menders, except garment	2	2	0	-1.5	0	0	28,370	L	30.1	H	L	Moderate-term on-the-job training	HS/SC	61.1	30.1	8.8
49-9094	Locksmiths and safe repairers[1]	26	32	6	22.1	4	1	32,020	H	28.3	VL	L	Moderate-term on-the-job training	HS/SC	56.1	32.6	0.0
49-9095	Manufactured building and mobile home installers	12	11	0	-2.9	1	0	25,080	L	19.7	VH	L	Moderate-term on-the-job training	HS	78.9	17.0	0.0
49-9096	Riggers[1]	12	12	0	-.3	1	0	39,220	H	0.0	H	L	Short-term on-the-job training	HS/SC	76.1	20.7	0.0
49-9097	Signal and track switch repairers[1]	7	7	0	-5.1	0	0	50,150	VH	10.8	VL	VL	Moderate-term on-the-job training	HS/SC	61.1	30.1	8.8
49-9098	Helpers--Installation, maintenance, and repair workers	163	183	19	11.8	52	6	22,270	L	.1	VH	H	Short-term on-the-job training	HS	76.9	17.7	0.0
49-9099	Installation, maintenance, and repair workers, all other	168	181	13	7.5	11	2	32,940	H	21.5	H	L	Moderate-term on-the-job training	HS/SC	61.1	30.1	8.8
51-0000	**Production occupations**	**10,675**	**10,147**	**-528**	**-4.9**	**1,433**	**232**	**—**	**—**	**3.3**	**—**	**—**	**—**	**—**	**—**	**—**	**—**
51-1000	Supervisors, production workers	699	665	-34	-4.8	46	12	—	—	2.4	—	—	—	—	—	—	—
51-1011	First-line supervisors/managers of production and operating workers	699	665	-34	-4.8	46	12	47,300	VH	2.4	VL	VL	Work experience in a related occupation	HS/SC	52.9	32.2	14.9
51-2000	Assemblers and fabricators	2,075	1,982	-93	-4.5	403	42	—	—	1.4	—	—	—	—	—	—	—
51-2011	Aircraft structure, surfaces, rigging, and systems assemblers[1]	28	32	4	12.8	7	1	45,410	H	0.0	VL	VL	Moderate-term on-the-job training	HS/SC	58.7	35.3	0.0
51-2020	Electrical, electronics, and electromechanical assemblers	297	227	-70	-23.5	38	5	—	—	0.0	—	—	—	—	—	—	—
51-2021	Coil winders, tapers, and finishers	23	16	-7	-30.5	3	0	26,300	L	.1	VH	VL	Short-term on-the-job training	HS/SC	69.0	25.5	5.5

See footnotes at end of table.

Table III–1. Occupational employment and job openings data, 2006–16, and worker characteristics, 2006 — Continued
(Numbers in thousands)

Code	2006 National Employment Matrix occupation and code	Employment 2006	Employment 2016	Employment change, 2006–16 Numeric	Employment change, 2006–16 Percent	Annual average job openings due to growth and total replacement needs, 2006–16	Annual average job openings due to growth and net replacement needs, 2006–16	2006 median annual wages Dollars	2006 median annual wages Rank	Percent self-employed, 2006	Unemployment rate	Percent part-time	Most significant source of postsecondary education or training[2]	Educational attainment cluster[3]	Percent of workers aged 25 to 44, by educational attainment[4]: High school or less	Some college	College or higher
51-2022	Electrical and electronic equipment assemblers	213	156	-57	-26.8	27	4	25,560	L	0.0	VH	VL	Short-term on-the-job training	HS/SC	69.0	25.5	5.5
51-2023	Electromechanical equipment assemblers	60	55	-5	-9.1	8	1	27,560	L	0.0	VH	VL	Short-term on-the-job training	HS/SC	69.0	25.5	5.5
51-2031	Engine and other machine assemblers[1]	45	41	-4	-8.6	9	1	33,250	H	0.0	VL	VL	Short-term on-the-job training	HS/SC	69.3	27.6	0.0
51-2041	Structural metal fabricators and fitters[1]	103	103	0	-.2	21	2	30,290	L	2.0	L	VL	Moderate-term on-the-job training	HS/SC	56.9	33.6	0.0
51-2090	Miscellaneous assemblers and fabricators	1,602	1,579	-23	-1.4	330	34	—	—	1.7	—	—	—	—	—	—	—
51-2091	Fiberglass laminators and fabricators	33	35	2	6.2	7	1	25,980	L	1.6	VH	VL	Moderate-term on-the-job training	HS/SC	70.8	24.5	4.7
51-2092	Team assemblers	1,274	1,275	1	.1	264	27	24,190	L	1.7	VH	VL	Moderate-term on-the-job training	HS/SC	70.8	24.5	4.7
51-2093	Timing device assemblers, adjusters, and calibrators	3	2	0	-7.6	1	0	28,830	L	2.3	VH	VL	Moderate-term on-the-job training	HS/SC	70.8	24.5	4.7
51-2099	Assemblers and fabricators, all other	292	266	-25	-8.7	58	6	26,730	L	1.6	VH	VL	Moderate-term on-the-job training	HS/SC	70.8	24.5	4.7
51-3000	Food processing occupations	705	764	59	8.4	106	27	—	—	1.8	—	—	—	—	—	—	—
51-3011	Bakers	149	164	15	10.0	31	5	22,030	L	4.3	H	H	Long-term on-the-job training	HS/SC	70.3	21.7	8.0
51-3020	Butchers and other meat, poultry, and fish processing workers	398	431	34	8.5	48	16	—	—	1.1	—	—	—	—	—	—	—
51-3021	Butchers and meat cutters	131	134	3	1.9	15	4	26,930	L	1.1	H	L	Long-term on-the-job training	HS	82.9	15.3	1.8
51-3022	Meat, poultry, and fish cutters and trimmers	144	160	16	10.9	18	6	20,370	VL	1.1	H	L	Short-term on-the-job training	HS	82.9	15.3	1.8
51-3023	Slaughterers and meat packers	122	138	16	12.7	16	5	21,690	L	1.2	H	L	Moderate-term on-the-job training	HS	82.9	15.3	1.8
51-3090	Miscellaneous food processing workers	158	169	10	6.5	27	6	—	—	1.1	—	—	—	—	—	—	—
51-3091	Food and tobacco roasting, baking, and drying machine operators and tenders	19	21	2	10.8	4	1	23,510	L	0.0	H	VL	Short-term on-the-job training	HS/SC	68.6	28.0	0.0
51-3092	Food batchmakers	95	105	10	10.9	16	3	23,100	L	1.7	VH	H	Short-term on-the-job training	HS/SC	72.1	23.3	4.7
51-3093	Food cooking machine operators and tenders[1]	44	42	-2	-4.7	7	2	21,280	L	.2	VH	L	Short-term on-the-job training	HS/SC	69.9	25.9	0.0
51-4000	Metal workers and plastic workers	2,258	2,087	-171	-7.6	290	46	—	—	2.3	—	—	—	—	—	—	—
51-4010	Computer control programmers and operators	158	153	-6	-3.6	15	2	—	—	0.0	—	—	—	—	—	—	—
51-4011	Computer-controlled machine tool operators, metal and plastic[1]	141	136	-4	-3.0	13	2	31,670	H	0.0	H	VL	Moderate-term on-the-job training	HS/SC	49.5	44.6	5.9
51-4012	Numerical tool and process control programmers[1]	18	16	-2	-8.4	2	0	42,480	H	0.0	H	VL	Work experience in a related occupation	HS/SC	49.5	44.6	5.9
51-4020	Forming machine setters, operators, and tenders, metal and plastic	161	140	-20	-12.7	14	4	—	—	.7	—	—	—	—	—	—	—
51-4021	Extruding and drawing machine setters, operators, and tenders, metal and plastic[1]	94	87	-7	-7.2	8	3	28,250	L	.1	H	VL	Moderate-term on-the-job training	HS	78.7	18.2	0.0
51-4022	Forging machine setters, operators, and tenders, metal and plastic[1]	31	22	-9	-30.3	2	1	28,980	L	0.0	VH	VL	Moderate-term on-the-job training	HS/SC	72.1	26.1	0.0
51-4023	Rolling machine setters, operators, and tenders, metal and plastic[1]	36	32	-4	-11.8	3	1	31,050	H	3.1	H	VL	Moderate-term on-the-job training	HS	82.4	16.2	0.0

See footnotes at end of table.

Table III-1. Occupational employment and job openings data, 2006–16, and worker characteristics, 2006 — Continued
(Numbers in thousands)

Code	2006 National Employment Matrix occupation and code	Employment 2006	Employment 2016	Employment change, 2006–16 Numeric	Employment change, 2006–16 Percent	Annual average job openings due to growth and total replacement needs, 2006–16	Annual average job openings due to growth and net replacement needs, 2006–16	2006 median annual wages Dollars	2006 median annual wages Rank	Percent self-employed, 2006	Unemployment rate	Percent part-time	Most significant source of postsecondary education or training[2]	Educational attainment cluster[3]	Percent of workers aged 25 to 44, by educational attainment[4] High school or less	Some college	College or higher
51-4030	Machine tool cutting setters, operators, and tenders, metal and plastic	513	425	-88	-17.1	70	10	—	—	.8	—	—	—	—	—	—	—
51-4031	Cutting, punching, and press machine setters, operators, and tenders, metal and plastic	272	231	-40	-14.9	31	7	26,340	L	.5	VH	VL	Moderate-term on-the-job training	HS/SC	76.7	21.6	0.0
51-4032	Drilling and boring machine tool setters, operators, and tenders, metal and plastic[1]	43	33	-9	-22.2	6	1	29,870	L	0.0	H	VL	Moderate-term on-the-job training	HS/SC	71.0	0.0	0.0
51-4033	Grinding, lapping, polishing, and buffing machine tool setters, operators, and tenders, metal and plastic	101	85	-16	-15.7	18	1	28,080	L	1.1	H	VL	Moderate-term on-the-job training	HS/SC	72.9	24.4	0.0
51-4034	Lathe and turning machine tool setters, operators, and tenders, metal and plastic	68	52	-16	-23.3	10	1	32,160	H	2.5	H	VL	Moderate-term on-the-job training	HS/SC	76.8	22.8	0.0
51-4035	Milling and planing machine setters, operators, and tenders, metal and plastic[1]	29	23	-6	-21.0	5	0	31,570	H	0.0	VH	VL	Moderate-term on-the-job training	HS/SC	72.6	24.0	3.4
51-4041	Machinists	397	384	-12	-3.1	40	6	34,770	H	1.7	L	VL	Long-term on-the-job training	HS/SC	59.5	37.3	3.2
51-4050	Metal furnace and kiln operators and tenders	33	27	-6	-18.3	10	1	—	—	0.0	—	—	—	—	—	—	—
51-4051	Metal-refining furnace operators and tenders	18	15	-3	-19.0	5	0	32,640	H	0.0	H	VL	Moderate-term on-the-job training	HS/SC	76.6	20.4	0.0
51-4052	Pourers and casters, metal	15	12	-3	-17.4	4	0	29,570	L	0.0	H	VL	Moderate-term on-the-job training	HS/SC	76.6	20.4	0.0
51-4060	Model makers and patternmakers, metal and plastic	16	15	-1	-5.9	3	0	—	—	4.5	—	—	—	—	—	—	—
51-4061	Model makers, metal and plastic[1]	9	8	-1	-6.3	2	0	42,050	H	4.8	H	VL	Long-term on-the-job training	HS/SC	68.9	24.4	0.0
51-4062	Patternmakers, metal and plastic[1]	7	7	0	-5.5	2	0	35,380	H	4.2	H	VL	Long-term on-the-job training	HS/SC	68.9	24.4	0.0
51-4070	Molders and molding machine setters, operators, and tenders, metal and plastic	171	148	-23	-13.6	34	4	—	—	.9	—	—	—	—	—	—	—
51-4071	Foundry mold and coremakers	15	11	-3	-22.7	3	0	28,740	L	1.0	H	VL	Moderate-term on-the-job training	HS/SC	72.2	25.1	0.0
51-4072	Molding, coremaking, and casting machine setters, operators, and tenders, metal and plastic	157	137	-20	-12.8	31	4	25,560	L	.9	H	VL	Moderate-term on-the-job training	HS/SC	72.2	25.1	0.0
51-4081	Multiple machine tool setters, operators, and tenders, metal and plastic[1]	97	97	0	.3	16	2	30,530	L	0.0	VH	VL	Moderate-term on-the-job training	HS/SC	72.6	24.0	3.4
51-4111	Tool and die makers	101	91	-10	-9.6	5	1	44,290	H	3.6	L	VL	Long-term on-the-job training	HS/SC	42.9	52.4	4.6
51-4120	Welding, soldering, and brazing workers	462	484	22	4.8	69	12	—	—	6.3	—	—	—	—	—	—	—
51-4121	Welders, cutters, solderers, and brazers	409	430	21	5.1	61	11	31,400	H	6.3	H	VL	Postsecondary vocational award	HS/SC	73.4	24.7	1.9
51-4122	Welding, soldering, and brazing machine setters, operators, and tenders	53	54	2	3.0	8	1	30,980	H	6.7	H	VL	Postsecondary vocational award	HS/SC	73.4	24.7	1.9

See footnotes at end of table.

Table III–1. Occupational employment and job openings data, 2006–16, and worker characteristics, 2006 — Continued
(Numbers in thousands)

Code	2006 National Employment Matrix occupation and code	Employment 2006	Employment 2016	Employment change, 2006–16 Numeric	Employment change, 2006–16 Percent	Annual average job openings due to growth and total replacement needs, 2006–16	Annual average job openings due to growth and net replacement needs, 2006–16	2006 median annual wages Dollars	2006 median annual wages Rank	Percent self-employed, 2006	Unemployment rate	Percent part-time	Most significant source of postsecondary education or training[2]	Educational attainment cluster[3]	Percent of workers aged 25 to 44, by educational attainment[4]: High school or less	Some college	College or higher
51-4190	Miscellaneous metalworkers and plastic workers	150	122	-28	-18.4	15	3	—	—	3.6	—	—	—	—	—	—	—
51-4191	Heat treating equipment setters, operators, and tenders, metal and plastic[1]	27	23	-4	-14.8	3	0	30,850	H	0.0	H	VL	Moderate-term on-the-job training	HS/SC	68.6	24.4	0.0
51-4192	Lay-out workers, metal and plastic[1]	10	8	-2	-19.8	1	0	33,600	H	0.0	H	VL	Moderate-term on-the-job training	HS/SC	72.6	24.0	3.4
51-4193	Plating and coating machine setters, operators, and tenders, metal and plastic	42	37	-5	-12.2	4	1	27,470	L	.1	H	VL	Moderate-term on-the-job training	HS/SC	78.6	20.7	0.0
51-4194	Tool grinders, filers, and sharpeners[1]	22	18	-4	-19.4	2	0	30,640	H	19.1	VL	L	Moderate-term on-the-job training	HS/SC	59.7	38.1	0.0
51-4199	Metal workers and plastic workers, all other	49	36	-12	-25.1	5	1	34,710	H	2.3	H	VL	Moderate-term on-the-job training	HS/SC	72.6	24.0	3.4
51-5000	Printing occupations	389	343	-46	-11.8	33	7	—	—	1.8	—	—	—	—	—	—	—
51-5010	Bookbinders and bindery workers	72	57	-15	-21.3	8	1	—	—	1.3	—	—	—	—	—	—	—
51-5011	Bindery workers	65	51	-14	-21.8	8	1	25,570	L	1.3	H	L	Short-term on-the-job training	HS/SC	70.4	22.6	7.1
51-5012	Bookbinders	7	6	-1	-16.9	1	0	30,260	L	1.2	H	L	Moderate-term on-the-job training	HS/SC	70.4	22.6	7.1
51-5020	Printers	317	286	-31	-9.7	24	6	—	—	1.9	—	—	—	—	—	—	—
51-5021	Job printers	48	44	-4	-9.3	2	0	32,410	H	3.3	H	L	Long-term on-the-job training	HS/SC	62.0	31.3	6.7
51-5022	Prepress technicians and workers	71	56	-15	-21.1	10	1	33,310	H	0.0	H	H	Postsecondary vocational award	HS/SC	45.8	38.3	15.9
51-5023	Printing machine operators	198	186	-11	-5.7	12	4	30,990	H	2.2	H	VL	Moderate-term on-the-job training	HS/SC	66.2	28.4	5.5
51-6000	Textile, apparel, and furnishings occupations	873	777	-97	-11.1	117	17	—	—	11.8	—	—	—	—	—	—	—
51-6011	Laundry and dry-cleaning workers	239	262	23	9.7	39	8	17,850	VL	8.0	H	H	Moderate-term on-the-job training	HS	79.1	15.7	5.2
51-6021	Pressers, textile, garment, and related materials	77	74	-3	-4.4	10	1	17,800	VL	2.9	H	H	Short-term on-the-job training	HS	87.9	9.3	2.8
51-6031	Sewing machine operators	233	170	-63	-27.2	36	2	18,810	VL	7.6	VH	L	Moderate-term on-the-job training	HS	82.3	13.2	4.5
51-6040	Shoe and leather workers	20	17	-3	-15.6	3	0	—	—	41.5	—	—	—	—	—	—	—
51-6041	Shoe and leather workers and repairers[1]	16	14	-2	-10.3	2	0	20,450	VL	52.4	VL	VL	Long-term on-the-job training	HS	78.9	0.0	0.0
51-6042	Shoe machine operators and tenders[1]	4	3	-1	-35.8	1	0	21,910	L	0.0	VH	L	Moderate-term on-the-job training	HS	82.0	0.0	0.0
51-6050	Tailors, dressmakers, and sewers	77	76	-2	-2.4	12	1	—	—	48.7	—	—	—	—	—	—	—
51-6051	Sewers, hand	23	21	-3	-12.2	3	0	20,370	VL	58.4	H	H	Short-term on-the-job training	HS/SC	62.2	23.8	14.1
51-6052	Tailors, dressmakers, and custom sewers	54	55	1	1.9	9	1	22,910	L	44.5	H	H	Long-term on-the-job training	HS/SC	62.2	23.8	14.1
51-6060	Textile machine setters, operators, and tenders	122	88	-34	-27.9	10	3	—	—	1.9	—	—	—	—	—	—	—
51-6061	Textile bleaching and dyeing machine operators and tenders[1]	19	14	-6	-30.2	2	0	23,290	L	0.0	VH	VL	Moderate-term on-the-job training	HS	83.5	11.8	0.0
51-6062	Textile cutting machine setters, operators, and tenders[1]	19	14	-5	-27.4	2	1	21,620	L	0.0	H	L	Moderate-term on-the-job training	HS	83.5	11.8	0.0
51-6063	Textile knitting and weaving machine setters, operators, and tenders	40	28	-12	-30.9	2	1	24,290	L	5.8	VH	L	Long-term on-the-job training	HS	83.9	14.0	0.0

See footnotes at end of table.

Table III–1. Occupational employment and job openings data, 2006–16, and worker characteristics, 2006 — Continued
(Numbers in thousands)

Code	2006 National Employment Matrix occupation and code	Employment		Employment change, 2006–16		Annual average job openings due to growth and total replacement needs, 2006–16	Annual average job openings due to growth and net replacement needs, 2006–16	2006 median annual wages		Percent self-employed, 2006	Unemployment rate	Percent part-time	Most significant source of postsecondary education or training[2]	Educational attainment cluster[3]	Percent of workers aged 25 to 44, by educational attainment[4]		
		2006	2016	Numeric	Percent			Dollars	Rank						High school or less	Some college	College or higher
51-6064	Textile winding, twisting, and drawing out machine setters, operators, and tenders	43	33	-11	-24.3	4	1	23,050	L	0.0	VH	VL	Moderate-term on-the-job training	HS	80.7	18.6	0.0
51-6090	Miscellaneous textile, apparel, and furnishings workers	106	92	-14	-13.5	7	2	—	—	14.9	—	—	—	—	—	—	—
51-6091	Extruding and forming machine setters, operators, and tenders, synthetic and glass fibers[1]	18	15	-3	-17.6	1	0	28,670	L	0.0	H	L	Moderate-term on-the-job training	HS	75.3	14.5	10.1
51-6092	Fabric and apparel patternmakers[1]	9	7	-3	-28.6	1	0	32,730	H	6.1	L	L	Long-term on-the-job training	HS	75.3	14.5	10.1
51-6093	Upholsterers	55	50	-5	-9.0	3	1	27,230	L	25.5	L	L	Long-term on-the-job training	HS	77.4	19.1	0.0
51-6099	Textile, apparel, and furnishings workers, all other	24	21	-4	-14.8	3	1	22,950	L	5.2	VH	L	Short-term on-the-job training	HS	75.3	14.5	10.1
51-7000	Woodworkers	370	380	11	2.9	40	11	—	—	11.9	—	—	—	—	—	—	—
51-7011	Cabinetmakers and bench carpenters	149	153	4	2.8	10	5	27,010	L	14.0	L	VL	Long-term on-the-job training	HS/SC	71.7	24.2	4.1
51-7021	Furniture finishers	31	30	-1	-3.1	10	1	25,010	L	20.3	H	L	Long-term on-the-job training	HS/SC	71.8	22.9	0.0
51-7030	Model makers and patternmakers, wood	4	2	-2	-40.3	0	0	—	—	0.0	—	—	—	—	—	—	—
51-7031	Model makers, wood[1]	2	1	-1	-40.8	0	0	28,470	L	0.0	L	L	Long-term on-the-job training	HS/SC	68.5	21.3	10.2
51-7032	Patternmakers, wood[1]	2	1	-1	-39.9	0	0	31,510	H	0.0	L	L	Long-term on-the-job training	HS/SC	68.5	21.3	10.2
51-7040	Woodworking machine setters, operators, and tenders	165	173	9	5.4	18	5	—	—	4.8	—	—	—	—	—	—	—
51-7041	Sawing machine setters, operators, and tenders, wood	65	68	2	3.8	6	2	24,280	L	8.0	VH	VL	Moderate-term on-the-job training	HS	84.0	14.1	0.0
51-7042	Woodworking machine setters, operators, and tenders, except sawing	100	106	6	6.4	12	3	23,940	L	2.7	VH	VL	Moderate-term on-the-job training	HS	81.9	15.3	0.0
51-7099	Woodworkers, all other	20	21	0	1.6	2	0	22,580	L	43.0	L	L	Moderate-term on-the-job training	HS/SC	68.5	21.3	10.2
51-8000	Plant and system operators	325	327	2	.7	27	10	—	—	.5	—	—	—	—	—	—	—
51-8010	Power plant operators, distributors, and dispatchers	47	48	1	2.0	2	2	—	—	0.0	—	—	—	—	—	—	—
51-8011	Nuclear power reactor operators	4	4	0	10.6	0	0	69,370	VH	0.0	VL	VL	Long-term on-the-job training	HS/SC/C	36.1	43.6	20.4
51-8012	Power distributors and dispatchers	9	8	0	-4.9	0	0	62,590	VH	0.0	VL	VL	Long-term on-the-job training	HS/SC/C	36.1	43.6	20.4
51-8013	Power plant operators	35	36	1	2.7	2	1	55,000	VH	0.0	VL	VL	Long-term on-the-job training	HS/SC/C	36.1	43.6	20.4
51-8021	Stationary engineers and boiler operators	45	47	2	3.4	2	1	46,040	H	0.0	L	VL	Long-term on-the-job training	HS/SC	55.9	34.0	10.1
51-8031	Water and liquid waste treatment plant and system operators	111	126	15	13.8	10	3	36,070	H	1.3	VL	VL	Long-term on-the-job training	HS/SC	51.7	40.6	7.8
51-8090	Miscellaneous plant and system operators	122	106	-15	-12.6	13	3	—	—	.1	—	—	—	—	—	—	—
51-8091	Chemical plant and system operators	53	45	-8	-15.3	6	1	49,080	VH	.1	VL	VL	Long-term on-the-job training	HS/SC	52.2	41.1	6.7
51-8092	Gas plant operators	12	11	-1	-9.9	1	0	53,670	VH	.1	VL	VL	Long-term on-the-job training	HS/SC	52.2	41.1	6.7
51-8093	Petroleum pump system operators, refinery operators, and gaugers	42	36	-6	-13.4	4	1	52,380	VH	.1	VL	VL	Long-term on-the-job training	HS/SC	52.2	41.1	6.7
51-8099	Plant and system operators, all other	14	14	0	-2.5	2	0	46,270	H	.1	VL	VL	Long-term on-the-job training	HS/SC	52.2	41.1	6.7

See footnotes at end of table.

Table III–1. Occupational employment and job openings data, 2006–16, and worker characteristics, 2006 — Continued
(Numbers in thousands)

Code	2006 National Employment Matrix occupation and code	Employment 2006	Employment 2016	Employment change, 2006–16 Numeric	Employment change, 2006–16 Percent	Annual average job openings due to growth and total replacement needs, 2006–16	Annual average job openings due to growth and net replacement needs, 2006–16	2006 median annual wages Dollars	2006 median annual wages Rank	Percent self-employed, 2006	Unemployment rate	Percent part-time	Most significant source of postsecondary education or training[2]	Educational attainment cluster[3]	Percent of workers aged 25 to 44, by educational attainment[4]: High school or less	Some college	College or higher
51-9000	Other production occupations	2,981	2,822	-159	-5.3	370	62	—	—	3.0	—	—	—	—	—	—	—
51-9010	Chemical processing machine setters, operators, and tenders	97	94	-3	-3.6	3	2	—	—	1.0	—	—	—	—	—	—	—
51-9011	Chemical equipment operators and tenders	53	51	-2	-3.9	1	1	40,290	H	1.1	VL	VL	Moderate-term on-the-job training	HS/SC	52.8	33.1	14.1
51-9012	Separating, filtering, clarifying, precipitating, and still machine setters, operators, and tenders	44	43	-1	-3.2	1	1	34,970	H	1.0	VL	VL	Moderate-term on-the-job training	HS/SC	52.8	33.1	14.1
51-9020	Crushing, grinding, polishing, mixing, and blending workers	230	215	-16	-6.8	30	4	—	—	.8	—	—	—	—	—	—	—
51-9021	Crushing, grinding, and polishing machine setters, operators, and tenders	42	37	-5	-11.9	5	1	28,080	L	.9	H	VL	Moderate-term on-the-job training	HS/SC	75.2	20.4	4.4
51-9022	Grinding and polishing workers, hand	45	42	-3	-7.1	6	1	23,880	L	.9	H	VL	Moderate-term on-the-job training	HS/SC	75.2	20.4	4.4
51-9023	Mixing and blending machine setters, operators, and tenders	143	136	-7	-5.1	19	2	29,330	L	.8	H	VL	Moderate-term on-the-job training	HS/SC	75.2	20.4	4.4
51-9030	Cutting workers	107	98	-9	-8.4	5	2	—	—	1.6	—	—	—	—	—	—	—
51-9031	Cutters and trimmers, hand	29	27	-2	-6.0	1	0	22,330	L	1.7	VH	L	Short-term on-the-job training	HS	80.7	16.0	3.3
51-9032	Cutting and slicing machine setters, operators, and tenders	79	71	-7	-9.3	4	1	27,930	L	1.6	VH	L	Moderate-term on-the-job training	HS	80.7	16.0	3.3
51-9041	Extruding, forming, pressing, and compacting machine setters, operators, and tenders	81	75	-7	-8.0	8	1	27,710	L	.5	VH	VL	Moderate-term on-the-job training	HS/SC	75.8	21.4	0.0
51-9051	Furnace, kiln, oven, drier, and kettle operators and tenders	32	29	-3	-8.7	2	1	30,320	L	14.9	VH	VL	Moderate-term on-the-job training	HS/SC	59.4	33.8	0.0
51-9061	Inspectors, testers, sorters, samplers, and weighers	491	457	-35	-7.0	75	7	29,420	L	1.5	H	VL	Moderate-term on-the-job training	HS/SC	53.4	33.1	13.5
51-9071	Jewelers and precious stone and metal workers	52	51	-1	-2.2	7	1	29,750	L	50.6	L	L	Postsecondary vocational award	HS/SC	52.6	31.1	16.3
51-9080	Medical, dental, and ophthalmic laboratory technicians	95	100	5	5.3	6	2	—	—	9.2	—	—	—	—	—	—	—
51-9081	Dental laboratory technicians	53	55	2	3.7	3	1	32,580	H	13.3	L	L	Long-term on-the-job training	HS/SC	42.5	46.0	11.5
51-9082	Medical appliance technicians	12	13	1	9.4	1	0	31,180	H	13.3	L	L	Long-term on-the-job training	HS/SC	42.5	46.0	11.5
51-9083	Ophthalmic laboratory technicians	29	31	2	6.6	2	1	25,460	L	0.0	L	L	Moderate-term on-the-job training	HS/SC	42.5	46.0	11.5
51-9111	Packaging and filling machine operators and tenders	386	365	-21	-5.4	80	7	22,990	L	.2	VH	VL	Short-term on-the-job training	HS	80.0	15.4	4.6
51-9120	Painting workers	192	184	-8	-4.2	10	4	—	—	3.8	—	—	—	—	—	—	—
51-9121	Coating, painting, and spraying machine setters, operators, and tenders	106	93	-14	-12.9	5	2	26,830	L	3.8	H	VL	Moderate-term on-the-job training	HS/SC	75.4	20.8	3.8
51-9122	Painters, transportation equipment	54	59	5	8.4	3	2	35,680	H	3.8	H	VL	Moderate-term on-the-job training	HS/SC	75.4	20.8	3.8
51-9123	Painting, coating, and decorating workers	31	32	1	3.6	2	1	22,970	L	3.7	H	VL	Short-term on-the-job training	HS/SC	75.4	20.8	3.8
51-9130	Photographic process workers and processing machine operators	73	40	-33	-45.4	8	3	—	—	.7	—	—	—	—	—	—	—

See footnotes at end of table.

Table III–1. Occupational employment and job openings data, 2006–16, and worker characteristics, 2006 — Continued
(Numbers in thousands)

2006 National Employment Matrix occupation and code		Employment		Employment change, 2006–16		Annual average job openings due to growth and total replacement needs, 2006–16	Annual average job openings due to growth and net replacement needs, 2006–16	2006 median annual wages		Percent self-employed, 2006	Unemployment rate	Percent part-time	Most significant source of postsecondary education or training[2]	Educational attainment cluster[3]	Percent of workers aged 25 to 44, by educational attainment[4]		
		2006	2016	Numeric	Percent			Dollars	Rank						High school or less	Some college	College or higher
51-9131	Photographic process workers	24	15	-9	-36.3	3	1	23,280	L	.7	VH	H	Moderate-term on-the-job training	HS/SC	42.2	39.4	18.5
51-9132	Photographic processing machine operators	49	25	-25	-49.8	5	2	19,500	VL	.6	VH	H	Short-term on-the-job training	HS/SC	42.2	39.4	18.5
51-9141	Semiconductor processors[1]	42	37	-5	-12.9	6	1	32,860	H	0.0	VH	VL	Associate degree	HS/SC	71.9	23.3	4.8
51-9190	Miscellaneous production workers	1,102	1,078	-23	-2.1	131	27	—	—	2.6	—	—	—	—	—	—	—
51-9191	Cementing and gluing machine operators and tenders[1]	23	21	-2	-9.2	4	1	25,170	L	0.0	H	L	Moderate-term on-the-job training	HS	79.2	19.2	0.0
51-9192	Cleaning, washing, and metal pickling equipment operators and tenders[1]	16	14	-2	-9.8	3	0	22,850	L	0.0	VH	VL	Moderate-term on-the-job training	HS/SC	68.5	30.1	0.0
51-9193	Cooling and freezing equipment operators and tenders[1]	11	10	-1	-6.8	2	0	23,880	L	0.0	VH	VL	Moderate-term on-the-job training	HS/SC	71.9	23.3	4.8
51-9194	Etchers and engravers[1]	14	13	-1	-4.8	2	0	25,590	L	16.9	H	H	Long-term on-the-job training	HS/SC	58.6	24.2	0.0
51-9195	Molders, shapers, and casters, except metal and plastic[1]	56	57	1	1.3	6	1	25,010	L	24.2	H	L	Moderate-term on-the-job training	HS/SC	69.1	20.8	10.1
51-9196	Paper goods machine setters, operators, and tenders	113	93	-21	-18.2	8	3	31,490	H	0.0	H	VL	Moderate-term on-the-job training	HS/SC	71.8	23.9	0.0
51-9197	Tire builders[1]	23	20	-3	-12.0	4	1	38,120	H	0.0	VL	VL	Moderate-term on-the-job training	HS/SC	71.2	26.9	0.0
51-9198	Helpers--Production workers	542	539	-3	-.5	49	13	20,740	VL	.2	VH	H	Short-term on-the-job training	HS	80.8	15.2	4.0
51-9199	Production workers, all other	305	312	7	2.3	54	7	24,890	L	3.8	VH	VL	Moderate-term on-the-job training	HS/SC	71.9	23.3	4.8
53-0000	**Transportation and material moving occupations**	**10,233**	**10,695**	**462**	**4.5**	**1,928**	**295**	—	—	**4.7**	—	—	—	—	—	—	—
53-1000	Supervisors, transportation and material moving workers	414	461	47	11.4	31	13	—	—	1.5	—	—	—	—	—	—	—
53-1011	Aircraft cargo handling supervisors	6	7	1	23.3	1	0	39,840	H	2.0	L	VL	Work experience in a related occupation	HS/SC	46.6	36.5	16.9
53-1021	First-line supervisors/managers of helpers, laborers, and material movers, hand	182	205	23	12.5	14	6	39,570	H	1.4	L	VL	Work experience in a related occupation	HS/SC	46.6	36.5	16.9
53-1031	First-line supervisors/managers of transportation and material-moving machine and vehicle operators	226	249	23	10.2	17	7	48,330	VH	1.5	L	VL	Work experience in a related occupation	HS/SC	46.6	36.5	16.9
53-2000	Air transportation occupations	137	154	17	12.4	7	6	—	—	1.8	—	—	—	—	—	—	—
53-2010	Aircraft pilots and flight engineers	107	121	14	13.0	5	5	—	—	2.3	—	—	—	—	—	—	—
53-2011	Airline pilots, copilots, and flight engineers	79	90	10	12.9	4	3	141,090	VH	2.5	VL	L	Bachelor's degree	SC/C	5.9	20.5	73.6
53-2012	Commercial pilots	28	31	4	13.2	1	1	57,480	VH	1.9	VL	L	Postsecondary vocational award	SC/C	5.9	20.5	73.6
53-2020	Air traffic controllers and airfield operations specialists	30	33	3	10.5	1	1	—	—	0.0	—	—	—	—	—	—	—
53-2021	Air traffic controllers[1]	25	28	3	10.2	1	1	117,240	VH	0.0	L	VL	Long-term on-the-job training	SC/C	12.8	54.8	32.4
53-2022	Airfield operations specialists[1]	5	5	1	11.8	0	0	37,630	H	0.0	L	VL	Long-term on-the-job training	SC/C	12.8	54.8	32.4
53-3000	Motor vehicle operators	4,335	4,704	368	8.5	637	112	—	—	8.8	—	—	—	—	—	—	—
53-3011	Ambulance drivers and attendants, except emergency medical technicians[1]	22	26	5	21.7	4	1	20,370	VL	.1	VL	H	Moderate-term on-the-job training	HS/SC	53.2	38.2	0.0
53-3020	Bus drivers	653	721	67	10.3	87	15	—	—	1.4	—	—	—	—	—	—	—

See footnotes at end of table.

Table III–1. Occupational employment and job openings data, 2006–16, and worker characteristics, 2006 — Continued
(Numbers in thousands)

Code	2006 National Employment Matrix occupation and code	Employment		Employment change, 2006–16		Annual average job openings due to growth and total replacement needs, 2006–16	Annual average job openings due to growth and net replacement needs, 2006–16	2006 median annual wages		Percent self-employed, 2006	Unemployment rate	Percent part-time	Most significant source of postsecondary education or training[2]	Educational attainment cluster[3]	Percent of workers aged 25 to 44, by educational attainment[4]		
		2006	2016	Numeric	Percent			Dollars	Rank						High school or less	Some college	College or higher
53-3021	Bus drivers, transit and intercity	198	223	25	12.5	27	5	32,090	H	1.3	L	VH	Moderate-term on-the-job training	HS/SC	60.8	34.9	4.3
53-3022	Bus drivers, school	455	497	42	9.3	60	10	24,820	L	1.4	L	VH	Moderate-term on-the-job training	HS/SC	60.8	34.9	4.3
53-3030	Driver/sales workers and truck drivers	3,356	3,614	258	7.7	491	88	—	—	9.0	—	—	—	—	—	—	—
53-3031	Driver/sales workers	445	421	-24	-5.3	58	8	20,770	VL	9.5	H	L	Short-term on-the-job training	HS/SC	70.7	25.2	4.1
53-3032	Truck drivers, heavy and tractor-trailer	1,860	2,053	193	10.4	279	52	35,040	H	8.8	H	L	Moderate-term on-the-job training	HS/SC	70.7	25.2	4.1
53-3033	Truck drivers, light or delivery services	1,051	1,140	89	8.4	154	28	25,300	L	9.3	H	L	Short-term on-the-job training	HS/SC	70.7	25.2	4.1
53-3041	Taxi drivers and chauffeurs	229	258	30	13.0	36	6	20,350	VL	29.5	H	H	Short-term on-the-job training	HS/SC	57.4	27.4	15.2
53-3099	Motor vehicle operators, all other	76	85	9	11.4	19	2	22,710	L	1.9	H	VH	Short-term on-the-job training	HS/SC	70.2	23.5	0.0
53-4000	Rail transportation occupations	125	127	2	1.4	9	5	—	—	0.0	—	—	—	—	—	—	—
53-4010	Locomotive engineers and operators	47	48	1	2.9	4	2	54,150	VH	0.0	VL	VL	Moderate-term on-the-job training	HS/SC	48.7	42.4	8.9
53-4021	Railroad brake, signal, and switch operators[1]	25	22	-3	-11.4	2	1	48,860	VH	0.0	L	VL	Moderate-term on-the-job training	HS/SC	44.9	49.8	0.0
53-4031	Railroad conductors and yardmasters[1]	40	44	4	9.1	3	2	55,530	VH	0.0	VL	VL	Moderate-term on-the-job training	HS/SC	37.7	51.7	10.6
53-4041	Subway and streetcar operators[1]	7	8	1	12.1	1	0	48,980	VH	0.0	L	VL	Moderate-term on-the-job training	HS/SC	40.4	49.1	0.0
53-4099	Rail transportation workers, all other[1]	7	6	-1	-18.7	0	0	39,150	H	0.0	L	VL	Moderate-term on-the-job training	HS/SC	40.4	49.1	0.0
53-5000	Water transportation occupations	84	98	14	16.1	13	4	—	—	3.1	—	—	—	—	—	—	—
53-5011	Sailors and marine oilers[1]	33	38	5	15.7	9	2	30,630	H	.1	VH	VL	Short-term on-the-job training	HS/SC	56.7	26.1	17.2
53-5020	Ship and boat captains and operators	37	43	6	17.3	3	2	—	—	7.0	—	—	—	—	—	—	—
53-5021	Captains, mates, and pilots of water vessels	34	40	6	17.9	3	1	53,430	VH	6.8	H	VL	Work experience in a related occupation	HS/SC/C	54.9	24.2	20.9
53-5022	Motorboat operators	3	3	0	10.9	0	0	32,350	H	9.1	H	VL	Moderate-term on-the-job training	HS/SC/C	54.9	24.2	20.9
53-5031	Ship engineers[1]	15	17	2	14.1	1	1	54,820	VH	0.0	VH	VL	Work experience in a related occupation	HS/SC	56.7	26.1	17.2
53-6000	Other transportation workers	312	351	39	12.6	76	14	—	—	1.6	—	—	—	—	—	—	—
53-6011	Bridge and lock tenders[1]	4	4	0	-3.2	0	0	39,010	H	0.0	L	VL	Short-term on-the-job training	HS/SC	49.8	42.7	7.4
53-6021	Parking lot attendants	135	152	16	12.1	44	5	17,320	VL	1.6	H	VH	Short-term on-the-job training	HS/SC	56.7	29.7	13.6
53-6031	Service station attendants	96	108	12	12.6	27	6	17,750	VL	.5	VH	H	Short-term on-the-job training	HS/SC	67.5	26.3	6.1
53-6041	Traffic technicians	7	8	1	9.9	0	0	37,140	H	1.5	L	VL	Short-term on-the-job training	HS/SC	49.8	42.7	7.4
53-6051	Transportation inspectors	26	31	4	16.4	2	1	50,390	VH	5.9	L	VL	Work experience in a related occupation	HS/SC	45.0	40.2	14.8
53-6099	Transportation workers, all other	44	49	6	13.3	2	1	30,180	L	1.9	L	VL	Short-term on-the-job training	HS/SC	49.8	42.7	7.4
53-7000	Material moving occupations	4,825	4,800	-25	-.5	1,155	142	—	—	1.7	—	—	—	—	—	—	—
53-7011	Conveyor operators and tenders[1]	50	46	-4	-7.3	6	1	27,220	L	0.0	H	VL	Short-term on-the-job training	HS/SC	64.3	32.3	0.0
53-7021	Crane and tower operators	46	48	1	2.8	3	1	39,040	H	.4	H	VL	Long-term on-the-job training	HS/SC	71.6	26.2	0.0
53-7030	Dredge, excavating, and loading machine operators	85	92	7	8.1	7	2	—	—	15.1	—	—	—	—	—	—	—
53-7031	Dredge operators	2	2	0	6.7	0	0	33,820	H	16.4	H	VL	Moderate-term on-the-job training	HS	78.8	17.7	3.5
53-7032	Excavating and loading machine and dragline operators	80	87	7	8.3	7	2	32,930	H	14.9	H	VL	Moderate-term on-the-job training	HS	78.8	17.7	3.5
53-7033	Loading machine operators, underground mining	3	3	0	4.5	0	0	37,250	H	19.4	H	VL	Moderate-term on-the-job training	HS	78.8	17.7	3.5

See footnotes at end of table.

Table III-1. Occupational employment and job openings data, 2006–16, and worker characteristics, 2006 — Continued
(Numbers in thousands)

2006 National Employment Matrix occupation and code		Employment		Employment change, 2006–16		Annual average job openings due to growth and total replacement needs, 2006–16	Annual average job openings due to growth and net replacement needs, 2006–16	2006 median annual wages		Percent self-employed, 2006	Unemployment rate	Percent part-time	Most significant source of postsecondary education or training[2]	Educational attainment cluster[3]	Percent of workers aged 25 to 44, by educational attainment[4]		
		2006	2016	Numeric	Percent			Dollars	Rank						High school or less	Some college	College or higher
53-7041	Hoist and winch operators[1]	3	3	0	-1.2	0	0	33,620	H	0.0	VH	VL	Moderate-term on-the-job training	HS/SC	64.3	32.3	0.0
53-7051	Industrial truck and tractor operators	637	624	-13	-2.0	90	16	27,270	L	.3	VH	VL	Short-term on-the-job training	HS	79.0	19.3	1.8
53-7060	Laborers and material movers, hand	3,766	3,741	-25	-.7	997	114	—	—	1.5	—	—	—	—	—	—	—
53-7061	Cleaners of vehicles and equipment	368	420	52	14.0	132	19	18,060	VL	7.4	VH	H	Short-term on-the-job training	HS	82.8	14.8	2.5
53-7062	Laborers and freight, stock, and material movers, hand	2,416	2,466	50	2.1	630	82	21,220	VL	1.1	VH	H	Short-term on-the-job training	HS/SC	71.6	23.8	4.5
53-7063	Machine feeders and offbearers	148	125	-22	-15.2	24	3	22,640	L	0.0	H	L	Short-term on-the-job training	HS/SC	72.6	23.9	0.0
53-7064	Packers and packagers, hand	834	730	-104	-12.4	211	10	17,650	VL	.4	VH	L	Short-term on-the-job training	HS	83.1	14.1	2.9
53-7070	Pumping station operators	29	25	-4	-12.9	5	1	—	—	2.6	—	—	—	—	—	—	—
53-7071	Gas compressor and gas pumping station operators	4	3	-1	-17.5	1	0	45,400	H	3.5	VL	VL	Moderate-term on-the-job training	HS/SC	73.2	25.2	0.0
53-7072	Pump operators, except wellhead pumpers	11	9	-1	-12.5	2	0	39,800	H	2.9	VL	VL	Moderate-term on-the-job training	HS/SC	73.2	25.2	0.0
53-7073	Wellhead pumpers	14	13	-2	-11.9	3	1	36,150	H	2.2	VL	VL	Moderate-term on-the-job training	HS/SC	73.2	25.2	0.0
53-7081	Refuse and recyclable material collectors	136	146	10	7.4	38	5	28,970	L	6.1	VH	L	Short-term on-the-job training	HS	77.1	19.7	3.1
53-7111	Shuttle car operators[1]	3	3	0	-8.3	0	0	39,060	H	0.0	H	VL	Short-term on-the-job training	HS/SC	70.4	24.1	5.5
53-7121	Tank car, truck, and ship loaders[1]	16	18	2	9.2	5	0	31,970	H	0.0	VH	VL	Moderate-term on-the-job training	HS/SC	70.4	24.1	5.5
53-7199	Material moving workers, all other	54	54	0	.7	4	1	30,270	L	.9	H	VL	Moderate-term on-the-job training	HS/SC	70.4	24.1	5.5

[1] One or more Current Population Survey (CPS) proxy occupations are used to estimate CPS-based data.
[2] An occupation is placed into one of 11 categories that best describes the postsecondary education or training needed by most workers to become fully qualified in the occupation.
[3] The job types are presented in the following categories: HS = high school occupations, HS/SC = high school/some college occupations, SC = some college occupations, HS/SC/C = high school/some college/college occupations, SC/C = some college/college occ
[4] Based on the average of 2005-06 American Community Survey data for those who responded as currently employed and had a valid occupation code.
NOTE: Codes for describing the ranked variables are: NH = Very high, H = High, L = Low, and VL = Very low. A dash indicates data are not applicable. Quartile ranking data ranges are available at http://www.bls.gov/emp/empqrank.htm.

See footnotes at end of table.

Table III-2. Employment for occupations excluded in the public National Employment Matrix and the corresponding line item, 2006
(Numbers in thousands)

2006 National Employment Matrix occupation code and title		Occupation type	2006 employment
25-1000	Postsecondary teachers	Line item	1,672
25-1011	Business teachers, postsecondary	Exclude	82
25-1021	Computer science teachers, postsecondary	Exclude	44
25-1022	Mathematical science teachers, postsecondary	Exclude	54
25-1031	Architecture teachers, postsecondary	Exclude	7
25-1032	Engineering teachers, postsecondary	Exclude	40
25-1041	Agricultural sciences teachers, postsecondary	Exclude	13
25-1042	Biological science teachers, postsecondary	Exclude	65
25-1043	Forestry and conservation science teachers, postsecondary	Exclude	3
25-1051	Atmospheric, earth, marine, and space sciences teachers, postsecondary	Exclude	11
25-1052	Chemistry teachers, postsecondary	Exclude	24
25-1053	Environmental science teachers, postsecondary	Exclude	5
25-1054	Physics teachers, postsecondary	Exclude	15
25-1061	Anthropology and archeology teachers, postsecondary	Exclude	6
25-1062	Area, ethnic, and cultural studies teachers, postsecondary	Exclude	9
25-1063	Economics teachers, postsecondary	Exclude	15
25-1064	Geography teachers, postsecondary	Exclude	5
25-1065	Political science teachers, postsecondary	Exclude	17
25-1066	Psychology teachers, postsecondary	Exclude	37
25-1067	Sociology teachers, postsecondary	Exclude	20
25-1069	Social sciences teachers, postsecondary, all other	Exclude	7
25-1071	Health specialties teachers, postsecondary	Exclude	145
25-1072	Nursing instructors and teachers, postsecondary	Exclude	46
25-1081	Education teachers, postsecondary	Exclude	67
25-1082	Library science teachers, postsecondary	Exclude	5
25-1111	Criminal justice and law enforcement teachers, postsecondary	Exclude	12
25-1112	Law teachers, postsecondary	Exclude	15
25-1113	Social work teachers, postsecondary	Exclude	10
25-1121	Art, drama, and music teachers, postsecondary	Exclude	88
25-1122	Communications teachers, postsecondary	Exclude	29
25-1123	English language and literature teachers, postsecondary	Exclude	72
25-1124	Foreignlanguage and literature teachers, postsecondary	Exclude	30
25-1125	History teachers, postsecondary	Exclude	26
25-1126	Philosophy and religion teachers, postsecondary	Exclude	25
25-1191	Graduate teaching assistants	Exclude	144
25-1192	Home economics teachers, postsecondary	Exclude	5
25-1193	Recreation and fitness studies teachers, postsecondary	Exclude	20
25-1194	Vocational education teachers, postsecondary	Exclude	119
25-1199	All other postsecondary teachers	Exclude	333
29-1060	Physicians and surgeons	Line item	633
29-1061	Anesthesiologists	Exclude	35
29-1062	Family and general practitioners	Exclude	133
29-1063	Internists, general	Exclude	60
29-1064	Obstetricians and gynecologists	Exclude	27
29-1065	Pediatricians, general	Exclude	35
29-1066	Psychiatrists	Exclude	30
29-1067	Surgeons	Exclude	64
29-1069	Physicians and surgeons, all other	Exclude	250
39-3099	Entertainment attendants and related workers, all other	Exclude	44
45-1000	Supervisors, farming, fishing, and forestry workers	Line item	53
45-1011	First-line supervisors/managers of farming, fishing, and forestry workers	Exclude	52
45-1012	Farm labor contractors	Exclude	1
53-4010	Locomotive engineers and operators	Line item	47
53-4011	Locomotive engineers	Exclude	40
53-4012	Locomotive firers	Exclude	1
53-4013	Rail yard engineers, dinkey operators, and hostlers	Exclude	6

Chapter IV. Factors Affecting Industry Employment and Occupational Utilization, 2006–16

Occupational employment may change over time, for several reasons. For example, an occupation's employment could increase because of growing demand for goods and services produced by industries in which the employment is concentrated. Alternatively, increases in the utilization of an occupation in those industries could boost the occupation's overall employment. This chapter presents information about both categories of factors—those affecting industry employment and occupational utilization within industries—that drive changes in occupational employment.

Industry employment

Many assumptions underlie the Bureau of Labor Statistics (BLS) projections of the aggregate economy and of industry output, productivity, and employment. Often, these assumptions bear specifically on macroeconomic factors, such as the aggregate unemployment rate, the anticipated time path of labor productivity, and expectations regarding the Federal budget surplus or deficit. Other assumptions deal with factors that affect industry-specific measures of economic activity.

Detailed industry employment projections are based largely on time-series models, which, by their very nature, project future economic behavior on the basis of a continuation of economic relationships that held in the past. For the most part, the determinants of industry employment are expressed both in the structure of the models' equations and as adjustments imposed on the specific equations to ensure that the models are indeed making a smooth transition from actual historical data to projected results. However, one of the most important steps associated with the preparation of the BLS projections is a detailed review of the results by analysts who have studied recent economic trends in specific industries. In some cases, the results of the aggregate and industry models are modified because of the analysts' judgment that historical relationships need to be redefined in some manner.

As discussed in chapter II, the 2002–12 projections were the first to incorporate the 2002 North American Industry Classification System (NAICS). Table IV–1 presents historical and projected information about employment and output for aggregate and detailed industries. Industry sector employment projections prepared in the Division of Industry Employment Projections (DIEP) used a comprehensive modeling technique that estimates output as well as employment. More detailed industry employment projections based on historical time series information are included in the matrix and are consistent with their parent industry sector; however, projections of output were not developed for these industries. Specific factors that underlie the projections of industry employment for DIEP sectors are presented in table IV–2 to allow the user to better understand the rationale behind projected changes in industry employment and output.

Occupational utilization

BLS projections of wage and salary employment are developed within the framework of an industry-occupation matrix, which shows the occupational distribution in each industry—the proportion of each industry's employment which each occupation comprises. Historical data indicate that the occupational distribution within industries shifts over time as the utilization of some occupations changes relative to that of other occupations.

Among the various factors that can affect the utilization of workers in an occupation in particular industries are technology, business practices, the mix of goods and services produced, the size of business establishments, and offshore outsourcing to lower-wage foreign countries. BLS staff analyze each occupation in the matrix to identify the factors that are likely to cause an increase or decrease in utilization of the occupation within a particular industry in the future. The analyses incorporate judgments about new trends that may influence occupational utilization, such as the use of the Internet and electronic commerce. Table IV–3 contains brief descriptions of the factors underlying changes in occupational utilization within industries projected to occur between 2006 and 2016. Occupations appear in order by Standard Occupational Classification code. Although all detailed occupations were analyzed, utilization of many occupations was projected to remain unchanged. These occupations are not included in the table. In addition, factors are discussed only for those industries with the highest share of an occupation's employment.

In developing the projections, BLS staff made hundreds of analytical judgments of the kind set forth in the preceding paragraph. To maintain consistency among analysts, guidelines for changing the proportion of an industry's employment which an occupation comprises were established as follows: small change = ±10 percent; moderate change = ±20 percent; large change = ±35 percent; very large change = ±50 percent.

Table IV–1. Employment and output by industry, 1996, 2006, and projected 2016

2002 NAICS coverage	Industry title	Employment: Thousands of jobs 1996	Employment: Thousands of jobs 2006	Employment: Thousands of jobs 2016	Employment: Change 1996–2006	Employment: Change 2006–2016	Employment: Average annual rate of change 1996–2006	Employment: Average annual rate of change 2006–2016	Output: Billions of chained 2000 dollars 1996	Output: Billions of chained 2000 dollars 2006	Output: Billions of chained 2000 dollars 2016	Output: Average annual rate of change 1996–2006	Output: Average annual rate of change 2006–2016
N.A.	Nonagriculture wage and salary[1]	120,371	136,912	151,962	16,541	15,050	1.3	1.0	14,880	19,998	26,757	3.0	3.0
210000	Mining	556	619	609	62	-10	1.1	-.2	213	242	269	1.3	1.0
211000	Oil and gas extraction	147	136	134	-11	-2	-.8	-.2	144	142	152	-.1	.7
212000	Mining, except oil and gas	249	221	231	-28	10	-1.2	.4	47	52	67	1.0	2.4
212100	Coal mining	91	79	79	-12	0	-1.4	0.0	21	23	27	1.1	1.4
212200	Metal ore mining	51	33	35	-18	3	-4.3	.8	9	8	11	-2.2	4.3
212300	Nonmetallic mineral mining and quarrying	108	110	116	1	7	.1	.6	17	21	27	2.4	2.2
213000	Support activities for mining	160	262	244	102	-17	5.0	-.7	24	46	52	6.5	1.2
220000	Utilities	640	549	518	-91	-31	-1.5	-.6	309	323	354	.5	.9
221100	Electric power generation, transmission and distribution	464	397	376	-67	-21	-1.5	-.5	230	266	303	1.5	1.3
221200	Natural gas distribution	137	106	87	-31	-19	-2.5	-1.9	74	52	45	-3.4	-1.3
221300	Water, sewage and other systems	39	46	54	7	9	1.6	1.7	7	7	10	1.2	2.7
230000	Construction	5,536	7,689	8,470	2,153	781	3.3	1.0	741	899	1,031	2.0	1.4
236000	Construction of buildings	1,380	1,806	2,031	426	225	2.7	1.2	-	-	-	-	-
236100	Residential building construction	663	1,018	1,140	354	123	4.4	1.1	-	-	-	-	-
236200	Nonresidential building construction	717	789	891	72	103	1.0	1.2	-	-	-	-	-
237000	Heavy and civil engineering construction	800	983	1,044	183	61	2.1	.6	-	-	-	-	-
237100	Utility system construction	317	426	454	108	29	3.0	.7	-	-	-	-	-
237130	Power and communication line and related structures construction	101	135	144	34	9	2.9	.6	-	-	-	-	-
237200	Land subdivision	81	97	96	16	-1	1.8	-.1	-	-	-	-	-
237300	Highway, street, and bridge construction	288	349	374	62	25	2.0	.7	-	-	-	-	-
237900	Other heavy and civil engineering construction	114	112	120	-3	8	-.2	.7	-	-	-	-	-
238000	Specialty trade contractors	3,355	4,900	5,394	1,544	495	3.9	1.0	-	-	-	-	-
238100	Foundation, structure, and building exterior contractors	755	1,132	1,269	376	137	4.1	1.1	-	-	-	-	-
238110	Poured concrete foundation and structure contractors	164	249	279	85	31	4.2	1.2	-	-	-	-	-
238140	Masonry contractors	171	258	285	87	27	4.2	1.0	-	-	-	-	-
238160	Roofing contractors	169	201	232	32	31	1.8	1.5	-	-	-	-	-
238200	Building equipment contractors	1,483	2,006	2,204	523	198	3.1	.9	-	-	-	-	-
238210	Electrical contractors	715	904	971	189	68	2.4	.7	-	-	-	-	-
238220	Plumbing, heating, and air-conditioning contractors	673	983	1,102	310	120	3.9	1.2	-	-	-	-	-
238290	Other building equipment contractors	95	120	130	25	11	2.4	.9	-	-	-	-	-
238300	Building finishing contractors	680	1,036	1,124	356	88	4.3	.8	-	-	-	-	-

See footnotes at end of table.

Table IV–1. Employment and output by industry, 1996, 2006, and projected 2016 — Continued

2002 NAICS coverage	Industry title	Employment: Thousands of jobs 1996	2006	2016	Change 1996–2006	2006–2016	Average annual rate of change 1996–2006	2006–2016	Output: Billions of chained 2000 dollars 1996	2006	2016	Average annual rate of change 1996–2006	2006–2016
238310	Drywall and insulation contractors	248	375	398	127	23	4.2	.6	-	-	-	-	-
238320	Painting and wall covering contractors	186	244	266	59	22	2.8	.9	-	-	-	-	-
238900	Other specialty trade contractors	437	726	799	289	72	5.2	1.0	-	-	-	-	-
31-33	Manufacturing	17,237	14,197	12,695	-3,039	-1,503	-1.9	-1.1	3,611	4,146	5,264	1.4	2.4
311000	Food manufacturing	1,562	1,484	1,489	-78	5	-.5	0.0	385	461	551	1.8	1.8
311100	Animal food manufacturing	56	50	43	-6	-8	-1.0	-1.7	20	26	35	2.8	3.0
311200	Grain and oilseed milling	69	61	51	-9	-9	-1.3	-1.6	38	43	52	1.2	1.8
311300	Sugar and confectionery product manufacturing	99	75	61	-25	-14	-2.8	-2.0	23	24	28	.7	1.5
311400	Fruit and vegetable preserving and specialty food manufacturing	210	177	156	-33	-22	-1.7	-1.3	46	53	66	1.4	2.3
311500	Dairy product manufacturing	134	132	127	-2	-5	-.1	-.4	58	65	76	1.2	1.6
311600	Animal slaughtering and processing	486	509	569	23	60	.5	1.1	99	127	155	2.6	2.0
311700	Seafood product preparation and packaging	53	40	36	-13	-4	-2.7	-1.2	9	10	11	1.6	1.2
311800	Bakeries and tortilla manufacturing	306	281	285	-26	4	-.9	.1	43	52	58	1.9	1.2
311900	Other food manufacturing	149	160	163	11	3	.7	.2	52	61	70	1.7	1.4
312000	Beverage and tobacco product	204	195	171	-10	-24	-.5	-1.3	135	118	109	-1.3	-.8
312100	Beverage manufacturing	166	171	156	5	-16	.3	-1.0	70	80	89	1.4	1.1
312200	Tobacco manufacturing	38	23	16	-15	-8	-4.8	-4.0	66	39	22	-5.1	-5.6
313000	Textile mills	443	196	134	-248	-62	-7.8	-3.7	52	32	25	-4.7	-2.4
313100	Fiber, yarn, and thread mills	87	48	38	-38	-10	-5.7	-2.3	12	8	8	-3.1	-.3
313200	Fabric mills	233	90	61	-143	-29	-9.1	-3.8	28	15	11	-6.0	-3.4
313300	Textile and fabric finishing and fabric coating mills	124	58	34	-66	-23	-7.3	-5.0	12	9	6	-3.4	-3.0
314000	Textile product mills	216	161	141	-55	-20	-2.9	-1.3	29	30	31	.4	.4
314100	Textile furnishings mills	126	90	79	-36	-11	-3.3	-1.3	19	21	23	1.3	.8
314900	Other textile product mills	91	71	62	-20	-9	-2.4	-1.3	10	9	8	-1.3	-.8
315000	Apparel manufacturing	743	238	110	-505	-129	-10.7	-7.5	67	36	20	-6.2	-5.5
315100	Apparel knitting mills	98	34	20	-64	-14	-10.0	-5.1	12	5	3	-7.6	-4.8
315200	Cut and sew apparel manufacturing	605	186	77	-419	-108	-11.1	-8.4	51	28	15	-5.9	-5.9
315900	Apparel accessories and other apparel manufacturing	41	19	12	-22	-7	-7.3	-4.1	5	3	2	-5.8	-3.8
316000	Leather and allied product manufacturing	94	37	20	-57	-17	-8.8	-6.0	10	5	3	-6.2	-5.7
316200	Footwear manufacturing	48	17	8	-31	-9	-9.7	-7.3	4	2	1	-8.2	-8.4
321000	Wood product manufacturing	583	560	527	-23	-33	-.4	-.6	85	95	105	1.1	1.0
321100	Sawmills and wood preservation	133	119	94	-15	-24	-1.2	-2.3	26	27	27	.5	0.0
321200	Veneer, plywood, and engineered wood product manufacturing	110	120	131	10	10	.9	.8	19	21	24	1.0	1.7
321900	Other wood product manufacturing	339	322	302	-18	-19	-.5	-.6	40	47	53	1.5	1.2

See footnotes at end of table.

Table IV–1. Employment and output by industry, 1996, 2006, and projected 2016 — Continued

2002 NAICS coverage	Industry title	Employment							Output				
		Thousands of jobs			Change		Average annual rate of change		Billions of chained 2000 dollars			Average annual rate of change	
		1996	2006	2016	1996–2006	2006–2016	1996–2006	2006–2016	1996	2006	2016	1996–2006	2006–2016
322000	Paper manufacturing	631	469	367	-162	-102	-2.9	-2.4	159	147	143	-.8	-.3
322100	Pulp, paper, and paperboard mills	216	136	94	-80	-42	-4.5	-3.6	72	70	68	-.2	-.3
322200	Converted paper product manufacturing	415	333	274	-82	-60	-2.2	-2.0	87	77	75	-1.2	-.3
323000	Printing and related support activities	816	636	497	-180	-139	-2.5	-2.4	99	84	73	-1.7	-1.3
324000	Petroleum and coal products manufacturing	137	114	88	-23	-26	-1.8	-2.6	223	268	295	1.9	1.0
325000	Chemical manufacturing	985	869	848	-116	-21	-1.2	-.2	398	450	556	1.2	2.1
325100	Basic chemical manufacturing	224	148	124	-77	-23	-4.1	-1.7	102	115	130	1.2	1.2
325200	Resin, synthetic rubber, and artificial synthetic fibers and filaments manufacturing	141	105	84	-36	-21	-2.9	-2.3	62	63	67	.1	.7
325300	Pesticide, fertilizer, and other agricultural chemical manufacturing	50	39	30	-11	-9	-2.4	-2.4	21	21	17	-.2	-2.1
325400	Pharmaceutical and medicine manufacturing	229	292	362	64	69	2.5	2.2	99	123	186	2.1	4.3
325500	Paint, coating, and adhesive manufacturing	76	67	62	-9	-5	-1.2	-.8	26	25	27	-.3	.9
325600	Soap, cleaning compound, and toilet preparation manufacturing	127	113	104	-15	-9	-1.2	-.8	52	67	87	2.6	2.7
325900	Other chemical product and preparation manufacturing	137	105	82	-32	-23	-2.6	-2.5	36	37	41	.4	1.0
326000	Plastics and rubber products manufacturing	920	797	764	-123	-33	-1.4	-.4	150	168	239	1.1	3.6
326100	Plastics product manufacturing	708	638	651	-71	13	-1.0	.2	119	139	208	1.6	4.1
326200	Rubber product manufacturing	212	159	114	-52	-46	-2.8	-3.3	32	29	30	-.9	.3
327000	Nonmetallic mineral product manufacturing	517	508	507	-9	-1	-.2	0.0	88	98	115	1.2	1.5
327100	Clay product and refractory manufacturing	84	61	54	-23	-6	-3.2	-1.1	10	9	10	-1.1	1.2
327200	Glass and glass product manufacturing	142	103	87	-39	-16	-3.1	-1.6	21	25	28	1.5	1.2
327300	Cement and concrete product manufacturing	200	248	266	48	18	2.2	.7	36	43	52	1.7	1.8
331000	Primary metal manufacturing	639	462	336	-177	-126	-3.2	-3.1	157	150	157	-.5	.5
331100	Iron and steel mills and ferroalloy manufacturing	153	94	64	-58	-31	-4.7	-3.9	52	55	58	.6	.6
331200	Steel product manufacturing from purchased steel	70	60	52	-10	-8	-1.6	-1.4	18	15	16	-1.8	.8
331300	Alumina and aluminum production and processing	99	73	50	-26	-22	-3.0	-3.6	33	34	33	.1	-.2
331400	Nonferrous metal (except aluminum) production and processing	102	73	50	-29	-23	-3.3	-3.7	27	19	19	-3.7	.2
331500	Foundries	216	162	120	-54	-42	-2.8	-3.0	27	29	30	.9	.4
332000	Fabricated metal product manufacturing	1,648	1,554	1,365	-94	-189	-.6	-1.3	235	247	278	.5	1.2
332100	Forging and stamping	139	113	86	-26	-27	-2.0	-2.7	23	25	25	.8	.2

See footnotes at end of table.

Table IV–1. Employment and output by industry, 1996, 2006, and projected 2016 — Continued

2002 NAICS coverage	Industry title	Employment							Output				
		Thousands of jobs			Change		Average annual rate of change		Billions of chained 2000 dollars			Average annual rate of change	
		1996	2006	2016	1996–2006	2006–2016	1996–2006	2006–2016	1996	2006	2016	1996–2006	2006–2016
332200	Cutlery and handtool manufacturing	78	54	40	-24	-14	-3.6	-3.0	12	9	9	-2.5	-.8
332300	Architectural and structural metals manufacturing.....	370	415	437	45	23	1.1	.5	49	59	71	2.0	1.8
332400	Boiler, tank, and shipping container manufacturing	107	92	82	-16	-10	-1.5	-1.1	22	21	22	-.7	.6
332500	Hardware manufacturing.	53	34	24	-19	-11	-4.4	-3.6	11	10	8	-1.5	-1.3
332600	Spring and wire product manufacturing	82	58	42	-23	-16	-3.3	-3.2	8	8	8	-.1	.2
332700	Machine shops; turned product; and screw, nut, and bolt manufacturing ..	343	352	283	9	-69	.3	-2.2	42	45	61	.8	3.0
332710	Machine shops..............	240	266	222	26	-44	1.0	-1.8	-	-	-	-	-
332720	Turned product and screw, nut, and bolt manufacturing	103	87	61	-17	-25	-1.7	-3.4	-	-	-	-	-
332800	Coating, engraving, heat treating, and allied activities	158	149	120	-9	-29	-.6	-2.2	18	20	24	1.4	1.4
332900	Other fabricated metal product manufacturing ...	318	287	252	-31	-36	-1.0	-1.3	50	49	50	-.1	.2
333000	Machinery manufacturing.	1,467	1,192	1,045	-275	-146	-2.1	-1.3	248	281	335	1.3	1.8
333100	Agriculture, construction, and mining machinery manufacturing	220	222	207	1	-15	.1	-.7	48	60	84	2.4	3.4
333200	Industrial machinery manufacturing	169	123	101	-46	-22	-3.2	-2.0	36	34	30	-.6	-1.2
333300	Commercial and service industry machinery manufacturing	146	111	97	-35	-14	-2.7	-1.3	25	22	20	-1.5	-1.0
333400	Ventilation, heating, air-conditioning, and commercial refrigeration equipment manufacturing	187	160	145	-27	-15	-1.6	-1.0	30	35	46	1.8	2.7
333500	Metalworking machinery manufacturing	280	203	166	-77	-37	-3.2	-2.0	29	27	29	-.7	.5
333600	Engine, turbine, and power transmission equipment manufacturing	113	100	84	-12	-17	-1.1	-1.8	23	38	48	5.0	2.4
333900	Other general purpose machinery manufacturing	352	273	246	-79	-27	-2.5	-1.0	57	64	76	1.3	1.7
334000	Computer and electronic product manufacturing ...	1,747	1,316	1,159	-430	-157	-2.8	-1.3	321	493	1,214	4.4	9.4
334100	Computer and peripheral equipment manufacturing	305	199	132	-106	-67	-4.2	-4.0	52	135	867	9.9	20.5
334200	Communications equipment manufacturing	238	144	145	-93	1	-4.9	0.0	66	78	116	1.6	4.1
334300	Audio and video equipment manufacturing	53	32	25	-21	-7	-5.0	-2.3	8	10	13	1.8	3.1
334400	Semiconductor and other electronic component manufacturing	607	463	399	-144	-64	-2.7	-1.5	107	163	543	4.3	12.8
334500	Navigational, measuring, electromedical, and control instruments manufacturing	489	438	418	-52	-20	-1.1	-.5	87	107	140	2.1	2.7

See footnotes at end of table.

Table IV–1. Employment and output by industry, 1996, 2006, and projected 2016 — Continued

2002 NAICS coverage	Industry title	Employment							Output				
		Thousands of jobs			Change		Average annual rate of change		Billions of chained 2000 dollars			Average annual rate of change	
		1996	2006	2016	1996–2006	2006–2016	1996–2006	2006–2016	1996	2006	2016	1996–2006	2006–2016
334600	Manufacturing and reproducing magnetic and optical media	56	41	40	-15	-2	-3.0	-.4	8	12	15	3.7	2.3
335000	Electrical equipment, appliance, and component manufacturing	591	436	355	-155	-81	-3.0	-2.0	106	105	116	-.1	1.1
335100	Electric lighting equipment manufacturing	82	59	43	-23	-16	-3.2	-3.2	12	13	14	1.0	.6
335200	Household appliance manufacturing	111	82	61	-29	-21	-3.0	-2.9	20	25	30	2.4	1.8
335300	Electrical equipment manufacturing	217	156	126	-61	-29	-3.3	-2.1	35	30	32	-1.6	.6
335900	Other electrical equipment and component manufacturing	181	139	125	-42	-14	-2.6	-1.1	39	37	42	-.5	1.2
336000	Transportation equipment manufacturing	1,974	1,765	1,651	-209	-114	-1.1	-.7	525	657	863	2.3	2.8
336100	Motor vehicle manufacturing	285	236	226	-49	-10	-1.9	-.4	193	278	385	3.7	3.3
336200	Motor vehicle body and trailer manufacturing	155	180	176	25	-4	1.5	-.2	22	27	36	1.7	2.9
336300	Motor vehicle parts manufacturing	800	654	516	-146	-138	-2.0	-2.3	166	190	205	1.3	.7
336400	Aerospace product and parts manufacturing	514	472	497	-43	25	-.9	.5	111	123	166	1.0	3.1
336500	Railroad rolling stock manufacturing	33	28	23	-5	-5	-1.7	-1.8	7	7	10	-.4	3.9
336600	Ship and boat building	145	156	174	10	18	.7	1.1	16	21	35	2.8	5.0
336900	Other transportation equipment manufacturing	41	40	40	-1	0	-.2	0.0	9	14	23	4.1	5.3
337000	Furniture and related product manufacturing ...	604	556	521	-47	-36	-.8	-.7	58	79	93	3.1	1.6
337100	Household and institutional furniture and kitchen cabinet manufacturing	397	374	346	-24	-28	-.6	-.8	35	46	51	2.8	1.2
337110	Wood kitchen cabinet and countertop manufacturing	120	177	195	58	18	4.0	1.0	-	-	-	-	-
337120	Household and institutional furniture manufacturing	277	196	150	-81	-46	-3.4	-2.6	-	-	-	-	-
337200	Office furniture (including fixtures) manufacturing ..	158	132	123	-25	-9	-1.7	-.7	18	26	31	3.7	2.0
337900	Other furniture related product manufacturing ...	49	51	52	1	1	.2	.2	6	8	10	2.9	2.6
339000	Miscellaneous manufacturing	716	652	600	-64	-52	-.9	-.8	101	147	219	3.9	4.0
339100	Medical equipment and supplies manufacturing ..	298	309	312	11	4	.4	.1	44	77	117	5.8	4.3
339900	Other miscellaneous manufacturing	418	343	287	-75	-56	-2.0	-1.8	57	70	102	2.1	3.8
339910	Jewelry and silverware manufacturing	62	41	24	-22	-17	-4.2	-5.1	-	-	-	-	-
420000	Wholesale trade	5,522	5,898	6,326	376	429	.7	.7	654	1,042	1,703	4.8	5.0
423000	Merchant wholesalers, durable goods	2,978	3,077	3,371	99	294	.3	.9	-	-	-	-	-
423100	Motor vehicle and motor vehicle parts and supplies merchant wholesalers	343	349	385	7	35	.2	1.0	-	-	-	-	-

See footnotes at end of table.

Table IV–1. Employment and output by industry, 1996, 2006, and projected 2016 — Continued

2002 NAICS coverage	Industry title	Employment: Thousands of jobs 1996	2006	2016	Change 1996–2006	2006–2016	Average annual rate of change 1996–2006	2006–2016	Output: Billions of chained 2000 dollars 1996	2006	2016	Average annual rate of change 1996–2006	2006–2016
423200	Furniture and home furnishing merchant wholesalers	104	117	123	14	6	1.2	.5	-	-	-	-	-
423300	Lumber and other construction materials merchant wholesalers	195	265	294	69	29	3.1	1.1	-	-	-	-	-
423400	Professional and commercial equipment and supplies merchant wholesalers	627	654	750	27	96	.4	1.4	-	-	-	-	-
423500	Metal and mineral (except petroleum) merchant wholesalers	130	128	136	-2	8	-.1	.6	-	-	-	-	-
423600	Electrical and electronic goods merchant wholesalers	376	344	396	-31	52	-.9	1.4	-	-	-	-	-
423700	Hardware, and plumbing and heating equipment and supplies merchant wholesalers	228	255	279	27	24	1.1	.9	-	-	-	-	-
423800	Machinery, equipment, and supplies merchant wholesalers	688	676	693	-12	17	-.2	.2	-	-	-	-	-
423820	Farm and garden machinery and equipment merchant wholesalers	106	101	95	-5	-6	-.5	-.6	-	-	-	-	-
423900	Miscellaneous durable goods merchant wholesalers	288	288	316	1	28	0.0	.9	-	-	-	-	-
424000	Merchant wholesalers, nondurable goods	1,978	2,040	2,087	62	47	.3	.2	-	-	-	-	-
424100	Paper and paper product merchant wholesalers	171	153	157	-19	4	-1.2	.3	-	-	-	-	-
424200	Drugs and druggists' sundries merchant wholesalers	149	211	242	61	31	3.5	1.4	-	-	-	-	-
424300	Apparel, piece goods, and notions merchant wholesalers	165	150	146	-15	-4	-.9	-.2	-	-	-	-	-
424400	Grocery and related product wholesalers	657	709	736	52	27	.8	.4	-	-	-	-	-
424500	Farm product raw material merchant wholesalers	88	73	53	-15	-20	-1.9	-3.1	-	-	-	-	-
424600	Chemical and allied products merchant wholesalers	130	133	146	3	13	.2	1.0	-	-	-	-	-
424700	Petroleum and petroleum products merchant wholesalers	124	101	70	-23	-31	-2.0	-3.6	-	-	-	-	-
424800	Beer, wine, and distilled alcoholic beverage merchant wholesalers	119	152	161	33	9	2.5	.6	-	-	-	-	-
424900	Miscellaneous nondurable goods merchant wholesalers	376	361	377	-15	17	-.4	.5	-	-	-	-	-
425000	Wholesale electronic markets and agents and brokers	567	781	868	214	87	3.3	1.1	-	-	-	-	-
44-45	Retail trade	14,143	15,319	16,006	1,177	687	.8	.4	824	1,305	1,892	4.7	3.8
441000	Motor vehicle and parts dealers	1,686	1,908	2,104	222	196	1.2	1.0	-	-	-	-	-
441100	Automobile dealers	1,113	1,247	1,388	134	141	1.1	1.1	-	-	-	-	-

See footnotes at end of table.

Table IV–1. Employment and output by industry, 1996, 2006, and projected 2016 — Continued

2002 NAICS coverage	Industry title	Employment							Output				
		Thousands of jobs			Change		Average annual rate of change		Billions of chained 2000 dollars			Average annual rate of change	
		1996	2006	2016	1996–2006	2006–2016	1996–2006	2006–2016	1996	2006	2016	1996–2006	2006–2016
441200	Other motor vehicle dealers	101	169	220	68	51	5.3	2.7	-	-	-	-	-
441300	Automotive parts, accessories, and tire stores	471	492	496	21	4	.4	.1	-	-	-	-	-
442000	Furniture and home furnishings stores	474	589	633	114	44	2.2	.7	-	-	-	-	-
442100	Furniture stores	259	300	297	40	-3	1.5	-.1	-	-	-	-	-
442200	Home furnishings stores	215	289	336	74	47	3.0	1.5	-	-	-	-	-
443000	Electronics and appliance stores	470	538	532	68	-7	1.4	-.1	-	-	-	-	-
444000	Building material and garden equipment and supplies dealers	1,007	1,323	1,638	315	315	2.8	2.2	-	-	-	-	-
444100	Building material and supplies dealers	858	1,176	1,507	318	331	3.2	2.5	-	-	-	-	-
444200	Lawn and garden equipment and supplies stores	150	147	131	-3	-16	-.2	-1.1	-	-	-	-	-
445000	Food and beverage stores	2,928	2,828	2,823	-100	-5	-.3	-0.0	-	-	-	-	-
445100	Grocery stores	2,535	2,463	2,479	-72	16	-.3	.1	-	-	-	-	-
445200	Specialty food stores	258	229	211	-30	-18	-1.2	-.8	-	-	-	-	-
445300	Beer, wine, and liquor stores	135	137	133	2	-4	.1	-.3	-	-	-	-	-
446000	Health and personal care stores	826	956	1,041	129	85	1.5	.9	-	-	-	-	-
446110	Pharmacies and drug stores	605	703	778	98	76	1.5	1.0	-	-	-	-	-
447000	Gasoline stations	946	861	716	-85	-146	-.9	-1.8	-	-	-	-	-
448000	Clothing and clothing accessories stores	1,221	1,439	1,504	218	65	1.7	.4	-	-	-	-	-
448100	Clothing stores	868	1,090	1,190	223	99	2.3	.9	-	-	-	-	-
448200	Shoe stores	196	182	149	-14	-33	-.7	-2.0	-	-	-	-	-
448300	Jewelry, luggage, and leather goods stores	157	167	165	10	-1	.6	-.1	-	-	-	-	-
451000	Sporting goods, hobby, book, and music stores	614	647	627	32	-20	.5	-.3	-	-	-	-	-
451100	Sporting goods, hobby, and musical instrument stores	388	457	478	69	22	1.7	.5	-	-	-	-	-
451110	Sporting goods stores	186	229	253	43	23	2.1	1.0	-	-	-	-	-
451200	Book, periodical, and music stores	227	190	149	-37	-41	-1.8	-2.4	-	-	-	-	-
452000	General merchandise stores	2,657	2,913	3,172	256	259	.9	.9	-	-	-	-	-
452100	Department stores	1,645	1,551	1,438	-94	-113	-.6	-.8	-	-	-	-	-
452900	Other general merchandise stores	1,012	1,362	1,735	350	373	3.0	2.4	-	-	-	-	-
453000	Miscellaneous store retailers	874	885	797	11	-88	.1	-1.0	-	-	-	-	-
453100	Florists	119	95	67	-23	-28	-2.1	-3.4	-	-	-	-	-
453200	Office supplies, stationery, and gift stores	406	379	300	-26	-79	-.7	-2.3	-	-	-	-	-
453300	Used merchandise stores	85	114	122	29	8	3.0	.7	-	-	-	-	-
453900	Other miscellaneous store retailers	266	297	308	31	11	1.1	.4	-	-	-	-	-
454000	Nonstore retailers	439	434	421	-4	-14	-.1	-.3	-	-	-	-	-
454100	Electronic shopping and mail-order houses	200	243	295	44	52	2.0	2.0	-	-	-	-	-

See footnotes at end of table.

Table IV–1. Employment and output by industry, 1996, 2006, and projected 2016 — Continued

2002 NAICS coverage	Industry title	Employment							Output				
		Thousands of jobs			Change		Average annual rate of change		Billions of chained 2000 dollars			Average annual rate of change	
		1996	2006	2016	1996–2006	2006–2016	1996–2006	2006–2016	1996	2006	2016	1996–2006	2006–2016
454200	Vending machine operators	69	49	30	-21	-18	-3.5	-4.6	-	-	-	-	-
454300	Direct selling establishments	170	143	95	-27	-47	-1.7	-3.9	-	-	-	-	-
48-49	Transportation and warehousing	3,936	4,466	4,962	530	496	1.3	1.1	523	670	890	2.5	2.9
481000	Air transportation	526	487	522	-39	35	-.8	.7	97	144	237	4.0	5.1
481100	Scheduled air transportation	486	441	472	-45	31	-1.0	.7	-	-	-	-	-
481200	Nonscheduled air transportation	40	45	50	6	5	1.4	1.0	-	-	-	-	-
482000	Rail transportation	225	225	213	0	-12	0.0	-.5	43	37	49	-1.4	2.7
483000	Water transportation	51	64	76	13	12	2.3	1.7	29	23	29	-2.6	2.7
483100	Deep sea, coastal, and great lakes water transportation	32	41	50	9	9	2.4	2.1	-	-	-	-	-
483200	Inland water transportation	19	23	26	5	3	2.2	1.1	-	-	-	-	-
484000	Truck transportation	1,282	1,437	1,595	155	158	1.1	1.0	179	261	338	3.8	2.6
484100	General freight trucking	924	1,004	1,117	80	113	.8	1.1	-	-	-	-	-
484200	Specialized freight trucking	359	433	478	75	45	1.9	1.0	-	-	-	-	-
485000	Transit and ground passenger transportation	339	394	438	55	44	1.5	1.1	26	32	39	2.3	1.8
485100	Urban transit systems	33	40	45	7	5	2.0	1.2	-	-	-	-	-
485200	Interurban and rural bus transportation	23	20	20	-3	1	-1.4	.4	-	-	-	-	-
485300	Taxi and limousine service	68	70	75	2	6	.2	.8	-	-	-	-	-
485400	School and employee bus transportation	137	170	186	33	17	2.2	.9	-	-	-	-	-
485500	Charter bus industry	31	30	34	-1	3	-.2	1.1	-	-	-	-	-
485900	Other transit and ground passenger transportation	48	65	77	17	12	3.1	1.7	-	-	-	-	-
486000	Pipeline transportation	51	39	26	-12	-13	-2.7	-3.8	27	24	21	-1.4	-1.4
487000	Scenic and sightseeing transportation	23	27	35	4	8	1.5	2.5	2	2	3	.8	1.1
488000	Support activities for transportation	446	571	668	125	97	2.5	1.6	41	49	54	1.6	1.1
488100	Support activities for air transportation	109	155	188	46	33	3.6	1.9	-	-	-	-	-
488300	Support activities for water transportation	90	100	111	10	11	1.1	1.1	-	-	-	-	-
488400	Support activities for road transportation	53	81	87	28	6	4.3	.8	-	-	-	-	-
488500	Freight transportation arrangement	149	180	223	31	43	1.9	2.2	-	-	-	-	-
492000	Couriers and messengers	540	585	603	46	18	.8	.3	47	63	83	2.9	2.8
492100	Couriers	489	534	549	45	15	.9	.3	-	-	-	-	-
492200	Local messengers and local delivery	51	51	54	1	3	.1	.6	-	-	-	-	-
493000	Warehousing and storage	452	636	786	185	150	3.5	2.1	31	40	58	2.4	3.8
510000	Information	2,940	3,055	3,267	115	212	.4	.7	634	1,006	1,683	4.7	5.3
511000	Publishing industries	927	904	932	-24	29	-.3	.3	165	274	461	5.2	5.3

See footnotes at end of table.

Table IV–1. Employment and output by industry, 1996, 2006, and projected 2016 — Continued

2002 NAICS coverage	Industry title	Employment							Output				
		Thousands of jobs			Change		Average annual rate of change		Billions of chained 2000 dollars			Average annual rate of change	
		1996	2006	2016	1996–2006	2006–2016	1996–2006	2006–2016	1996	2006	2016	1996–2006	2006–2016
511100	Newspaper, periodical, book, and directory publishers	752	660	611	-92	-49	-1.3	-.8	118	132	167	1.1	2.4
511110	Newspaper publishers	423	361	309	-62	-52	-1.6	-1.5	-	-	-	-	-
511200	Software publishers	175	243	321	69	78	3.4	2.8	49	153	420	12.0	10.6
512000	Motion picture, video, and sound recording industries	335	378	414	43	36	1.2	.9	70	81	116	1.5	3.7
512100	Motion picture and video industries	306	357	396	51	39	1.6	1.0	-	-	-	-	-
512130	Motion picture and video exhibition	122	135	134	12	-1	1.0	-.1	-	-	-	-	-
512200	Sound recording industries	29	20	18	-9	-3	-3.4	-1.3	-	-	-	-	-
515000	Broadcasting (except internet)	309	331	363	22	31	.7	.9	59	73	99	2.1	3.1
515100	Radio and television broadcasting	239	241	253	2	12	.1	.5	-	-	-	-	-
515110	Radio broadcasting	113	114	114	1	0	.1	0.0	-	-	-	-	-
515120	Television broadcasting	127	128	139	1	12	.1	.9	-	-	-	-	-
515200	Cable and other subscription programming	70	90	110	20	20	2.6	2.0	-	-	-	-	-
517000	Telecommunications	997	973	1,022	-24	49	-.2	.5	301	470	759	4.6	4.9
517100	Wired telecommunications carriers	603	478	379	-125	-99	-2.3	-2.3	-	-	-	-	-
517200	Wireless telecommunications carriers (except satellite)	110	200	282	90	82	6.2	3.5	-	-	-	-	-
517300	Telecommunications resellers	172	129	134	-43	5	-2.9	.4	-	-	-	-	-
517500	Cable and other program distribution	95	144	198	50	54	4.3	3.2	-	-	-	-	-
516,8,9	Internet and other information services	372	469	536	97	67	2.3	1.3	41	109	248	10.3	8.5
516000	Internet publishing and broadcasting	21	35	50	14	15	5.1	3.7	-	-	-	-	-
518000	Internet service providers, Web search portals, and data processing services	312	383	437	72	54	2.1	1.3	-	-	-	-	-
518100	Internet service providers and Web search portals	60	122	89	62	-33	7.4	-3.1	-	-	-	-	-
518200	Data processing, hosting, and related services	252	262	348	10	86	.4	2.9	-	-	-	-	-
519000	Other information services	39	51	50	12	-2	2.7	-.3	-	-	-	-	-
52-53	Financial activities	6,969	8,363	9,570	1,395	1,207	1.8	1.4	1,726	2,621	3,762	4.3	3.7
520000	Finance and insurance	5,154	6,184	6,999	1,029	815	1.8	1.2	-	-	-	-	-
521-2	Monetary authorities, credit intermediation, and related activities	2,391	2,958	3,196	567	238	2.2	.8	415	660	946	4.7	3.7
521000	Monetary authorities - central bank	23	22	19	-1	-2	-.6	-1.0	-	-	-	-	-
522000	Credit intermediation and related activities	2,368	2,937	3,177	569	240	2.2	.8	-	-	-	-	-
522100	Depository credit intermediation	1,691	1,803	1,879	112	76	.6	.4	-	-	-	-	-
522200	Nondepository credit intermediation	514	784	867	270	83	4.3	1.0	-	-	-	-	-

See footnotes at end of table.

Table IV–1. Employment and output by industry, 1996, 2006, and projected 2016 — Continued

2002 NAICS coverage	Industry title	Employment							Output				
		Thousands of jobs			Change		Average annual rate of change		Billions of chained 2000 dollars			Average annual rate of change	
		1996	2006	2016	1996–2006	2006–2016	1996–2006	2006–2016	1996	2006	2016	1996–2006	2006–2016
522290	Other nondepository credit intermediation, including real estate credit and consumer lending	304	556	629	252	73	6.2	1.2	-	-	-	-	-
522300	Activities related to credit intermediation	163	350	430	186	81	7.9	2.1	-	-	-	-	-
523000	Securities, commodity contracts, and other financial investments and related activities	590	816	1,192	227	376	3.3	3.9	112	351	958	12.1	10.6
523100-200	Securities and commodity contracts, brokerages, and exchanges	431	510	743	79	233	1.7	3.8	-	-	-	-	-
523900	Other financial investment activities	159	307	450	148	143	6.8	3.9	-	-	-	-	-
524000	Insurance carriers and related activities	2,108	2,316	2,488	208	172	.9	.7	-	-	-	-	-
524100	Insurance carriers	1,382	1,428	1,463	46	35	.3	.2	289	355	406	2.1	1.3
524120	Direct insurance (except life, health, and medical) carriers	558	601	616	43	15	.7	.2	-	-	-	-	-
524200	Agencies, brokerages, and other insurance related activities	726	888	1,025	162	137	2.0	1.4	88	104	153	1.6	4.0
524210	Insurance agencies and brokerages	547	660	755	113	95	1.9	1.3	-	-	-	-	-
524290	Other insurance related activities	179	228	270	49	42	2.4	1.7	-	-	-	-	-
525000	Funds, trusts, and other financial vehicles	66	93	122	28	29	3.6	2.8	57	72	90	2.4	2.2
525100	Insurance and employee benefit funds	37	48	59	11	10	2.7	2.0	-	-	-	-	-
525900	Other investment pools and funds	29	45	64	16	19	4.6	3.6	-	-	-	-	-
530000	Real estate and rental and leasing	1,814	2,180	2,571	365	392	1.9	1.7	-	-	-	-	-
531000	Real estate	1,206	1,503	1,796	298	293	2.2	1.8	665	847	1,007	2.5	1.7
531100	Lessors of real estate	586	599	660	13	61	.2	1.0	-	-	-	-	-
531200	Offices of real estate agents and brokers	247	381	461	134	80	4.4	1.9	-	-	-	-	-
531300	Activities related to real estate	373	523	675	151	152	3.5	2.6	-	-	-	-	-
532000	Rental and leasing services	588	647	739	60	91	1.0	1.3	-	-	-	-	-
532100	Automotive equipment rental and leasing	180	200	229	20	30	1.0	1.4	26	30	34	1.2	1.2
5322-3	Consumer goods rental and general rental centers	320	326	361	6	35	.2	1.0	20	24	34	1.7	3.6
532200	Consumer goods rental	266	267	296	2	29	.1	1.0	-	-	-	-	-
532300	General rental centers	55	59	65	4	6	.8	1.0	-	-	-	-	-
532400	Commercial and industrial machinery and equipment rental and leasing	88	122	148	34	27	3.3	2.0	33	43	54	2.9	2.3
533000	Lessors of nonfinancial intangible assets (except copyrighted works)	21	29	37	8	8	3.3	2.4	63	139	278	8.3	7.2
540000	Professional, scientific, and technical services	5,337	7,372	9,494	2,035	2,122	3.3	2.6	770	1,149	1,607	4.1	3.4
541100	Legal services	968	1,173	1,285	205	111	1.9	.9	172	192	214	1.1	1.1

See footnotes at end of table.

Table IV–1. Employment and output by industry, 1996, 2006, and projected 2016 — Continued

2002 NAICS coverage	Industry title	Employment							Output				
		Thousands of jobs			Change		Average annual rate of change		Billions of chained 2000 dollars			Average annual rate of change	
		1996	2006	2016	1996–2006	2006–2016	1996–2006	2006–2016	1996	2006	2016	1996–2006	2006–2016
541200	Accounting, tax preparation, bookkeeping, and payroll services	730	889	1,072	160	183	2.0	1.9	82	97	110	1.7	1.3
541300	Architectural, engineering, and related services	1,025	1,386	1,731	361	345	3.1	2.3	136	210	276	4.4	2.8
541380	Testing laboratories	122	146	182	24	36	1.8	2.2	-	-	-	-	-
541400	Specialized design services	107	136	179	29	44	2.4	2.8	18	27	40	4.0	4.2
541500	Computer systems design and related services	701	1,278	1,768	577	489	6.2	3.3	97	156	230	4.8	4.0
541600	Management, scientific, and technical consulting services	517	921	1,639	404	718	5.9	5.9	87	171	318	7.0	6.4
541700	Scientific research and development services	473	593	649	121	55	2.3	.9	59	127	216	7.9	5.5
541710	Research and development in the physical, engineering, and life sciences	414	529	581	116	52	2.5	.9	-	-	-	-	-
541720	Research and development in the social sciences and humanities	59	64	68	5	4	.8	.5	-	-	-	-	-
541800	Advertising and related services	414	458	520	44	62	1.0	1.3	57	77	97	3.1	2.3
541900	Other professional, scientific, and technical services	402	537	651	135	114	2.9	1.9	63	96	132	4.3	3.3
541920	Photographic services	88	80	79	-8	-1	-.9	-.1	-	-	-	-	-
541940	Veterinary services	176	278	371	102	93	4.7	2.9	-	-	-	-	-
550000	Management of companies and enterprises	1,703	1,809	2,080	107	270	.6	1.4	227	435	592	6.7	3.1
560000	Administrative and support and waste management and remediation services	6,422	8,370	10,070	1,949	1,700	2.7	1.9	348	553	800	4.8	3.8
561000	Administrative and support services	6,140	8,023	9,647	1,883	1,623	2.7	1.9	302	494	724	5.0	3.9
561100	Office administrative services	247	363	456	116	93	3.9	2.3	31	74	129	9.2	5.7
561200	Facilities support services	80	123	179	43	56	4.4	3.8	8	11	12	3.0	.8
561300	Employment services	2,601	3,657	4,348	1,056	692	3.5	1.7	83	134	186	4.9	3.4
561400	Business support services	678	791	950	112	160	1.5	1.9	41	61	93	4.1	4.3
561420	Telephone call centers	365	383	371	18	-12	.5	-.3	-	-	-	-	-
561500	Travel arrangement and reservation services	294	227	230	-67	3	-2.6	.1	26	30	30	1.5	.1
561510	Travel agencies	165	108	101	-57	-7	-4.2	-.7	-	-	-	-	-
561600	Investigation and security services	612	761	923	149	163	2.2	2.0	23	36	58	4.7	4.9
561610	Investigation, guard, and armored car services	543	649	776	106	127	1.8	1.8	-	-	-	-	-
561620	Security systems services	69	111	147	43	36	5.0	2.8	-	-	-	-	-
561700	Services to buildings and dwellings	1,362	1,797	2,161	436	364	2.8	1.9	62	106	162	5.5	4.4
561710	Exterminating and pest control services	81	99	115	17	16	1.9	1.5	-	-	-	-	-
561730	Landscaping services	378	658	817	280	159	5.7	2.2	-	-	-	-	-

See footnotes at end of table.

Table IV–1. Employment and output by industry, 1996, 2006, and projected 2016 — Continued

2002 NAICS coverage	Industry title	Employment: Thousands of jobs 1996	2006	2016	Change 1996–2006	2006–2016	Average annual rate of change 1996–2006	2006–2016	Output: Billions of chained 2000 dollars 1996	2006	2016	Average annual rate of change 1996–2006	2006–2016
561900	Other support services....	266	305	399	39	94	1.4	2.7	30	43	55	3.7	2.6
562000	Waste management and remediation services......	282	347	424	65	77	2.1	2.0	46	59	75	2.6	2.4
562100	Waste collection.............	93	130	157	38	27	3.5	1.9	24	30	36	2.4	1.8
562200-900	Waste treatment and disposal and waste management services....	190	217	267	27	50	1.4	2.1	22	29	39	2.8	2.9
562200	Waste treatment and disposal..................	106	102	124	-4	22	-.4	1.9	-	-	-	-	-
562900	Remediation and other waste management services..........................	84	115	143	31	29	3.2	2.3	-	-	-	-	-
610000	Education services...........	2,078	2,918	3,527	841	609	3.5	1.9	124	157	191	2.4	2.0
611100	Elementary and secondary schools.........	599	847	1,001	248	154	3.5	1.7	26	30	34	1.5	1.2
611200-300	Junior colleges, colleges, universities, and professional schools......	1,170	1,537	1,824	368	287	2.8	1.7	72	95	114	2.8	1.8
611400-700	Other educational services..........................	309	534	703	225	168	5.6	2.8	26	33	44	2.4	2.9
620000	Health care and social assistance.....................	11,605	14,920	18,954	3,315	4,034	2.5	2.4	865	1,211	1,720	3.4	3.6
621000	Ambulatory health care services..........................	3,940	5,283	6,844	1,343	1,561	3.0	2.6	401	593	890	4.0	4.1
621100-300	Offices of health practitioners..................	2,629	3,508	4,365	879	857	2.9	2.2	286	433	643	4.2	4.0
621100	Offices of physicians.......	1,604	2,154	2,687	550	534	3.0	2.2	-	-	-	-	-
621200	Offices of dentists..........	611	784	960	173	176	2.5	2.0	-	-	-	-	-
621300	Offices of other health practitioners..................	415	571	718	156	147	3.2	2.3	-	-	-	-	-
621310	Offices of chiropractors...	84	114	140	31	26	3.2	2.1	-	-	-	-	-
621320	Offices of optometrists....	77	99	117	22	18	2.6	1.7	-	-	-	-	-
621330	Offices of mental health practitioners (except physicians).....................	51	55	66	4	11	.7	1.9	-	-	-	-	-
621340	Offices of physical, occupational and speech therapists, and audiologists............	149	222	291	73	69	4.1	2.7	-	-	-	-	-
621390	Offices of all other health practitioners..................	54	80	103	26	23	4.1	2.5	-	-	-	-	-
621600	Home health care services..........................	667	867	1,348	200	481	2.7	4.5	36	48	83	3.0	5.6
621400, 500, 900	Outpatient, laboratory, and other ambulatory care services.................	644	908	1,131	264	223	3.5	2.2	79	113	164	3.5	3.8
621400	Outpatient care centers...	340	489	609	149	119	3.7	2.2	-	-	-	-	-
621420	Outpatient mental health and substance abuse centers...............	118	157	194	40	37	2.9	2.1	-	-	-	-	-
621500	Medical and diagnostic laboratories...................	149	202	236	53	34	3.1	1.6	-	-	-	-	-
621900	Other ambulatory health care services.......	154	216	286	62	70	3.4	2.8	-	-	-	-	-
621910	Ambulance services.......	94	129	164	36	34	3.3	2.4	-	-	-	-	-
621990	All other ambulatory health care services.......	60	87	122	26	35	3.7	3.5	-	-	-	-	-
622000	Hospitals, private............	3,773	4,427	5,119	654	692	1.6	1.5	292	397	543	3.1	3.2
623000	Nursing and residential care facilities.................	2,380	2,901	3,588	521	687	2.0	2.1	98	119	146	1.9	2.1
623100	Nursing care facilities......	1,448	1,584	1,759	136	174	.9	1.0	64	72	84	1.2	1.6

See footnotes at end of table.

Table IV–1. Employment and output by industry, 1996, 2006, and projected 2016 — Continued

2002 NAICS coverage	Industry title	Employment							Output				
		Thousands of jobs			Change		Average annual rate of change		Billions of chained 2000 dollars			Average annual rate of change	
		1996	2006	2016	1996–2006	2006–2016	1996–2006	2006–2016	1996	2006	2016	1996–2006	2006–2016
623200-900	Residential care facilities	932	1,317	1,829	385	513	3.5	3.3	34	47	62	3.2	2.9
623200	Residential mental retardation, mental health and substance abuse facilities	375	512	674	138	161	3.2	2.8	-	-	-	-	-
623210	Residential mental retardation facilities	260	346	445	86	98	2.9	2.5	-	-	-	-	-
623220	Residential mental health and substance abuse facilities	114	166	229	52	63	3.8	3.3	-	-	-	-	-
623300	Community care facilities for the elderly	428	639	960	212	321	4.1	4.1	-	-	-	-	-
623900	Other residential care facilities	129	165	196	36	31	2.5	1.7	-	-	-	-	-
624000	Social assistance	1,512	2,309	3,404	797	1,095	4.3	4.0	74	103	149	3.4	3.8
624100-300	Individual, family, community, and vocational rehabilitation services	953	1,502	2,326	549	823	4.7	4.5	-	-	-	-	-
624100	Individual and family services	545	974	1,687	429	713	6.0	5.7	30	44	68	3.7	4.5
624120	Services for the elderly and persons with disabilities	230	493	860	263	367	7.9	5.7	-	-	-	-	-
624200, 300	Community, and vocational rehabilitation services	408	529	639	120	110	2.6	1.9	14	22	32	4.2	4.0
624200	Community food and housing, and emergency and other relief services	94	129	153	36	24	3.3	1.7	-	-	-	-	-
624300	Vocational rehabilitation services	315	399	485	85	86	2.4	2.0	-	-	-	-	-
624400	Child day care services	559	807	1,078	248	272	3.7	2.9	29	38	50	2.8	2.8
710000	Arts, entertainment, and recreation	1,522	1,927	2,522	405	595	2.4	2.7	131	185	274	3.5	4.0
711000	Performing arts, spectator sports, and related industries	329	399	478	70	79	2.0	1.8	56	62	84	1.1	3.0
711100	Performing arts companies	115	121	120	5	-1	.5	-.1	10	9	10	-.8	.8
711200	Spectator sports	109	131	162	22	31	1.9	2.1	18	24	31	2.5	2.8
711300-400	Promoters of events, and agents and managers	72	100	131	28	31	3.3	2.8	11	14	18	2.0	2.9
711500	Independent artists, writers, and performers	32	47	65	15	18	3.9	3.3	16	16	24	-.1	4.5
712000	Museums, historical sites, and similar institutions	89	124	167	35	44	3.4	3.1	5	7	10	2.8	3.7
713000	Amusement, gambling, and recreation industries	1,105	1,404	1,877	300	472	2.4	2.9	70	116	182	5.2	4.6
713100	Amusement parks and arcades	148	153	202	5	49	.3	2.8	-	-	-	-	-
713200	Gambling industries	121	137	227	16	90	1.3	5.2	-	-	-	-	-
713900	Other amusement and recreation industries	836	1,115	1,447	278	333	2.9	2.6	-	-	-	-	-
713940	Fitness and recreational sports centers	349	507	673	158	166	3.8	2.9	-	-	-	-	-
720000	Accommodation and food services	9,254	11,216	12,494	1,962	1,278	1.9	1.1	427	555	635	2.6	1.4
721000	Accommodation	1,699	1,833	2,088	135	254	.8	1.3	115	139	170	2.0	2.0

See footnotes at end of table.

Table IV–1. Employment and output by industry, 1996, 2006, and projected 2016 — Continued

2002 NAICS coverage	Industry title	Employment							Output				
		Thousands of jobs			Change		Average annual rate of change		Billions of chained 2000 dollars			Average annual rate of change	
		1996	2006	2016	1996–2006	2006–2016	1996–2006	2006–2016	1996	2006	2016	1996–2006	2006–2016
721100	Traveler accommodation, including hotels and motels	1,653	1,770	2,018	117	248	.7	1.3	-	-	-	-	-
721120	Casino hotels	253	283	329	31	46	1.2	1.5	-	-	-	-	-
721200	RV (recreational vehicle) parks and recreational camps	38	54	61	16	7	3.6	1.3	-	-	-	-	-
722000	Food services and drinking places	7,556	9,383	10,407	1,827	1,024	2.2	1.0	313	415	465	2.9	1.1
722100	Full-service restaurants	3,545	4,447	4,881	902	434	2.3	.9	-	-	-	-	-
722200	Limited-service eating places	3,197	4,019	4,548	822	529	2.3	1.2	-	-	-	-	-
722300	Special food services	453	556	645	103	90	2.1	1.5	-	-	-	-	-
722400	Drinking places (alcoholic beverages)	361	362	333	1	-29	0.0	-.8	-	-	-	-	-
810000	Other services	5,435	6,235	7,077	800	843	1.4	1.3	370	439	551	1.7	2.3
811000	Repair and maintenance	1,136	1,249	1,453	113	204	1.0	1.5	144	176	223	2.0	2.4
811100	Automotive repair and maintenance	781	887	1,094	106	207	1.3	2.1	90	106	132	1.7	2.2
811110	Automotive mechanical and electrical repair and maintenance	370	401	474	31	73	.8	1.7	-	-	-	-	-
811120	Automotive body, paint, interior, and glass repair	227	258	298	31	41	1.3	1.5	-	-	-	-	-
811190	Other automotive repair and maintenance	185	229	322	44	93	2.2	3.5	-	-	-	-	-
811200	Electronic and precision equipment repair and maintenance	110	104	94	-6	-10	-.5	-1.0	18	20	20	.8	.2
811300	Commercial and industrial machinery and equipment (except automotive and electronic) repair and maintenance	160	179	191	19	12	1.1	.7	17	29	45	5.5	4.4
811400	Personal and household goods repair and maintenance	84	78	73	-6	-5	-.7	-.6	19	21	26	.7	2.2
812000	Personal and laundry services	1,166	1,284	1,415	118	131	1.0	1.0	96	122	167	2.5	3.1
812100	Personal care services	454	585	649	131	64	2.6	1.0	29	40	56	3.5	3.3
812200	Death care services	126	137	154	10	18	.8	1.2	13	11	12	-1.5	.6
812300	Drycleaning and laundry services	378	344	346	-34	2	-.9	.1	20	21	23	.3	1.0
812900	Other personal services	207	218	265	12	47	.6	2.0	33	50	77	4.1	4.3
813000	Religious, grantmaking, civic, professional, and similar organizations	2,389	2,899	3,373	510	474	2.0	1.5	118	128	147	.8	1.4
813100	Religious organizations	1,310	1,666	1,981	356	316	2.4	1.7	47	49	56	.5	1.3
813200-300	Grantmaking and giving services and social advocacy organizations	251	321	367	70	46	2.5	1.4	15	18	22	2.3	1.9
813200	Grantmaking and giving services	104	142	164	38	21	3.1	1.4	-	-	-	-	-
813300	Social advocacy organizations	147	178	203	32	25	2.0	1.3	-	-	-	-	-
813400-900	Civic, social, professional, and similar organizations	828	913	1,025	85	112	1.0	1.2	57	60	69	.5	1.4
813400	Civic and social organizations	394	413	457	19	44	.5	1.0	-	-	-	-	-

See footnotes at end of table.

Table IV–1. Employment and output by industry, 1996, 2006, and projected 2016 — Continued

2002 NAICS coverage	Industry title	Employment: Thousands of jobs 1996	2006	2016	Change 1996–2006	2006–2016	Average annual rate of change 1996–2006	2006–2016	Output: Billions of chained 2000 dollars 1996	2006	2016	Average annual rate of change 1996–2006	2006–2016
813900	Business, professional, labor, political, and similar organizations	434	500	568	66	68	1.4	1.3	-	-	-	-	-
813930	Labor unions and similar labor organizations	140	134	131	-6	-4	-.4	-.3	-	-	-	-	-
814000	Private households	744	803	837	58	34	.8	.4	13	13	15	.4	.9
N.A.	Federal Government	2,877	2,728	2,626	-149	-103	-.5	-.4	580	715	761	2.1	.6
491100	Postal Service	867	770	757	-97	-13	-1.2	-.2	58	58	62	-.1	.7
N.A.	Federal electric utilities	26	23	23	-4	0	-1.5	.1	9	10	12	1.4	1.5
N.A.	Federal enterprises except the Postal Service and electric utilities	97	45	27	-52	-19	-7.3	-5.2	8	7	8	-1.3	1.2
N.A.	Federal government except enterprises	1,887	1,891	1,819	4	-71	0.0	-.4	506	641	680	2.4	.6
N.A.	Federal defense government	597	492	434	-105	-59	-1.9	-1.3	274	358	385	2.7	.7
N.A.	Federal non-defense government except enterprises	1,290	1,399	1,386	109	-13	.8	-.1	152	192	192	2.4	0.0
N.A.	Federal Government capital services	-	-	-	-	-	-	-	80	90	102	1.1	1.3
N.A.	State and local government	16,662	19,262	20,696	2,600	1,434	1.5	.7	1,159	1,436	1,749	2.2	2.0
N.A.	Local government passenger transit	206	256	317	50	61	2.2	2.2	7	9	10	1.6	1.8
N.A.	Local government enterprises except passenger transit	1,093	1,266	1,347	173	81	1.5	.6	111	132	176	1.8	2.9
N.A.	Local government hospitals	648	650	679	2	30	0.0	.4	47	65	87	3.4	2.9
N.A.	Local government educational services	6,592	7,939	8,450	1,346	512	1.9	.6	349	418	449	1.8	.7
N.A.	Local government excluding enterprises, educational services, and hospitals	3,517	4,072	4,542	555	470	1.5	1.1	277	350	437	2.4	2.2
N.A.	State government enterprises	1,824	1,876	1,879	52	4	.3	0.0	15	19	25	2.2	2.9
N.A.	State government hospitals	376	361	346	-15	-15	-.4	-.4	34	47	61	3.5	2.5
N.A.	State government educational services	1,911	2,295	2,586	384	291	1.8	1.2	125	159	189	2.4	1.8
N.A.	State government excluding enterprises, educational services, and hospitals	496	549	549	53	1	1.0	0.0	125	135	179	.8	2.9
N.A.	State and local government capital services	-	-	-	-	-	-	-	71	103	140	3.9	3.0
N.A.	Owner-occupied dwellings	-	-	-	-	-	-	-	680	920	1,229	3.1	2.9
110000	Agriculture, forestry, fishing, and hunting[2]	2,731	2,139	1,966	-592	-173	-2.4	-.8	236	267	331	1.3	2.2
111000	Crop production	1,166	898	759	-268	-139	-2.6	-1.7	89	107	148	1.9	3.3
112000	Animal production	1,238	922	904	-316	-18	-2.9	-.2	96	112	138	1.6	2.1
113100-3200	Forestry	18	19	21	1	1	.5	.6	5	5	5	-1.4	-.4

See footnotes at end of table.

Table IV–1. Employment and output by industry, 1996, 2006, and projected 2016 — Continued

2002 NAICS coverage	Industry title	Employment: Thousands of jobs 1996	2006	2016	Change 1996–2006	2006–2016	Average annual rate of change 1996–2006	2006–2016	Output: Billions of chained 2000 dollars 1996	2006	2016	Average annual rate of change 1996–2006	2006–2016
113300	Logging	121	95	76	-26	-19	-2.4	-2.2	27	25	23	-.9	-.9
114000	Fishing, hunting and trapping	62	49	39	-13	-10	-2.3	-2.2	7	6	4	-1.5	-2.9
115000	Support activities for agriculture and forestry	126	155	167	29	12	2.1	.7	13	12	14	-.4	1.1
N.A.	Nonagriculture self-employed and unpaid family worker[3]	9,368	9,772	10,462	404	690	.4	.7	-	-	-	-	-
N.A.	Secondary wage and salary jobs in agriculture and private household industries[4]	177	178	185	2	7	.1	.4	-	-	-	-	-
N.A.	Secondary jobs as a self-employed or unpaid family worker[5]	2,043	1,619	1,646	-425	27	-2.3	.2	-	-	-	-	-
N.A.	**Total[6,7]**	**134,690**	**150,620**	**166,220**	**15,930**	**15,600**	**1.1**	**1.0**	**15,120**	**20,265**	**27,094**	**3.0**	**2.9**

[1] Includes wage and salary data from the Current Employment Statistics survey, except private households, which is from the Current Population Survey. Logging workers are excluded.

[2] Includes agriculture, forestry, fishing, and hunting wage and salary, self-employed, and unpaid family workers data from the Current Population Survey, except logging, which is from Current Employment Statistics survey. Government wage and salary workers are excluded.

[3] Comparable estimate of output growth is not available.

[4] Workers who hold a secondary wage and salary job in agricultural production, forestry, fishing, and private household industries.

[5] Workers who hold a secondary job as a self-employed or unpaid family worker.

[6] Employment data for wage and salary workers are from the BLS Current Employment Statistics survey, which counts jobs, whereas self-employed, unpaid family workers, and agriculture, forestry, fishing, and hunting are from the Current Population Survey (household survey), which counts workers.

[7] Output subcategories do not necessarily add to higher categories as a by product of chain-weighting.

Notes: Dash indicates data not available. Due to rounding, detailed employment and output may not add to totals.

See footnotes at end of table.

Table IV–2. Factors affecting industry output and employment, 2006–16

2002 NAICS coverage	2006 Industry title	Factors affecting output and employment
210000	**Mining**	
211000	Oil and gas extraction	Output is used in petroleum refining and by gas utilities industries. Although industry output decreased during the 1996-2006 period, it is projected to grow at a relatively slow rate over the next 10 years. This turnaround is due to an increase in prices, as well as increase in worldwide demand. Slightly declining employment growth is projected because of improved extraction techniques and other productivity gains.
212100	Coal mining	Output is used in the production of electricity and primary steel products. Demand is expected to increase on the world market, leading to continued output growth. Improvements in productivity and an increase in mining in western States, where coal is easier to access, are expected to contribute to virtually no growth in employment.
212200	Metal ore mining	Output is used in a large variety of manufactured goods. Output is expected to reverse the previous decade's decline and grow faster than GDP due to high prices , which compensate for the high cost of extraction, making metal mining profitable again. Employment also is expected to increase only slightly, however, as the U.S. industry contracts out work and productivity gains continue.
212300	Nonmetallic mineral mining and quarrying	Output is used in new residential and maintenance construction and concrete products industries. This industry is expected to increase output slowly. Productivity improvement will be less than in the previous decade, as many processes are already highly automated. In addition, little consolidation is possible due to the geographical dispersion within the industry, resulting in a slight increase in employment.
213000	Support activities for mining	Output is primarily used by the oil and gas extraction industry, but is consumed in all mining operations. Production is expected to increase moderately, mirroring the oil and gas extraction industry. Employment is projected to decrease slightly, however, as productivity increases slightly due to the introduction of new technologies and drilling techniques.
220000	**Utilities**	
2211000	Electric power generation, transmission and distribution	Output is consumed by individuals and is used as an input in virtually all industries. Output in this industry is expected to grow slower than GDP. The demand for electric energy in the U.S. is projected to continue to rise over the next 10 years, although less rapidly due to increases in energy efficiency. Although employment is projected to continue to decline slightly as a result of continued productivity growth, the rate will be less than the previous decade.
221200	Natural gas distribution	The output from this industry is consumed by individuals and by industries, including gas and combined utility services. Output is expected to fall due to continued pressure from regulation, although at a slower rate than the previous decade. Employment is projected to fall at a similar rate, as efficiency has leveled off.
221300	Water, sewage and other systems	Output is consumed by individuals and is used as an input in other industries. This industry is expected to increase output as the population grows in rural areas and the overall population growth. Employment is expected to grow slightly faster than that of the overall economy, primarily because of the industry's relatively stable productivity growth.
230000	**Construction**	
230000	Construction	Output is expected to grow more slowly than GDP and more slowly than in the recent past because of a decline in residential building from historic highs. The positive growth is due to continued nonresidential activity, even as residential activity slows. Employment is also projected to continue to grow because of the positive output growth and the traditional low productivity gains.
310000–330000	**Manufacturing**	
311000	**Food Manufacturing**	
311100	Animal food manufacturing	Output is used in the production of pet food and agriculture. Output is expected to increase because of an increasing number of households with pets. Employment, however, is expected to decrease because of continuing large advances in productivity. Technology and automation of food processing plants and techniques will continue to be adopted throughout the projections period.
311200	Grain and oilseed milling	Output is used in the livestock industry, is consumed by individuals, and is exported. Industry output is expected to grow as productivity increases. Employment is projected to fall slightly, which also is the result of productivity growth.
311300	Sugar and confectionery product manufacturing	Output is used by other food industries and is consumed by individuals. Output is expected to grow slower than GDP. Productivity is expected to increase, driving a decline in employment as it takes less people to do the same work.
311400	Fruit and vegetable preserving and specialty food manufacturing	Output is used in eating and drinking establishments and is consumed by individuals. Industry output is expected to grow at pace with GDP. Employment is projected to show a slight decline as a result of high productivity growth due to new technologies and processes.
311500	Dairy product manufacturing	Output is consumed by individuals and is used by eating and drinking establishments. Output is expected to increase more slowly than GDP. Improved technology and productivity growth is expected to contribute to a slight decline in employment.
311600	Animal slaughtering and processing	Output is used by eating and drinking establishments and is consumed by individuals. Industry output is expected to grow at a rate almost equal to GDP growth. Because this industry is relatively labor intensive, productivity growth rates are expected to be small. Employment is therefore projected to continue to grow at a rate comparable to the employment growth for the overall economy.
311700	Seafood product preparation and packaging	Output is consumed by individuals and is used by eating and drinking establishments. Industry output is expected to rise more slowly than GDP, but to remain positive as per capita consumption remains strong. Employment is expected to fall slightly as a result of improvements in productivity; however the rates will be less than the previous decade as most efficiency gains have been realized.

Table IV–2. Factors affecting industry output and employment, 2006–16 — Continued

2002 NAICS coverage	2006 Industry title	Factors affecting output and employment
311800	Bakeries and tortilla manufacturing	Output is consumed by individuals and is used by eating and drinking establishments. Industry output is expected to grow at a positive rate, but slower than GDP. The industry traditionally is more labor intensive, and productivity is projected to grow at roughly the same rate as industry output. Consequently employment is projected to grow very slightly.
311900	Other food manufacturing	This industry group includes snack food manufacturing, coffee and tea manufacturing, seasoning and dressing, and other miscellaneous food manufacturing. Output is consumed by individuals and is used in eating and drinking establishments. Population growth, rising incomes, and successful marketing will affect this industry; output is expected to grow at a rate slower than GDP. Employment is projected to grow slightly, as modest productivity growth occurs.
312100	Beverage manufacturing	Output is consumed by individuals and eating and drinking establishments. This industry is projected to grow more slowly than GDP, and employment is projected to decrease slightly because of increases in productivity. Automation of packaging and filling will continue to affect the productivity in this industry.
312200	Tobacco manufacturing	Output is consumed by individuals, is used by other firms in the tobacco industry, and is exported. Industry output is expected to continue to fall dramatically, even faster than it did in the preceding decade, due to decreased consumption and tighter restrictions. Employment is projected to fall, although at a slightly slower rate than output. This is projected to be one of the most rapidly declining industries, in terms of employment, over the 2006-16 projection period.
313000	**Textile Manufacturing**	
313100	Fiber, yarn, and thread mills	Output is used in the apparel and textile and furniture industries. This industry is projected to decline, mostly because of increasing imports. China is expected to dominate much of the market; they have low labor costs and efficient production techniques. Employment in this industry is projected to fall not only as a result of declining U.S. production, but also because of increasing productivity.
313200	Fabric mills	Output is used in the apparel and textile and furniture industries. Imports are expected to continue to grow, causing domestic production to fall. Productivity growth is expected to flatten; an increased proportion of design and management functions within the industry will slow productivity growth. Consolidation among the textile producers and cost pressures are projected to result in declining employment.
313300	Textile and fabric finishing and fabric coating mills	Output is used in the apparel and textile and furniture industries. Domestic production is expected to fall in this industry as a result of increasing imports. Employment is projected to fall because of declining output and pressure to reduce costs, as well as continuing productivity growth. This is projected to be one of the most rapidly declining industries, in terms of employment, over the 2006-16 projection period.
314100	Textile furnishings mills	Output is consumed by individuals and other industries. Like other textile industries, this industry is facing severe pressures from imports, resulting in only slight growth in output. Because productivity is expected to grow faster than output, employment is projected to fall.
314900	Other textile product mills	Output is consumed by individuals and is used in other industries. Imports will remain high; however, as prices have been on the rise, imports are expected to have less of an effect on this industry, resulting in only a slight decline in output growth. Productivity growth, however, is expected to maintain positive growth, contributing to declining employment.
315000	**Apparel Manufacturing**	
315100	Apparel knitting mills	Output is consumed by individuals and is used in the cut-and-sew apparel industries. The proliferation of trade agreements with China, Mexico, India, Caribbean, and Sub-Saharan countries will have a significant effect on this industry; output is expected to fall, although less than in the previous decade. In addition, productivity growth is projected to further the decline of employment in this industry, although this decline will be less than the previous decade. This is projected to be one of the most rapidly declining industries, in terms of employment, over the 2006-16 projection period.
315200	Cut and sew apparel manufacturing	Output is consumed by individuals. Industry output is expected to fall as a result of increasing imports, primarily from China. Productivity growth is projected to continue to be strong, although half the rate of the previous decade. This will lead to continued large declines in employment, although less than that of the previous decade. This is projected to be one of the ten most rapidly declining industries, in terms of employment, over the 2006-16 projection period.
315900	Apparel accessories and other apparel manufacturing	Output is consumed by individuals. Output is expected to continue to fall, but at a slower rate than it did in the preceding decade. Productivity is expected to continue to grow but also at a slower rate that the previous decade. The combination of decreased output and positive productivity growth will cause continuing declines in employment. This is projected to be one of the most rapidly declining industries, in terms of employment, over the 2006-16 projection period.
316100, 316900	Leather and hide tanning and finishing, and other leather and allied product manufacturing	Output is used in other leather industries and motor vehicle parts industry. Industry output is projected to fall because of an increasing share of imports. Continued productivity improvements contribute to declining employment. This is projected to be one of the most rapidly declining industries, in terms of employment, over the 2006-16 projection period.
316200	Footwear manufacturing	Output is consumed mostly by individuals. Industry output is expected to fall dramatically. Imports will satisfy most of the demand for this product. Employment is projected to fall as a result of declining production and increasing productivity. This is projected to be one of the most rapidly declining industries, in terms of employment, over the 2006-16 projection period.
321000	**Wood product manufacturing**	
321100	Sawmills and wood preservation	Output is used in the construction industry, primarily for new single-unit housing, and by individuals. Output is expected to have zero growth. Productivity is projected to continue to grow causing a decline in employment.
321200	Veneer, plywood, and engineered wood product manufacturing	Output is used as an input in residential construction. It is projected to grow more slowly than GDP. Productivity is projected to grow at a comparable rate to the preceding decade, but still slower than output. The overall result is expected to be marginal growth in employment.

Table IV–2. Factors affecting industry output and employment, 2006–16 — Continued

2002 NAICS coverage	2006 Industry title	Factors affecting output and employment
321900	Other wood product manufacturing	Output is used in the construction industry. It is expected to grow slower than GDP. Productivity growth is expected to be slightly higher than output in this industry, resulting in a slight decline in employment.
322000	**Paper manufacturing**	
322100	Pulp, paper, and paperboard mills	Output is used as an input to paper and printing industries. This industry is projected to show slightly negative growth in output. Employment is projected to fall because of continued, but slower than the previous decade, growth in productivity. Consolidation and increased level of computerization are expected to contribute heavily to projected trends for output, productivity, and employment.
322200	Converted paper product manufacturing	Output is used by individuals and as an input to other industries, especially wholesale and retail trade. Industry output is expected to show just under flat growth. Productivity is expected to increase at a faster rate than the previous decade, resulting in negative employment growth for the current projections period.
323000	Printing and related support activities	Output is purchased by commercial printing, publishing, and advertising industries, and is projected to decline at a comparable rate to the previous decade. Modest productivity growth, the result of increasing computerization, is expected to combine with rising imports and the increasing use of the Internet to diminish employment overall.
324000	Petroleum and coal products manufacturing	Output is consumed by individuals and as an input to electric utilities, and transportation industries. Industry output is expected to show modest growth. Employment is projected to fall because of productivity growing faster than output.
325000	Basic chemical manufacturing	Output is used as an input in the chemical, plastics, and petroleum-refining industries. Output is expected to fall slightly as a result of increasing imports. Employment is projected to fall because of decreasing production and increasing productivity due to machine automation.
321000	**Chemical Manufacturing**	
325200	Resin, synthetic rubber, and artificial synthetic fibers and filaments manufacturing	Output is used as an input in a variety of other manufacturing industries, including plastics and textiles. Output is expected to grow only slightly due to cheaper labor overseas. Employment is projected to continue to fall as productivity growth improves.
325300	Pesticide, fertilizer, and other agricultural chemical manufacturing	Output is used in the agricultural industries. Industry output is projected to fall slightly due to cheaper foreign labor overseas generating higher imports. While there will be slight productivity gains, employment is projected to fall primarily due to decreased output.
325400	Pharmaceutical and medicine manufacturing	Output is consumed by individuals and is used the medical services industries. Industry output is projected to grow at a rate double that of the previous decade. The aging of the population is expected to contribute to increasing demand in this industry. Employment is projected to increase at the same rate as the previous decade but slower than output over the projection period because of relatively strong productivity growth.
325500	Paint, coating, and adhesive manufacturing	Output is used in manufacturing and construction industries. Industry output is expected to show some growth over the projection period. . Improved productivity is expected to cause a decline in employment.
325600	Soap, cleaning compound, and toilet preparation manufacturing	Output is used as an input in manufacturing and construction industries. Industry output is projected to continue to grow comparably to the previous decade. Employment growth is projected to fall slightly because continued productivity improvements will outpace the demand growth.
325900	Other chemical product and preparation manufacturing	Output is used as an input in manufacturing and construction industries. Industry output is projected to continue to grow comparably to the previous decade. Employment is expected to decline as productivity improvements continue.
326000	**Plastics and rubber products manufacturing**	
326100	Plastics product manufacturing	Output is used as an input in many industries. Demand is expected to grow as manufacturers continue to substitute plastic products for other materials. Despite strong output growth, employment is projected to grow only slightly, as computer-controlled automation and other technological improvements contribute to strong productivity growth.
326200	Rubber product manufacturing	Output is used as an input in construction, motor vehicles, and textiles industries. Industry output is projected to grow very slightly. Employment is projected to fall as output is expected to show little growth and productivity continues to improve.
327000	Nonmetallic mineral product manufacturing	
327100	Clay product and refractory manufacturing	Output is used in construction and manufacturing industries. Industry output is expected to grow; demand in the construction industry for these goods is projected to remain strong, a reversal from the previous decade. Employment however is projected to continue to fall, but at a slower rate than the previous decade, as productivity is expected to grow in this industry.
327200	Glass and glass product manufacturing	Output is consumed by beverage, prepared foods, motor vehicle, and other manufacturing industries. Output is expected to continue to grow, but at less than half the rate of GDP growth. Employment is projected to fall as productivity growth remains strong due to investment in new plants.

Table IV–2. Factors affecting industry output and employment, 2006–16 — Continued

2002 NAICS coverage	2006 Industry title	Factors affecting output and employment
327300	Cement and concrete product manufacturing	Output is used in the construction industry and owner-occupied dwellings. Industry output is projected to increase slower than GDP, due in large part to the continued growth in construction. Employment is projected to continue to increase, but at a third of the rate in the previous decade. This is due to a turnaround in productivity compared to the same period.
327400, 327900	Lime, gypsum and other nonmetallic mineral product manufacturing	Output is used in the construction industry and owner occupied dwellings and is projected to grow just under half that of GDP. Employment is projected to essentially remain flat with only slight growth.
331000	**Primary metal manufacturing**	
331100	Iron and steel mills and ferroalloy manufacturing	Output is used in manufacturing industries. Industry output is projected to grow slower than GDP due to strong foreign competition. Productivity growth is projected to continue to be strong, resulting in declining employment. This is projected to be one of the most rapidly declining industries, in terms of employment, over the 2006-16 projection period.
331200	Steel product manufacturing from purchased steel	Output is used in manufacturing industries. Output is projected to grow very modestly because of increased imports. Employment is projected to decline as the modest growth in output is not enough to offset the expected increases in productivity.
331300	Alumina and aluminum production and processing	Output is used in metal cans and shipping containers, fabricated structural metal products, semiconductors and electronic components, and other manufacturing industries. Output is expected to decline slightly. Employment is projected to decline because of continued improvements in productivity.
331400	Nonferrous metal (except aluminum) production and processing	Output is used in manufacturing industries. Industry output is projected to essentially remain flat. Employment is projected to fall as a result of little or no growth in output and continued improvements in productivity. .
331500	Foundries	Output is used primarily in the motor vehicle parts industry and other industrial sectors. The next decade projects a slight increase in output, but employment will continue to decrease as productivity improvements are expected to continue.
332000	**Fabricated metal product manufacturing**	
332100	Forging and stamping	Output is used in manufacturing industries, including construction, utilities, and oil and gas extraction industries. Output is projected to grow only slightly. Productivity is projected to grow, such that there is expected to be a decline in employment.
332200	Cutlery and hand tool manufacturing	Output is primarily purchased by individuals. Industry output is projected to decrease slightly. Employment is projected to decline because the rate of growth for productivity will exceed that of output.
332300	Architectural and structural metals manufacturing	Output is mostly used in construction. Industry output is projected to grow at roughly two-thirds the rate of GDP. Employment is projected to increase slightly because of relatively low growth in productivity.
332400	Boiler, tank, and shipping container manufacturing	Output is used in construction and manufacturing industries, including light gauge metal shipping containers. Output is projected to grow slightly; demand is projected to continue to grow as the shipping of goods increases. Because productivity is projected to grow more quickly than output, employment is expected to fall.
332500	Hardware manufacturing	Output is used mostly in the construction and manufacturing industries. Industry output is projected to decline. Employment is projected to fall because decreased output combined with continued positive productivity growth.
332600	Spring and wire product manufacturing	Output is used in the construction and motor vehicle and aircraft industries. Output is expected to show little or no growth. Continued productivity growth will cause a decline in projected employment.
332700	Machine shops; turned product; and screw, nut, and bolt manufacturing	Output is purchased by motor vehicle manufacturers and repairers, aircraft producers, and other industrial manufacturers. Output is projected to grow at a faster rate than GDP. Productivity is expected to grow even faster than output, as the industry continues to invest in new technologies, resulting in declining employment.
332800	Coating, engraving, heat treating, and allied activities	Output is used in a variety of manufacturing industries, including electronic components, motor vehicle parts, and communication equipment. Output is projected to increase at approximately the half the rate as GDP. Employment is projected to decrease because of continued productivity growth.
332900	Other fabricated metal product manufacturing	Output is used in the construction industry and is consumed by both individuals and businesses. Industry output is expected to remain flat. Employment is projected to decline because of continued productivity gains.
333000	**Machinery manufacturing**	
333100	Agriculture, construction, and mining machinery manufacturing	Output is purchased as investment by construction, crude petroleum, coal mining, and other manufacturing industries. Continued demand in the construction, mining, and petroleum industries due to high commodity prices and strong demand from record crop prices will contribute to high output growth. However further gains in productivity will cause a slight decline in employment.

Table IV–2. Factors affecting industry output and employment, 2006–16 — Continued

2002 NAICS coverage	2006 Industry title	Factors affecting output and employment
333200	Industrial machinery manufacturing	Output is used as investment in the food, printing and publishing, paper, and other manufacturing industries. Many of these industries, including paper and textiles are expected to face increased international competition, resulting in downward pressure on demand. Other industries, such as petroleum refining machinery and food processing machinery will increase their demand. The net result is negative growth in output. Employment is projected to fall because of relatively strong productivity growth.
333300	Commercial and service industry machinery manufacturing	Output from this industry is purchased for investment and personal consumption purposes. An increasing amount of imports is expected to put pressure on this industry, resulting in a decrease in output. Employment also is projected to fall because of shrinking output as well as increasing productivity due to replacement of machinery with electronic devices that perform similar functions at once.
333400	Ventilation, heating, air-conditioning, and commercial refrigeration equipment manufacturing	Output is used in production in the motor vehicles and construction industries. It is also purchased as an investment by retail trade and eating and drinking establishments. Output is projected to grow at approximately the same rate as GDP as construction is expected to grow, although somewhat slower than from historic peaks, and as replacement of aging HVAC equipment becomes necessary. Improved production techniques are expected to result in higher productivity such that employment is projected to fall.
333500	Metalworking machinery manufacturing	Output is purchased as investment by construction, crude petroleum, coal mining, and other manufacturing industries. This industry is susceptible to import pressures, because transportation costs are low; however the need for highly skilled employees and the fact that proximity to the manufacturing site is important results in some limits on foreign sourcing. As a result, output growth is expected to be very limited. New technologies are expected to increase productivity, resulting in a decrease in employment. This is projected to be one of the most rapidly declining industries, in terms of employment, over the 2006-16 projection period.
333600	Engine, turbine, and power transmission equipment manufacturing	Output is mostly used as an intermediate input to other industries and is exported. The growth of domestic electricity generation and trucking fleets, as well as replacement needs, are expected to contribute to the growth of output in this industry. Because industry output is projected to grow slightly slower than GDP and productivity improvements are expected to continue, employment is projected to decrease.
333900	Other general purpose machinery manufacturing	Output is purchased as an investment by public utilities, chemical, construction, steel, and mining industries and is used as an intermediate input in heavy manufacturing sectors. Output is projected to grow more slowly than GDP. Productivity growth is projected to continue such that employment is expected to continue to fall, although at a slower rate than in the previous decade.
334000	**Computer and electronic product manufacturing**	
334100	Computer and peripheral equipment manufacturing	Output is purchased as a capital investment by many industries including retail trade, finance and insurance, and business services. Output is projected to continue growing rapidly. This is due in large part to extremely large productivity gains, which are typical of this industry. Employment is projected to decrease, although not as rapidly as it did in the preceding decade. Again, this is due to large productivity gains which outpace output increases. This is projected to be one of the most rapidly declining industries, in terms of employment, over the 2006-16 projection period.
334200	Communications equipment manufacturing	Output is purchased primarily as investment in air transportation, broadcasting, and communications industries. It is also used as an input to the aircraft missiles, space vehicles, construction, and communications industries. Industry output is projected to grow approximately twice as fast as GDP. Much of this is due to productivity improvements. Employment is expected to remain flat.
334300	Audio and video equipment manufacturing	Output is primarily purchased by individuals. Industry output is projected to grow slightly faster than GDP. Because productivity growth rates are expected to continue at an even faster rate, due to pressure from foreign competitors, employment is projected to decline.
334400	Semiconductor and other electronic component manufacturing	Output is used as an input in communications equipment, computers, and telephone equipment industries. It is also exported. Output is projected to increase significantly faster than GDP. Much of the increase is due to rapidly rising exports. Productivity growth is expected to continue at an even higher pace, as processes continue to be automated. The productivity growth along with research and development being moved overseas, are expected to result in a decline in employment.
334500	Navigational, measuring, electromedical, and control instruments manufacturing	Output is used mostly by the defense, aerospace, ship and transportation industries. This industry is expected to grow at approximately the same rate as GDP. An increase in the number of satellites and global positioning systems in the use of navigational systems are expected to influence growth in this industry. Productivity is projected to continue to grow such that employment is expected to increase only slightly.
334600	Manufacturing and reproducing magnetic and optical media	Output is used in construction, motor vehicles, lighting and wiring equipment, computers, and communications industries. Industry output is projected to grow at a rate slightly below that of GDP. Productivity growth is projected to continue at a slightly faster pace than output, resulting in a slight decrease in the level of employment.
335000	**Electrical equipment, appliance, and component manufacturing**	
335100	Electric lighting equipment manufacturing	Output is purchased by construction, motor vehicle producers, and individuals. Industry output is projected to grow only slightly. Productivity is projected to grow relatively fast; as a result, employment is expected to continue to fall.
335200	Household appliance manufacturing	Output is purchased mainly by individuals, and by the real estate and construction industries. Industry output is projected to grow at about half of the rate of GDP. Employment is projected to continue to decline as a result of strong productivity growth.

Table IV–2. Factors affecting industry output and employment, 2006–16 — Continued

2002 NAICS coverage	2006 Industry title	Factors affecting output and employment
335300	Electrical equipment manufacturing	Output is consumed as a capital investment by electric utilities. It is also used as an input by electrical and non-electrical machinery producers. Output is projected to grow very slowly, as imports continue to rise. Productivity improvements are expected to continue; employment is projected to continue to decline as it did in the preceding decade.
335900	Other electrical equipment and component manufacturing	Output is purchased as an investment by construction and the motor vehicles and parts industries. It is also purchased by individuals for consumption and is used as an intermediate input in a variety of industries. Industry output is projected to grow at approximately half the rate of GDP. Continuing productivity growth is expected to result in a decline in employment.
336000	**Transportation equipment manufacturing**	
336100	Motor vehicle manufacturing	Output is purchased by consumers and as investment. Output is projected to faster than GDP. US companies are expected to continue to lose market share to foreign automotive manufacturers. In addition, both domestic and foreign makers are looking to locations overseas for cheaper labor. As a result, employment is projected to decline slightly. Productivity is expected to increase, although not as fast as it did in the preceding decade.
336200	Motor vehicle body and trailer manufacturing	Output is purchased in the motor vehicle manufacturing industry, by various intermediate industries, and by consumers. Output in this industry is projected to grow slightly faster than GDP; however employment will decline very slightly, as productivity growth is expected to continue because of automation and advanced manufacturing methods and because of strong foreign competition.
336300	Motor vehicle parts manufacturing	Output is used in the motor vehicle manufacturing industry and in various intermediate industries. Consumers also purchase parts for their vehicles. Output is projected to grow slowly. With the pressure to source parts from foreign producers, and as productivity continues to grow because of improved technology, employment is projected to decline.
336400	Aerospace product and parts manufacturing	Output is purchased by defense, is exported, and is used in the production of aircraft and missiles. Industry output is projected to grow faster than GDP. Greater defense aerospace production and an improving trend in civilian aircraft demand will contribute to the growth in this industry. Employment is expected to increase modestly.
336500	Railroad rolling stock manufacturing	Output is purchased as an investment or is used as an intermediate input in the rail transportation industry. Although industry output is projected to grow mush faster than GDP, productivity is projected to improve at such an extremely high rate that employment is expected to continue to decline.
336600	Ship and boat building	Output is consumed by the military, by individuals, and as an investment in water transport and energy industries. Output is projected to grow at approximately twice the rate as GDP. The Oil Pollution Act of 1990 requires all tankers and tank barges converted to double hulls by 2015; many vessels will need to be refitted. In addition, the rapidly aging Navy fleet will also support a significant increase in production. A modest increase in employment is projected.
336900	Other transportation equipment manufacturing	Output is consumed by individuals and the military. Industry output is projected to increase, as the demand for motorcycles, bicycles, golf carts, and other recreation type vehicles increases. Productivity is projected to improve; employment is expected to increase very slightly in this industry.
337000	**Furniture and related product manufacturing**	
337100	Household and institutional furniture and kitchen cabinet manufacturing	Output is purchased by individuals and the construction industry. The growth of industry output is expected to slow. Furniture production is facing strong import competition from foreign manufacturers. Productivity is projected to grow only modestly, such that there is expected to be a slight decline in employment.
337200	Office furniture (including fixtures) manufacturing	Output is typically purchased as an investment by offices. Industry output is projected to slow. It is expected that the growth of administrative and support services will support demand for this industry, but will be offset by competition from foreign manufacturers. Employment is projected to decrease slightly as a result of increases in productivity.
337900	Other furniture related product manufacturing	Output is purchased mainly by individuals and as an investment in some industries. Output is projected to grow more slowly than GDP. Slightly slower growth in productivity is projected to cause a small increase in employment.
339000	**Miscellaneous manufacturing**	
3391	Medical equipment and supplies manufacturing	Output is consumed as a capital purchase or as an intermediate input by hospitals and other medical services. Output is projected to continue to grow faster than GDP, although the rate of growth is expected to be slightly less than the preceding decade because of some offshoring of production and research and development. Employment is projected to continue to grow slowly; again offshoring is expected to have some effect on employment.
3399	Other miscellaneous manufacturing	Output is consumed as an input in a variety of industries such as apparel and retail trade. Output is projected to grow faster than the growth rate of GDP. Employment is projected to fall, however, since productivity is expected to grow faster than output.
420000	**Wholesale Trade**	
420000	Wholesale trade	Output is consumed as a trade margin on goods sold at various stages of production. Output is projected to grow about twice as fast as GDP. However, big box retailers are expected to put some downward pressure on this industry. Improved technology, such as electronic data interchange and radio frequency identification tags are expected to make storage, tracking, and shipping more efficient and lessen the demand for employment. Employment is still projected to increase slightly in the next decade, since output is expected to grow faster than productivity.
440000–450000	**Retail Trade**	
440000–450000	Retail trade	Output is consumed as a trade margin on goods sold to individuals. Industry output is projected to grow faster than GDP. Productivity is projected to increase because of gains in technology, and employment is projected to increase slightly.

Table IV–2. Factors affecting industry output and employment, 2006–16 — Continued

2002 NAICS coverage	2006 Industry title	Factors affecting output and employment
480000–490000	**Transportation and warehousing**	
481000	Air transportation	Output is consumed by individuals and as a transportation margin on the shipment of goods. Output is projected to grow in the United States and abroad as GDP and the population increase. Cargo traffic is expected to increase with the economy, as are growing world trade and the demand for seats on commercial planes. Productivity is projected to continue to grow, but at a slower rate than it did in the previous decade. Since output is projected to grow faster than productivity, employment is expected to increase modestly.
482000	Rail transportation	Output is consumed as a transportation margin on nearly all manufactured products and on public utilities, and by individuals. Output is projected to grow at approximately the same rate as GDP. Demand for railroad freight service is expected to increase as the economy expands. Intermodal systems, which utilize trains to transport goods over longer distances, should come into greater use. Employment is projected to fall slightly as productivity increases faster than output. Improvements in productivity include more widespread use of computers for tracking, dispatching, and monitoring trains.
483000	Water transportation	Output is consumed as a transportation margin on shipping goods to market, and by individuals. Output is projected to grow more slowly than GDP. Plans to introduce more ferries along the congested coasts to ease the burden on highways, in addition to a likely increase in shipments of primary products for energy industry, especially coal, are expected to help expand output and employment on internal U.S. waterways. Productivity is projected to increase only slightly, resulting in employment growth.
484000	Truck transportation	Output is consumed as a transportation margin on shipping goods to market, and by individuals. Output is projected to grow at approximately the same rate as GDP as the population increases. No growth in productivity is expected, and employment is projected to increase.
485000	Transit and ground passenger transportation	Output is consumed by individuals, businesses, and by state and local governments for school transportation. Output is expected to grow slower than GDP. Demand is expected to increase with population growth. Employment is projected to grow slightly, since productivity growth is expected to be very slow.
486000	Pipeline transportation	Output is consumed as a transportation margin on the shipment of petroleum. Output and employment are projected to fall, as productivity grows.
487000	Scenic and sightseeing transportation	Output is purchased by individuals and some is used as an input in various industries. Industry output is projected to grow slower than GDP. Retirement of the baby boomers is expected to drive the demand in this industry. Employment also is projected to grow faster than economy-wide employment. Productivity growth is expected, but it will not be as fast as the growth in output.
488000	Support activities for transportation	Output is purchased by other transportation industries, and is used as an input in other industries. Output is expected to grow slower than GDP; packaging, freight, cargo arrangement, and other transportation-related services are expected to play a key role in logistics management. No productivity growth is projected, however, as security concerns and resulting increases in operating and fuel costs are expected to increase the overhead; employment is projected to continue to grow.
492000	Couriers and messengers	Output is consumed by businesses and individuals. Industry output is projected to grow at the same rate as GDP. The courier industry has been affected positively by the growth of e-commerce and catalog sales. However, the increasing use of email and fax machines has had a negative effect on the messenger industry, which is expected to temper employment growth.
493000	Warehousing and storage	Output is consumed as a transportation margin on shipping goods to market, and by individuals. Output is projected to grow faster than GDP. Manufacturers are expected to continue to outsource distribution functions to warehousing companies. Inventory management and just-in-time shipping, as well as the expansion of electronic commerce are expected to increase demand for the logistical services of the warehousing industry. Productivity is projected to grow at less than half the rate of output, resulting in an increase in employment.
510000	**Information**	
511100	Newspaper, periodical, book, and directory publishers	Output is purchased mostly by individuals. Industry output is projected to increase at a slower rate than GDP. Increased market activity is expected in custom publishing and ethnic publications; however publishers try to temper new hires to keep costs low as pressure to increase online content is being felt. Productivity is projected to grow faster than output, resulting in a slight decline in employment.
511200	Software publishers	Output is purchased as an investment and is used as intermediate input to many industries. Output is projected to continue to grow significantly faster than GDP due in part to increasing reliance on information technology and falling prices for computers and hardware. Productivity growth is expected to continue, but not as rapidly as output; employment in this industry also is projected to grow faster than economy-wide employment.
512000	Motion picture, video, and sound recording industries	Output in this industry is consumed as an input to motion picture theaters and to the television broadcasting industry. Output is projected to increase as a growing population continues to enjoy movies as entertainment. Productivity is projected to increase, but at a slower rate than output; consequently, employment is projected to increase.
515000	Broadcasting (except internet)	Output is purchased mostly by individuals and as in intermediate input in the broadcasting and telecommunications industries. Output is projected to grow faster than GDP. Cable and other subscription services are expected to grow rapidly; however, there is uncertainty over what direction media forms should take. Employment is projected to increase as a result of productivity growing more slowly than output.
517000	Telecommunications	Output is consumed by individuals, government, business, and other institutions. Industry output is projected to grow faster than GDP. New products and the bundling of services by growing cable distribution companies are expected to force the current wireline companies to rethink their entire structure and favor wireless, cable, and satellite companies. Productivity is projected to grow more slowly than output, resulting in a small increase in employment.

Table IV-2. Factors affecting industry output and employment, 2006–16 — Continued

2002 NAICS coverage	2006 Industry title	Factors affecting output and employment
516000, 518000, 519000	Internet and other information services	Output is used as an intermediate input by many other industries; some output is consumed by individuals. This industry is projected to grow much faster than GDP; the internet is expected to expand and branch out as the amount of data generated continues to increase. Data processing, web hosting, and related services should see strong growth. Productivity is projected to continue to grow at a rapid pace as well. However, it is not expected to grow as fast as output; employment is projected to continue to grow in this industry, but at a slower rate than the previous decade.
520000	**Finance and Insurance**	
521000, 522000	Monetary authorities, credit intermediation, and related activities	Output is consumed by individuals and by firms. Industry output is projected to grow faster than GDP. This sector is basically comprised of 2 different components: Depository Credit Intermediation, which includes banks, and Nondepository Credit Intermediation. This includes credit card companies and financing companies such as GE Capital and GMAC. The Credit institutions have captured a larger marker share of the two. Productivity is projected to grow slower than output, resulting in an increase in employment.
523000	Securities, commodity contracts, and other financial investments and related activities	Output is consumed by individuals and by financial firms. Output is projected to grow much faster than GDP. Population growth and baby boomers increasing their savings activities are expected to increase demand. Several factors are in place for fairly rapid increases in productivity including further consolidations, efficiency, technology and automation. Productivity growth, while strong, is expected to be slower than output growth. As a result, employment is projected to increase. This is projected to be one of the fastest growing industries, in terms of employment, over the 2006-2016 projection period.
524100	Insurance carriers	Output is purchased by individuals and a variety of intermediate industries. Industry output is projected to increase as a growing population demands more insurance of all kinds, particularly health insurance. Productivity is expected to increase at a slightly slower rate than output, and employment is projected to increase slightly as a consequence. Cost pressures, internet policies, and industry-specific software allowing employees to work more efficiently are expected to temper employment growth.
524200	Agencies, brokerages, and other insurance related activities	Output is purchased mostly by the insurance carrier industry. Output is projected to grow; a continuing trend of brokers and agencies taking away business from insurance carriers is expected, as the number of independent sales agencies and third party administration of insurance and pension fund companies increase. Employment also is projected to continue to increase as productivity is expected to grow more slowly than output.
525000	Funds, trusts, and other financial vehicles	Output is purchased mostly by individuals. Output is projected to increase slower than GDP. Productivity growth is projected to fall, resulting in strong growth in employment.
530000	**Real estate and rental and leasing**	
531000	Real estate	Output is purchased by individuals and businesses as rent, real estate commissions, or fees. Output is projected to continue growing as the demographic composition of the population changes and the need for various types of suitable housing increases. Employment in this industry is projected to increase, since output is expected to grow faster than productivity.
532100	Automotive equipment rental and leasing	Output is purchased by individuals and a variety of industries. Output is projected to increase because of firms' preference for leasing and renting motor vehicles. In addition, many equipment rental companies are expected to offer a mix of services, including rental, sales, dealership, and repair. Employment is projected to increase in response to the expansion of services and relatively slow productivity growth.
532200, 532300	Consumer goods rental and general rental centers	Output is purchased primarily by individuals. Output is projected to grow faster than GDP. Growth in this industry is affected by consumers' preferences for leasing or renting over purchasing; smaller capital outlays are often required when renting or leasing. Employment is projected to increase slightly, as productivity is expected to grow relatively slowly.
532400	Commercial and industrial machinery and equipment rental and leasing	Output is purchased as an intermediate input. Output is projected to grow at a faster rate than productivity, resulting in healthy employment growth.
533000	Lessors of non-financial intangible assets (except copyrighted works)	Output is used as an intermediate input and is exported. Establishments in this industry are engaged in assigning rights to assets, such as patents, trademarks, brand names, and franchise agreements. Industry output is projected to continue to demonstrate rapid growth. Productivity levels also are projected to rise rapidly, but at a lower rate than output, resulting in strong growth in employment.
540000	**Professional, scientific, and technical services**	
541100	Legal services	Output is purchased by individuals and by a wide variety of industries. Output is expected to increase as growth is stimulated by increased litigation as a result of a rise in the amount and complexity of business practices. Employment is projected to increase slightly, since productivity is expected to grow more slowly than output. The increasing utilization of paralegals in legal services and the trend toward hiring more in-house lawyers are expected to increase employment.
541200	Accounting, tax preparation, bookkeeping, and payroll services	Output is purchased by individuals and by a variety of industries. Industry output is projected to increase as the rest of the economy grows. Productivity is projected to grow slowly, resulting in employment growth.
541300	Architectural, engineering, and related services	Output is purchased as an investment and is used as an intermediate input to many industries. Output is projected to continue to increase, but not as rapidly as it did in the 1990's. Employment is also projected to grow at a slower rate than it did in the previous decade. Spending on large-scale residential projects is expected to slow.

Table IV–2. Factors affecting industry output and employment, 2006–16 — Continued

2002 NAICS coverage	2006 Industry title	Factors affecting output and employment
541400	Specialized design services	Output is purchased by most industries and by individuals. Industry output is projected to increase faster than GDP. Productivity also is projected to grow, but at a slower rate than output, resulting in strong employment growth. New computer graphics software better facilitates graphic design and layout. Industrial design of certain products increasingly is expected to occur overseas. Interior design is not expected to be as susceptible to offshoring, but only accounts for a small share of the industry.
541500	Computer systems design and related services	Output is used as an intermediate input and is purchased as an investment. Output is projected to continue to grow rapidly. Factors affecting this industry include the expansion of intranets, increased need for remote access, and the growing importance of security. Productivity also is projected to increase slightly; employment is projected to continue to experience strong growth, although not as quickly as it did in the preceding decade. This is projected to be one of the fastest growing industries, in terms of employment, over the 2006-2016 projection period.
541600	Management, scientific, and technical consulting services	Output is used as an intermediate input in many industries. This industry is projected to continue to grow strongly as more companies hire consultants for various projects. Planning and logistics, compliance with government, environmental, and employee benefits and workplace safety continue to play a role in the necessity for these services. Factors affecting this industry include the expansion of companies looking to consultants for everything from human resource advice, how to best manage employee benefits, and security concerns. Some productivity growth is expected, although employment is projected to continue growing at a healthy rate. This is projected to be one of the fastest growing industries, in terms of employment, over the 2006-16 projection period.
541700	Scientific research and development services	Output is used as an intermediate good, primarily by the federal government, and is consumed by individuals. Output is projected to continue to grow much faster than GDP. Research and development in the physical sciences and engineering should grow faster as manufacturing industries outsource their research and development. Social sciences and humanities are less sensitive to business cycles, are generally more stable and should grow at a slower pace as they are not directly linked to new technology development and industrial output. Employment is projected to grow at a relatively slow pace as a result of large gains in productivity.
541800	Advertising and related services	Output is purchased by retail and wholesale trade, eating and drinking establishments, real estate, and the management of companies and enterprises. Industry output is expected to continue to grow. New opportunities created by the internet, international business-markets, and firms' further specialization are expected to contribute to growth in this industry. Productivity growth is expected to moderate, resulting in accelerating employment growth.
541900	Other professional, scientific, and technical services	Output is purchased primarily purchased as an intermediate input and by individuals for personal consumption. Output is projected to grow faster than GDP. Employment is projected to grow, although not as quickly as output. Growth of the veterinary medical care, as well as professional, scientific, and technical services, particularly in areas such as wealth forecasting and appraisal services, are expected to drive demand. Photographic services are expected to increase slowly as improvements in camera technology and reduced prices allow more consumers to take photographs for themselves, and as more commercial photographers work as self-employed contract workers.
550000	**Management of companies and enterprises**	
550000	Management of companies and enterprises	Output is used as an intermediate input, and is exported. Output Is projected to continue to grow faster than GDP. Productivity also is projected to continue growing rapidly, although not as quickly as output. Employment is expected to increase.
560000	**Administrative and support and waste management and remediation services**	
561100	Office administrative services	Output is primarily consumed as an intermediate input in a variety of industries. Output is projected to grow rapidly, although at a slower rate than the previous decade. Employment and productivity are projected to increase.
561200	Facilities support services	Output is consumed as an intermediate input to both manufacturing and services. Output is expected to increase only slightly, as businesses realize the importance of maintaining, securing, and efficiently operating their facilities. Productivity is projected to decrease, causing employment to increase faster than output. This is projected to be one of the fastest growing industries, in terms of employment, over the 2006-2016 projection period.
561300	Employment services	Output is purchased as an intermediate input in many industries. Output is projected to grow faster than GDP. Since productivity growth is expected to grow more slowly than output, employment also is projected to increase. By expanding the categories of workers they offer, temporary help services and employment placement agencies continue to change the way the business economy endures business cycles, helping to fuel industry employment growth.
561400	Business support services	Many intermediate industries purchase business services. Output is projected to continue to increase more rapidly than GDP. Productivity also is projected to grow rapidly, although not as fast as output. As a result, employment also is expected to increase.
561500	Travel arrangement and reservation services	Output is purchased by individuals and as an intermediate input. Industry output is projected to grow minimally, as is employment. The majority of growth in this sector is expected in other services, which include tour operators, condominium time-share exchange services, ticket offices, ticket agencies, and reservation services.
561600	Investigation and security services	Output is used primarily as an intermediate input in various business services. Output is projected to grow faster than GDP. Productivity is projected to grow, but more slowly than output, so employment is projected to rise. Increased globalization of business and finance, the ever-increasing value to business of information, heightened security concerns, and overwhelmed law enforcement are expected to contribute to growth in investigation, guard, and armored car services. An increase in employment background checks and demand for investigative services to solve internet-based crimes such as identity theft, intellectual property theft, and harassment have also contributed to the growth in this industry.
561700	Services to buildings and dwellings	Output is purchased by individuals and many industries including real estate, educational services, and hotels. Output is projected to continue to grow, as the growth in the number of residential and commercial properties is expected to continue demanding the services of this industry. Employment also is projected to grow, but not as quickly as output because of productivity improvements. As residential construction in warmer States grows, so does expected demand for these services.

Table IV-2. Factors affecting industry output and employment, 2006–16 — Continued

2002 NAICS coverage	2006 Industry title	Factors affecting output and employment
561900	Other support services	Output is used as an intermediate input to various business services. Industry output is projected to grow at about the same rate as GDP. Employment growth is projected to accelerate relative to the previous decade, as a result of slowing productivity growth.
562100	Waste collection	Output is consumed by various industries and by individuals. Output and employment are both projected to increase. Demand for waste collection is expected to increase with new residential construction, as more communities implement or mandate recycling of materials. Automated and semi-automated collection methods are expected to contribute to productivity improvements, but demand for services are expected to result in employment growth.
562200, 562900	Waste treatment and disposal and waste management services	Output is consumed by various industries. Industry output is expected to grow at about the same rate as GDP. Employment Is projected to grow slower than output because of small productivity gains. As people produce more waste, the need for landfills and material recovery facilities is expected to continue. Optical sorters and other labor-saving technologies are being implemented at recycling facilities. However, these improvements are not expected to have a significant effect on productivity growth for the entire industry.
610000	**Educational services, private**	
611100	Elementary and secondary schools	Output is consumed by individuals, and is projected to grow at a rate comparable to the previous decade. Declining productivity, which is typical for this industry, and a greater share of kindergarten through 12th grade students attending private schools, which usually have lower pupil per staff ratios, are expected to cause employment to grow.
611200, 611300	Junior colleges, colleges, universities, and professional schools	Output is consumed by individuals and by government. Output is projected to grow as the college-aged population increases, and as workers in the labor force utilize this industry for skills improvement, on-going education, and career transitions. Productivity is projected to grow very slightly, and employment is projected to grow at about the same rate as output.
611400, 611500, 611600, 611700	Other educational services	Output is purchased by individuals and by government. Output is projected to grow with strong demand for self enrichment education, as the baby boomers enter retirement, and for educational consulting, exam preparation, and tutoring services. Productivity is expected to essentially remain flat, which is expected to cause an increase in employment growth.
620000	**Health care and social assistance**	
621100, 621200, 621300	Offices of health practitioners	Output is consumed almost entirely by individuals. This industry is projected to grow faster than GDP, as an expected increase in the elderly population increases demand for physician care. Productivity gains are expected in areas such as medical record keeping; however, employment is projected to increase.
621600	Home health care services	Output is consumed entirely by individuals. Output is projected to grow at twice the growth rate of GDP, while employment is projected to grow almost as fast as industry output. Output and employment are expected to grow as a result of more patients receiving routine and post-operative care at home in order to contain costs. Relatively little work in this industry can be improved through technology, and new technology is usually slow to be implemented. This is projected to be one of the fastest growing industries, in terms of employment, over the 2006-2016 projection period.
621400, 621500, 621900	Outpatient, laboratory, and other ambulatory care services	Output is consumed mostly by individuals. Output is projected to grow faster than GDP. Employment also is projected increase, as productivity gains are not expected to match the high demand for services. More patients are being treated in specialty outpatient clinics, such as kidney dialysis centers or mental health facilities, rather than hospitals. Demand for outpatient services is expected to increase with the projected growth of the elderly population. Ambulance services also are also expected to increase with a growing population, especially the elderly segment, and higher utilization of emergency care is expected by patients without insurance.
622000	Hospitals, private	Output is consumed by individuals, and is projected to increase as the population ages. Employment also is projected to increase, as productivity gains are not expected to match the high demand for services. The largest sector, general medical and surgical hospitals, is projected to grow in line with overall industry. Specialty hospitals are expected to grow faster than the industry average as more patients seek treatment in these facilities.
623100	Nursing care facilities	Output is purchased by individuals, and is expected to increase faster than it did in the previous decade. Despite a growing elderly population, many are living longer with fewer illnesses and are expected to either have home health care or live in assisted living facilities, thus dampening growth. Employment is projected to increase slightly slower than the rate of output growth, as productivity gains are expected to be minor.
623200, 623300, 623900	Residential care facilities	Output is consumed by individuals, and is expected to continue to grow faster than GDP. Employment also is expected to grow rapidly, as productivity declines slightly. Demand for residential care services is expected to increase among the active elderly who prefer to live in assisted living facilities instead of nursing homes. This is projected to be one of the fastest growing industries, in terms of employment, over the 2006-2016 projection period.
624100	Individual and family services	Output is consumed by individuals and is expected to grow faster than during the previous decade, as it is driven primarily by expected growth in the population of the elderly. Employment is expected to grow at an even faster rate, because of declining productivity. This is projected to be one of the fastest growing industries, in terms of employment, over the 2006-2016 projection period.
624200, 624300	Community, and vocational rehabilitation services	Output is consumed by individuals, and is expected to grow at a comparable rate to the previous decade. Employment is expected to grow more slowly than over the previous decade.
624400	Child day care services	Output is consumed entirely by individuals. Output is expected to continue to grow as the number of women in the workforce grows and the baby boom echo enters child-bearing years. Formal child care is expected to be favored over self-employed care, such as nannies. Employment also is expected to grow as productivity grows at a slower rate than output. This is projected to be one of the fastest growing industries, in terms of employment, over the 2006-2016 projection period.

Table IV-2. Factors affecting industry output and employment, 2006–16 — Continued

2002 NAICS coverage	2006 Industry title	Factors affecting output and employment
710000	**Arts, entertainment, and recreation**	
711100	Performing arts companies	Output is purchased by individuals, by food services and drinking places, and as an input to other industries. Output is projected to increase slower than GDP. Attendance at performing arts events has not grown significantly in recent decades; this trend should continue. "All other performing arts companies" is expected to continue to grow more rapidly than "theater companies and dinner theaters." Because the former industry sector includes musical groups and artists, carnivals, and circuses, all of which cater strongly to a young demographic, it is expected to get a boost from the echo boom generation. Productivity is projected to increase faster than output, however, resulting in a very small decline in employment growth.
711200	Spectator sports	Output is consumed by individuals and by radio and television broadcasting. Output is projected to grow as a larger population with more leisure time continues to be interested in sports as a form of entertainment. Productivity gains in this industry are expected to be minimal; as a result, employment is projected to grow slightly slower than output.
711300, 711400	Promoters of events, and agents and managers	Output is consumed by individuals, independent artists, writers, performers, and as an input to other industries. Industry output is projected to grow at roughly the same rate as GDP. Productivity gains in this industry are expected to be minimal; as a result, employment is projected to grow slightly slower than output.
711500	Independent artists, writers, and performers	Output is consumed mostly as an input to performing arts companies. Output is projected to grow faster than GDP. Productivity growth also is expected to be strong, however not as strong as output. Wage and salary employment is projected to comprise approximately 15 percent of the total employment in this industry. This type of employment typically includes administrative support for artists, writers, and performers. Employment for all jobs, including self-employed workers and unpaid family workers, is projected to grow at roughly the same rate as economy-wide employment. This is projected to be one of the fastest growing industries, in terms of employment, over the 2006-2016 projection period.
712000	Museums, historical sites, and similar institutions	Output is consumed by individuals and is projected to continue to grow as public interest in science, art, and history increases because of growth in both leisure time and disposable income. This has had a positive income effect on museums, resulting in investments in capital improvements in the form of expansions and renovations. Employment is projected to increase, as productivity grows more slowly than output. This is projected to be one of the fastest growing industries, in terms of employment, over the 2006-2016 projection period.
713000	Amusement, gambling, and recreation industries	Output is purchased by individuals and is expected to continue to grow as the increasing numbers or retirees spend more time and money on leisure activities. Productivity is projected to grow, but at a slower rate than output, resulting in employment increasing faster than the economy-wide rate. This is projected to be one of the fastest growing industries, in terms of employment, over the 2006-2016 projection period.
720000	**Accommodation and food services**	
721000	Accommodation	Output is consumed by individuals and businesses and is projected to grow because of demand for short-term lodging. Because this is a labor-intensive industry with a largely hourly-wage workforce, productivity should grow slower than output; therefore, as output increases, so too does employment.
722000	Food services and drinking places	Output is consumed primarily by individuals. Output is expected to increase as a result of demographic factors such as increases in population, growth of personal income, increased leisure time, and a rise in the number of dual-income families. Much of the food services industry is labor-intensive and does not lend itself well to productivity enhancements. Many of the productivity gains already have been realized, resulting in no growth. As a result, employment is projected to increase.
810000	**Other services (except government)**	
811000	**Repair and maintenance services**	
811100	Automotive repair and maintenance	Output is consumed primarily by individuals, and is projected to increase with the number of cars and trucks on the road in need of maintenance. Productivity is projected to grow with the increase in embedded electrical components and computer systems within new cars that make diagnosis easier. Employment is expected to increase, however, as productivity gains are not expected to overtake output growth. Factors, such as an increase in the durability of cars and slower growth in the driving age population, are also expected to keep growth at a moderate level over the next ten years.
811200	Electronic and precision equipment repair and maintenance	Output is purchased as an input to many industries, and is consumed by individuals. Output is projected to remain flat over the next decade. Automated repair and self-repairing equipment are expected to contribute to productivity growth and declining employment.
811300	Commercial and industrial machinery and equipment (except automotive and electronic) repair and maintenance	Output is used as an intermediate input to many industries. Industry output is projected to continue to grow faster than GDP. Productivity in this industry is projected to grow faster than average as the industry becomes more automated and dependent on machines to do more work. . Employment is projected to continue to grow slightly as the need for industrial repair workers grows.
811400	Personal and household goods repair and maintenance	Output is used as an intermediate input in telecommunications and other industries, and is consumed by individuals. Output is projected to continue to grow. Productivity is projected to increase at approximately the same rate as output, resulting in flat employment growth.
812000	**Personal and laundry services**	
812100	Personal care services	Output is consumed mostly by individuals. Output is expected to continue to grow as the population grows, as incomes rise, and as demand for personal care increases. Productivity is projected to grow slower than output, resulting in employment growth that is slightly faster that economy-wide employment growth.

Table IV–2. Factors affecting industry output and employment, 2006–16 — Continued

2002 NAICS coverage	2006 Industry title	Factors affecting output and employment
812200	Death care services	Output is purchased mainly by individuals. Output is projected to continue to grow as the population grows and the number of deaths increases. Employment also is projected to increase because of declining productivity.
812300	Dry-cleaning and laundry services	Output is used mainly by individuals, but is also contracted for by other industries, such as eating and drinking places. Output is expected to grow as the affluent population requiring these services increases. Central dry-cleaning facilities that process work for multiple stores are expected to contribute to productivity growth at the same rate as output, resulting in flat employment growth.
812900	Other personal services	Output is purchased by individuals and is expected to continue to grow as the population increases; demand for services such as parking lots and garages is expected to influence much of the growth in this industry. There are expected to be some productivity gains, but output is projected to grow much faster. Employment in this industry is projected to grow almost twice as fast as the rate for economy-wide employment.
813000	Religious, grantmaking, civic, professional, and similar organizations	
813100	Religious organizations	Output is consumed entirely by individuals. Output is projected to grow faster than it did in the preceding decade. Growing demand for religious advocacy groups is expected to continue. Employment is projected to continue to increase, as productivity is expected to remain flat.
813200, 813300	Grantmaking and giving services and social advocacy organizations	Output is consumed mostly by individuals and is projected to continue to grow at a healthy rate. An increasingly affluent population involved in advocacy groups for causes such as human rights and conservation is expected to continue to fuel the growth in this industry. Productivity is expected to increase as the application of modern information technology is incorporated into communications, marketing, fundraising, decision-making and management. Productivity is not expected to rise as quickly as output. As a result, employment is projected to grow.
813400, 813900	Civic, social, professional, and similar organizations	Output is consumed mostly by individuals and is expected to increase slightly faster than the population because of rising demand for professional networking and political organizations. Employment is projected to grow at approximately the same rate as output, primarily because of stagnant productivity growth.
814000	**Private household services**	
814000	Private households	Output is purchased by individuals and is expected to grow modestly. Government regulation of the workplace makes the use of private household workers expensive, relative to hiring specialized firms. Employment is projected to increase slightly over the next decade, as is productivity.
NA	**Federal Government**	
491000	Postal Service	Output is consumed as an intermediate input by most industries, and by individuals. Output is projected to grow slowly; growth is expected to stem from an increase in package deliveries, but be offset by increasing competition from alternative delivery systems and productivity improvements. Employment is projected to decline slightly as a result of automation, competition from alternative delivery systems, and the increasing use of electronic communications. An increase in the number of rural routes is expected to only partially offset the negative impacts to employment from the other factors.
NA	Federal electric utilities	Output is projected to increase as the number of end users grows. Many older workers are retiring, which should lead to increased hours on the part of workers who remain. Productivity is projected to grow slightly slower than output, resulting in flat employment growth.
NA	Federal enterprises except the Postal Service and electric utilities	Output is directed mostly to the finance industries and is projected to grow as the demand for federal services increases. Productivity is projected to continue to grow much faster than output, resulting in a decline in employment. This is projected to be one of the most rapidly declining industries, in terms of employment, over the 2006-16 projection period.
NA	Federal defense government	Output is allocated to defense compensation and is projected to increase only slightly, and much slower than the previous decade. Employment is expected to continue declining, as further outsourcing continues to meet the increased security demands for the War on Terror and as productivity grows.
NA	Federal non-defense government except enterprises	Output is allocated to non-defense compensation and is projected to remain flat, much slower than the previous decade. A slight employment decline is expected as productivity grows by a slight amount and the government implements the Program Assessment Rating Tool to measure the effectiveness of programs.
NA	Federal Government capital services	Output is projected to grow slightly. No employment is counted in this sector.
NA	**State and local government**	
NA	Local government passenger transit	As towns and cities continue to grow, this industry is expected to develop and expand transit systems such as light rail and bus service in metropolitan areas. In addition, declining productivity growth is expected to result in increasing employment.
NA	Local government enterprises except passenger transit	Output is consumed mostly by individuals. Output is projected to grow faster than it did in the preceding decade. Employment is projected to continue to increase, but at a slower rate as a result of changing demand.
NA	Local government hospitals	Output is projected to increase as health care for the elderly and uninsured in government hospitals rises. Employment is projected to increase marginally. Recent employment gains are due to an overall increase in demand for health care, especially among the uninsured and Medicare/ Medicaid patients who use government hospitals.

Table IV–2. Factors affecting industry output and employment, 2006–16 — Continued

2002 NAICS coverage	2006 Industry title	Factors affecting output and employment
NA	Local government educational services	Output growth is expected to result from increased spending on education as all levels of government continue to focus on performance of students in kindergarten through12th grade. Growth is expected to moderate due to the low level of enrollment growth as the baby boom echo exits the public school system. Low productivity growth is expected to cause employment to increase about as quickly as output.
NA	Local government excluding enterprises, educational services, and hospitals	Output is projected to continue to grow as it did in the previous decade, spurred by increasing demand for services from local governments, largely as a result of population increases. Employment also is projected to have positive growth, but at a slightly reduced rate from the previous decade. Local governments increasingly outsource non-core functions, and Homeland Security-related employment growth is expected to continue.
NA	State government enterprises	Output is expected to grow more rapidly than in the previous decade. Productivity is expected to grow at about the same rate as output, resulting in flat employment growth. This is a deceleration from the previous decade due mostly to competition from the private sector.
NA	State government hospitals	Output is projected to grow. Recent gains in output appear to be caused by uninsured and underinsured patients seeking treatment in government hospitals instead of more expensive private facilities. Improvements in productivity are expected to result in slightly declining employment. Most employment in this industry is in state psychiatric hospitals which have been declining for years as more patients are treated in outpatient facilities; this trend is expected to continue.
NA	State government educational services	Output, which is based on state spending on higher education, is projected to grow as enrollments continue to increase, both among traditional college students and among current workers who take classes for new job skills or new careers. Employment growth is expected to result from increased enrollments, and also from institutions hiring more part-time adjunct faculty. Demographic factors are expected to cause output to grow slightly slower than in the previous decade.
NA	State government excluding enterprises, educational services, and hospitals	Output is projected to grow at a much faster rate than the past decade. Employment is projected to be flat, however, as productivity gains are not expected to match output growth. In addition, growth in Medicaid spending is expected to crowd out other State government services that would employ more workers.
NA	State and local government capital services	Output is projected to grow more slowly than it did in the previous decade, but faster than GDP. There is no employment in this sector.
NA	**Owner-occupied dwellings**	
NA	Owner-occupied dwellings	Output is projected to grow at about the same rate as the previous decade. There is no employment in this sector.
110000	**Agriculture, forestry, fishing, and hunting**	
111000	Crop production	Output is expected to grow faster than GDP. Employment is projected to fall as a result of increasing productivity, foreign competition, increasing consolidation of farms, increased immigration enforcement, and a decline in the number of self-employed farmers and unpaid family workers.
112000	Animal production	Output is expected to grow slower than GDP. Employment is projected to continue to decline due to the continued consolidation of ranches, which is expected to occur more slowly than in the preceding decade as most of the consolidation is complete. The expected increase in productivity from consolidation is expected to be offset, as enforced immigration laws raise the official count of workers. This increase in official workers coupled with the re-opening of foreign markets for U.S. beef, boosting output, is expected to slow the previous decade's employment decline and result in nearly flat job growth over the projection period.
113100-113200	Forestry	Output is traditionally purchased by the logging industry. Output will only slightly decrease as global competition is expected to contribute to little or no growth in U.S. production and because many of the larger, corporate logging companies have sold off their forest holdings. Although demand by traditional customers will decrease, employment is projected to increase slightly because of the growth in "Green" industry and because massive infestations of insects will result in the need to replace trees. Productivity is expected to continue to decline, as this industry is a relatively labor-intensive, but at a slower rate than the previous decade due to increased price pressures from the remaining logging industry.
113300	Logging	Output is comprised by the cutting and transporting of timber and/or wood chips and is used in the production of pulp, paper, and veneer and plywood industries. Output is expected to have slightly negative growth due to the continued digitization of media and a recent trade pact with Canada that will allow uncontested lumber imports into the U.S. Employment is projected to decline because of increases in productivity from bigger logging machinery.
114000	Fishing, hunting and trapping	Output is used in food production, and is consumed by individuals. Output is projected to decline more rapidly than the previous period and employment is projected to decrease because of imports, an increase in fish farming, and declines in the level of fish stocks in U.S. waters due to bottom-trawling, over fishing, and pollution.
115000	Support activities for agriculture and forestry	Output is used in the agricultural and livestock industries. The industry is projected to grow more slowly than GDP. Overall, employment is expected to grow slowly as farms and ranches get larger and increasingly hire out specialized workers from this industry to perform tasks previously done by self-employed farmers.

Note: Economy-wide annual rate of change is 2.8 percent for GDP and 1.0 percent for employment.

Note: Not all detailed industries that are included in table IV–1 are included.

Table IV–3 Factors affecting occupational utilization, 2006–16

Matrix code	Matrix occupation title	Factors affecting occupational utilization
11-1011	Chief executives	Small decreases are expected in all industries because as the size of firms grows chief executives will oversee larger staffs.
11-1021	General and operations managers	A small decrease is expected for all industries except the Federal Government. Employment of general and operations managers is expected to grow more slowly than their staffs as firms assign these managers greater responsibility in an effort to cut costs.
11-1031	Legislators	As the number of legislators remains generally fixed while employment in other parts of government grows, small decreases are expected in local governments.
11-2011	Advertising and promotions managers	Small decreases in all industries except advertising and related services are expected due to outsourcing of services.
11-2031	Public relations managers	Small increases in advertising and related services are expected as contracting to public relations services grows.
11-3061	Purchasing managers	Small decreases are expected in the Federal Government, except the post office, and in local governments as purchasing work is increasingly contracted out to private firms. Small decreases are expected in manufacturing of motor vehicle parts and in wholesaling of professional and commercial equipment supplies as purchasing work is offshored and consolidated.
11-9011	Farm, ranch, and other agricultural managers	A moderate increase in crop production is expected due to consolidation of farms and the increased demand for corn for ethanol.
11-9021	Construction managers	A moderate increase is expected in nonresidential building construction. As large-scale commercial construction projects become more complex and sophisticated a greater number of specialized managers will be required to handle the many specific tasks at hand, such as worker safety, financial and cost management, quality assurance, zoning laws and regulations, litigation, environmental protection, and handling of contractors.
11-9041	Engineering managers	Small increases are expected in semiconductor and other electronic component manufacturing and aerospace product and parts manufacturing due to the increasing employment of engineers in those industries.
11-9051	Food service managers	A small decrease in limited-service eating places is expected as the number of limited-service chains expands and food service management becomes more regionally controlled. A small decrease in special food services is expected due to consolidation. A small decrease in hotels is expected due to an increase in limited-service hotels.
11-9081	Lodging managers	A small increase in hotels is expected due to an increase in limited-service hotels with smaller staffs.
11-9121	Natural sciences managers	Small increases are expected in research and development in the physical, engineering, and life sciences due to the relatively faster growth of scientists in this industry relative to engineers, especially related to biological science.
11-9141	Property, real estate, and community association managers	Small increases are expected in activities related to real estate and lessors of real estate as professional third-party management becomes more prevalent.
13-1022	Wholesale and retail buyers, except farm products	Small decreases are expected across all industries because of mergers and consolidation within the retail industry.
13-1023	Purchasing agents, except wholesale, retail, and farm products	Small decreases expected in government at all levels as this work is outsourced to private firms. In the private sector, small decreases are expected in many industries because of offshoring and consolidation.
13-1031	Claims adjusters, examiners, and investigators	A small increase in other insurance-related activities is expected as more insurance carrying members of the public are seeking their own estimations from public adjusters due to the increasing problem with insurance fraud.
13-1032	Insurance appraisers, auto damage	A small increase in direct insurance (except life, health, and medical) carriers is expected as more auto policies and drivers on the roads lead to more claims being filed. A small decrease is expected in other insurance related activities as more appraisers become more likely to work for insurance carriers.
13-1051	Cost estimators	Small increases are expected all industries as the project-cost process continues to become increasingly complex.
13-1071	Employment, recruitment, and placement specialists	A small decrease is expected in employment services as recruiting agencies increasingly adopt computerized human resource information systems that make workers more productive.
13-1072	Compensation, benefits, and job analysis specialists	A small increase is expected in many industries as firms are forced to analyze and alter benefits in response to their growing costs.
13-1079	Human resources, training, and labor relations specialists, all other	A small increase is expected for almost all industries as employers increasingly seek the services of these workers to find, retain, and train both new and existing employees as well as to handle labor relations.
13-1081	Logisticians	Small increases across all industries are expected due to the increasingly widespread use of logisticians to increase workplace efficiencies.

Table IV–3 Factors affecting occupational utilization, 2006–16 — Continued

Matrix code	Matrix occupation title	Factors affecting occupational utilization
13-1199	Business operation specialists, all other	Small increases are expected in all industries as organizations strive to become more efficient and streamline their operations.
13-2011	Accountants and auditors	Small increases in accounting, tax preparation, bookkeeping, and payroll services; management of companies and enterprises; management, scientific, and technical consulting services; and office administrative services are expected due to the Sarbanes-Oxley Act of 2002 that requires more financial disclosure through formal independent reporting of company statistics. Accountants will be the ones completing these reports. Small increases in State and local governments and other financial investment activities are expected due to more accounting and auditing that arises from an increasing population and the elderly population. A small decrease in the Federal government is expected due to increased outsourcing. A small increase in computer systems design and related services is expected as more accountants and auditors play a larger role in developing business information systems.
13-2041	Credit analysts	Small decreases across all industries are expected due to increased automation.
13-2051	Financial analysts	A small increase in the other financial activities industry and a moderate increase in the securities and commodities contracts intermediation and brokerage industry are expected as financial markets grow more complex.
13-2052	Personal financial advisors	Moderate increases are expected in the other financial activities industry; securities and commodities contracts intermediation and brokerage industry; depository credit intermediation industry; and other investment pools and funds industry as a result of the growing demand for financial services and financial planning because of the shift from defined benefit retirement plans to defined contribution plans.
13-2061	Financial examiners	A moderate increase is expected in monetary authorities-central bank as the Federal Reserve continues to increase regulation.
13-2071	Loan counselors	A small decrease is expected in all industries as increased automation of the loan process and customer self-service will lessen demand for loan counselors.
13-2072	Loan officers	A small decrease is expected in activities related to credit intermediation; credit card issuing and sales financing; and other nondepository credit intermediation, including real estate credit and consumer lending. The increased use of credit scoring and online loan applications will limit growth for this occupation relative to others within these industries. A small increase should occur in depository credit intermediation as many banks are expanding their networks of local branches.
13-2082	Tax preparers	A moderate decrease is expected to occur in accounting, tax preparation, bookkeeping, and payroll services due to the use of tax preparation software.
15-1021	Computer programmers	Moderate decreases in all industries are expected due to improved productivity caused by technology and the offshore outsourcing of some programming work.
15-1031	Computer software engineers, applications	Moderate increases across all industries are expected due to growing demand for software.
15-1032	Computer software engineers, systems software	Small increases across all industries are expected to meet the growing demand for system software.
15-1041	Computer support specialists	Small decreases are expected in computer systems design and related services, professional and commercial equipment and supplies merchant wholesalers, and software publishers due to increased off-shoring. A small increase is expected in computer and software stores to meet small business demand for added services.
15-1051	Computer systems analysts	Small increases are expected in all industries due to increased demand for the efficient application of existing and new technologies.
15-1061	Database administrators	Small increases are expected in all industries as databases are becoming more complex, requiring more database administrators to manage and improve them.
15-1071	Network and computer systems administrators	Small increases are expected across all industries as organizations develop and expand network, Internet, and intranet systems.
15-1081	Network systems and data communications analysts	Large increases are expected all industries because of the continued expansion of wireless networks, firms' growing reliance on Web sites, and a greater emphasis on the security and protection of digital information.
15-2011	Actuaries	A moderate increase in management of companies and enterprises is expected due to the increasing practice of conducting investment risk analyses.
17-2011	Aerospace engineers	Small increases across all industries are expected due to an increased emphasis on defense and the development of new aircraft designs.
17-2031	Biomedical engineers	Small increases across all industries are expected as biotechnology shifts from research to production.
17-2041	Chemical engineers	Small increases across all industries are expected due to increasing work in nanotechnology and biotechnology.
17-2071	Electrical engineers	A small increase is expected in electric power generation, transmission and distribution as grid expansion and maintenance become more important.
17-2081	Environmental engineers	Small increases in engineering, surveying, mapping, building inspection, and drafting services and remediation and other waste management services are expected due to increasing demands for environmental impact studies and remediation services.

Table IV–3 Factors affecting occupational utilization, 2006–16 — Continued

Matrix code	Matrix occupation title	Factors affecting occupational utilization
17-2112	Industrial engineers	Moderate increases across all industries are expected as competition in manufacturing industries will drive increasing demand for industrial engineers to optimize production.
17-2121	Marine engineers and naval architects	Small decreases in engineering, surveying, mapping, building inspection, and drafting services are expected because employment of marine engineers and naval architects is concentrated in the portion of the industry supplying marine design services, which is not expected to grow as fast as the rest of the industry.
17-2131	Materials engineers	Small increases across all industries are expected because the increasingly complex nature of materials will increase the need for these workers.
17-2151	Mining and geological engineers, including mining safety engineers	A small increase in oil and gas extraction is expected due to the increasing proportion of mining engineers involved in locating and extracting oil and gas. A small decrease in engineering, surveying, mapping, building inspection, and drafting services is expected as the mining and geological segment of this industry is expected to grow more slowly than the industry as a whole.
17-2161	Nuclear engineers	A small increase is expected in electric power generation, transmission, and distribution in preparation for the possible construction of new nuclear power plants.
17-2171	Petroleum engineers	A small increase in oil and gas extraction is expected due to increased investment in locating and extracting oil and gas reserves.
17-3011	Architectural and civil drafters	A small decrease is expected across all industries as improved CADD and modeling software will lessen the need for drafters.
17-3012	Electrical and electronics drafters	A small decrease is expected in engineering, surveying, mapping, building inspection, and drafting services as improved CADD software will likely make these workers more productive and lessen the need for these workers as compared to other occupations in the industry.
17-3013	Mechanical drafters	A small decrease is expected in engineering, surveying, mapping, building inspection, and drafting services as improved CADD software will likely make these workers more productive and lessen the need for these workers as compared to other occupations in the industry.
17-3019	Drafters, all other	A small decrease is expected in engineering, surveying, mapping, building inspection, and drafting services as improved CADD software will likely make these workers more productive and lessen the need for these workers as compared to other occupations in the industry.
17-3022	Civil engineering technicians	A small decrease in engineering, surveying, mapping, building inspection, and drafting services is expected due to productivity increases.
17-3025	Environmental engineering technicians	Small increases in remediation and other waste management services are expected due to the higher growth in the remediation portion of this industry where this occupation is concentrated.
17-3026	Industrial engineering technicians	Small increases across all industries are expected as this occupation is utilized to optimize production processes.
19-1012	Food scientists and technologists	Small increases across all industries are expected due to increased demand for food products and enhanced food safety procedures.
19-1021	Biochemists and biophysicists	A small increase in research and development in the physical, engineering, and life sciences is expected due to the increasing use of R & D services.
19-1022	Microbiologists	A small increase in research and development in the physical, engineering, and life sciences is expected due to increases in contracting out work to this industry.
19-1023	Zoologists and wildlife biologists	A small increase in research and development in the physical, engineering, and life sciences is expected due to increases in contracting out work to this industry.
19-1029	Biological scientists, all other	A small increase in research and development in the physical, engineering, and life sciences is expected due to increases in contracting out work to this industry.
19-1031	Conservation scientists	A moderate increase in the Federal government, excluding postal service, should occur because the Federal government is increasingly replacing foresters with conservation scientists.
19-1032	Foresters	A small increase in State government, excluding education and hospitals, should occur as more foresters in this industry are providing consulting services to private land-owners, the number of whom are increasing due to a large number of land sell-offs from timber companies.
19-1041	Epidemiologists	Small increases in State government, excluding education and hospitals and local government, excluding education and hospitals, due to growing public health concerns are expected.
19-1042	Medical scientists, except epidemiologists	Small increases in colleges, universities, and professional schools, public and private and research and development in the physical, engineering, and life sciences are expected due to increases in grant funding and in research and development services.
19-1099	All other life scientists	A small increase in research and development in the physical, engineering, and life sciences is expected due to the rapid growth in biological research.
19-2031	Chemists	An expected small decrease in pharmaceutical and medicine manufacturing and a small increase in research and development in the physical, engineering, and life sciences and testing laboratories is due to the expected contracting out of services.
19-2032	Materials scientists	Small increases in research and development in the physical, engineering, and life sciences are expected due contracting out research related to nanotechnology.

Table IV-3 Factors affecting occupational utilization, 2006–16 — Continued

Matrix code	Matrix occupation title	Factors affecting occupational utilization
19-2041	Environmental scientists and specialists, including health	A small increase in engineering, surveying, mapping, building inspection, and drafting services is expected due to increases in the contracting out of services.
19-2042	Geoscientists, except hydrologists and geographers	A small increase in oil and gas extraction is expected due to the increased efforts to locate reserves in smaller or more isolated areas.
19-2043	Hydrologists	A small increase in engineering, surveying, mapping, building inspection, and drafting services is expected due to increased concerns over water supply.
19-3011	Economists	A moderate decrease in management, scientific, and technical consulting services is expected because firms are looking for more specialized consultants, such as financial analysts, rather than economists.
19-3021	Market research analysts	Small increases in management, scientific, and technical consulting services and marketing research, public opinion polling, and all other professional, scientific, and technical services industries is expected. As companies look to decrease costs, much market research will be outsourced to consulting firms, increasing the share of market research analysts in those firms.
19-3031	Clinical, counseling, and school psychologists	A small increase in outpatient mental health and substance abuse centers is expected as the use of psychologists to help prevent and treat addictions becomes accepted.
19-4021	Biological technicians	Small increases are expected in research and development in the physical, engineering, and life sciences and testing laboratories due to increased contracting out of R&D and testing services and in colleges, universities, and professional schools, public and private, to support increasing research emphasis.
19-4031	Chemical technicians	Small increases in testing laboratories are expected due to increased contracting out.
19-4041	Geological and petroleum technicians	Small increases in oil and gas extraction are expected due to the increased efforts to locate reserves in smaller or more isolated areas.
19-4051	Nuclear technicians	Small increases in electric power generation, transmission, and distribution are expected due to increasing interest in servicing aging plants and in planning new plants.
19-4091	Environmental science and protection technicians, including health	Small increases are expected in engineering, surveying, mapping, building inspection, and drafting services due to increased interest in environmental impact studies and site remediation.
19-4092	Forensic science technicians	Moderate increases across all industries are expected due to increasing utilization of forensic techniques among law enforcement agencies.
21-1011	Substance abuse and behavioral disorder counselors	A large increase in outpatient mental health and substance abuse centers, and small increases in residential mental health and substance abuse facilities and in psychiatric and substance abuse hospitals, public and private are expected as substance abuse treatment increasingly becomes favored over prison time and becomes socially more acceptable.
21-1012	Educational, vocational, and school counselors	A moderate increase in junior colleges, public and private, is expected as greater emphasis is placed on student counseling.
21-1014	Mental health counselors	Small increases are expected in outpatient mental health and substance abuse centers and in residential mental health and substance abuse facilities due to the increasing preference and use of counselors over the more expensive services of psychologists and psychiatrists.
21-1022	Medical and public health social workers	A moderate increase in home health care services is expected as people choose to live in their homes longer. A small increase in nursing care facilities is expected as people with debilitating illnesses live longer. A small decrease in general medical and surgical hospitals, public and private, is expected as work shifts to those in other more affordable occupations.
21-1023	Mental health and substance abuse social workers	Large increases in residential mental health and substance abuse facilities and small increases in outpatient mental health and substance abuse centers are expected as mental health and substance abuse social workers become a lower-cost alternative to treatment by psychologists and psychiatrists.
21-1091	Health educators	Moderate increases in child, youth, and all other individual and family services; outpatient care centers, except mental health and substance abuse; grantmaking and giving services; and social advocacy organizations are expected due to increasing public awareness efforts and attempts to promote health research or social policy advocacy.
21-1092	Probation officers and correctional treatment specialists	A small increase is expected in State governments, excluding education and hospitals, driven by the need to supervise the large number of people who will be released from prison over the next decade and those who are sentenced to probation rather than prison.
21-1093	Social and human service assistants	Small to large increases are expected in industries providing direct services to youth, elderly, or residential facility clients due to cost containment efforts. A small decrease in State government is expected due to contracting out. Small decreases in child day care services and administrative service agencies are expected due to preferences for more highly skilled and educated social workers.

Table IV–3 Factors affecting occupational utilization, 2006–16 — Continued

Matrix code	Matrix occupation title	Factors affecting occupational utilization
21-1099	Community and social service specialists, all other	Moderate increases are expected in child, youth, and all other individual and family services; social advocacy organizations; and community food and housing, and emergency and other relief services due to a preference for these workers in place of more educated social workers.
23-1011	Lawyers	Moderate increases are expected in State and local government as more staff attorneys are needed to handle the rising number of caseloads and to deal with a growing number of regulatory issues.
23-2011	Paralegals and legal assistants	Small increases in all industries are expected as firms substitute relatively lower cost paralegals for lawyers and law clerks.
23-2091	Court reporters	A small increase is expected in collection agencies and all other business support services as this industry will employ more court reporters to record and secure records of pretrial depositions, arbitrations, board of director meetings, stockholder meetings, and convention business sessions.
23-2092	Law clerks	Small decreases are expected in all industries as firms replace law clerks with paralegals in an effort to contain the costs of delivering legal services.
23-2093	Title examiners, abstractors, and searchers	Small decreases are expected in all industries because of increased productivity caused by electronic databases. Additionally, tasks once handled by title examiners are now handled by paralegals.
25-1000	Postsecondary teachers	Small increases across all industries are expected as faculty will grow faster than support occupations due to use of part-time faculty; also, growth in programs catering to working adults require fewer support workers.
25-2011	Preschool teachers, except special education	Small increases in elementary and secondary schools, public and private, are expected as States run more preschool programs out of existing school buildings.
25-2012	Kindergarten teachers, except special education	Small increases in elementary and secondary schools, public and private, are expected as States transition to full day kindergarten and as the population of young children grows faster than that of all students combined.
25-2021	Elementary school teachers, except special education	Small increases in elementary and secondary schools, public and private, are expected as the population of elementary aged students grows faster than that of older students.
25-2023	Vocational education teachers, middle school	Small decreases in elementary and secondary schools, public and private, are expected as curricula shift focus to core skills and leave less time for vocational skills subject matter.
25-2032	Vocational education teachers, secondary school	Small decreases in elementary and secondary schools, public and private, are expected as curricula shift focus to core skills and leave less time for vocational skills subject matter.
25-2041	Special education teachers, preschool, kindergarten, and elementary school	Small increases in elementary and secondary schools, public and private, are expected due to increasing enrollment at this grade level and increased identification of students needing special education services.
25-2042	Special education teachers, middle school	Small increases in elementary and secondary schools, public and private, are expected due to increasing enrollment at this grade level and increased identification of students needing special education services.
25-4021	Librarians	Moderate decreases are expected in colleges, universities, and professional schools, public and private, and junior colleges, public and private, because increased use of electronic cataloging and the Internet will result in a declining need for librarian services compared to technician services. A small decrease in local government, excluding education and hospitals is expected as some work shifts to support staff and because of steady or declining budgets.
25-4031	Library technicians	Small decreases are expected in colleges, universities, and professional schools, public and private, and junior colleges, public and private, because decreases in library services provided by these institutions will be countered by increased ability of technicians to handle most patron requests.
25-9011	Audio-visual collections specialists	Moderate decreases across all industries are expected as the need for specialists to catalogue and operate multimedia resources decreases because more workers are expected to become familiar with it.
25-9021	Farm and home management advisors	There should be a small decrease across all industries as fewer funds are allocated for this occupation's services.
25-9031	Instructional coordinators	Moderate increases are expected in elementary and secondary schools, public and private and State and local governments, excluding education and hospitals, because the focus on accountability will necessitate continual review of curricula and teaching methods to improve educational achievement.
27-1014	Multi-media artists and animators	A small increase is expected in most industries. As computer animation becomes more advanced consumers will demand more realistic looking film and games which requires more skilled employees. A moderate increase is expected in advertising and related services as more films require more advanced special effects which will increase the need for multimedia artists and animators. A moderate increase is also expected in motion picture and video production and distribution, as many more films require more advanced special effects.
27-1022	Fashion designers	Moderate increases in apparel, piece goods, and notions merchant wholesalers and small increases in cut and sew apparel manufacturing are expected as manufacturers keep design work in house and outsource production work.

Table IV–3 Factors affecting occupational utilization, 2006–16 — Continued

Matrix code	Matrix occupation title	Factors affecting occupational utilization
27-1024	Graphic designers	Small increases in advertising and related services and newspaper publishers are expected as Internet advertising grows. Small decreases in specialized design services are expected as improving technology enables others to do design work.
27-1025	Interior designers	A small increase in specialized design services is expected as retailers contract these firms to do their interior designs. A small decrease in furniture stores and home furnishings stores is expected as retailers contract design firms to do their interior design work.
27-2031	Dancers	A small decrease is expected in musical groups and all other performing arts companies, because of a reduction in concert dance settings. However, a small increase is expected in amusement and recreation industries because of the increased popularity of recreational dance and dance-for-fitness.
27-2032	Choreographers	Moderate decreases are expected in all industries where choreographers are employed because employment growth of choreographers should be less than employment growth of other occupations because typically there is only one per establishment.
27-2041	Music directors and composers	A small increase is expected among independent artists, writers, and performers as the increased use of the Internet has made it easier for independent music directors and composers to present their work.
27-3011	Radio and television announcers	Small decreases are expected across all industries as increased consolidation and technology have made syndication and pre-recorded shows more common, reducing the need for radio and television announcers.
27-3012	Public address system and other announcers	Small decreases are expected across all industries. Because few of these workers are needed per establishment, the employment of this occupation will grow more slowly than the employment other occupations that are found in the same industries.
27-3022	Reporters and correspondents	A small increase in newspaper publishers is expected. There is consolidation in the industry but reporters and correspondents are generally not the ones whose jobs are being cut.
27-3031	Public relations specialists	Small increases in advertising and related services are expected as outsourcing from other industries continues.
27-3041	Editors	A small decrease in periodical publishers and all other book and directory publishers, business associations, and colleges and universities due to contracting out of editorial services.
27-3091	Interpreters and translators	Small increases are expected in most industries as globalization increases demand for interpreters and translators.
27-4011	Audio and video equipment technicians	A small increase is expected across most industries (except motion picture and video production and distribution, and television broadcasting) to reflect the growing amount of audio and video equipment in use; more audio and video technicians will have to be hired to maintain the equipment.
27-4012	Broadcast technicians	A small increase is expected in the television broadcasting industry. Because of the upcoming deadline for the mandatory switch to digital broadcasting, many stations will have to hire additional broadcast technicians.
27-4013	Radio operators	A moderate decrease is expected in all industries as improvements in technology and the increased use of digital signals reduce the need for radio operators.
27-4031	Camera operators, television, video, and motion picture	A small decrease is expected in television broadcasting as many studios are switching to automated cameras under the control of a single operator.
27-4032	Film and video editors	A small decrease is expected in television broadcasting as the increased use of disc-based cameras allows more editing to be done by camera operators or reporters in the field.
29-1031	Dietitians and nutritionists	A moderate decrease in nursing care facilities should result from contracting out of dietician services and as dietetic technicians replace dietitians. Small decreases are expected in general medical and surgical hospitals, public and private and local government, excluding education and hospitals, as the result of contracting out of dietitian services.
29-1041	Optometrists	There should be a small decrease in offices of physicians as more assistants are taking over the job duties of this profession.
29-1051	Pharmacists	A small increase is expected in pharmacies and drug stores and general medical and surgical hospitals as the demand for prescription drugs grows. Moderate increases are expected in electronic shopping and mail-order houses as more people buy drugs through the Internet; moderate increases also are expected in grocery stores, department stores and other general merchandise stores as these stores add more pharmacies.
29-1062	Family and general practitioners	A small decrease is expected in offices of physicians as nurses and physicians assistants take over some responsibilities of physicians
29-1063	Internists, general	A small decrease is expected in offices of physicians as nurses and physicians assistants take over some responsibilities of physicians
29-1065	Pediatricians, general	A small decrease is expected in offices of physicians as nurses and physicians assistants take over some responsibilities of physicians
29-1067	Surgeons	A small decrease is expected in offices of physicians as nurses and physicians assistants take over some responsibilities of physicians
29-1071	Physician assistants	A small increase is expected to occur in offices of physicians as physicians increasingly use physician's assistants in their offices.
29-1081	Podiatrists	A moderate decrease is expected to occur in offices of physicians and offices of all other health practitioners due to the lack of insurance coverage for podiatric medicine services.

Table IV–3 Factors affecting occupational utilization, 2006–16 — Continued

Matrix code	Matrix occupation title	Factors affecting occupational utilization
29-1111	Registered nurses	A small increase across most industries is expected because nurses provide a cost-effective alternative to physicians and other higher-wage occupations. A small decrease is expected in home health care services as advances in medical technology make it increasingly possible for lower-skilled workers, such as home health aides, to provide a lower-cost alternative for many of the duties RNs used to be responsible for.
29-1122	Occupational therapists	Small increases are expected in nursing care facilities and general medical hospitals, public and private, will result from growth in services for the elderly in these industries.
29-1123	Physical therapists	Small increases are expected in general medical and surgical hospitals and nursing care facilities due to an increase in the elderly population which will need physical therapy services.
29-1124	Radiation therapists	Small increases are expected in general medical and surgical hospitals, public and private, and offices of physicians due to increases in the number of people receiving radiation treatments.
29-1125	Recreational therapists	A small decrease is expected in all industries due to cost containment efforts.
29-1126	Respiratory therapists	As respiratory technicians become more involved in direct patient care, small increases are expected in general medical and surgical hospitals, specialty hospitals, and nursing care facilities. A moderate increase in the consumer goods and rental industry is expected because of the increases in respiratory care services related to the rental of oxygen equipment.
29-1127	Speech-language pathologists	A moderate decrease is expected in the offices of physical, occupational and speech therapists, and audiologists as the portion of the industry employing speech-language pathologists are expected to grow more slowly than other sectors of the industry.
29-1131	Veterinarians	A small increase is expected in veterinary services as pet owners increasingly view companion pets as a member of the family and are more willing to spend on advanced veterinary medical care.
29-2011	Medical and clinical laboratory technologists	As hospitals and physicians' offices continue to outsource laboratory services to medical and diagnostic laboratories, small decreases are expected in general medical and surgical hospitals and the offices of physicians, and a moderate increase is expected in medical and diagnostic laboratories. A moderate increase is also expected for all other ambulatory health care services, as blood blanks constitute a growing proportion of this industry.
29-2012	Medical and clinical laboratory technicians	A small decrease is expected in offices of physicians as hospitals and physicians' offices continue to outsource laboratory services to medical and diagnostic laboratories.
29-2021	Dental hygienists	A small increase is expected in offices of dentists as dentists continue to hire more hygienists to handle routine tasks, allowing the dentist to visit more patients and handle more demanding tasks.
29-2031	Cardiovascular technologists and technicians	A small increase is expected in all industries due to the aging population and the importance of treating heart disease.
29-2032	Diagnostic medical sonographers	A small increase in offices of physicians is expected as more third-party payers encourage outpatient care.
29-2034	Radiologic technologists and technicians	A small increase in outpatient care facilities is expected as more third-party payers encourage the use of outpatient care facilities.
29-2052	Pharmacy technicians	A moderate increase is expected in pharmacies and drug stores and general medical and surgical hospitals as the demand for prescription drugs grows. Moderate increases are expected in electronic shopping and mail-order houses as more people buy drugs through the Internet; moderate increases also are expected in department stores and other general merchandise stores and a large increase is expected in grocery stores as these stores add more pharmacies.
29-2054	Respiratory therapy technicians	A small decrease is expected in all industries as respiratory care is becoming less technical and more focused on direct patient care, which is provided by respiratory therapists.
29-2055	Surgical technologists	Small increases are expected in general medical, and surgical hospitals; in offices of physicians; and in outpatient care centers as surgical technologists replace nurses during surgery.
29-2056	Veterinary technologists and technicians	A small increase is expected in veterinary services as veterinary technicians take on more advanced tasks formerly conducted by veterinarians. Also, veterinary technicians will continue to replace less skilled veterinary assistants at animal clinics and hospitals.
29-2061	Licensed practical and licensed vocational nurses	A small increase is expected in nursing care facilities. The elderly in better health will choose home health care or assisted living facilities as an alternative to nursing care facilities, leaving those with the worst health in nursing care facilities who will require more highly-skilled workers, such as LPNs, to care for them. A moderate decrease is expected to occur in general medical and surgical hospitals and a small decrease is expected in offices of physicians as the demand for more highly-skilled RNs increases and lower-cost workers such as nursing aides will be able to perform many of the same duties as LPNs. A small decrease is expected in home health care services as an increasingly healthy elderly population will demand home health care services for health problems that are less severe than those in the past. This, combined with increasing technology, will allow lower-skilled workers, such as home health aides, to provide a lower-cost alternative to LPNs. A small decrease also is expected in community care facilities for the elderly as most health needs of the elderly can be handled through regular visits from home health aides.
29-2071	Medical records and health information technicians	A small increase is expected in outpatient care centers as the increased use of outpatient services preferred by third-party payers will cause increased growth in outpatient facilities procedures and the need to transcribe these procedures.
29-2081	Opticians, dispensing	A small increase in other general merchandise stores is expected as more of these retailers expand into eye care and hire dispensing opticians for related products.

Table IV–3 Factors affecting occupational utilization, 2006–16 — Continued

Matrix code	Matrix occupation title	Factors affecting occupational utilization
29-2091	Orthotists and prosthetists	Small increases are expected in medical equipment and supplies manufacturing and cosmetic, beauty supply, and all other health and personal care stores reflecting evidence that complications from diseases with increasing prevalence, such as diabetes, will lead to increased demand for prostheses.
29-9091	Athletic trainers	General medical and surgical hospitals, public and private and offices of physical, occupational and speech therapists, and audiologists are both expected to experience small increases because athletic trainers provide a cost-efficient option for treatment and rehabilitation of injuries. Elementary and secondary schools, public and private are also expected to have a small increase as an increasing emphasis on the health of students is leading to more athletic trainers being placed in schools.
31-1011	Home health aides	Residential mental retardation facilities, community care facilities for the elderly, and services for the elderly and persons with disabilities are all expected to experience a small increase as patients are expected to receive less round-the-clock care and more care via visits from home health aides.
31-1012	Nursing aides, orderlies, and attendants	A small increase in general medical and surgical hospitals, public and private is expected as nursing aides will be a cost-effective substitute for LPNs. Community care facilities for the elderly is expected to have a small decrease as more home health aides treat the elderly.
31-2011	Occupational therapist assistants	A small increase is expected in general medical and surgical hospitals, public and private, and offices of physical, occupational and speech therapists, and audiologists due to the growing elderly population which will cause increased demand for therapy services. In addition, occupational therapists will delegate more job tasks to occupational therapist assistants.
31-2021	Physical therapist assistants	A moderate increase in general medical and surgical hospitals, public and private and small increases in nursing care facilities and home health care are expected as the result of growth in demand for physical therapy services by the elderly population.
31-9091	Dental assistants	A small increase will occur in offices of dentists as dentists will continue to hire more dental assistants and delegate easier tasks to them, allowing the dentists to visit more patients and spend time on more complex tasks.
31-9092	Medical assistants	A small increase is expected to occur across all industries. These cost-effective workers will continue to be used in the place of other occupations such as LPNs or nursing aides.
31-9094	Medical transcriptionists	A small decrease in general, medical, and surgical hospitals and in physicians' offices is expected as more transcription work is contracted out overseas and as investment in speech-recognition technology allowing for the nearly real-time dissemination of medical reports and charts increases.
31-9095	Pharmacy aides	Moderate decreases across all industries are expected due to increased use of pharmacy technicians instead of pharmacy aides.
31-9096	Veterinary assistants and laboratory animal caretakers	Small decreases are expected across all industries as more skilled veterinary technicians and technologists become the preferred form of help for veterinarians.
33-1011	First-line supervisors/ managers of correctional officers	A small increase is expected in Federal and State governments because of expectations of increasing prison populations .
33-3021	Detectives and criminal investigators	A moderate increase is expected in the Federal government, excluding postal service and small increases are expected in State and local governments because of population growth and heightened concerns over security.
33-9021	Private detectives and investigators	A small increase is expected in investigation, guard, and armored car services as businesses increasingly seek to protect proprietary information and as background checks become more common. A small increase is expected in legal services as businesses seek to protect information; as firms investigate to find evidence in corporate scandals and information leaks; and as computer forensics become increasingly important for evidence.
33-9032	Security guards	Moderate decreases in department stores and small decreases in hotels (except casino), motels, and all other traveler accommodation are expected as these industries increasingly contract out services.
33-9091	Crossing guards	Small decreases across all industries are expected as enrollment growth is expected to be slower in areas with the most widespread use of crossing guards.
33-9099	Protective service workers, all other	Small increases are expected in Federal and State Government due to population growth and security concerns.
35-1011	Chefs and head cooks	A small decrease is expected in limited service eating places and a moderate decrease is expected in fitness and recreational sports centers due to the growth of restaurant chains and fitness facilities that will limit the growth of chefs and head cooks in favor of lower-level cooks.
35-1012	First-line supervisors/ managers of food preparation and serving workers	A moderate increase is expected in grocery stores due to increases in the prepared foods and salad bar departments.
35-2011	Cooks, fast food	A moderate increase is expected in grocery stores due to increases in the prepared foods and salad bar departments.
35-2012	Cooks, institution and cafeteria	A small decrease is expected in elementary and secondary schools, public and private, and general medical and surgical hospitals, public and private, due to contracting out of food services. A small increase is expected in special food service due to contracting food services to this industry.
35-2019	Cooks, all other	A small decrease should occur across all industries because kitchens are highly structured. Staffing changes will occur by specific type of cook rather than in an all other category.

Table IV–3 Factors affecting occupational utilization, 2006–16 — Continued

Matrix code	Matrix occupation title	Factors affecting occupational utilization
35-2021	Food preparation workers	A small increase is expected in limited-service eating places as food preparation workers are needed to portion or assemble sandwiches, salads, and other foods. A moderate increase is expected in grocery stores due to increases in the prepared foods and salad bar departments.
35-3011	Bartenders	A small increase in full-service restaurants is expected as a growing number of full-service restaurants are highlighting specialty drink menus and offering lighter fare or smaller meals at the bar to introduce patrons to the full menu, thus requiring more bartenders to serve a growing customer base.
35-3021	Combined food preparation and serving workers, including fast food	An expected small increase in grocery stores is due to the increase of prepared food departments.
35-3031	Waiters and waitresses	A small decrease in hotels is expected to reflect the growing trend towards limited-service hotels without restaurants.
35-9011	Dining room and cafeteria attendants and bartender helpers	A small decrease in hotels is expected to reflect the growing trend towards limited-service hotels without restaurants.
35-9021	Dishwashers	A small decrease is expected in limited-service eating places due to expected increases in carry-out orders. A small decrease in hotels is expected to reflect the growing trend towards limited-service hotels without restaurants.
35-9031	Hosts and hostesses, restaurant, lounge, and coffee shop	A small decrease in hotels is expected to reflect the growing trend towards limited-service hotels without restaurants.
37-1011	First-line supervisors/managers of housekeeping and janitorial workers	Small decreases are expected in elementary and secondary schools, public and private; colleges, universities, and professional schools, public and private; local government, excluding education and hospitals; community care facilities for the elderly; and lessors of real estate due to these workers being increasingly contracted out in these industries, stemming from a desire to cut costs.
37-2011	Janitors and cleaners, except maids and housekeeping cleaners	There should be small decreases in colleges, universities, and professional schools, public and private; local government, excluding education and hospitals; and lessors of real estate, due to these workers being increasingly contracted out in these industries, stemming from a desire to cut costs.
39-1012	Slot key persons	A small decrease is expected in casino hotels and a moderate decrease is expected in gambling industries as the increased use of computerized and cashless slot machines will lessen the need for slot key persons.
39-3021	Motion picture projectionists	A small decrease is expected in all industries as digital screens and projectors require fewer motion picture projectionists to operate them.
39-5011	Barbers	A large decrease in employment in personal care services is expected as men are going to hairdressers, rather than barbers, in larger numbers.
39-5091	Makeup artists, theatrical and performance	A large increase in all industries is expected due to an anticipated increase in demand for theatrical and performance makeup services.
39-5094	Skin care specialists	A moderate increase is expected in personal care services. As the population ages, they will increasingly engage in personal indulgences such as skin care treatments to combat the effects of aging.
39-6011	Baggage porters and bellhops	A small decrease is expected in hotels due to expected increase in limited-service hotels which don't use bellhops. A small decrease is expected in scheduled air transportation as security concerns, nationalization of airport security operations, and airline cost cutting will lead to a greater realignment of staff.
39-6012	Concierges	A small decrease in hotels is expected to reflect the growing trend towards limited-service hotels.
39-6022	Travel guides	A small increase should occur in tour operators and all other travel arrangement and reservation services reflecting the greater demand for travel guides and tour services by a more mobile and affluent population.
39-9011	Child care workers	Small increases in child day care services; elementary and secondary schools, public and private; religious organizations; and civic and social organizations are expected as organizations increasingly provide child care services to members, employees, and the public.
39-9021	Personal and home care aides	Small increases are expected in home health care services, services for the elderly and persons with disabilities, and vocational rehabilitation services as home-based services and cost-containment concerns increase. A moderate decrease is expected in residential mental retardation facilities as principal care shifts to workers in other occupations. A moderate decrease is also expected in community care facilities for the elderly as these facilities focus more on day care than home care.
39-9031	Fitness trainers and aerobics instructors	A large increase is expected in employment in hospitals as more fitness centers are built in these institutions.
39-9032	Recreation workers	Small decreases across all industries are expected due to tight budgets.
41-2011	Cashiers, except gaming	Small decreases across all industries are expected as self-checkout and automation become more common and as the popularity of on-line purchasing increases.

Table IV–3 Factors affecting occupational utilization, 2006–16 — Continued

Matrix code	Matrix occupation title	Factors affecting occupational utilization
41-2012	Gaming change persons and booth cashiers	Spectator sports, casino hotels, and gambling industries are all expected to experience a moderate decrease and local government a small decrease as the increased use of cashless slots will lessen the need for change persons and booth cashiers.
41-2021	Counter and rental clerks	Small increases across all industries are expected as businesses strive to improve customer service.
41-2022	Parts salespersons	A small decrease is expected across all industries as the Internet and other electronic ordering systems will reduce the need for these workers.
41-3011	Advertising sales agents	Moderate increases are expected across most industries. As advertisers become more creative about where and how they advertise, they will need sales agents in all mediums to sell advertising space and time.
41-3021	Insurance sales agents	A small increase is expected in insurance agencies and brokerages as agents take on more tasks previously done by other occupations.
41-3031	Securities, commodities, and financial services sales agents	A small decrease is expected in the securities and commodities contract intermediation and brokerage industry because of continuing automation of brokerage activities. A small increase is expected in depository credit intermediation as many banks are becoming more heavily involved in the securities industry because of deregulation of financial services.
41-3099	Sales representatives, services, all other	A small increase is expected in all industries as businesses that sell services employ a growing share of sales representatives to generate new business.
41-9041	Telemarketers	A moderate decrease across all industries is expected as new technologies are allowing people to block telemarketer phone calls.
43-2011	Switchboard operators, including answering service	Moderate decreases are expected in all industries due to increasing automation of switchboards and outsourcing to call centers in other countries.
43-2021	Telephone operators	Large decreases are expected in all industries because of increased automation, wider availability of mobile Internet access, and outsourcing to foreign call centers.
43-3021	Billing and posting clerks and machine operators	Small decreases across all industries are expected due to increased automation.
43-3031	Bookkeeping, accounting, and auditing clerks	Small increases in accounting, tax preparation, bookkeeping, and payroll services are expected due to increased use of these workers compared to more highly paid professional workers.
43-3041	Gaming cage workers	A moderate decrease is expected across all industries as increased use of ticket slot machines and self-cash out machines will limit growth for this occupation relative to others involved in gambling.
43-3051	Payroll and timekeeping clerks	A small decrease is expected in most industries due to outsourcing. A small increase in accounting, tax preparation, bookkeeping, and payroll services is expected due to increased work contracted to this industry.
43-3061	Procurement clerks	A small decrease is expected in building material and supply dealers as procurement work is sent offshore or consolidated. Small decreases are also expected in Federal and State governments as procurement work is contracted out.
43-4011	Brokerage clerks	A small decrease is expected in all industries except depository credit intermediation because of automation and increased responsibility of stockbrokers.
43-4041	Credit authorizers, checkers, and clerks	Moderate decreases across all industries are expected due to increased automation.
43-4051	Customer service representatives	Small to moderate increases are expected across all industries as firms put more emphasis on improving the quality of their customer service.
43-4061	Eligibility interviewers, government programs	A small increase is expected in Federal government, excluding postal service as the retirement of baby boomers will require more interviewers to deal with the increases in the number of people who apply for social security and Medicare programs.
43-4071	File clerks	A very large decrease is expected across all industries due to automation and the increased use of electronic files.
43-4111	Interviewers, except eligibility and loan	A moderate decrease is expected in marketing research, public opinion polling, and all other professional, scientific, and technical services as increases in the use of online surveys will lessen the need for interviews conducted over the phone.
43-4121	Library assistants, clerical	Small decreases in colleges, universities, and professional schools and junior colleges, public and private, are expected due to decreases in staff services and increases in staff abilities to meet patron needs.
43-4131	Loan interviewers and clerks	A small decrease should occur in all industries as automation will increase productivity so that fewer workers will be required to process, check, and authorize applications than in the past.
43-4141	New accounts clerks	A moderate decrease is expected across all industries due to an increase in customer self service in opening new accounts as well as the duties of a new account clerk being consolidated into the duties of other more general positions such as customer service representatives.
43-4151	Order clerks	Large decreases are expected in all industries except electronic shopping and mail-order houses as electronic commerce continues to expand, affecting all transactions between consumers, business, and government, thereby reducing the need for order clerks.

Table IV–3 Factors affecting occupational utilization, 2006–16 — Continued

Matrix code	Matrix occupation title	Factors affecting occupational utilization
43-4171	Receptionists and information clerks	A small decrease in employment services is expected, as this industry continues shift away from the traditional clerical and administrative workers.
43-4199	Information and record clerks, all other	Moderate decreases across all industries are expected due to increased automation.
43-5021	Couriers and messengers	A small decrease is expected across all industries, as couriers and messengers will continue to be adversely affected by the more widespread use of electronic information-handling technologies such as e-mail, fax, and scanning of checks and other paper documents.
43-5032	Dispatchers, except police, fire, and ambulance	Small decreases are expected in all industries because of increased use of automated dispatching devices, such as computers and GPS, that make the dispatching function more efficient.
43-5041	Meter readers, utilities	Small decreases across all industries due to the introduction of remote meter reading technology that eliminates the function of this occupation.
43-5053	Postal service mail sorters, processors, and processing machine operators	There should be a small decrease in the postal service industry as the work performed by this occupation becomes increasingly automated.
43-5081	Stock clerks and order fillers	Small or moderate decreases are expected across all industries as computers are increasingly used for inventory control and the installation of automated order equipment increases the efficiency of making up orders.
43-5111	Weighers, measurers, checkers, and samplers, recordkeeping	A moderate decrease is expected across all industries due to the increased use of automated equipment that performs the functions of this occupation.
43-6014	Secretaries, except legal, medical, and executive	A small decrease should occur across all industries due to advances in technology which allow these workers to take on more duties, while other duties are automated.
43-9011	Computer operators	A large decrease is expected in all industries as older systems that require operators are replaced and technological advances make it possible to automate the remaining systems.
43-9021	Data entry keyers	A moderate decrease in all industries is expected as technology allows other workers to enter data.
43-9022	Word processors and typists	A moderate decrease in all industries is expected as technology allows word processing and other typing tasks to be performed by other workers.
43-9041	Insurance claims and policy processing clerks	An expected small decrease in all industries as technology allows more functions once done by these clerks to get taken over by customer service representatives or insurance professionals.
43-9051	Mail clerks and mail machine operators, except postal service	A moderate to large decrease is expected in most industries. As the popularity of electronic communications continues to grow fewer people will use formal post mail. A small decrease is expected in advertising and related services due to outsourcing to this industry.
43-9071	Office machine operators, except computer	A moderate decrease in all industries is expected due to advanced technology and automation which allows other workers to complete tasks formerly done by these workers.
43-9199	Office and administrative support workers, all other	There should be a moderate decrease across all industries because of advances in office technology, allowing these workers to be more productive and take on more duties.
45-2011	Agricultural inspectors	There should be a small increase in State government, excluding education and hospitals, as more States are conducting their own food inspections, taking over for the Federal Government. A small decrease in the Federal Government is expected as a result.
45-4021	Fallers	There should be a small decrease in the logging industry due to automation.
45-4022	Logging equipment operators	A small increase in logging is expected to occur, as the development of more logging equipment as an alternative to manually bringing down trees will result in a greater need for workers to run the machinery.
47-2011	Boilermakers	A small increase is expected all industries except plumbing, heating, and air conditioning contractors because many new clean-burning coal power plants are expected to be built over the projection period. Also, antiquated boilers in the commercial and industrial sectors are requiring more repair and replacement.
47-2041	Carpet installers	A small decrease is expected in all industries as more durable flooring products such as wood and tile increase in popularity. Additionally, many do-it-yourself homeowners are increasingly taking advantage of easy-to-install laminate floors as an alternative to carpet.
47-2042	Floor layers, except carpet, wood, and hard tiles	A moderate decrease is expected in all industries because of loss of market share to other flooring types, such as laminate, wood, and tile.

Table IV–3 Factors affecting occupational utilization, 2006–16 — Continued

Matrix code	Matrix occupation title	Factors affecting occupational utilization
47-2043	Floor sanders and finishers	A small decrease is expected in all industries as the increased use of prefinished flooring replaces some sanded-in-place flooring.
47-2044	Tile and marble setters	Small increases are expected in all industries as tile gains popularity relative to other building materials in both homes and nonresidential buildings.
47-2111	Electricians	A large decrease should occur in employment services as electricians are increasingly likely be self-employed or hired by specialty trade contractors, which decreases the need for them to find work through the employment services industry.
47-2142	Paperhangers	A moderate decrease is expected in all industries as wallpaper is increasingly viewed as outdated and a greater number of people choose cheaper, more modern decorative paint finishes over wall coverings. Additionally, homeowners are able to take advantage of easy application materials if they do choose wallpaper.
47-2152	Plumbers, pipefitters, and steamfitters	A small increase is expected in the water and sewer system and all other utility system construction industry due to expected increases in power plant construction. Also, some are likely to be used as a replacement for boilermakers in this industry.
47-3014	Helpers—Painters, paperhangers, plasterers, and stucco masons	A small decrease is expected in all industries as demand shifts away from unskilled helpers toward more specialized skilled labor.
47-4011	Construction and building inspectors	A small increase in engineering, surveying, mapping, building inspection, and drafting services is expected as engineering and architectural advances, coupled with more stringent building codes, will lead to more inspectors needed to ensure compliance with codes and safety.
47-4041	Hazardous materials removal workers	A small decrease is expected in all industries as lead and asbestos remediation has been ongoing since the 1970's and continues to wind down, and Superfund projects will become limited because of limited federal funding.
47-4061	Rail-track laying and maintenance equipment operators	A small increase is expected in rail transportation as their services are becoming more important for rail operations.
47-4071	Septic tank servicers and sewer pipe cleaners	There should be a small decrease in the remediation and other waste management services industry due to productivity gains.
47-4099	Construction and related workers, all other	A moderate decrease in employment services should occur as many of the workers in this broad category are being reclassified to specific occupations within this industry.
47-5011	Derrick operators, oil and gas	Small decreases in oil and gas extraction are expected due to continued contracting out of this work.
47-5012	Rotary drill operators, oil and gas	Small decreases in oil and gas extraction are expected due to continued contracting out of this work.
47-5013	Service unit operators, oil, gas, and mining	Small decreases in oil and gas extraction are expected due to continued contracting out of this work.
47-5051	Rock splitters, quarry	A moderate increase in nonmetallic mineral mining and quarrying is expected. Dimension stone demand is likely to increase at a faster rate than other types of stone in this industry, and is also more labor intensive, yielding a faster growth for this occupation than for others in the industry.
49-2021	Radio mechanics	Small decreases across all industries are expected due to use of increasingly reliable radio equipment and more overlap with cell phone systems. The increasing use of wireless systems should somewhat offset those decreases.
49-2022	Telecommunications equipment installers and repairers, except line installers	A large increase in electrical contractors is expected because telecommunications and cable companies will outsource more of their work to them.
49-2091	Avionics technicians	A small increase is expected in aerospace product and parts manufacturing as these firms increasingly perform repairs. A small decrease is expected in scheduled air transportation and the Federal government, excluding postal service, as these industries increasingly outsource repair work to third-party maintenance contractors (foreign and domestic).
49-2092	Electric motor, power tool, and related repairers	Small decreases across all industries are expected due to greater reliability and easier repair of motors.
49-2094	Electrical and electronics repairers, commercial and industrial equipment	Small increases across all industries are expected due to the growing dependence on commercial and industrial equipment.

Table IV–3 Factors affecting occupational utilization, 2006–16 — Continued

Matrix code	Matrix occupation title	Factors affecting occupational utilization
49-2097	Electronic home entertainment equipment installers and repairers	Small decrease across all industries are expected as home electronic equipment becomes cheaper and more reliable, making it less expensive to replace than repair.
49-3011	Aircraft mechanics and service technicians	A small increase is expected in support activities for air transportation as services are contracted in to this industry. A moderate increase is expected in aerospace product and parts manufacturing as these firms increasingly perform repairs. Small decreases are expected in scheduled and nonscheduled air transportation and the Federal government, excluding postal service, as repair work is increasingly outsourced.
49-3021	Automotive body and related repairers	A small decrease is expected in automobile dealers as dealers focus on maintenance and engine service, and contract out auto body work.
49-3023	Automotive service technicians and mechanics	A small decrease is expected in gasoline stations as these establishments are getting out of the repair business. A small increase is expected in automotive dealerships as dealers try to add value to their vehicles through aftermarket services such as maintenance and repair.
49-3031	Bus and truck mechanics and diesel engine specialists	A small increase in automotive mechanical and electrical repair and maintenance due to an increased need to service diesel powered automobiles.
49-3041	Farm equipment mechanics	Moderate decreases in all industries except farm and garden machinery and equipment merchant wholesalers, which is expected to experience a small increase, as repair work is shifted to merchant wholesalers of farm and garden machinery and equipment.
49-3042	Mobile heavy equipment mechanics, except engines	A moderate increase is expected in the metal ore mining, as this industry becomes more mechanized and requires more mechanics. A moderate increase is also expected with merchant wholesalers of industrial machinery, equipment, and supplies as increasing numbers of wholesalers offer maintenance and repair services to customers: this equipment and machinery are increasingly becoming so complex that only manufacturer-trained mechanics are able to repair it.
49-3043	Rail car repairers	A small increase is expected in rail transportation. Productivity increases in this industry will lead to a relative increase in employment.
49-3052	Motorcycle mechanics	A small decrease in other motor vehicle dealers is expected because motorcycle dealers are not expected to be as large a growth area as other types of motor vehicle dealers.
49-3093	Tire repairers and changers	A moderate increase is expected in the automotive parts, accessories, and tire stores industry as this is a prominent maintenance duty for these establishments and those duties are expected to be required more often as cars are on the road longer. A small decrease is expected in most other industries because of longer-lasting tires and job duties being folded into other workers' duties.
49-9012	Control and valve installers and repairers, except mechanical door	There should be a small increase in the electric power generation, transmission, and distribution as more workers will be needed to fix and maintain the large number of power plants being built to meet energy demand.
49-9031	Home appliance repairers	A small decrease is expected in department stores and appliance, TV, and all other electronics stores as these firms scale back their repair services. A small increase is expected in personal and household goods repair and maintenance as most establishments that offer home appliance repair will contract work to this industry.
49-9041	Industrial machinery mechanics	Moderate increases across all industries are expected due to increasing automation in the manufacturing sector which requires more maintenance. In addition, many maintenance positions are being consolidated into broader, more flexible positions like industrial maintenance mechanics.
49-9044	Millwrights	Small increases across all industries are expected because millwrights will be needed to build and maintain the growing number of automated machines used in manufacturing.
49-9051	Electrical power-line installers and repairers	Small increases across most industries are expected due to increased demand for electrical power which will require more power lines.
49-9061	Camera and photographic equipment repairers	A small decreases is expected in all industries as the prices of new cameras fall, leading users to replace rather than repair cameras.
49-9062	Medical Equipment Repairers	A small increase is expected in all industries, as medical equipment becomes more complicated.
49-9064	Watch repairers	A small decrease is expected in all industries as watches are generally replaced rather than repaired.
49-9069	All other precision instrument and equipment repairers	Moderate increases in the electronic and precision equipment repair and maintenance industry because of increasing automation of high tech manufacturing.
49-9095	Manufactured building and mobile home installers	There should be a small decrease across all industries due to an expected decreased demand for manufactured and mobile homes.

Table IV–3 Factors affecting occupational utilization, 2006–16 — Continued

Matrix code	Matrix occupation title	Factors affecting occupational utilization
51-2021	Coil winders, tapers, and finishers	Moderate decreases across all industries are expected due to increasing automation.
51-2022	Electrical and electronic equipment assemblers	Moderate decreases across all industries are expected due to increasing automation, use of robotics, and foreign competition.
51-2099	All other assemblers and fabricators	Small decreases across all industries are expected as those in this occupation become more likely to be classified as team assemblers or in another more specific assembly occupation.
51-3011	Bakers	A small increase is expected in bakeries and tortilla manufacturing; outsourcing to bakeries by large grocery stores should continue to grow as artisan and specialty breads continue to gain in popularity.
51-3093	Food cooking machine operators and tenders	A small decrease is expected in all industries as automation will continue to increase productivity and negatively impact employment.
51-4011	Computer-controlled machine tool operators, metal and plastic	Small increases across all industries are expected due to shifts from manual operations to use of computer-numerical-controlled machines.
51-4022	Forging machine setters, operators, and tenders, metal and plastic	Moderate decreases across all industries are expected due to increasing automation and more productive manufacturing techniques.
51-4023	Rolling machine setters, operators, and tenders, metal and plastic	Small increases in iron and steel mills and ferroalloy manufacturing are expected due to increased skill needs as the structure of the industry shifts from integrated mills to minimills.
51-4031	Cutting, punching, and press machine setters, operators, and tenders, metal and plastic	Expected small decreases across all industries except employment services are due to increasing automation.
51-4032	Drilling and boring machine tool setters, operators, and tenders, metal and plastic	Small decreases across all industries are expected due to increasing automation.
51-4034	Lathe and turning machine tool setters, operators, and tenders, metal and plastic	Small decreases across all industries are expected due to increasing automation.
51-4035	Milling and planing machine setters, operators, and tenders, metal and plastic	Small decreases across all industries are expected due to increasing automation.
51-4041	Machinists	Small increases across all industries are expected because machinists will take over much of the work of lower-skilled machining occupations.
51-4072	Molding, coremaking, and casting machine setters, operators, and tenders, metal and plastic	Small decreases across all industries, except foundries, are expected due to automation and increased productivity.
51-4081	Multiple machine tool setters, operators, and tenders, metal and plastic	Small increases are expected across all industries can be expected because employers prefer the flexibility of hiring those who can work more than one machine.
51-4111	Tool and die makers	Small increases across all industries can be expected because the occupation is essential for automation.
51-4121	Welders, cutters, solderers, and brazers	Small increases across all industries can be expected as welding applications continue to expand due to technological improvements.
51-4122	Welding, soldering, and brazing machine setters, operators, and tenders	Small increases are expected across all industries such as motor vehicles parts manufacturing; architectural and structural metals manufacturing; and agricultural, construction, and mining, machinery manufacturing industries due to the expanding uses of machine welding equipment.

Table IV–3 Factors affecting occupational utilization, 2006–16 — Continued

Matrix code	Matrix occupation title	Factors affecting occupational utilization
51-4192	Lay-out workers, metal and plastic	Moderate decreases across all industries are expected duo to improvements in manufacturing techniques.
51-4194	Tool grinders, filers, and sharpeners	A small decrease across all industries is expected due to an increased propensity to replace rather than repair tools.
51-4199	All other metal workers and plastic workers	Moderate decreases are expected across all industries are expected due to increased automation and greater productivity.
51-5011	Bindery workers	A small decrease in all industries except employment services is expected due to outsourcing opportunities and increased productivity through automation.
51-5021	Job printers	A large increase is expected in advertising and related services because many in this industry are finding it cheaper to produce their own print advertisements on a small scale using new technology.
51-5022	Prepress technicians and workers	A small decrease is expected across all industries as the job duties for prepress technicians have been simplified, digitized, and automated to the point where other workers (newspaper editors, desktop publishers at magazines, and some trained customer service representatives) are performing job duties that had been those of prepress technicians.
51-6031	Sewing machine operators	A small decrease should occur in apparel accessories and other apparel manufacturing and apparel knitting mills, as the work of this occupation is expected to be outsourced faster than other occupations in these industries.
51-6051	Sewers, hand	A small decrease should occur across all industries due to the offshoring of this occupation to other countries who can perform these functions at a lower cost.
51-6052	Tailors, dressmakers, and custom sewers	There should be a small increase in personal and household goods repair and maintenance, as clients who use these workers' services in this industry will continue to demand them at the same rate even as overall industry employment decreases. A small increase should also occur in drycleaning and laundry services as the services offered by this occupation become increasingly important for these businesses.
51-6091	Extruding and forming machine setters, operators, and tenders, synthetic and glass fibers	A small decrease should occur across all industries due to productivity improvements.
51-6099	All other textile, apparel, and furnishings workers	A small decrease should occur across all industries, except janitorial and all other services to buildings and dwellings, because of the productivity gains.
51-7031	Model makers, wood	Increasing use of automated machinery is expected to make for a large decrease in all industries.
51-7032	Patternmakers, wood	Increasing use of automated machinery is expected to make for a large decrease in all industries.
51-7041	Sawing machine setters, operators, and tenders, wood	As wood sawing and cutting becomes more automated and machinery more complex, small increases across all industries are expected for operators and tenders.
51-7042	Woodworking machine setters, operators, and tenders, except sawing	Small increases in all industries are expected as a result of increased use of machinery in wood manufacturing.
51-8092	Gas plant operators	Small increases are expected in all industries because there is usually only one plant operator per facility so it is not often possible to eliminate gas plant operators.
51-9021	Crushing, grinding, and polishing machine setters, operators, and tenders	Small decreases across all industries are expected due to automation.
51-9031	Cutters and trimmers, hand	There should be a small increase across all industries as this occupation is difficult to automate, leading to a continued demand for these services relative to other occupations in the employing industries.
51-9081	Dental laboratory technicians	Offices of dentists is expected to experience a small decrease as dentists are more likely to contract work out to dental laboratories.
51-9082	Medical appliance technicians	Small increases are expected in medical equipment and supplies manufacturing and cosmetic, beauty supply, and all other health and personal care stores reflecting evidence that complications from diseases with increasing prevalence, such as diabetes, are leading to increased demand for prostheses.
51-9083	Ophthalmic laboratory technicians	A small decrease is expected in offices of physicians as automation is making these workers more efficient.
51-9111	Packaging and filling machine operators and tenders	A small decrease is expected in all industries due to productivity improvements.

Table IV–3 Factors affecting occupational utilization, 2006–16 — Continued

Matrix code	Matrix occupation title	Factors affecting occupational utilization
51-9121	Coating, painting, and spraying machine setters, operators, and tenders	Small decreases across all industries can be expected due to increased automation and improved productivity.
51-9122	Painters, transportation equipment	Small decreases expected in automobile dealers because fewer dealerships are expected to do collision repairs and small decreases expected in motor vehicle body and trailer manufacturing because of automation.
51-9131	Photographic process workers	A large decrease is expected across all industries as many photographers are processing their own pictures with increases in digital photography and the better editing software now available.
51-9132	Photographic processing machine operators	Very large decreases are expected in all industries as digital technology makes it easier for individuals to print, copy, and alter photographs with the use of personal computers and equipment.
51-9192	Cleaning, washing, and metal pickling equipment operators and tenders	A small decrease is expected in all industries due to productivity improvements.
51-9193	Cooling and freezing equipment operators and tenders	A small decrease is expected in all industries due to productivity improvements.
53-1011	Aircraft cargo handling supervisors	A small increase in the ratio of aircraft cargo handling supervisors in all industries is expected as demand rises for the rapid movement of goods and products by air, both domestically and internationally.
53-2021	Air traffic controllers	A small increase is expected in the Federal government due to an anticipated increase in commercial aircraft traffic.
53-3031	Driver/sales workers	Small decreases across all industries are expected due an expected shift toward the use of sales persons rather than driver/sales workers.
53-4013	Rail yard engineers, dinkey operators, and hostlers	A large decrease in rail transportation is expected as this occupation is being automated through such technology as remote control of engines.
53-4099	Rail transportation workers, all other	A moderate decrease is expected in rail transportation due to productivity improvements.
53-6011	Bridge and lock tenders	A small decrease across all industries is expected due to the phase-out of many draw bridges.
53-6021	Parking lot attendants	Small decreases across all industries are expected due to increasing use of self-validating/self-serve parking systems.
53-6051	Transportation inspectors	Small increases across all industries are expected due to increasing security concerns.
53-7011	Conveyor operators and tenders	Small decreases are expected in all industries except warehousing and storage due to the phase out of conveyors needing tending.
53-7051	Industrial truck and tractor operators	Small decreases across all industries are expected due to continued emphasis on operational efficiencies.
53-7062	Laborers and freight, stock, and material movers, hand	Small decreases across all industries are expected due to automation.
53-7063	Machine feeders and offbearers	Small decreases across all industries are expected due to automation.
53-7064	Packers and packagers, hand	Moderate decreases across all industries are expected due to automation.
53-7072	Pump operators, except wellhead pumpers	Small decreases across all industries are expected due to automation.
53-7073	Wellhead pumpers	Small decreases across all industries are expected due to automation.
53-7081	Refuse and recyclable material collectors	Small decreases across all industries are expected due to automation.
53-7111	Shuttle car operators	Small decreases across all industries are expected due to automation.
53-7199	Material moving workers, all other	Small decreases across all industries are expected due to automation.

Chapter V. Estimating Occupational Replacement Needs

Projections of job growth provide valuable insight into future employment opportunities because each new job created is an opening for a worker entering an occupation. However, opportunities also result when workers leave their occupations and need to be replaced. In most occupations, these replacements provide more job openings than employment growth does.

To suit the needs of different users, the Bureau of Labor Statistics (BLS) produces two estimates of replacement needs:

- *Total replacement needs* estimate the number of openings resulting from the flow of workers out of an occupation, without regard to the number of workers entering over the same period. This estimate sometimes is used to identify occupations with high rates of workers departing. Total replacement needs also can be used to roughly approximate the number of openings expected for any reason. However, because experienced workers seeking to reenter the occupation will fill some of those openings, it is not a good measure of opportunities for people seeking to enter the occupation for the first time.

- *Net replacement needs* estimate the number of workers leaving an occupation who will need to be replaced by relatively younger workers. It often is used to approximate openings stemming from retirements and from the need to replace workers who permanently leave an occupation for other reasons. This number added to openings due to job growth roughly estimates opportunities for workers entering an occupation for the first time. And because workers new to an occupation often need training, this estimate may be used to assess the minimum number of workers who will need to be trained for the occupation. Because the estimate is limited to opportunities created by relatively older workers leaving the occupation, it may underestimate openings for new entrants, especially in occupations where many people permanently leave the occupation at younger ages.

Neither of these estimates counts workers who change jobs but remain in the same occupation. There are many openings advertised that would not be included in the estimates because those openings are created by workers switching jobs but staying in the same occupation.

To develop estimates of replacements, BLS used data from the Current Population Survey (CPS), a household survey that collects demographic and employment information about individuals[1]. Although the data source was the same for both types of replacement needs estimates, different methods were used. This chapter summarizes the specific methods used to estimate total and net separations and replacements.

[1] CPS data uses occupational codes consistent with the U.S. Census Bureau, but the occupational employment projections use more detailed occupational codes from the 2000 Standard Occupational Classification (SOC) system. To apply CPS data to the occupations in the projections matrix, analysts identified the CPS occupations that were equivalent to, or included in, the detailed SOC occupation.

Developing estimates of total separations and replacements

Total, or gross, separations measure the flow of workers out of an occupation, without regard to those entering it. To estimate the number of workers who changed their occupation over the year, analysts used data from the January 2006 CPS supplement, which asked workers that question directly. To estimate the number of workers who stopped working altogether, monthly survey data from August 2004 to July 2006 were used to match individuals' employment data from one month to the same month the following year[2].

If employment in an occupation grew or remained the same, the number of separations was equal to the number of workers replaced over the year. If employment declined, however, that decline was subtracted from the number of separations to determine replacements.

Next, the number of replacements was divided by employment in the first year to determine the replacement rate over the year. To estimate future replacement needs, this historical rate was multiplied by projected employment for the midpoint of the 2006–16 decade.

There are limitations to this method of measuring separations and replacements. The CPS is conducted to obtain current data on the labor force status of individuals, rather than to measure changes over time. One limitation, for example, is that since the CPS collects data by household, data cannot be collected on the original individuals in the household if they have moved. Thus, movers are excluded from calculations of total separations, which may bias separations downward since people who move are more likely to have changed occupations or labor force status. Deaths also are excluded, further downward biasing the estimates.

Because the CPS is a sample survey, sampling error also must be considered. Data on total separations for occupations with fewer than 50,000 employees were judged unreliable because of the limited number of observations in the sample. Data for the remaining occupations were examined individually for cases where data appeared unreliable, such as when replacement rates differed greatly from previously developed rates or from the rates of similar occupations. In these cases, analysts used data from proxies: either a related occupation or a summary occupational group.

Developing estimates of net separations and replacements

Estimates of net separations account for the net effect of workers flowing into and out of an occupation as they age. This measure often is used as a rough estimate of opportunities for workers entering an occupation for the first time. Since these workers often need training to enter the occupation, this estimate also represents the minimum number of workers who will need to be trained for an occupation.

[2] CPS sample design includes surveying a household for 4 months, not contacting that household for 8 months, and then surveying it again for another 4 months. As a result, half of the sample from an individual year is in the first year of being included, and will be re-contacted the following year.

Figure 1. Total and net occupational entrants and separations

Figure 1 illustrates the differences between total and net separations. For each age group, the figure shows total and net occupational entrants and separations. Most of the younger age groups exhibit an excess of total entrants over total separations as more young people begin working in an occupation than leave the occupation. This excess is referred to as *net entrants*. Likewise, the excess of total separations over total entrants in older age groups is referred to as *net separations*.

Total separations:

- Occur in all age groups
- Are independant of the total number of entrants
- Identify all of the normal movements out of occupations

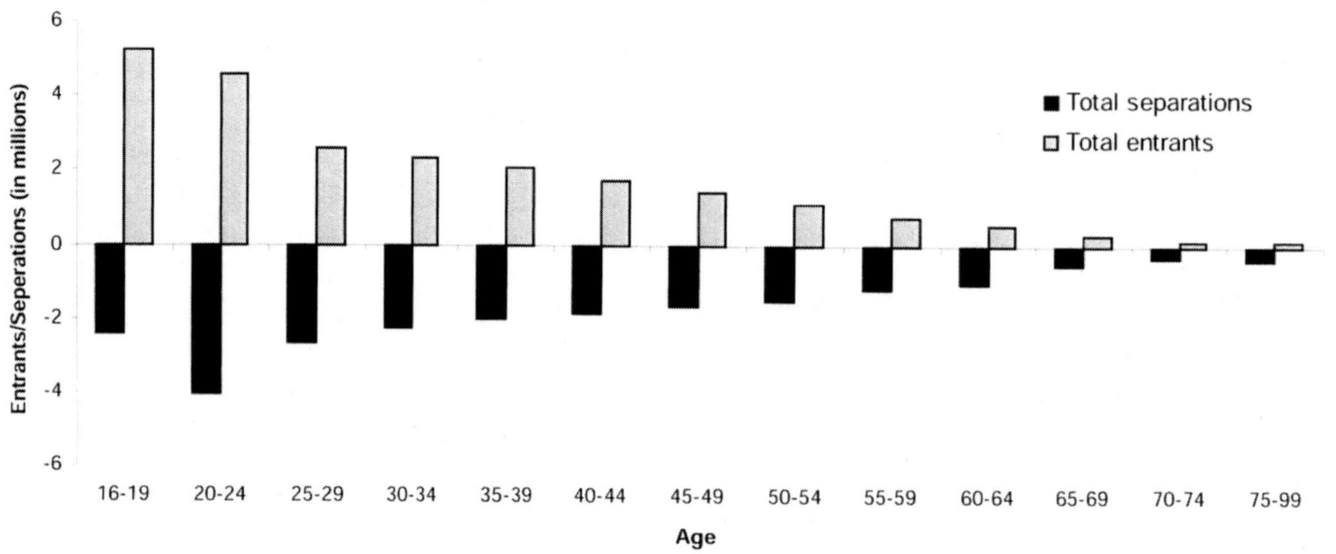

Net separations:

- Occur only when total separations exceed total entrants within an age group
- For an occupation, are the sum of separations for each age group
- Exclude information about net entrants

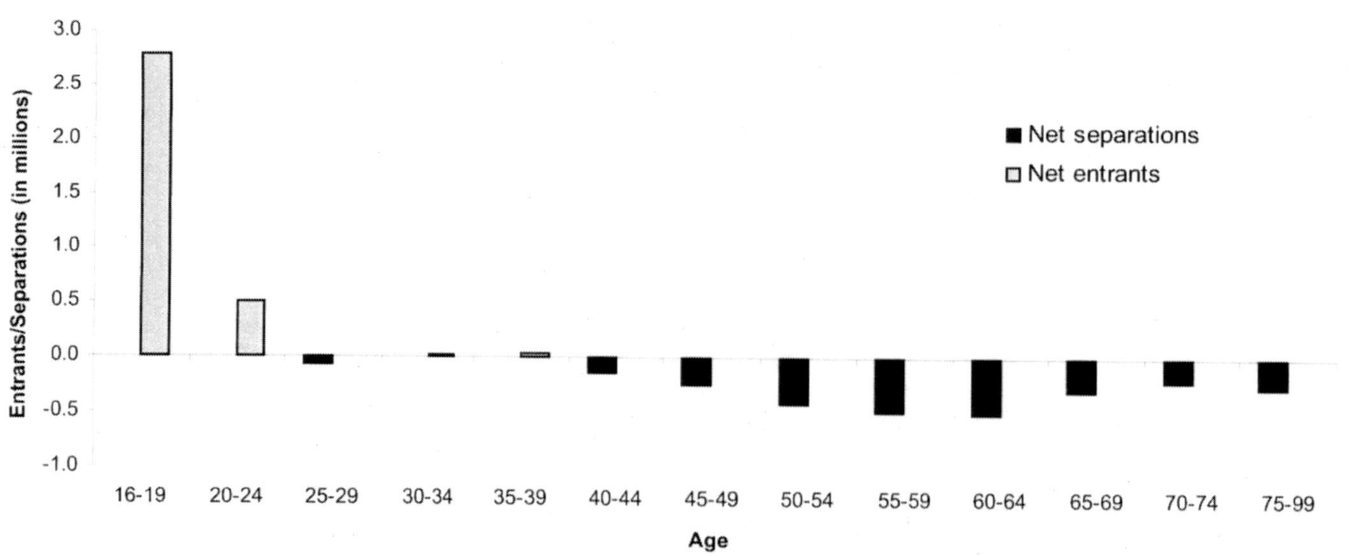

Table V–1. Net separations for registered nurses and for waiters and waitresses, by age group, 2001–2006

(Numbers in thousands)

2001 employment[1]		2006 employment[2]		Net change, 2001–06	Net separations, 2001–06	Separation rate[3], 2001–06 (percent)
Age	Number	Age	Number			
Registered nurses						
16–99	2,139	—	2,435	296	110	5.2
		16–20	4	4		
16–19	1	21–24	73	71	0	0
20–24	60	25–29	200	140	0	0
25–29	211	30–34	297	86	0	0
30–34	269	35–39	299	30	0	0
35–39	340	40–44	399	59	0	0
40–44	411	45–49	419	8	0	0
45–49	350	50–54	359	9	0	0
50–54	239	55–59	224	–15	15	6.4
55–59	145	60–64	111	–35	35	23.8
60–64	77	65–69	36	–41	41	53.0
65–69	23	70–74	11	–12	12	52.8
70–74	9	75–79	3	–5	5	60.7
75–99	4	80–99	2	–2	2	54.0
Waiters and waitresses						
16–99	1,790	—	1,903	113	500	27.9
		16–20	540	540		
16–19	406	21–24	478	72	0	0
20–24	510	25–29	258	–251	251	49.3
25–29	239	30–34	159	–80	80	33.6
30–34	165	35–39	124	–41	41	24.9
35–39	152	40–44	113	–39	39	25.7
40–44	118	45–49	90	–27	27	23.2
45–49	74	50–54	56	–18	18	24.0
50–54	52	55–59	36	–16	16	31.2
55–59	32	60–64	24	–8	8	24.2
60–64	24	65–69	12	–12	12	49.0
65–69	11	70–74	7	–4	4	35.6
70–74	7	75–79	4	–2	2	35.0
75–99	3	80–99	1	–2	2	64.1

[1] 2001 data are averages of 1997, 1998, 1999, 2000, and 2001.
[2] 2006 data are averages of 2002, 2003, 2004, 2005, and 2006.
[3] Separation rates were calculated by dividing net separations by 2001 employment.
Note: Age group data may not sum to age 16–99 total due to rounding.

To increase the sample size and reduce cyclical fluctuations, employment data from 5 years (1997, 1998, 1999, 2000, and 2001) were averaged and used as the base year employment[3]. Similarly, employment data from 2002, 2003, 2004, 2005, and 2006 were averaged and used to represent employment 5 years later. To simplify this discussion, the 1997–2001 averages are referred to as 2001 data, and the 2002–06 averages are referred to as 2006 data.

BLS analysts developed estimates of net separations by comparing the level of occupational employment for 13 different age cohorts at two points in time, 5 years apart. Specifically, in a given occupation, employment data for each age group in 2001 were compared with corresponding data for the group 5 years older in 2006. A decline in employment for an age cohort is a measure of net separations for that cohort, while an increase is a measure of net entrants. For example, the number of registered nurses aged 20 to 24 in 2001 was compared to the number of registered nurses aged 25 to 29 in 2006. (See table V–1) The employment in 2006 was greater, indicating that more individuals aged 20 to 24 in 2001 entered than had left the occupation. Thus, for this age group net separations were recorded as zero. For registered nurses in the cohort aged 50 to 54 in 2001, however, employment declined through 2006, indicating that there were net separations for the group. For each occupation, net separations from each age cohort were summed to develop an estimate of overall net separations for the occupation.

In most occupations, net separations occur only in the older age groups, usually above age 45. This pattern typically reflects retirements. In some occupations, however, net separations happen in younger age groups. A high number of separations of young workers often occurs in occupations that have relatively low entrance requirements and pay relatively low wages. Young workers often take jobs in such occupations while obtaining additional education or training; when these workers qualify for a higher paying occupation, they transfer. Waiters and waitresses are an example of this type of occupation, as shown in table V–1, where net separations occurred for all except the youngest age cohort.

Next, BLS analysts estimated net replacements. Net replacements were equal to net separations unless employment declined between 2001 and 2006. Declines in employment were subtracted from the net separations in groups aged 16–49, because younger workers are more likely to be affected by adverse economic conditions. If the employment decline was greater than those separations, the remaining decline was subtracted from the net separations of those aged 50 and over. The resulting age-specific net replacements were divided by 2001 employment in each age group to calculate a historical 5-year net replacement rate for each group.

These historical replacement rates were used to estimate replacement needs during the 2006–16 decade. First, replacement needs for the first 5 years were calculated in each age cohort. Then, that number of people leaving was used to estimate the number of people remaining in the cohort in 2011. Next, that estimate was multiplied by the historical replacement rate to calculate replacement needs for the next 5 years. Finally, the future replacement needs were summed, and future overall replacement rates for each occupation were computed.

[3] Data from 1997–99 used 1990 Census codes, while data from 2000 to present uses 2000 Census codes. However, data from 2000–02 were coded on both systems, which made it possible to develop a crosswalk and estimate employment for 1997–99 using the 2000 Census codes. Thus, all analysis is done using 2000 Census codes.

Table V–2. Net replacement data for registered nurses, by age group, 2006–16
(Numbers in thousands)

Age	2006 employment[1]	Net replacements, 2006–11	Net replacement rate, 2001–06 (percent)	Number remaining, 2011	Net replacements, 2011–16	Net replacements, 2006–16	Net replacement rate, 2006–16 (percent)
16–99	2,435	163	5.2	—	239	402	16.5
16–19	2	0	0	0	0	0	—
20–24	75	0	0	2	0	0	—
25–29	200	0	0	75	0	0	—
30–34	297	0	0	200	0	0	—
35–39	299	0	0	297	0	0	—
40–44	399	0	0	299	0	0	—
45–49	419	0	0	399	0	0	—
50–54	359	23	6.4	419	27	50	—
55–59	224	53	23.8	336	80	133	—
60–64	111	59	53	170	90	149	—
65–69	36	19	52.8	52	28	47	—
70–74	11	7	60.7	17	10	17	—
75–99	6	3	54	7	4	7	—

[1] 2006 data are averages of 2002, 2003, 2004, 2005, and 2006.
Note: Age group data may not sum to age 16–99 total due to rounding.

Specifically, net replacement needs were calculated for 2006–11 by multiplying 2006 employment for each age group by its historical replacement rate. The number of workers remaining in 2011 for each age cohort was calculated by subtracting the number of workers from that age cohort who left (assumed to be equal to 2006–11 replacements) from 2006 employment for the age cohort. For example, table V–2 shows the number of workers remaining 2011 for registered nurses aged 55 to 59 to be 336,000. This was calculated by subtracting the 23,000 net replacements in 2006–11 for those aged 50–54 from the 359,000 employed in that age group in 2006. The younger age group was looked at because the 2006 workforce will age by 2011, and so the cohort must be moved forward.

Then, net replacements for 2011–16 were calculated by multiplying the historical replacement rate for each age group by the number of workers remaining in that age group in 2011. Summing the number of net replacements for each of the 5-year periods, 2006–11 and 2011–16, provided an estimate of net replacements over the 10-year projection period. The 2006–16 net replacement rates were calculated by dividing net replacements for 2006–16 by 2006 employment. Dividing the net replacements for 2006–16 by 10 yielded the annual average net replacement needs.

Just as in the development of total replacements, some estimates of net replacements used the replacement rates of proxy occupations. For large occupations, the CPS data averaged over 5 years provides reliable employment data for each age group. However, for small occupations (fewer than 10,000 workers in 2006), the sample is too small and the net replacement data are unreliable. Data also were deemed unreliable for some other occupations which had larger employment when there was an irregular distribution of net replacements among the age groups or when the net replacement rates were inconsistent with rates for similar occupations.

Table V–3 presents 2005–06 total and projected 2006–16 net replacement rates for OES-based matrix occupations and shows 2006–16 annual average total and net replacement needs. The table notes when proxy occupations were used.

Frequently asked questions about replacement needs

Q. What is the difference between total and net replacement needs?
A. Total replacement needs measure the total number of openings that result from workers leaving the occupation, without regard to the workers who reenter that occupation. Net replacement needs measure the number of relatively older workers who leave an occupation and are replaced by relatively younger workers. Total replacement needs are higher, because they also include openings that may be filled by workers who reenter an occupation after a period of separation and by older workers who are new entrants to the occupation. However, since these scenarios do not create opportunities for younger workers, they are not included in net replacement needs.

Q. How should total and net replacement needs be used?
A. There are many different uses for total and net replacement needs. For example, total replacement needs can be used to study which occupations see more worker turnover and which offer more total openings. Net replacements are often used to learn what job opportunities will be like for future workers, to use in career guidance, and to estimate training needs for future workers.

Q. Why are the estimates of growth and net replacement needs described as providing a minimum measure of training needs?
A. The number of new entrants needed is underestimated due to relatively younger workers permanently leaving an occupation and relatively older workers entering the occupation for the first time. Even if growth and net replacement needs perfectly measured the need for new entrants, training needs would still be underestimated because some people who complete training do not enter the occupation for which they qualify.

Q. Do the 2006–16 projected net replacement needs assume that future labor market behavior will not change from past patterns?
A. Yes, the projected net replacement needs assume workers will continue to retire and otherwise exit an occupation at similar ages as have been observed in the recent past. 2001–06 occupation- and age-specific rates are used in calculating the projected rates. The 2001–06 rates are applied to current occupational age-distribution data to estimate replacement needs for the future. The result is an occupation-specific replacement rate that captures the impact of demographic, but not behavioral, changes.

Q. Are separations the same as replacement needs?
A. In most occupations, yes. If employment declined during the historical period, however, separations will exceed replacement needs by the decline in employment. When employment is declining, not all people who separate from an occupation are replaced.

Q. Should a projected decline in employment be subtracted from replacement needs to estimate job opportunities?
A. No. If employment is projected to decline, the number of opportunities resulting from growth is zero, and replacement needs constitute the only source of opportunities. When employment declines, separations increase both because it is more likely that individuals lose their jobs and, in the case of net separations, because fewer are entering the occupation. Replacement needs already capture these effects by reducing separations by declines in employment. They should not be further reduced by projected employment declines.

Q. If employment is declining rapidly, is it possible for replacement needs to be zero?
A. In the extreme case, yes. For example, assume that, in a limited geographic area, a single firm is the sole employer of tool and die makers. If the firm ceases operations, all tool and die makers in the area will leave the occupation; separations will equal the decline in employment, and there will be no replacement needs. On a national scale, however, a situation like this is highly unlikely because not all areas of the country share the same market conditions.

Q. Are there any data on replacement needs by industry?
A. No, estimates of replacement needs are created only for occupations. The Bureau of Labor Statistics does have a survey that collects data on current job openings and labor turnover by industry. For more information, see the Job Openings and Labor Turnover Survey program Web site: **http://www.bls.gov/jlt/home.htm**. The Bureau also has a program that estimates gross job gains and losses by industry. For more information, see the Business Employment Dynamics program Web site: **http://www.bls.gov/bdm/home.htm**.

Table V-3. Total and net replacement rates and annual average projected replacement needs, 2006–16
(Numbers in thousands)

2006 National Employment Matrix code and title		Total employment, 2006	Replacement rate (percent)		Annual average replacement needs, 2006–16	
			Total, 2005–06	Net, 2006–16	Total	Net
00-0000	Total, all occupations	150,620	15.9	22.1	25,186	3,336
11-1300	Management, business, and financial occupations	15,397	9.7	18.6	1,578	287
11-0000	Management occupations	8,789	9.2	19.8	832	174
11-1000	Top executives	2,187	6.0	24.6	133	54
11-1011	Chief executives	402	5.0	27.3	20	11
11-1021	General and operations managers	1,720	6.3	24.1	109	41
11-1031	Legislators[1]	65	5.1	19.0	3	1
11-2000	Advertising, marketing, promotions, public relations, and sales managers	583	9.5	22.3	59	13
11-2011	Advertising and promotions managers[1]	47	5.5	22.2	3	1
11-2020	Marketing and sales managers	486	9.9	22.2	51	11
11-2021	Marketing managers	167	9.9	22.2	18	4
11-2022	Sales managers	318	9.9	22.2	33	7
11-2031	Public relations managers[1]	50	9.2	23.3	5	1
11-3000	Operations specialties managers	1,474	8.9	21.0	138	31
11-3011	Administrative services managers	247	6.4	26.4	17	7
11-3021	Computer and information systems managers	264	9.3	16.2	27	4
11-3031	Financial managers	506	9.5	14.5	51	7
11-3040	Human resources managers	136	10.6	18.8	15	3
11-3041	Compensation and benefits managers	49	10.6	18.8	6	1
11-3042	Training and development managers	29	10.6	18.8	3	1
11-3049	Human resources managers, all other	58	10.6	18.8	7	1
11-3051	Industrial production managers	157	9.7	34.5	15	5
11-3061	Purchasing managers	70	9.9	28.6	7	2
11-3071	Transportation, storage, and distribution managers	94	6.3	29.7	6	3
11-9000	Other management occupations	4,545	10.7	16.8	503	76
11-9010	Agricultural managers	1,317	11.6	8.7	147	11
11-9011	Farm, ranch, and other agricultural managers	258	6.9	7.3	18	2
11-9012	Farmers and ranchers	1,058	12.8	9.0	130	10
11-9021	Construction managers	487	6.9	15.5	37	8
11-9030	Education administrators	443	10.8	27.9	51	12
11-9031	Education administrators, preschool and child care center/program	56	10.8	27.9	7	2
11-9032	Education administrators, elementary and secondary school	226	10.8	27.9	25	6
11-9033	Education administrators, postsecondary	131	10.8	27.9	15	4
11-9039	Education administrators, all other	30	10.8	27.9	3	1
11-9041	Engineering managers	187	3.1	20.2	6	4
11-9051	Food service managers	350	16.0	23.6	58	8
11-9061	Funeral directors	29	11.7	24.0	4	1
11-9071	Gaming managers[1]	4	10.1	18.7	([2])	([2])
11-9081	Lodging managers	71	6.2	22.0	5	2
11-9111	Medical and health services managers	262	9.7	18.7	28	5
11-9121	Natural sciences managers[1]	41	7.4	21.9	3	1
11-9131	Postmasters and mail superintendents[1]	26	6.3	24.1	2	1
11-9141	Property, real estate, and community association managers	329	12.7	13.8	45	5
11-9151	Social and community service managers	130	14.1	19.1	21	2
11-9199	Managers, all other	870	10.9	19.9	98	17
13-0000	Business and financial operations occupations	6,608	10.4	17.1	746	113
13-1000	Business operations specialists	3,860	11.6	17.3	484	67
13-1011	Agents and business managers of artists, performers, and athletes	25	14.2	27.3	4	1
13-1020	Buyers and purchasing agents	460	9.5	21.4	44	10
13-1021	Purchasing agents and buyers, farm products[1]	16	10.6	13.0	2	([2])
13-1022	Wholesale and retail buyers, except farm products	157	12.7	22.4	20	4
13-1023	Purchasing agents, except wholesale, retail, and farm products	287	7.8	21.4	22	6
13-1030	Claims adjusters, appraisers, examiners, and investigators	319	6.1	25.5	20	8
13-1031	Claims adjusters, examiners, and investigators	305	6.1	25.5	19	8
13-1032	Insurance appraisers, auto damage	13	6.1	25.5	1	([2])

See footnotes at end of table.

Table V–3. Total and net replacement rates and annual average projected replacement needs, 2006–16 — Continued
(Numbers in thousands)

2006 National Employment Matrix code and title		Total employment, 2006	Replacement rate (percent)		Annual average replacement needs, 2006–16	
			Total, 2005–06	Net, 2006–16	Total	Net
13-1041	Compliance officers, except agriculture, construction, health and safety, and transportation	237	6.0	11.7	15	3
13-1051	Cost estimators	221	14.2	20.5	34	5
13-1061	Emergency management specialists	12	11.2	10.7	1	([2])
13-1070	Human resources, training, and labor relations specialists	732	13.9	21.5	111	16
13-1071	Employment, recruitment, and placement specialists	197	13.9	21.5	30	4
13-1072	Compensation, benefits, and job analysis specialists	110	13.9	21.5	17	2
13-1073	Training and development specialists	210	13.9	21.5	32	5
13-1079	Human resources, training, and labor relations specialists, all other	214	13.9	21.5	32	5
13-1081	Logisticians	83	9.1	14.9	8	1
13-1111	Management analysts	678	14.7	17.1	111	12
13-1121	Meeting and convention planners[1]	51	13.0	20.0	7	1
13-1199	Business operation specialists, all other	1,043	11.2	10.7	129	11
13-2000	Financial specialists	2,748	8.8	16.8	261	46
13-2011	Accountants and auditors	1,274	8.1	17.6	112	22
13-2021	Appraisers and assessors of real estate	101	4.4	20.0	5	2
13-2031	Budget analysts[1]	62	9.3	23.1	6	1
13-2041	Credit analysts[1]	67	4.5	38.2	3	3
13-2050	Financial analysts and advisors	501	6.6	11.2	38	6
13-2051	Financial analysts	221	8.5	5.7	22	1
13-2052	Personal financial advisors	176	4.7	9.0	10	2
13-2053	Insurance underwriters	104	5.8	26.8	6	3
13-2061	Financial examiners[1]	26	8.1	17.6	2	([2])
13-2070	Loan counselors and officers	406	12.7	10.8	54	4
13-2071	Loan counselors	33	12.7	10.8	4	([2])
13-2072	Loan officers	373	12.7	10.8	50	4
13-2080	Tax examiners, collectors, preparers, and revenue agents	181	17.1	21.1	30	4
13-2081	Tax examiners, collectors, and revenue agents	81	5.3	25.4	4	2
13-2082	Tax preparers	100	27.2	17.6	26	2
13-2099	Financial specialists, all other	129	7.9	26.7	11	3
15-2900	Professional and related occupations	29,819	9.6	20.3	3,111	606
15-0000	Computer and mathematical science occupations	3,313	8.3	22.0	309	73
15-1000	Computer specialists	3,200	8.2	21.9	295	70
15-1011	Computer and information scientists, research	25	8.4	26.5	2	1
15-1021	Computer programmers	435	6.6	20.9	28	9
15-1030	Computer software engineers	857	5.8	14.6	59	12
15-1031	Computer software engineers, applications	507	5.8	14.6	36	7
15-1032	Computer software engineers, systems software	350	5.8	14.6	23	5
15-1041	Computer support specialists	552	15.3	30.9	90	17
15-1051	Computer systems analysts	504	8.4	26.5	49	13
15-1061	Database administrators	119	3.6	10.7	5	1
15-1071	Network and computer systems administrators	309	8.2	22.8	29	7
15-1081	Network systems and data communications analysts	262	6.4	20.4	21	5
15-1099	Computer specialists, all other	136	8.4	26.5	12	4
15-2000	Mathematical science occupations	114	11.1	25.4	13	3
15-2011	Actuaries[1]	18	13.9	36.1	3	1
15-2021	Mathematicians[1]	3	13.9	24.7	([2])	([2])
15-2031	Operations research analysts	58	8.3	20.1	5	1
15-2041	Statisticians[1]	22	13.9	31.2	3	1
15-2090	Miscellaneous mathematical science occupations	12	13.9	24.7	2	([2])
15-2091	Mathematical technicians[1]	1	13.9	24.7	([2])	([2])
15-2099	Mathematical scientists, all other[1]	10	13.9	24.7	2	([2])
17-0000	Architecture and engineering occupations	2,583	6.6	22.6	180	58
17-1000	Architects, surveyors, and cartographers	232	10.4	22.6	26	5
17-1010	Architects, except naval	160	6.3	18.9	11	3
17-1011	Architects, except landscape and naval	132	6.3	18.9	9	2

See footnotes at end of table.

Table V-3. Total and net replacement rates and annual average projected replacement needs, 2006–16 — Continued
(Numbers in thousands)

2006 National Employment Matrix code and title		Total employment, 2006	Replacement rate (percent)		Annual average replacement needs, 2006–16	
			Total, 2005–06	Net, 2006–16	Total	Net
17-1012	Landscape architects	28	6.3	18.9	2	1
17-1020	Surveyors, cartographers, and photogrammetrists	72	19.2	30.9	15	2
17-1021	Cartographers and photogrammetrists	12	19.2	30.9	3	([2])
17-1022	Surveyors	60	19.2	30.9	13	2
17-2000	Engineers	1,512	4.8	22.9	77	35
17-2011	Aerospace engineers[1]	90	5.9	19.8	6	2
17-2021	Agricultural engineers[1]	3	6.1	22.8	([2])	([2])
17-2031	Biomedical engineers[1]	14	9.4	22.8	2	([2])
17-2041	Chemical engineers[1]	30	5.9	25.4	2	1
17-2051	Civil engineers	256	4.1	26.4	11	7
17-2061	Computer hardware engineers	79	4.0	30.7	3	2
17-2070	Electrical and electronics engineers	291	3.7	23.2	11	7
17-2071	Electrical engineers	153	3.7	23.2	6	4
17-2072	Electronics engineers, except computer	138	3.7	23.2	5	3
17-2081	Environmental engineers[1]	54	5.9	29.3	4	2
17-2110	Industrial engineers, including health and safety	227	3.2	24.1	8	5
17-2111	Health and safety engineers, except mining safety engineers and inspectors	25	3.2	24.1	1	1
17-2112	Industrial engineers	201	3.2	24.1	7	5
17-2121	Marine engineers and naval architects[1]	9	4.1	26.4	([2])	([2])
17-2131	Materials engineers[1]	22	5.9	23.3	1	1
17-2141	Mechanical engineers	226	5.0	21.7	11	5
17-2151	Mining and geological engineers, including mining safety engineers[1]	7	5.2	22.8	([2])	([2])
17-2161	Nuclear engineers[1]	15	5.9	22.8	1	([2])
17-2171	Petroleum engineers[1]	17	5.2	25.9	1	([2])
17-2199	Engineers, all other	170	8.5	11.8	15	2
17-3000	Drafters, engineering, and mapping technicians	840	8.9	22.2	77	19
17-3010	Drafters	253	13.1	28.6	34	7
17-3011	Architectural and civil drafters	116	13.1	28.6	16	3
17-3012	Electrical and electronics drafters	35	13.1	28.6	5	1
17-3013	Mechanical drafters	78	13.1	28.6	10	2
17-3019	Drafters, all other	25	13.1	28.6	3	1
17-3020	Engineering technicians, except drafters	511	6.9	19.5	36	10
17-3021	Aerospace engineering and operations technicians	9	6.9	19.5	1	([2])
17-3022	Civil engineering technicians	91	6.9	19.5	7	2
17-3023	Electrical and electronic engineering technicians	170	6.9	19.5	12	3
17-3024	Electro-mechanical technicians	16	6.9	19.5	1	([2])
17-3025	Environmental engineering technicians	21	6.9	19.5	2	([2])
17-3026	Industrial engineering technicians	75	6.9	19.5	5	1
17-3027	Mechanical engineering technicians	48	6.9	19.5	3	1
17-3029	Engineering technicians, except drafters, all other	82	6.9	19.5	6	2
17-3031	Surveying and mapping technicians	76	8.2	18.9	7	1
19-0000	Life, physical, and social science occupations	1,407	10.1	23.8	152	33
19-1000	Life scientists	258	7.1	27.2	19	7
19-1010	Agricultural and food scientists	33	4.4	30.6	2	1
19-1011	Animal scientists	5	4.4	30.6	([2])	([2])
19-1012	Food scientists and technologists	12	4.4	30.6	1	([2])
19-1013	Soil and plant Scientists	16	4.4	30.6	1	([2])
19-1020	Biological scientists	87	6.1	20.3	5	2
19-1021	Biochemists and biophysicists	20	6.1	20.3	1	([2])
19-1022	Microbiologists	17	6.1	20.3	1	([2])
19-1023	Zoologists and wildlife biologists	20	6.1	20.3	1	([2])
19-1029	Biological scientists, all other	29	6.1	20.3	2	1
19-1030	Conservation scientists and foresters	33	5.2	29.5	2	1
19-1031	Conservation scientists[1]	20	5.2	29.5	1	1

See footnotes at end of table.

Table V–3. Total and net replacement rates and annual average projected replacement needs, 2006–16 — Continued
(Numbers in thousands)

2006 National Employment Matrix code and title		Total employment, 2006	Replacement rate (percent)		Annual average replacement needs, 2006–16	
			Total, 2005–06	Net, 2006–16	Total	Net
19-1032	Foresters[1]	13	5.2	29.5	1	(2)
19-1040	Medical scientists	92	9.2	31.0	9	3
19-1041	Epidemiologists	5	9.2	31.0	(2)	(2)
19-1042	Medical scientists, except epidemiologists	87	9.2	31.0	9	3
19-1099	Life scientists, all other	14	9.2	31.0	1	(2)
19-2000	Physical scientists	267	6.7	25.3	19	7
19-2010	Astronomers and physicists	18	7.0	24.4	1	(2)
19-2011	Astronomers[1]	2	7.0	24.4	(2)	(2)
19-2012	Physicists[1]	17	7.0	24.4	1	(2)
19-2021	Atmospheric and space scientists[1]	9	7.0	24.4	1	(2)
19-2030	Chemists and materials scientists	93	9.4	26.4	9	2
19-2031	Chemists	84	9.4	26.4	8	2
19-2032	Materials scientists	10	9.4	26.4	1	(2)
19-2040	Environmental scientists and geoscientists	123	5.2	25.9	7	3
19-2041	Environmental scientists and specialists, including health	83	5.2	25.9	5	2
19-2042	Geoscientists, except hydrologists and geographers	31	5.2	25.9	2	1
19-2043	Hydrologists	8	5.2	25.9	(2)	(2)
19-2099	Physical scientists, all other	24	3.7	19.1	1	(2)
19-3000	Social scientists and related occupations	530	10.1	14.0	58	7
19-3011	Economists[1]	15	9.4	29.4	1	(2)
19-3020	Market and survey researchers	261	15.6	6.8	45	2
19-3021	Market research analysts	234	15.6	6.8	40	2
19-3022	Survey researchers	27	15.6	6.8	5	(2)
19-3030	Psychologists	166	3.6	15.3	6	3
19-3031	Clinical, counseling, and school psychologists	152	3.6	15.3	6	2
19-3032	Industrial-organizational psychologists	2	3.6	15.3	(2)	(2)
19-3039	Psychologists, all other	12	3.6	15.3	(2)	(2)
19-3041	Sociologists[1]	4	9.4	16.6	(2)	(2)
19-3051	Urban and regional planners[1]	34	4.1	29.5	1	1
19-3090	Miscellaneous social scientists and related workers	51	6.1	31.9	3	2
19-3091	Anthropologists and archeologists	6	6.1	31.9	(2)	(2)
19-3092	Geographers	1	6.1	31.9	(2)	(2)
19-3093	Historians	3	6.1	31.9	(2)	(2)
19-3094	Political scientists	5	6.1	31.9	(2)	(2)
19-3099	Social scientists and related workers, all other	36	6.1	31.9	2	1
19-4000	Life, physical, and social science technicians	351	15.1	35.0	56	12
19-4011	Agricultural and food science technicians[1]	26	14.5	15.6	4	(2)
19-4021	Biological technicians	79	16.6	35.7	14	3
19-4031	Chemical technicians	61	5.8	33.4	4	2
19-4041	Geological and petroleum technicians[1]	12	14.5	37.8	2	(2)
19-4051	Nuclear technicians[1]	7	14.5	35.0	1	(2)
19-4061	Social science research assistants	18	17.7	38.0	3	1
19-4090	Other life, physical, and social science technicians	150	17.7	38.0	28	6
19-4091	Environmental science and protection technicians, including health	36	17.7	38.0	7	1
19-4092	Forensic science technicians	13	17.7	38.0	3	(2)
19-4093	Forest and conservation technicians	34	17.7	38.0	6	1
19-4099	Life, physical, and social science technicians, all other	66	17.7	38.0	12	3
21-0000	Community and social services occupations	2,386	13.5	16.9	359	40
21-1000	Counselors, social workers, and other community and social service specialists	1,843	15.3	17.5	315	32
21-1010	Counselors	635	18.4	19.8	129	13
21-1011	Substance abuse and behavioral disorder counselors	83	18.4	19.8	18	2
21-1012	Educational, vocational, and school counselors	260	18.4	19.8	51	5
21-1013	Marriage and family therapists	25	18.4	19.8	5	(2)
21-1014	Mental health counselors	100	18.4	19.8	21	2

See footnotes at end of table.

Table V-3. Total and net replacement rates and annual average projected replacement needs, 2006–16 — Continued
(Numbers in thousands)

2006 National Employment Matrix code and title		Total employment, 2006	Replacement rate (percent)		Annual average replacement needs, 2006–16	
			Total, 2005–06	Net, 2006–16	Total	Net
21-1015	Rehabilitation counselors	141	18.4	19.8	29	3
21-1019	Counselors, all other	27	18.4	19.8	5	1
21-1020	Social workers	595	9.7	21.1	64	13
21-1021	Child, family, and school social workers	282	9.7	21.1	30	6
21-1022	Medical and public health social workers	124	9.7	21.1	13	3
21-1023	Mental health and substance abuse social workers	122	9.7	21.1	14	3
21-1029	Social workers, all other	66	9.7	21.1	7	1
21-1090	Miscellaneous community and social service specialists	613	17.4	11.6	121	7
21-1091	Health educators	62	17.4	11.6	12	1
21-1092	Probation officers and correctional treatment specialists	94	17.4	11.6	17	1
21-1093	Social and human service assistants	339	17.4	11.6	69	4
21-1099	Community and social service specialists, all other	118	17.4	11.6	23	1
21-2000	Religious workers	543	7.4	15.0	44	8
21-2011	Clergy	404	6.2	13.4	27	5
21-2021	Directors, religious activities and education	99	8.7	22.9	10	2
21-2099	Religious workers, all other	39	16.6	11.0	7	([2])
23-0000	Legal occupations	1,222	6.1	17.5	79	21
23-1000	Lawyers, judges, and related workers	812	5.1	19.0	44	15
23-1011	Lawyers	761	5.1	19.0	41	14
23-1020	Judges, magistrates, and other judicial workers	51	5.1	19.0	3	1
23-1021	Administrative law judges, adjudicators, and hearing officers[1]	15	5.1	19.0	1	([2])
23-1022	Arbitrators, mediators, and conciliators[1]	8	5.1	19.0	([2])	([2])
23-1023	Judges, magistrate judges, and magistrates[1]	27	5.1	19.0	1	1
23-2000	Legal support workers	410	8.0	14.6	35	6
23-2011	Paralegals and legal assistants	238	6.6	13.2	17	3
23-2090	Miscellaneous legal support workers	173	10.0	16.6	18	3
23-2091	Court reporters	19	10.0	16.6	2	([2])
23-2092	Law clerks	37	10.0	16.6	4	1
23-2093	Title examiners, abstractors, and searchers	69	10.0	16.6	7	1
23-2099	Legal support workers, all other	48	10.0	16.6	5	1
25-0000	Education, training, and library occupations	9,034	11.8	19.7	1,142	178
25-1000	Postsecondary teachers	1,672	10.7	16.7	199	28
25-2000	Primary, secondary, and special education teachers	4,413	9.6	23.2	449	102
25-2010	Preschool and kindergarten teachers	607	13.5	16.5	92	10
25-2011	Preschool teachers, except special education	437	13.5	16.5	67	7
25-2012	Kindergarten teachers, except special education	170	13.5	16.5	25	3
25-2020	Elementary and middle school teachers	2,214	9.8	21.8	230	48
25-2021	Elementary school teachers, except special education	1,540	9.8	21.8	161	34
25-2022	Middle school teachers, except special and vocational education	658	9.8	21.8	68	14
25-2023	Vocational education teachers, middle school	16	9.8	21.8	2	([2])
25-2030	Secondary school teachers	1,133	8.2	29.8	95	34
25-2031	Secondary school teachers, except special and vocational education	1,038	8.2	29.8	87	31
25-2032	Vocational education teachers, secondary school	96	8.2	29.8	8	3
25-2040	Special education teachers	459	6.6	22.2	32	10
25-2041	Special education teachers, preschool, kindergarten, and elementary school	219	6.6	22.2	16	5
25-2042	Special education teachers, middle school	102	6.6	22.2	7	2
25-2043	Special education teachers, secondary school	138	6.6	22.2	9	3
25-3000	Other teachers and instructors	1,078	20.0	10.7	229	12
25-3011	Adult literacy, remedial education, and GED teachers and instructors	76	20.0	10.7	16	1
25-3021	Self-enrichment education teachers	261	20.0	10.7	58	3
25-3099	Teachers and instructors, all other	741	20.0	10.7	155	8
25-4000	Librarians, curators, and archivists	307	15.6	37.0	49	11
25-4010	Archivists, curators, and museum technicians	27	10.2	43.2	3	1
25-4011	Archivists	6	10.2	43.2	1	([2])
25-4012	Curators	10	10.2	43.2	1	([2])
25-4013	Museum Technicians and Conservators	11	10.2	43.2	1	([2])

See footnotes at end of table.

Table V–3. Total and net replacement rates and annual average projected replacement needs, 2006–16 — Continued
(Numbers in thousands)

2006 National Employment Matrix code and title		Total employment, 2006	Replacement rate (percent)		Annual average replacement needs, 2006–16	
			Total, 2005–06	Net, 2006–16	Total	Net
25-4021	Librarians	158	11.4	27.1	18	4
25-4031	Library technicians	121	22.2	48.6	28	6
25-9000	Other education, training, and library occupations	1,563	13.0	15.9	215	25
25-9011	Audio-visual collections specialists	7	12.8	13.7	1	(2)
25-9021	Farm and home management advisors	15	12.8	13.7	2	(2)
25-9031	Instructional coordinators	129	12.8	13.7	18	2
25-9041	Teacher assistants	1,312	13.1	16.3	180	21
25-9099	Education, training, and library workers, all other	99	12.8	13.7	13	1
27-0000	Arts, design, entertainment, sports, and media occupations	2,677	12.8	24.3	362	65
27-1000	Art and design occupations	821	9.5	25.7	82	21
27-1010	Artists and related workers	218	11.1	23.4	26	5
27-1011	Art directors	78	11.1	23.4	9	2
27-1012	Craft artists	9	11.1	23.4	1	(2)
27-1013	Fine artists, including painters, sculptors, and illustrators	30	11.1	23.4	4	1
27-1014	Multi-media artists and animators	87	11.1	23.4	11	2
27-1019	Artists and related workers, all other	14	11.1	23.4	2	(2)
27-1020	Designers	603	8.9	26.6	56	16
27-1021	Commercial and industrial designers	48	8.9	26.6	4	1
27-1022	Fashion designers	20	8.9	26.6	2	1
27-1023	Floral designers	87	8.9	26.6	7	2
27-1024	Graphic designers	261	8.9	26.6	24	7
27-1025	Interior designers	72	8.9	26.6	7	2
27-1026	Merchandise displayers and window trimmers	87	8.9	26.6	8	2
27-1027	Set and exhibit designers	12	8.9	26.6	1	(2)
27-1029	Designers, all other	16	8.9	26.6	2	(2)
27-2000	Entertainers and performers, sports and related occupations	798	14.7	26.0	124	21
27-2010	Actors, producers, and directors	163	16.3	25.8	28	4
27-2011	Actors	70	27.1	20.6	20	1
27-2012	Producers and directors	93	8.1	29.7	8	3
27-2020	Athletes, coaches, umpires, and related workers	253	20.6	25.7	56	6
27-2021	Athletes and sports competitors	18	20.6	25.7	4	(2)
27-2022	Coaches and scouts	217	20.6	25.7	48	6
27-2023	Umpires, referees, and other sports officials	19	20.6	25.7	4	(2)
27-2030	Dancers and choreographers	40	6.1	55.2	3	2
27-2031	Dancers	20	6.1	55.2	1	1
27-2032	Choreographers	20	6.1	55.2	1	1
27-2040	Musicians, singers, and related workers	264	10.7	20.3	30	5
27-2041	Music directors and composers	68	10.7	20.3	8	1
27-2042	Musicians and singers	196	10.7	20.3	22	4
27-2099	Entertainers and performers, sports and related workers, all other	77	9.6	31.9	8	2
27-3000	Media and communication occupations	764	15.6	20.6	126	16
27-3010	Announcers	71	11.3	34.1	8	2
27-3011	Radio and television announcers	59	11.3	34.1	6	2
27-3012	Public address system and other announcers	12	11.3	34.1	1	(2)
27-3020	News analysts, reporters and correspondents	67	17.6	31.5	12	2
27-3021	Broadcast news analysts	8	17.6	31.5	1	(2)
27-3022	Reporters and correspondents	59	17.6	31.5	10	2
27-3031	Public relations specialists	243	17.7	7.5	47	2
27-3040	Writers and editors	306	15.2	24.6	49	8
27-3041	Editors	122	16.2	29.8	20	4
27-3042	Technical writers	49	12.1	30.2	7	1
27-3043	Writers and authors	135	15.5	18.0	22	2
27-3090	Miscellaneous media and communications workers	77	12.3	23.8	10	2
27-3091	Interpreters and translators	41	12.3	23.8	6	1
27-3099	Media and communication workers, all other	36	12.3	23.8	5	1
27-4000	Media and communication equipment occupations	294	9.6	25.5	30	7

See footnotes at end of table.

Table V–3. Total and net replacement rates and annual average projected replacement needs, 2006–16 — Continued
(Numbers in thousands)

2006 National Employment Matrix code and title		Total employment, 2006	Replacement rate (percent)		Annual average replacement needs, 2006–16	
			Total, 2005–06	Net, 2006–16	Total	Net
27-4010	Broadcast and sound engineering technicians and radio operators	105	6.2	32.5	7	3
27-4011	Audio and video equipment technicians	50	6.2	32.5	3	2
27-4012	Broadcast technicians	38	6.2	32.5	2	1
27-4013	Radio operators	2	6.2	32.5	(2)	(2)
27-4014	Sound engineering technicians	16	6.2	32.5	1	1
27-4021	Photographers	122	11.5	22.0	15	3
27-4030	Television, video, and motion picture camera operators and editors	47	11.2	18.6	6	1
27-4031	Camera operators, television, video, and motion picture	27	11.2	18.6	3	1
27-4032	Film and video editors	21	11.2	18.6	2	(2)
27-4099	Media and communication equipment workers, all other[1]	19	12.0	25.3	2	(2)
29-0000	Healthcare practitioners and technical occupations	7,198	6.7	18.9	528	136
29-1000	Health diagnosing and treating practitioners	4,460	5.6	16.7	278	75
29-1011	Chiropractors[1]	53	4.3	10.9	2	1
29-1020	Dentists	161	4.1	19.6	7	3
29-1021	Dentists, general[1]	136	4.1	19.6	6	3
29-1022	Oral and maxillofacial surgeons[1]	8	4.1	19.6	(2)	(2)
29-1023	Orthodontists[1]	9	4.1	19.6	(2)	(2)
29-1024	Prosthodontists[1]	1	4.1	19.6	(2)	(2)
29-1029	Dentists, all other specialists[1]	7	4.1	19.6	(2)	(2)
29-1031	Dietitians and nutritionists	57	7.6	25.3	5	1
29-1041	Optometrists[1]	33	4.1	17.1	1	1
29-1051	Pharmacists	243	4.1	17.3	11	4
29-1060	Physicians and surgeons	633	4.3	18.0	29	11
29-1071	Physician assistants	66	7.2	13.8	5	1
29-1081	Podiatrists[1]	12	4.3	34.0	1	(2)
29-1111	Registered nurses	2,505	6.2	16.5	175	41
29-1120	Therapists	570	5.7	14.6	36	8
29-1121	Audiologists[1]	12	6.7	11.5	1	(2)
29-1122	Occupational therapists	99	5.5	14.7	6	1
29-1123	Physical therapists	173	3.8	12.0	7	2
29-1124	Radiation therapists[1]	15	6.7	15.0	1	(2)
29-1125	Recreational therapists[1]	25	6.7	15.0	2	(2)
29-1126	Respiratory therapists	102	2.8	14.7	3	2
29-1127	Speech-language pathologists	110	8.7	19.3	10	2
29-1129	Therapists, all other	35	15.3	12.0	6	(2)
29-1131	Veterinarians[1]	62	4.3	19.6	3	1
29-1199	Health diagnosing and treating practitioners, all other[1]	65	3.8	17.1	3	1
29-2000	Health technologists and technicians	2,612	8.5	22.6	242	59
29-2010	Clinical laboratory technologists and technicians	319	5.3	15.1	18	5
29-2011	Medical and clinical laboratory technologists	167	5.3	15.1	9	3
29-2012	Medical and clinical laboratory technicians	151	5.3	15.1	9	2
29-2021	Dental hygienists	167	2.8	19.1	5	3
29-2030	Diagnostic related technologists and technicians	307	4.7	13.6	16	4
29-2031	Cardiovascular technologists and technicians	45	4.7	13.6	2	1
29-2032	Diagnostic medical sonographers	46	4.7	13.6	2	1
29-2033	Nuclear medicine technologists	20	4.7	13.6	1	(2)
29-2034	Radiologic technologists and technicians	196	4.7	13.6	10	3
29-2041	Emergency medical technicians and paramedics	201	7.1	11.4	16	2
29-2050	Health diagnosing and treating practitioner support technicians	549	13.7	30.5	85	17
29-2051	Dietetic technicians	25	13.7	30.5	4	1
29-2052	Pharmacy technicians	285	13.7	30.5	45	9
29-2053	Psychiatric technicians	62	13.7	30.5	8	2
29-2054	Respiratory therapy technicians	19	13.7	30.5	3	1
29-2055	Surgical technologists	86	13.7	30.5	13	3
29-2056	Veterinary technologists and technicians	71	13.7	30.5	12	2

See footnotes at end of table.

Table V-3. Total and net replacement rates and annual average projected replacement needs, 2006–16 — Continued
(Numbers in thousands)

2006 National Employment Matrix code and title		Total employment, 2006	Replacement rate (percent)		Annual average replacement needs, 2006–16	
			Total, 2005–06	Net, 2006–16	Total	Net
29-2061	Licensed practical and licensed vocational nurses	749	7.5	27.3	60	20
29-2071	Medical records and health information technicians[1]	170	19.5	27.1	36	5
29-2081	Opticians, dispensing	66	3.7	31.8	3	2
29-2090	Miscellaneous health technologists and technicians	85	3.8	7.9	3	1
29-2091	Orthotists and prosthetists	6	3.8	7.9	(2)	(2)
29-2099	Healthcare technologists and technicians, all other	79	3.8	7.9	3	1
29-9000	Other healthcare practitioners and technical occupations	126	6.5	19.0	9	2
29-9010	Occupational health and safety specialists and technicians	56	6.5	19.0	4	1
29-9011	Occupational health and safety specialists[1]	45	6.5	19.0	3	1
29-9012	Occupational health and safety technicians[1]	10	6.5	19.0	1	(2)
29-9090	Miscellaneous health practitioners and technical workers	70	6.5	19.0	5	1
29-9091	Athletic trainers[1]	17	6.5	19.0	1	(2)
29-9099	Healthcare practitioners and technical workers, all other[1]	53	6.5	19.0	4	1
31-3900	Service occupations	28,950	22.5	25.5	7,071	737
31-0000	Healthcare support occupations	3,723	16.2	10.7	685	40
31-1000	Nursing, psychiatric, and home health aides	2,296	18.7	8.9	489	21
31-1011	Home health aides	787	18.7	8.9	183	7
31-1012	Nursing aides, orderlies, and attendants	1,447	18.7	8.9	295	13
31-1013	Psychiatric aides	62	18.7	8.9	12	1
31-2000	Occupational and physical therapist assistants and aides	140	6.0	13.4	10	2
31-2010	Occupational therapist assistants and aides	33	7.1	15.3	3	1
31-2011	Occupational therapist assistants[1]	25	7.1	15.3	2	(2)
31-2012	Occupational therapist aides[1]	8	7.1	15.3	1	(2)
31-2020	Physical therapist assistants and aides	107	5.7	12.8	7	1
31-2021	Physical therapist assistants	60	5.7	12.8	4	1
31-2022	Physical therapist aides	46	5.7	12.8	3	1
31-9000	Other healthcare support occupations	1,287	12.9	13.4	186	17
31-9011	Massage therapists	118	5.3	11.4	7	1
31-9090	Miscellaneous healthcare support occupations	1,170	13.7	13.6	180	16
31-9091	Dental assistants	280	6.6	17.4	21	5
31-9092	Medical assistants	417	15.9	12.4	78	5
31-9093	Medical equipment preparers	45	15.9	12.4	8	1
31-9094	Medical transcriptionists	98	15.9	12.4	17	1
31-9095	Pharmacy aides	50	15.9	12.4	8	1
31-9096	Veterinary assistants and laboratory animal caretakers	75	15.9	12.4	13	1
31-9099	Healthcare support workers, all other	204	15.9	12.4	35	3
33-0000	Protective service occupations	3,163	12.4	27.6	421	87
33-1000	First-line supervisors/managers, protective service workers	233	8.1	27.5	20	6
33-1010	First-line supervisors/managers, law enforcement workers	133	8.8	30.1	12	4
33-1011	First-line supervisors/managers of correctional officers	40	8.8	27.3	4	1
33-1012	First-line supervisors/managers of police and detectives[1]	93	8.8	31.3	9	3
33-1021	First-line supervisors/managers of fire fighting and prevention workers[1]	52	5.7	31.3	3	2
33-1099	First-line supervisors/managers, protective service workers, all other	48	8.7	16.3	4	1
33-2000	Fire fighting and prevention workers	308	4.9	35.7	16	11
33-2011	Fire fighters	293	4.9	36.4	15	11
33-2020	Fire inspectors	16	3.4	22.6	1	(2)
33-2021	Fire inspectors and investigators	14	3.4	22.6	(2)	(2)
33-2022	Forest fire inspectors and prevention specialists	2	3.4	22.6	(2)	(2)
33-3000	Law enforcement workers	1,239	7.3	24.9	97	31
33-3010	Bailiffs, correctional officers, and jailers	460	10.3	22.9	51	11
33-3011	Bailiffs	19	10.3	22.9	2	(2)
33-3012	Correctional officers and jailers	442	10.3	22.9	49	10
33-3021	Detectives and criminal investigators	106	11.2	21.9	13	2
33-3031	Fish and game wardens[1]	8	7.2	25.0	1	(2)
33-3041	Parking enforcement workers[1]	11	7.2	25.0	1	(2)

See footnotes at end of table.

Table V–3. Total and net replacement rates and annual average projected replacement needs, 2006–16 — Continued
(Numbers in thousands)

2006 National Employment Matrix code and title		Total employment, 2006	Replacement rate (percent)		Annual average replacement needs, 2006–16	
			Total, 2005–06	Net, 2006–16	Total	Net
33-3050	Police officers	654	4.5	26.7	31	17
33-3051	Police and sheriff's patrol officers	648	4.5	26.7	31	17
33-3052	Transit and railroad police[1]	6	4.5	26.8	(2)	(2)
33-9000	Other protective service workers	1,382	19.3	28.3	288	39
33-9011	Animal control workers[1]	15	19.7	21.0	3	(2)
33-9021	Private detectives and investigators	52	11.3	19.4	6	1
33-9030	Security guards and gaming surveillance officers	1,049	18.1	20.3	206	21
33-9031	Gaming surveillance officers and gaming investigators	9	18.1	20.3	2	(2)
33-9032	Security guards	1,040	18.1	20.3	205	21
33-9090	Miscellaneous protective service workers	266	25.6	62.2	72	17
33-9091	Crossing guards	69	5.7	28.8	4	2
33-9092	Lifeguards, ski patrol, and other recreational protective service workers	114	32.1	74.0	40	8
33-9099	Protective service workers, all other	83	32.1	74.0	28	6
35-0000	Food preparation and serving related occupations	11,352	30.1	34.8	3,632	395
35-1000	Supervisors, food preparation and serving workers	932	15.6	8.2	153	8
35-1011	Chefs and head cooks	115	7.2	12.7	9	1
35-1012	First-line supervisors/managers of food preparation and serving workers	817	16.8	7.5	145	6
35-2000	Cooks and food preparation workers	2,998	26.6	29.4	843	88
35-2010	Cooks	2,097	25.4	27.1	559	57
35-2011	Cooks, fast food	629	25.4	27.1	167	17
35-2012	Cooks, institution and cafeteria	401	25.4	27.1	108	11
35-2013	Cooks, private household	5	25.4	27.1	1	(2)
35-2014	Cooks, restaurant	850	25.4	27.1	229	23
35-2015	Cooks, short order	195	25.4	27.1	51	5
35-2019	Cooks, all other	16	25.4	27.1	4	(2)
35-2021	Food preparation workers	902	29.3	34.7	284	31
35-3000	Food and beverage serving workers	6,081	32.7	38.4	2,126	234
35-3011	Bartenders	495	15.7	36.4	82	18
35-3020	Fast food and counter workers	3,036	37.9	27.8	1,248	84
35-3021	Combined food preparation and serving workers, including fast food	2,503	36.6	19.0	998	47
35-3022	Counter attendants, cafeteria, food concession, and coffee shop	533	44.6	69.4	250	37
35-3031	Waiters and waitresses	2,361	29.8	54.3	742	128
35-3041	Food servers, nonrestaurant	189	26.1	15.3	53	3
35-9000	Other food preparation and serving related workers	1,341	36.0	48.7	509	65
35-9011	Dining room and cafeteria attendants and bartender helpers	416	33.9	41.9	149	17
35-9021	Dishwashers	517	35.9	40.8	195	21
35-9031	Hosts and hostesses, restaurant, lounge, and coffee shop	351	38.5	68.3	142	24
35-9099	Food preparation and serving related workers, all other[1]	56	37.1	48.8	22	3
37-0000	Building and grounds cleaning and maintenance occupations	5,745	18.8	17.1	1,160	98
37-1000	Supervisors, building and grounds cleaning and maintenance workers	484	8.2	11.4	42	6
37-1011	First-line supervisors/managers of housekeeping and janitorial workers	282	9.0	14.7	27	4
37-1012	First-line supervisors/managers of landscaping, lawn service, and groundskeeping workers	202	7.0	6.8	15	1
37-2000	Building cleaning and pest control workers	3,941	19.2	19.1	810	75
37-2010	Building cleaning workers	3,872	19.5	19.0	805	74
37-2011	Janitors and cleaners, except maids and housekeeping cleaners	2,387	19.5	19.1	498	46
37-2012	Maids and housekeeping cleaners	1,470	19.4	18.8	304	28
37-2019	Building cleaning workers, all other	16	19.5	19.1	3	(2)
37-2021	Pest control workers	70	6.6	24.2	5	2
37-3000	Grounds maintenance workers	1,319	21.4	13.2	308	17
37-3010	Grounds maintenance workers	1,319	21.4	13.2	308	17
37-3011	Landscaping and groundskeeping workers	1,220	21.4	13.2	285	16
37-3012	Pesticide handlers, sprayers, and applicators, vegetation	31	21.4	13.2	7	(2)
37-3013	Tree trimmers and pruners	41	21.4	13.2	9	1
37-3019	Grounds maintenance workers, all other	28	21.4	13.2	6	(2)
39-0000	Personal care and service occupations	4,966	21.3	23.6	1,174	117

See footnotes at end of table.

Table V-3. Total and net replacement rates and annual average projected replacement needs, 2006–16 — Continued
(Numbers in thousands)

Code	2006 National Employment Matrix code and title	Total employment, 2006	Replacement rate (percent)		Annual average replacement needs, 2006–16	
			Total, 2005–06	Net, 2006–16	Total	Net
39-1000	Supervisors, personal care and service workers	268	13.8	21.0	40	6
39-1010	First-line supervisors/managers of gaming workers	54	10.1	18.7	6	1
39-1011	Gaming supervisors	34	10.1	18.7	4	1
39-1012	Slot key persons	20	10.1	18.7	2	(2)
39-1021	First-line supervisors/managers of personal service workers	215	14.8	21.6	34	5
39-2000	Animal care and service workers	200	17.7	16.4	39	3
39-2011	Animal trainers	43	12.0	17.2	6	1
39-2021	Nonfarm animal caretakers	157	19.3	16.1	33	3
39-3000	Entertainment attendants and related workers	546	29.0	46.9	176	26
39-3010	Gaming services workers	117	10.6	20.1	14	2
39-3011	Gaming dealers	84	10.6	20.1	10	2
39-3012	Gaming and sports book writers and runners	18	10.6	20.1	2	(2)
39-3019	Gaming service workers, all other	15	10.6	20.1	2	(2)
39-3021	Motion picture projectionists[1]	11	30.3	43.9	3	1
39-3031	Ushers, lobby attendants, and ticket takers[1]	103	30.3	70.2	34	7
39-3090	Miscellaneous entertainment attendants and related workers	315	35.4	49.4	125	16
39-3091	Amusement and recreation attendants	247	35.4	49.4	98	12
39-3092	Costume attendants	4	35.4	49.4	2	(2)
39-3093	Locker room, coatroom, and dressing room attendants	19	35.4	49.4	8	1
39-4000	Funeral service workers	42	15.8	23.7	7	1
39-4011	Embalmers	9	15.8	23.7	2	(2)
39-4021	Funeral attendants	33	15.8	23.7	6	1
39-5000	Personal appearance workers	825	10.0	12.1	88	10
39-5010	Barbers and cosmetologists	677	9.5	12.5	68	8
39-5011	Barbers	60	4.5	18.3	3	1
39-5012	Hairdressers, hairstylists, and cosmetologists	617	10.0	11.9	65	7
39-5090	Miscellaneous personal appearance workers	148	11.9	10.4	20	2
39-5091	Makeup artists, theatrical and performance	2	11.9	10.4	(2)	(2)
39-5092	Manicurists and pedicurists	78	11.9	10.4	11	1
39-5093	Shampooers	29	11.9	10.4	4	(2)
39-5094	Skin care specialists	38	11.9	10.4	5	(2)
39-6000	Transportation, tourism, and lodging attendants	232	17.6	20.4	43	5
39-6010	Baggage porters, bellhops, and concierges	69	21.8	12.8	16	1
39-6011	Baggage porters and bellhops	49	21.8	12.8	11	1
39-6012	Concierges	20	21.8	12.8	5	(2)
39-6020	Tour and travel guides	45	31.7	39.8	16	2
39-6021	Tour guides and escorts	40	31.7	39.8	14	2
39-6022	Travel guides	5	31.7	39.8	2	(2)
39-6030	Transportation attendants	118	9.6	17.4	12	2
39-6031	Flight attendants	97	9.6	17.4	10	2
39-6032	Transportation attendants, except flight attendants and baggage porters	21	9.6	17.4	2	(2)
39-9000	Other personal care and service workers	2,853	24.2	23.4	781	67
39-9011	Child care workers	1,388	29.6	28.7	447	40
39-9021	Personal and home care aides	767	22.5	16.9	216	13
39-9030	Recreation and fitness workers	555	16.9	18.7	102	10
39-9031	Fitness trainers and aerobics instructors	235	16.9	18.7	45	4
39-9032	Recreation workers	320	16.9	18.7	57	6
39-9041	Residential advisors	57	11.3	28.4	7	2
39-9099	Personal care and service workers, all other[1]	86	9.9	21.7	8	2
41-0000	Sales and related occupations	15,985	22.4	30.0	3,717	479
41-1000	Supervisors, sales workers	2,206	11.6	19.4	261	43
41-1011	First-line supervisors/managers of retail sales workers	1,676	12.5	21.0	214	35
41-1012	First-line supervisors/managers of non-retail sales workers	530	8.7	14.4	47	8
41-2000	Retail sales workers	8,719	29.7	37.4	2,674	326
41-2010	Cashiers	3,527	34.5	47.6	1,197	168

See footnotes at end of table.

Table V–3. Total and net replacement rates and annual average projected replacement needs, 2006–16 — Continued
(Numbers in thousands)

2006 National Employment Matrix code and title		Total employment, 2006	Replacement rate (percent)		Annual average replacement needs, 2006–16	
			Total, 2005–06	Net, 2006–16	Total	Net
41-2011	Cashiers, except gaming	3,500	34.5	47.6	1,187	166
41-2012	Gaming change persons and booth cashiers	27	34.5	47.6	10	1
41-2020	Counter and rental clerks and parts salespersons	715	21.6	29.2	165	21
41-2021	Counter and rental clerks	477	21.2	38.1	113	18
41-2022	Parts salespersons	238	22.3	11.2	52	3
41-2031	Retail salespersons	4,477	27.6	30.8	1,312	138
41-3000	Sales representatives, services	1,567	11.5	21.7	198	34
41-3011	Advertising sales agents	170	13.7	17.5	26	3
41-3021	Insurance sales agents	436	12.6	21.7	59	9
41-3031	Securities, commodities, and financial services sales agents	320	11.1	25.6	40	8
41-3041	Travel agents	101	12.8	7.0	13	1
41-3099	Sales representatives, services, all other	540	9.9	23.5	61	13
41-4000	Sales representatives, wholesale and manufacturing	1,973	8.8	22.1	182	44
41-4011	Sales representatives, wholesale and manufacturing, technical and scientific products	411	8.8	22.1	38	9
41-4012	Sales representatives, wholesale and manufacturing, except technical and scientific products	1,562	8.8	22.1	143	34
41-9000	Other sales and related workers	1,520	25.8	21.2	402	32
41-9010	Models, demonstrators, and product promoters	107	27.0	28.4	31	3
41-9011	Demonstrators and product promoters	105	27.0	28.4	31	3
41-9012	Models	2	27.0	28.4	1	(2)
41-9020	Real estate brokers and sales agents	564	12.4	16.0	74	9
41-9021	Real estate brokers	131	12.4	16.0	17	2
41-9022	Real estate sales agents	432	12.4	16.0	57	7
41-9031	Sales engineers[1]	76	8.5	25.2	7	2
41-9041	Telemarketers	395	56.2	35.2	211	14
41-9090	Miscellaneous sales and related workers	379	20.1	11.4	80	4
41-9091	Door-to-door sales workers, news and street vendors, and related workers	200	23.5	13.6	48	3
41-9099	Sales and related workers, all other	180	16.5	9.0	32	2
43-0000	Office and administrative support occupations	24,344	17.2	21.2	4,336	515
43-1000	Supervisors, office and administrative support workers	1,418	8.9	20.6	130	29
43-1011	First-line supervisors/managers of office and administrative support workers	1,418	8.9	20.6	130	29
43-2000	Communications equipment operators	209	23.2	19.8	45	4
43-2011	Switchboard operators, including answering service	177	23.7	20.9	40	4
43-2021	Telephone operators	27	19.5	12.5	4	(2)
43-2099	Communications equipment operators, all other[1]	4	23.2	19.0	1	(2)
43-3000	Financial clerks	4,007	14.5	20.1	616	81
43-3011	Bill and account collectors	434	22.5	15.1	109	7
43-3021	Billing and posting clerks and machine operators	542	14.4	12.8	80	7
43-3031	Bookkeeping, accounting, and auditing clerks	2,114	11.6	15.6	261	33
43-3041	Gaming cage workers[1]	18	21.3	26.7	4	(2)
43-3051	Payroll and timekeeping clerks	214	8.2	25.3	18	5
43-3061	Procurement clerks[1]	78	9.1	20.1	7	2
43-3071	Tellers	608	21.3	43.7	138	27
43-4000	Information and record clerks	5,738	20.9	25.3	1,269	145
43-4011	Brokerage clerks[1]	73	11.6	32.3	9	2
43-4021	Correspondence clerks[1]	17	22.3	25.7	4	(2)
43-4031	Court, municipal, and license clerks	115	12.7	22.8	15	3
43-4041	Credit authorizers, checkers, and clerks	69	13.3	30.8	9	2
43-4051	Customer service representatives	2,202	22.1	27.8	546	61
43-4061	Eligibility interviewers, government programs	112	9.6	17.4	11	2
43-4071	File clerks	234	27.0	26.5	50	6
43-4081	Hotel, motel, and resort desk clerks	219	30.2	40.5	72	9
43-4111	Interviewers, except eligibility and loan	221	22.4	26.3	52	6
43-4121	Library assistants, clerical	116	15.0	31.6	18	4
43-4131	Loan interviewers and clerks	256	15.8	17.3	40	4

See footnotes at end of table.

Table V-3. Total and net replacement rates and annual average projected replacement needs, 2006–16 — Continued
(Numbers in thousands)

2006 National Employment Matrix code and title		Total employment, 2006	Replacement rate (percent)		Annual average replacement needs, 2006–16	
			Total, 2005–06	Net, 2006–16	Total	Net
43-4141	New accounts clerks[1]	81	22.3	29.4	17	2
43-4151	Order clerks	271	19.6	20.9	47	6
43-4161	Human resources assistants, except payroll and timekeeping	168	9.4	7.4	17	1
43-4171	Receptionists and information clerks	1,173	24.6	24.5	314	29
43-4181	Reservation and transportation ticket agents and travel clerks	165	18.4	22.0	31	4
43-4199	Information and record clerks, all other	245	7.8	15.9	18	4
43-5000	Material recording, scheduling, dispatching, and distributing occupations	4,016	18.9	24.3	751	97
43-5011	Cargo and freight agents	86	9.2	27.2	9	2
43-5021	Couriers and messengers[1]	134	16.3	27.2	22	4
43-5030	Dispatchers	289	15.4	25.3	46	7
43-5031	Police, fire, and ambulance dispatchers	99	15.4	25.3	16	3
43-5032	Dispatchers, except police, fire, and ambulance	190	15.4	25.3	30	5
43-5041	Meter readers, utilities	47	16.6	31.7	7	1
43-5050	Postal service workers	615	4.4	22.4	27	14
43-5051	Postal service clerks	80	4.5	22.5	4	2
43-5052	Postal service mail carriers	338	4.8	29.3	16	10
43-5053	Postal service mail sorters, processors, and processing machine operators	198	3.6	10.7	7	2
43-5061	Production, planning, and expediting clerks	293	17.2	27.2	52	8
43-5071	Shipping, receiving, and traffic clerks	769	17.4	24.0	136	18
43-5081	Stock clerks and order fillers	1,705	26.8	23.7	439	40
43-5111	Weighers, measurers, checkers, and samplers, recordkeeping	79	18.3	26.2	14	2
43-6000	Secretaries and administrative assistants	4,241	12.2	15.9	538	68
43-6011	Executive secretaries and administrative assistants	1,618	12.2	15.9	211	26
43-6012	Legal secretaries	275	12.2	15.9	35	4
43-6013	Medical secretaries	408	12.2	15.9	54	7
43-6014	Secretaries, except legal, medical, and executive	1,940	12.2	15.9	237	31
43-9000	Other office and administrative support workers	4,715	20.3	19.3	987	91
43-9011	Computer operators	130	15.7	16.0	18	2
43-9020	Data entry and information processing workers	492	23.5	22.5	111	11
43-9021	Data entry keyers	313	25.9	24.6	79	8
43-9022	Word processors and typists	179	19.1	18.9	32	3
43-9031	Desktop publishers[1]	32	20.0	20.3	6	1
43-9041	Insurance claims and policy processing clerks	254	16.7	12.0	42	3
43-9051	Mail clerks and mail machine operators, except postal service	152	19.5	26.4	28	4
43-9061	Office clerks, general	3,200	21.3	18.3	725	59
43-9071	Office machine operators, except computer	94	8.9	33.0	8	3
43-9081	Proofreaders and copy markers[1]	18	20.0	20.0	4	(2)
43-9111	Statistical assistants[1]	23	20.0	43.7	5	1
43-9199	Office and administrative support workers, all other	320	12.8	22.2	39	7
45-0000	Farming, fishing, and forestry occupations	1,039	22.5	23.8	231	25
45-1000	Supervisors, farming, fishing, and forestry workers	53	22.4	18.5	12	1
45-2000	Agricultural workers	858	24.2	24.5	205	21
45-2011	Agricultural inspectors[1]	16	23.0	25.0	4	(2)
45-2021	Animal breeders[1]	11	23.0	24.0	2	(2)
45-2041	Graders and sorters, agricultural products	42	20.6	14.2	9	1
45-2090	Miscellaneous agricultural workers	790	24.4	25.0	190	20
45-2091	Agricultural equipment operators	59	24.4	25.0	14	1
45-2092	Farmworkers and laborers, crop, nursery, and greenhouse	603	24.4	25.0	145	15
45-2093	Farmworkers, farm and ranch animals	107	24.4	25.0	26	3
45-2099	Agricultural workers, all other	20	24.4	25.0	5	1
45-3000	Fishing and hunting workers	39	20.8	14.0	7	1
45-3011	Fishers and related fishing workers	38	20.8	14.0	7	1
45-3021	Hunters and trappers[1]	0	20.9	15.1	(2)	(2)
45-4000	Forest, conservation, and logging workers	88	7.3	24.3	6	2
45-4011	Forest and conservation workers	20	8.6	38.2	2	1
45-4020	Logging workers	69	6.8	20.2	5	1

See footnotes at end of table.

Table V-3. Total and net replacement rates and annual average projected replacement needs, 2006–16 — Continued
(Numbers in thousands)

2006 National Employment Matrix code and title		Total employment, 2006	Replacement rate (percent)		Annual average replacement needs, 2006–16	
			Total, 2005–06	Net, 2006–16	Total	Net
45-4021	Fallers	13	6.8	20.2	1	(2)
45-4022	Logging equipment operators	40	6.8	20.2	3	1
45-4023	Log graders and scalers	7	6.8	20.2	(2)	(2)
45-4029	Logging workers, all other	8	6.8	20.2	1	(2)
47-0000	Construction and extraction occupations	8,295	14.5	17.5	1,261	145
47-1000	Supervisors, construction and extraction workers	772	9.4	14.0	76	11
47-1011	First-line supervisors/managers of construction trades and extraction workers	772	9.4	14.0	76	11
47-2000	Construction trades and related workers	6,422	14.3	17.0	960	109
47-2011	Boilermakers	18	11.1	36.2	2	1
47-2020	Brickmasons, blockmasons, and stonemasons	182	9.7	20.9	18	4
47-2021	Brickmasons and blockmasons	158	9.7	20.9	16	3
47-2022	Stonemasons	24	9.7	20.9	2	(2)
47-2031	Carpenters	1,462	13.5	13.5	208	20
47-2040	Carpet, floor, and tile installers and finishers	196	9.2	14.5	18	3
47-2041	Carpet installers	73	9.2	14.5	7	1
47-2042	Floor layers, except carpet, wood, and hard tiles	29	9.2	14.5	3	(2)
47-2043	Floor sanders and finishers	14	9.2	14.5	1	(2)
47-2044	Tile and marble setters	79	9.2	14.5	8	1
47-2050	Cement masons, concrete finishers, and terrazzo workers	228	13.7	29.0	33	7
47-2051	Cement masons and concrete finishers	222	13.7	29.0	32	6
47-2053	Terrazzo workers and finishers	7	13.7	29.0	1	(2)
47-2061	Construction laborers	1,232	18.8	7.5	244	9
47-2070	Construction equipment operators	494	10.8	19.5	55	10
47-2071	Paving, surfacing, and tamping equipment operators	64	4.3	20.0	3	1
47-2072	Pile-driver operators[1]	6	11.3	19.4	1	(2)
47-2073	Operating engineers and other construction equipment operators	424	11.7	19.4	52	8
47-2080	Drywall installers, ceiling tile installers, and tapers	240	15.4	13.8	38	3
47-2081	Drywall and ceiling tile installers	186	15.4	13.8	30	3
47-2082	Tapers	54	15.4	13.8	9	1
47-2111	Electricians	705	10.1	25.7	74	18
47-2121	Glaziers[1]	55	9.9	16.8	6	1
47-2130	Insulation workers	61	18.7	22.8	12	1
47-2131	Insulation workers, floor, ceiling, and wall	32	18.7	22.8	6	1
47-2132	Insulation workers, mechanical	28	18.7	22.8	6	1
47-2140	Painters and paperhangers	473	19.5	17.8	98	8
47-2141	Painters, construction and maintenance	463	19.5	17.8	96	8
47-2142	Paperhangers[1]	10	19.7	17.5	2	(2)
47-2150	Pipelayers, plumbers, pipefitters, and steamfitters	569	12.0	20.6	72	12
47-2151	Pipelayers	67	12.0	20.6	8	1
47-2152	Plumbers, pipefitters, and steamfitters	502	12.0	20.6	63	10
47-2161	Plasterers and stucco masons	61	6.3	23.3	4	1
47-2171	Reinforcing iron and rebar workers[1]	30	13.0	25.1	4	1
47-2181	Roofers	156	21.6	22.9	36	4
47-2211	Sheet metal workers	189	15.6	24.3	30	5
47-2221	Structural iron and steel workers	72	8.8	32.5	7	2
47-3000	Helpers, construction trades	448	31.6	25.3	148	11
47-3010	Helpers, construction trades	448	31.6	25.3	148	11
47-3011	Helpers—Brickmasons, blockmasons, stonemasons, and tile and marble setters	65	31.6	25.3	22	2
47-3012	Helpers—Carpenters	109	31.6	25.3	36	3
47-3013	Helpers—Electricians	105	31.6	25.3	34	3
47-3014	Helpers—Painters, paperhangers, plasterers, and stucco masons	24	31.6	25.3	8	1
47-3015	Helpers—Pipelayers, plumbers, pipefitters, and steamfitters	85	31.6	25.3	28	2
47-3016	Helpers—Roofers	22	31.6	25.3	7	1
47-3019	Helpers, construction trades, all other	38	31.6	25.3	13	1
47-4000	Other construction and related workers	451	11.5	20.5	55	9

See footnotes at end of table.

Table V–3. Total and net replacement rates and annual average projected replacement needs, 2006–16 — Continued
(Numbers in thousands)

Code	2006 National Employment Matrix code and title	Total employment, 2006	Replacement rate (percent)		Annual average replacement needs, 2006–16	
			Total, 2005–06	Net, 2006–16	Total	Net
47-4011	Construction and building inspectors	110	8.9	18.5	11	2
47-4021	Elevator installers and repairers[1]	22	11.7	26.5	3	1
47-4031	Fence erectors[1]	32	7.2	20.1	2	1
47-4041	Hazardous materials removal workers	39	3.6	21.5	1	1
47-4051	Highway maintenance workers	145	15.5	18.2	23	3
47-4061	Rail-track laying and maintenance equipment operators[1]	15	11.7	24.5	2	(2)
47-4071	Septic tank servicers and sewer pipe cleaners[1]	24	11.7	20.1	3	(2)
47-4090	Miscellaneous construction and related workers	63	14.2	26.1	9	2
47-4091	Segmental pavers	1	14.2	26.1	(2)	(2)
47-4099	Construction and related workers, all other	62	14.2	26.1	9	2
47-5000	Extraction workers	202	11.0	24.1	22	5
47-5010	Derrick, rotary drill, and service unit operators, oil, gas, and mining	67	11.1	10.1	7	1
47-5011	Derrick operators, oil and gas[1]	19	11.1	10.1	2	(2)
47-5012	Rotary drill operators, oil and gas[1]	20	11.1	10.1	2	(2)
47-5013	Service unit operators, oil, gas, and mining[1]	28	11.1	10.1	3	(2)
47-5021	Earth drillers, except oil and gas	22	11.1	32.5	2	1
47-5031	Explosives workers, ordnance handling experts, and blasters[1]	5	11.1	29.6	1	(2)
47-5040	Mining machine operators	21	11.1	38.2	2	1
47-5041	Continuous mining machine operators	10	11.1	38.2	1	(2)
47-5042	Mine cutting and channeling machine operators	8	11.1	38.2	1	(2)
47-5049	Mining machine operators, all other	3	11.1	38.2	(2)	(2)
47-5051	Rock splitters, quarry	4	9.8	25.2	(2)	(2)
47-5061	Roof bolters, mining[1]	4	11.1	29.6	(2)	(2)
47-5071	Roustabouts, oil and gas[1]	44	11.1	29.6	5	1
47-5081	Helpers—Extraction workers[1]	25	11.1	29.6	3	1
47-5099	Extraction workers, all other	10	9.8	25.2	1	(2)
49-0000	Installation, maintenance, and repair occupations	5,883	9.8	16.1	601	95
49-1000	Supervisors of installation, maintenance, and repair workers	465	4.3	23.5	21	11
49-1011	First-line supervisors/managers of mechanics, installers, and repairers	465	4.3	23.5	21	11
49-2000	Electrical and electronic equipment mechanics, installers, and repairers	661	8.5	21.0	57	14
49-2011	Computer, automated teller, and office machine repairers	175	12.3	11.6	22	2
49-2020	Radio and telecommunications equipment installers and repairers	205	6.5	24.6	13	5
49-2021	Radio mechanics	7	6.5	24.6	(2)	(2)
49-2022	Telecommunications equipment installers and repairers, except line installers	198	6.5	24.6	13	5
49-2090	Miscellaneous electrical and electronic equipment mechanics, installers, and repairers	281	7.5	24.2	22	7
49-2091	Avionics technicians[1]	16	6.5	10.2	1	(2)
49-2092	Electric motor, power tool, and related repairers	25	10.5	37.6	3	1
49-2093	Electrical and electronics installers and repairers, transportation equipment[1]	21	7.3	21.5	2	(2)
49-2094	Electrical and electronics repairers, commercial and industrial equipment[1]	80	7.3	33.9	6	3
49-2095	Electrical and electronics repairers, powerhouse, substation, and relay[1]	22	7.3	33.9	2	1
49-2096	Electronic equipment installers and repairers, motor vehicles[1]	20	7.3	32.1	1	1
49-2097	Electronic home entertainment equipment installers and repairers[1]	40	7.3	9.3	3	(2)
49-2098	Security and fire alarm systems installers[1]	57	7.3	13.2	5	1
49-3000	Vehicle and mobile equipment mechanics, installers, and repairers	1,771	10.7	20.2	201	36
49-3011	Aircraft mechanics and service technicians	122	6.5	10.2	8	1
49-3020	Automotive technicians and repairers	979	11.9	21.1	125	21
49-3021	Automotive body and related repairers	183	18.3	23.7	35	4
49-3022	Automotive glass installers and repairers[1]	24	11.7	36.4	3	1
49-3023	Automotive service technicians and mechanics	773	10.4	20.1	86	15
49-3031	Bus and truck mechanics and diesel engine specialists	275	7.7	21.8	22	6
49-3040	Heavy vehicle and mobile equipment service technicians and mechanics	188	6.8	19.6	13	4
49-3041	Farm equipment mechanics	31	6.8	19.6	2	1

See footnotes at end of table.

Table V–3. Total and net replacement rates and annual average projected replacement needs, 2006–16 — Continued
(Numbers in thousands)

2006 National Employment Matrix code and title		Total employment, 2006	Replacement rate (percent)		Annual average replacement needs, 2006–16	
			Total, 2005–06	Net, 2006–16	Total	Net
49-3042	Mobile heavy equipment mechanics, except engines	131	6.8	19.6	9	3
49-3043	Rail car repairers	27	6.8	19.6	2	1
49-3050	Small engine mechanics	78	14.6	20.0	12	2
49-3051	Motorboat mechanics	24	14.6	20.0	4	(2)
49-3052	Motorcycle mechanics	21	14.6	20.0	3	(2)
49-3053	Outdoor power equipment and other small engine mechanics	33	14.6	20.0	5	1
49-3090	Miscellaneous vehicle and mobile equipment mechanics, installers, and repairers	128	14.3	19.9	20	3
49-3091	Bicycle repairers	9	14.3	19.9	1	(2)
49-3092	Recreational vehicle service technicians	14	14.3	19.9	2	(2)
49-3093	Tire repairers and changers	106	14.3	19.9	17	2
49-9000	Other installation, maintenance, and repair occupations	2,987	10.3	11.4	322	34
49-9010	Control and valve installers and repairers	58	8.9	17.5	5	1
49-9011	Mechanical door repairers[1]	15	8.9	17.5	1	(2)
49-9012	Control and valve installers and repairers, except mechanical door[1]	43	8.9	17.5	4	1
49-9021	Heating, air conditioning, and refrigeration mechanics and installers	292	8.9	17.5	27	5
49-9031	Home appliance repairers	57	7.2	22.6	4	1
49-9040	Industrial machinery installation, repair, and maintenance workers	1,794	10.2	5.5	192	10
49-9041	Industrial machinery mechanics	261	7.7	16.7	21	4
49-9042	Maintenance and repair workers, general	1,391	10.4	2.5	152	3
49-9043	Maintenance workers, machinery	84	18.0	16.0	15	1
49-9044	Millwrights	55	7.9	12.5	4	1
49-9045	Refractory materials repairers, except brickmasons	3	7.7	16.7	(2)	(2)
49-9050	Line installers and repairers	275	6.9	28.3	20	8
49-9051	Electrical power-line installers and repairers	112	4.8	31.5	6	4
49-9052	Telecommunications line installers and repairers	162	8.4	26.0	14	4
49-9060	Precision instrument and equipment repairers	68	3.7	28.0	3	2
49-9061	Camera and photographic equipment repairers[1]	4	3.7	28.0	(2)	(2)
49-9062	Medical equipment repairers[1]	38	3.7	28.0	2	1
49-9063	Musical instrument repairers and tuners[1]	6	3.7	28.0	(2)	(2)
49-9064	Watch repairers[1]	4	3.7	28.0	(2)	(2)
49-9069	Precision instrument and equipment repairers, all other[1]	16	3.7	28.0	1	(2)
49-9090	Miscellaneous installation, maintenance, and repair workers	442	15.4	16.1	71	7
49-9091	Coin, vending, and amusement machine servicers and repairers	48	10.3	27.7	5	1
49-9092	Commercial divers[1]	3	5.6	6.4	(2)	(2)
49-9093	Fabric menders, except garment	2	5.6	6.4	(2)	(2)
49-9094	Locksmiths and safe repairers[1]	26	10.3	19.4	3	1
49-9095	Manufactured building and mobile home installers	12	12.4	18.9	1	(2)
49-9096	Riggers[1]	12	5.6	6.4	1	(2)
49-9097	Signal and track switch repairers[1]	7	5.6	6.4	(2)	(2)
49-9098	Helpers--Installation, maintenance, and repair workers	163	29.0	23.5	50	4
49-9099	Installation, maintenance, and repair workers, all other	168	5.6	6.4	10	1
51-0000	Production occupations	10,675	13.6	20.2	1,416	216
51-1000	Supervisors, production workers	699	6.8	16.7	46	12
51-1011	First-line supervisors/managers of production and operating workers	699	6.8	16.7	46	12
51-2000	Assemblers and fabricators	2,075	19.9	20.1	403	42
51-2011	Aircraft structure, surfaces, rigging, and systems assemblers[1]	28	20.7	20.8	6	1
51-2020	Electrical, electronics, and electromechanical assemblers	297	14.4	17.0	38	5
51-2021	Coil winders, tapers, and finishers	23	14.4	17.0	3	(2)
51-2022	Electrical and electronic equipment assemblers	213	14.4	17.0	27	4
51-2023	Electromechanical equipment assemblers	60	14.4	17.0	8	1
51-2031	Engine and other machine assemblers[1]	45	20.2	23.9	9	1
51-2041	Structural metal fabricators and fitters[1]	103	20.2	17.3	21	2
51-2090	Miscellaneous assemblers and fabricators	1,602	20.7	20.8	329	33
51-2091	Fiberglass laminators and fabricators	33	20.7	20.8	7	1

See footnotes at end of table.

Table V-3. Total and net replacement rates and annual average projected replacement needs, 2006–16 — Continued
(Numbers in thousands)

2006 National Employment Matrix code and title		Total employment, 2006	Replacement rate (percent)		Annual average replacement needs, 2006–16	
			Total, 2005–06	Net, 2006–16	Total	Net
51-2092	Team assemblers	1,274	20.7	20.8	264	26
51-2093	Timing device assemblers, adjusters, and calibrators	3	20.7	20.8	1	([2])
51-2099	Assemblers and fabricators, all other	292	20.7	20.8	58	6
51-3000	Food processing occupations	705	13.6	29.2	100	21
51-3011	Bakers	149	19.1	21.1	30	3
51-3020	Butchers and other meat, poultry, and fish processing workers	398	10.7	31.7	45	13
51-3021	Butchers and meat cutters	131	10.7	31.7	14	4
51-3022	Meat, poultry, and fish cutters and trimmers	144	10.7	31.7	16	5
51-3023	Slaughterers and meat packers	122	10.7	31.7	14	4
51-3090	Miscellaneous food processing workers	158	15.5	30.6	25	5
51-3091	Food and tobacco roasting, baking, and drying machine operators and tenders	19	20.0	37.2	4	1
51-3092	Food batchmakers	95	14.7	25.5	15	2
51-3093	Food cooking machine operators and tenders[1]	44	15.5	38.8	7	2
51-4000	Metal workers and plastic workers	2,258	13.3	19.2	288	43
51-4010	Computer control programmers and operators	158	9.4	11.9	15	2
51-4011	Computer-controlled machine tool operators, metal and plastic[1]	141	9.4	11.9	13	2
51-4012	Numerical tool and process control programmers[1]	18	9.4	11.9	2	([2])
51-4020	Forming machine setters, operators, and tenders, metal and plastic	161	9.1	26.6	14	4
51-4021	Extruding and drawing machine setters, operators, and tenders, metal and plastic[1]	94	9.1	27.2	8	3
51-4022	Forging machine setters, operators, and tenders, metal and plastic[1]	31	9.1	31.6	2	1
51-4023	Rolling machine setters, operators, and tenders, metal and plastic[1]	36	9.1	20.7	3	1
51-4030	Machine tool cutting setters, operators, and tenders, metal and plastic	513	15.0	19.4	70	10
51-4031	Cutting, punching, and press machine setters, operators, and tenders, metal and plastic	272	12.2	24.0	31	7
51-4032	Drilling and boring machine tool setters, operators, and tenders, metal and plastic[1]	43	16.2	20.1	6	1
51-4033	Grinding, lapping, polishing, and buffing machine tool setters, operators, and tenders, metal and plastic	101	19.3	9.8	18	1
51-4034	Lathe and turning machine tool setters, operators, and tenders, metal and plastic	68	17.5	19.5	10	1
51-4035	Milling and planing machine setters, operators, and tenders, metal and plastic[1]	29	19.3	9.8	5	([2])
51-4041	Machinists	397	10.1	15.5	40	6
51-4050	Metal furnace and kiln operators and tenders	33	33.0	15.5	10	1
51-4051	Metal-refining furnace operators and tenders	18	33.0	15.5	5	([2])
51-4052	Pourers and casters, metal	15	33.0	15.5	4	([2])
51-4060	Model makers and patternmakers, metal and plastic	16	21.2	23.5	3	([2])
51-4061	Model makers, metal and plastic[1]	9	21.2	23.5	2	([2])
51-4062	Patternmakers, metal and plastic[1]	7	21.2	23.5	2	([2])
51-4070	Molders and molding machine setters, operators, and tenders, metal and plastic	171	21.2	23.5	34	4
51-4071	Foundry mold and coremakers	15	21.2	23.5	3	([2])
51-4072	Molding, coremaking, and casting machine setters, operators, and tenders, metal and plastic	157	21.2	23.5	31	4
51-4081	Multiple machine tool setters, operators, and tenders, metal and plastic[1]	97	16.2	20.1	16	2
51-4111	Tool and die makers	101	5.5	13.3	5	1
51-4120	Welding, soldering, and brazing workers	462	14.1	21.2	67	10
51-4121	Welders, cutters, solderers, and brazers	409	14.1	21.2	59	9
51-4122	Welding, soldering, and brazing machine setters, operators, and tenders	53	14.1	21.2	8	1
51-4190	Miscellaneous metalworkers and plastic workers	150	11.3	20.2	15	3
51-4191	Heat treating equipment setters, operators, and tenders, metal and plastic[1]	27	11.8	17.1	3	([2])
51-4192	Lay-out workers, metal and plastic[1]	10	11.8	17.1	1	([2])
51-4193	Plating and coating machine setters, operators, and tenders, metal and plastic	42	10.3	29.7	4	1
51-4194	Tool grinders, filers, and sharpeners[1]	22	11.8	17.1	2	([2])
51-4199	Metal workers and plastic workers, all other	49	11.6	15.9	5	1
51-5000	Printing occupations	389	8.9	17.9	33	7
51-5010	Bookbinders and bindery workers	72	13.0	14.2	8	1

See footnotes at end of table.

Table V–3. Total and net replacement rates and annual average projected replacement needs, 2006–16 — Continued
(Numbers in thousands)

2006 National Employment Matrix code and title		Total employment, 2006	Replacement rate (percent)		Annual average replacement needs, 2006–16	
			Total, 2005–06	Net, 2006–16	Total	Net
51-5011	Bindery workers	65	13.0	14.2	8	1
51-5012	Bookbinders	7	13.0	14.2	1	(2)
51-5020	Printers	317	8.0	18.8	24	6
51-5021	Job printers	48	4.1	9.6	2	(2)
51-5022	Prepress technicians and workers	71	15.8	15.7	10	1
51-5023	Printing machine operators	198	6.4	22.1	12	4
51-6000	Textile, apparel, and furnishings occupations	873	13.9	16.6	115	14
51-6011	Laundry and dry-cleaning workers	239	14.5	22.4	36	5
51-6021	Pressers, textile, garment, and related materials	77	13.5	7.3	10	1
51-6031	Sewing machine operators	233	17.8	9.6	36	2
51-6040	Shoe and leather workers	20	15.1	18.4	3	(2)
51-6041	Shoe and leather workers and repairers[1]	16	14.5	20.7	2	(2)
51-6042	Shoe machine operators and tenders[1]	4	17.8	9.6	1	(2)
51-6050	Tailors, dressmakers, and sewers	77	15.7	16.8	12	1
51-6051	Sewers, hand	23	15.7	16.8	3	(2)
51-6052	Tailors, dressmakers, and custom sewers	54	15.7	16.8	9	1
51-6060	Textile machine setters, operators, and tenders	122	9.6	22.0	10	3
51-6061	Textile bleaching and dyeing machine operators and tenders[1]	19	10.5	14.2	2	(2)
51-6062	Textile cutting machine setters, operators, and tenders[1]	19	10.5	33.4	2	1
51-6063	Textile knitting and weaving machine setters, operators, and tenders	40	6.8	28.8	2	1
51-6064	Textile winding, twisting, and drawing out machine setters, operators, and tenders	43	11.3	14.2	4	1
51-6090	Miscellaneous textile, apparel, and furnishings workers	106	7.4	18.8	7	2
51-6091	Extruding and forming machine setters, operators, and tenders, synthetic and glass fibers[1]	18	6.9	20.1	1	(2)
51-6092	Fabric and apparel patternmakers[1]	9	6.9	20.1	1	(2)
51-6093	Upholsterers	55	5.5	15.6	3	1
51-6099	Textile, apparel, and furnishings workers, all other	24	12.1	24.8	3	1
51-7000	Woodworkers	370	10.4	25.2	39	9
51-7011	Cabinetmakers and bench carpenters	149	6.2	29.7	9	4
51-7021	Furniture finishers	31	32.9	18.0	10	1
51-7030	Model makers and patternmakers, wood	4	9.9	21.5	(2)	(2)
51-7031	Model makers, wood[1]	2	9.9	21.5	(2)	(2)
51-7032	Patternmakers, wood[1]	2	9.9	21.5	(2)	(2)
51-7040	Woodworking machine setters, operators, and tenders	165	10.1	22.9	17	4
51-7041	Sawing machine setters, operators, and tenders, wood	65	8.8	19.9	6	1
51-7042	Woodworking machine setters, operators, and tenders, except sawing	100	10.9	24.9	11	2
51-7099	Woodworkers, all other	20	9.9	21.5	2	(2)
51-8000	Plant and system operators	325	7.7	23.7	25	8
51-8010	Power plant operators, distributors, and dispatchers	47	4.8	34.5	2	2
51-8011	Nuclear power reactor operators	4	4.8	34.5	(2)	(2)
51-8012	Power distributors and dispatchers	9	4.8	34.5	(2)	(2)
51-8013	Power plant operators	35	4.8	34.5	2	1
51-8021	Stationary engineers and boiler operators	45	3.8	16.9	2	1
51-8031	Water and liquid waste treatment plant and system operators	111	6.8	17.5	8	2
51-8090	Miscellaneous plant and system operators	122	11.4	27.7	13	3
51-8091	Chemical plant and system operators	53	11.4	27.7	6	1
51-8092	Gas plant operators	12	11.4	27.7	1	(2)
51-8093	Petroleum pump system operators, refinery operators, and gaugers	42	11.4	27.7	4	1
51-8099	Plant and system operators, all other	14	11.4	27.7	2	(2)
51-9000	Other production occupations	2,981	12.7	20.2	368	60
51-9010	Chemical processing machine setters, operators, and tenders	97	2.8	22.8	3	2
51-9011	Chemical equipment operators and tenders	53	2.8	22.8	1	1
51-9012	Separating, filtering, clarifying, precipitating, and still machine setters, operators, and tenders	44	2.8	22.8	1	1

See footnotes at end of table.

Table V–3. Total and net replacement rates and annual average projected replacement needs, 2006–16 — Continued
(Numbers in thousands)

2006 National Employment Matrix code and title		Total employment, 2006	Replacement rate (percent)		Annual average replacement needs, 2006–16	
			Total, 2005–06	Net, 2006–16	Total	Net
51-9020	Crushing, grinding, polishing, mixing, and blending workers	230	13.4	16.3	30	4
51-9021	Crushing, grinding, and polishing machine setters, operators, and tenders	42	13.4	16.3	5	1
51-9022	Grinding and polishing workers, hand	45	13.4	16.3	6	1
51-9023	Mixing and blending machine setters, operators, and tenders	143	13.4	16.3	19	2
51-9030	Cutting workers	107	5.3	15.2	5	2
51-9031	Cutters and trimmers, hand	29	5.3	15.2	1	([2])
51-9032	Cutting and slicing machine setters, operators, and tenders	79	5.3	15.2	4	1
51-9041	Extruding, forming, pressing, and compacting machine setters, operators, and tenders	81	9.7	18.4	8	1
51-9051	Furnace, kiln, oven, drier, and kettle operators and tenders	32	5.9	27.5	2	1
51-9061	Inspectors, testers, sorters, samplers, and weighers	491	15.9	14.8	75	7
51-9071	Jewelers and precious stone and metal workers	52	14.3	17.2	7	1
51-9080	Medical, dental, and ophthalmic laboratory technicians	95	6.0	18.8	6	2
51-9081	Dental laboratory technicians	53	6.0	18.8	3	1
51-9082	Medical appliance technicians	12	6.0	18.8	1	([2])
51-9083	Ophthalmic laboratory technicians	29	6.0	18.8	2	1
51-9111	Packaging and filling machine operators and tenders	386	21.2	18.6	80	7
51-9120	Painting workers	192	5.0	19.6	9	4
51-9121	Coating, painting, and spraying machine setters, operators, and tenders	106	5.0	19.6	5	2
51-9122	Painters, transportation equipment	54	5.0	19.6	3	1
51-9123	Painting, coating, and decorating workers	31	5.0	19.6	2	1
51-9130	Photographic process workers and processing machine operators	73	13.8	34.7	8	3
51-9131	Photographic process workers	24	13.8	34.7	3	1
51-9132	Photographic processing machine operators	49	13.8	34.7	5	2
51-9141	Semiconductor processors[1]	42	14.4	17.0	6	1
51-9190	Miscellaneous production workers	1,102	11.9	23.6	130	26
51-9191	Cementing and gluing machine operators and tenders[1]	23	17.0	26.3	4	1
51-9192	Cleaning, washing, and metal pickling equipment operators and tenders[1]	16	17.0	28.7	3	([2])
51-9193	Cooling and freezing equipment operators and tenders[1]	11	17.0	22.2	2	([2])
51-9194	Etchers and engravers[1]	14	15.8	18.5	2	([2])
51-9195	Molders, shapers, and casters, except metal and plastic[1]	56	10.2	22.2	6	1
51-9196	Paper goods machine setters, operators, and tenders	113	7.7	24.2	8	3
51-9197	Tire builders[1]	23	17.0	36.9	4	1
51-9198	Helpers--Production workers	542	9.0	24.6	49	13
51-9199	Production workers, all other	305	17.4	20.7	54	6
53-0000	Transportation and material moving occupations	10,233	17.8	22.6	1,864	231
53-1000	Supervisors, transportation and material moving workers	414	6.0	20.4	26	8
53-1011	Aircraft cargo handling supervisors	6	6.0	20.4	([2])	([2])
53-1021	First-line supervisors/managers of helpers, laborers, and material movers, hand	182	6.0	20.4	12	4
53-1031	First-line supervisors/managers of transportation and material-moving machine and vehicle operators	226	6.0	20.4	14	5
53-2000	Air transportation occupations	137	3.6	28.8	5	4
53-2010	Aircraft pilots and flight engineers	107	3.6	29.2	4	3
53-2011	Airline pilots, copilots, and flight engineers	79	3.6	29.2	3	2
53-2012	Commercial pilots	28	3.6	29.2	1	1
53-2020	Air traffic controllers and airfield operations specialists	30	3.6	27.3	1	1
53-2021	Air traffic controllers[1]	25	3.6	27.3	1	1
53-2022	Airfield operations specialists[1]	5	3.6	27.3	([2])	([2])
53-3000	Motor vehicle operators	4,335	13.2	16.7	597	73
53-3011	Ambulance drivers and attendants, except emergency medical technicians[1]	22	13.6	12.9	3	([2])
53-3020	Bus drivers	653	11.7	13.1	80	9
53-3021	Bus drivers, transit and intercity	198	11.7	13.1	25	3
53-3022	Bus drivers, school	455	11.7	13.1	56	6
53-3030	Driver/sales workers and truck drivers	3,356	13.3	17.7	463	60
53-3031	Driver/sales workers	445	13.3	17.7	58	8

See footnotes at end of table.

Table V-3. Total and net replacement rates and annual average projected replacement needs, 2006–16 — Continued
(Numbers in thousands)

2006 National Employment Matrix code and title		Total employment, 2006	Replacement rate (percent)		Annual average replacement needs, 2006–16	
			Total, 2005–06	Net, 2006–16	Total	Net
53-3032	Truck drivers, heavy and tractor-trailer	1,860	13.3	17.7	260	33
53-3033	Truck drivers, light or delivery services	1,051	13.3	17.7	145	19
53-3041	Taxi drivers and chauffeurs	229	13.6	12.9	33	3
53-3099	Motor vehicle operators, all other	76	22.8	15.8	18	1
53-4000	Rail transportation occupations	125	6.8	34.6	9	4
53-4010	Locomotive engineers and operators	47	6.8	30.7	3	1
53-4021	Railroad brake, signal, and switch operators[1]	25	6.8	34.7	2	1
53-4031	Railroad conductors and yardmasters[1]	40	6.8	38.9	3	2
53-4041	Subway and streetcar operators[1]	7	6.8	34.7	1	([2])
53-4099	Rail transportation workers, all other[1]	7	6.8	34.7	([2])	([2])
53-5000	Water transportation occupations	84	12.3	29.9	11	3
53-5011	Sailors and marine oilers[1]	33	22.7	35.4	8	1
53-5020	Ship and boat captains and operators	37	5.6	26.3	2	1
53-5021	Captains, mates, and pilots of water vessels	34	5.6	26.3	2	1
53-5022	Motorboat operators	3	5.6	26.3	([2])	([2])
53-5031	Ship engineers[1]	15	5.6	26.3	1	([2])
53-6000	Other transportation workers	312	21.8	32.0	72	10
53-6011	Bridge and lock tenders[1]	4	4.0	18.2	([2])	([2])
53-6021	Parking lot attendants	135	29.3	27.3	42	4
53-6031	Service station attendants	96	25.6	45.9	26	4
53-6041	Traffic technicians	7	4.0	18.2	([2])	([2])
53-6051	Transportation inspectors	26	5.9	33.6	2	1
53-6099	Transportation workers, all other	44	4.0	18.2	2	1
53-7000	Material moving occupations	4,825	23.7	26.9	1,143	130
53-7011	Conveyor operators and tenders[1]	50	13.4	17.3	6	1
53-7021	Crane and tower operators	46	5.3	17.9	2	1
53-7030	Dredge, excavating, and loading machine operators	85	7.1	15.9	6	1
53-7031	Dredge operators	2	7.1	15.9	([2])	([2])
53-7032	Excavating and loading machine and dragline operators	80	7.1	15.9	6	1
53-7033	Loading machine operators, underground mining	3	7.1	15.9	([2])	([2])
53-7041	Hoist and winch operators[1]	3	11.7	17.3	([2])	([2])
53-7051	Industrial truck and tractor operators	637	14.2	25.2	90	16
53-7060	Laborers and material movers, hand	3,766	26.3	27.7	987	104
53-7061	Cleaners of vehicles and equipment	368	32.3	38.2	127	14
53-7062	Laborers and freight, stock, and material movers, hand	2,416	25.6	32.0	626	77
53-7063	Machine feeders and offbearers	148	17.5	17.9	24	3
53-7064	Packers and packagers, hand	834	26.9	12.2	211	10
53-7070	Pumping station operators	29	18.6	39.6	5	1
53-7071	Gas compressor and gas pumping station operators	4	18.6	39.6	1	([2])
53-7072	Pump operators, except wellhead pumpers	11	18.6	39.6	2	([2])
53-7073	Wellhead pumpers	14	18.6	39.6	3	1
53-7081	Refuse and recyclable material collectors	136	26.1	27.1	37	4
53-7111	Shuttle car operators[1]	3	13.3	38.2	([2])	([2])
53-7121	Tank car, truck, and ship loaders[1]	16	25.6	17.7	4	([2])
53-7199	Material moving workers, all other	54	7.8	18.1	4	1

[1] One or more Current Population Survey (CPS) proxy occupations may be used to estimate CPS-based data.

[2] Less than 500.

See footnotes at end of table.

Chapter VI. Education and Training Statistics: Completions, by Field of Study

The National Center for Education Statistics (NCES), U.S. Department of Education, collected data in fall 2006 on the number of awards, degrees, and certificates completed during 2005–06, by type of educational program and detailed field of study through the Integrated Postsecondary Education Data System (IPEDS) Web-based data collection system. These data, covering the period from July 1, 2005, to June 30, 2006, are presented in table VI–1. NCES surveyed institutions of higher education that offered awards at the bachelor's degree level and higher, institutions with 2-year programs, and public and private institutions with programs of less than 2 years. The 2000 version of the Classification of Instructional Programs was used to categorize the data.

About 3.9 million postsecondary awards and degrees were earned during the 2005–06 academic year, an increase of about 923,000, or 31 percent, from 10 years earlier. Formal degrees earned included: 737,000 associate degrees; 1.6 million bachelor's degrees; 629,000 master's degrees (including 22,000 postbaccalaureate certificates); 72,000 doctoral degrees (including 15,000 postmaster's certificates); and 91,000 first professional degrees (including 1,000 first professional certificates). In addition, there were 363,000 nondegree formal awards for the completion of 1- to 4-year curricula during 2005–06, along with 379,000 awards for the completion of programs of less than 1 year. Both levels of awards saw moderate growth from 10 years earlier, with 1- to 4-year awards increasing by 13 percent and awards of less than 1 year by 21 percent. More than a third of both types of awards were earned in the field of health professions and related clinical sciences, with significant numbers also earned in personal and culinary services; mechanic and repair technologies/technicians; and business, management, marketing, and related support services.

About 737,000 associate degrees were earned during 2005–06, an increase of 31 percent from 10 years earlier. Three disciplines accounted for almost two-thirds of the degrees: liberal arts and sciences, general studies, and humanities; health professions and related clinical sciences; and business, management, marketing, and related support services. According to the middle alternative set of the most recent NCES projections, which uses a base year of 2004–05, the number of associate degrees earned is expected to grow by 9 percent through 2016-17.

Some 1,583,000 bachelor's degrees were earned during 2005–06, up about 34 percent from 1995-96. Business, management, marketing, and related support services accounted for about 21 percent of these degrees, while social sciences contributed 9 percent and education another 7 percent. Disciplines experiencing rapid growth over the past 10 years include computer and information sciences and support services (up about 100 percent); parks, recreation, leisure, and fitness studies (up about 85 percent); and visual and performing arts (up about 76 percent). NCES projects that the number of bachelor's degrees earned will grow by another 26 percent from 2004–05 to 2016–17.

Master's degrees earned totaled 606,000 in 2005–06, about 48 percent more than in 1995–96. More than half were earned in the fields of education and business, management, marketing, and related support services. These fields also accounted for the majority of gains in master's degrees earned over the last 10 years, with education degrees increasing by 70,000 (66 percent growth) and business, management, marketing, and related support services degrees increasing by 58,000 (61 percent growth). NCES projects the number of master's degrees earned to grow by 35 percent from 2004–05 to 2016–17. Data presented in table VI–1 include about 22,000 postbaccalaureate certificates earned in 2005–06, primarily from education programs.

The number of new doctoral degrees, 57,000, increased in 2005–06 by 27 percent from 10 years earlier. The most popular disciplines for doctoral degrees were education, engineering, health professions and related clinical sciences, and psychology, which together totaled more than half of all doctoral degrees and postmaster's certificates earned. NCES projects the number of doctoral degrees earned to grow by 32 percent from 2004–05 to 2016–17. Data presented in table VI–1 include about 15,000 postmaster's certificates earned in 2005–06, primarily from education programs.

The number of first professional degrees earned totaled approximately 89,000 during 2005–06, about 15 percent more than in 1995–96. Forty-nine percent were earned in legal professions and studies, 44 percent in health professions and related clinical sciences, and the remainder in theology and religious vocations. NCES projects the number of first professional degrees earned to grow by 30 percent from 2004–05 to 2016–17. Data presented in table VI–1 include about 1,000 first professional certificates earned in 2005–06, primarily from health professions and related clinical sciences programs.

Information on obtaining data on postsecondary education from NCES is available on the Internet. Visit the NCES site (**http://www.nces.ed.gov**) for the Digest of Education Statistics, IPEDS data from previous years, data from other statistical series, and more information on projections of education statistics.

Table VI–1. Earned awards and degrees, by field of study, 2005–06

2000 Classification of Instructional Program (CIP) code and title		Awards of less than 1 academic year	1- to 4- year awards	Associate degrees	Bachelor's degrees	Master's degrees or post-baccalaureate certificates	Doctoral degrees or post-master's certificates	First professional degrees or certificates
	Total, all programs	**379,104**	**362,819**	**736,818**	**1,582,839**	**628,748**	**72,072**	**90,663**
1.	**Agriculture, general**	**2,865**	**2,069**	**5,025**	**14,655**	**2,250**	**724**	**–**
1.00	Agriculture, general	16	8	409	1,426	261	8	–
1.01	Agricultural business and management	694	287	918	4,093	501	128	–
1.0101	Agricultural business and management, general	42	43	360	941	68	–	–
1.0102	Agribusiness/agricultural business operations	3	51	180	1,680	31	–	–
1.0103	Agricultural economics	–	–	23	876	381	128	–
1.0104	Farm/farm and ranch management	469	185	96	113	14	–	–
1.0105	Agricultural/farm supplies retailing and wholesaling	80	7	122	70	–	–	–
1.0106	Agricultural business technology	100	1	29	–	1	–	–
1.0199	Agricultural business and management, other	–	–	108	413	6	–	–
1.02	Agricultural mechanization	22	187	387	319	2	1	–
1.0201	Agricultural mechanization, general	2	6	88	290	1	–	–
1.0204	Agricultural power machinery operation	1	59	91	–	–	–	–
1.0205	Agricultural mechanics and equipment/machine technology	17	81	199	–	1	1	–
1.0299	Agricultural mechanization, other	2	41	9	29	–	–	–
1.03	Agricultural production operations	141	359	712	307	63	7	–
1.0301	Agricultural production operations, general	8	100	291	70	32	–	–
1.0302	Animal/livestock husbandry and production	43	157	270	165	–	–	–
1.0303	Aquaculture	51	3	16	44	21	4	–
1.0304	Crop production	21	9	32	26	10	3	–
1.0306	Dairy husbandry and production	–	40	23	–	–	–	–
1.0307	Horse husbandry/equine science and management	8	36	51	2	–	–	–
1.0399	Agricultural production operations, other	10	14	29	–	–	–	–
1.04	Agricultural and food products processing	8	4	6	91	3	1	–
1.05	Agricultural and domestic animal services	210	108	280	451	1	–	–
1.0504	Dog/pet/animal grooming	27	–	1	–	–	–	–
1.0505	Animal training	19	–	18	–	–	–	–
1.0507	Equestrian/equine studies	149	95	236	447	1	–	–
1.0508	Taxidermy/taxidermist	13	5	–	–	–	–	–
1.0599	Agricultural and domestic animal services, other	2	8	25	4	–	–	–
1.06	Applied horticulture/horticultural business services	1,652	1,011	1,802	683	27	15	–
1.0601	Applied horticulture/horticulture operations, general	942	506	657	188	15	10	–
1.0603	Ornamental horticulture	48	29	178	136	9	5	–
1.0604	Greenhouse operations and management	40	8	32	–	–	–	–
1.0605	Landscaping and groundskeeping	254	249	451	201	3	–	–

- None reported

Table VI–1. Earned awards and degrees, by field of study, 2005–06 — Continued

2000 Classification of Instructional Program (CIP) code and title		Awards of less than 1 academic year	1- to 4- year awards	Associate degrees	Bachelor's degrees	Master's degrees or post-baccalaureate certificates	Doctoral degrees or post-master's certificates	First professional degrees or certificates
1.0606	Plant nursery operations and management	102	27	52	–	–	–	–
1.0607	Turf and turfgrass management	36	92	326	142	–	–	–
1.0608	Floriculture/floristry operations and management	216	65	16	–	–	–	–
1.0699	Applied horticulture/horticultural business services, other	14	35	90	16	–	–	–
1.07	International agriculture	–	–	–	22	15	–	–
1.08	Agricultural public services	–	–	–	299	35	4	–
1.0801	Agricultural and extension education services	–	–	–	36	21	4	–
1.0802	Agricultural communication/ journalism	–	–	–	214	14	–	–
1.0899	Agricultural public services, other	–	–	–	49	–	–	–
1.09	Animal sciences	28	40	336	4,028	402	158	–
1.0901	Animal sciences, general	23	4	172	3,627	338	132	–
1.0902	Agricultural animal breeding	–	–	–	27	8	5	–
1.0903	Animal health	1	23	32	–	8	–	–
1.0904	Animal nutrition	–	–	–	–	7	4	–
1.0905	Dairy science	–	13	5	145	12	5	–
1.0906	Livestock management	–	–	–	13	–	–	–
1.0907	Poultry science	–	–	41	90	19	7	–
1.0999	Animal sciences, other	4	–	86	126	10	5	–
1.10	Food science and technology	–	37	43	762	297	138	–
1.1001	Food science	–	5	6	737	266	132	–
1.1002	Food technology and processing	–	32	36	5	7	–	–
1.1099	Food science and technology, other	–	–	1	20	24	6	–
1.11	Plant sciences	24	13	87	1,791	487	199	–
1.1101	Plant sciences, general	–	7	6	327	95	42	–
1.1102	Agronomy and crop science	–	3	15	420	167	75	–
1.1103	Horticultural science	17	1	55	836	101	46	–
1.1104	Agricultural and horticultural plant breeding	–	–	–	–	17	8	–
1.1105	Plant protection and integrated pest management	7	2	10	17	14	3	–
1.1106	Range science and management	–	–	1	126	44	9	–
1.1199	Plant sciences, other	–	–	–	65	49	16	–
1.12	Soil sciences	–	–	3	132	109	52	–
1.1201	Soil science and agronomy, general	–	–	3	122	99	47	–
1.1299	Soil sciences, other	–	–	–	10	10	5	–
1.99	Agriculture, agricultural operations, and related sciences, other	70	15	42	251	47	13	–
3.	**Natural resources and conservation**	**752**	**69**	**1,217**	**9,252**	**2,535**	**489**	**–**
3.01	Natural resources conservation and research	25	6	409	6,160	1,308	218	–
3.0101	Natural resources/conservation, general	16	6	312	1,022	248	57	–
3.0103	Environmental studies	7	–	46	3,178	465	48	–
3.0104	Environmental science	2	–	51	1,960	594	113	–
3.0199	Natural resources conservation and research, other	–	–	–	–	1	–	–
3.02	Natural resources management and policy	629	10	178	597	427	50	–

- None reported

Table VI–1. Earned awards and degrees, by field of study, 2005–06 — Continued

2000 Classification of Instructional Program (CIP) code	and title	Awards of less than 1 academic year	1- to 4- year awards	Associate degrees	Bachelor's degrees	Master's degrees or post-baccalaureate certificates	Doctoral degrees or post-master's certificates	First professional degrees or certificates
3.0201	Natural resources management and policy	14	9	56	346	339	32	–
3.0204	Natural resource economics	–	–	–	20	2	8	–
3.0205	Water, wetlands, and marine resources management	–	–	9	81	45	–	–
3.0206	Land use planning and management/development	–	–	7	47	36	8	–
3.0299	Natural resources management and policy, other	615	1	106	103	5	2	–
3.03	Fishing and fisheries sciences and management	11	–	61	179	78	21	–
3.05	Forestry	64	37	414	1,129	539	141	–
3.0501	Forestry, general	13	8	75	690	334	92	–
3.0502	Forest sciences and biology	–	–	–	168	122	25	–
3.0506	Forest management/forest resources management	3	7	56	98	23	7	–
3.0508	Urban forestry	–	–	36	35	6	–	–
3.0509	Wood science and wood products/pulp and paper technology	14	–	7	112	26	5	–
3.0510	Forest resources production and management	–	–	3	1	17	2	–
3.0511	Forest technology/technician	23	19	194	2	–	6	–
3.0599	Forestry, other	11	3	43	23	11	4	–
3.06	Wildlife and wildlands science and management	23	14	147	1,014	143	45	–
3.99	Natural resources and conservation, other	–	2	8	173	40	14	–
4.	**Architecture and related services**	**181**	**173**	**656**	**9,603**	**5,826**	**220**	**–**
4.02	Architecture and related services	–	–	50	5,721	3,130	100	–
4.03	City/urban, community and regional planning	–	–	–	695	2,036	90	–
4.04	Environmental design	–	–	–	941	19	17	–
4.05	Interior architecture	–	122	307	773	17	–	–
4.06	Landscape architecture	4	1	10	1,062	518	1	–
4.08	Architectural history and criticism	–	–	–	27	11	6	–
4.09	Architectural technology/ technician	130	50	211	25	–	–	–
4.99	Architecture and related services, other	47	–	78	359	95	6	–
5.	**Area, ethnic, cultural, and gender studies**	**407**	**114**	**126**	**10,133**	**2,266**	**312**	**–**
5.01	Area studies	253	37	5	5,509	1,446	221	–
5.0101	African studies	38	–	–	50	48	7	–
5.0102	American/United States studies/civilization	–	16	3	1,891	269	102	–
5.0103	Asian studies/civilization	27	–	1	699	144	1	–
5.0104	East Asian studies	6	5	–	472	156	19	–
5.0105	Central/Middle and Eastern European studies	–	–	–	6	19	5	–
5.0106	European studies/civilization	19	–	–	223	29	1	–
5.0107	Latin American studies	49	15	–	715	302	7	–
5.0108	Near and Middle Eastern studies	9	–	–	205	144	39	–
5.0109	Pacific area/Pacific rim studies	–	–	–	14	10	–	–
5.0110	Russian studies	22	–	–	163	79	15	–
5.0111	Scandinavian studies	–	–	–	33	8	–	–
5.0112	South Asian studies	–	–	–	19	16	3	–

- None reported

Table VI–1. Earned awards and degrees, by field of study, 2005–06 — Continued

2000 Classification of Instructional Program (CIP) code and title		Awards of less than 1 academic year	1- to 4- year awards	Associate degrees	Bachelor's degrees	Master's degrees or post-baccalaureate certificates	Doctoral degrees or post-master's certificates	First professional degrees or certificates
5.0113	Southeast Asian studies	–	–	–	3	22	–	–
5.0114	Western European studies	50	–	–	9	67	2	–
5.0115	Canadian studies	–	–	–	2	–	–	–
5.0118	Slavic studies	–	–	–	12	1	–	–
5.0120	Ural-Altaic and Central Asian studies	–	–	–	–	12	1	–
5.0122	Regional studies (US, Canadian, foreign)	–	–	1	17	3	4	–
5.0123	Chinese studies	10	–	–	33	11	–	–
5.0124	French studies	–	–	–	91	4	8	–
5.0125	German studies	–	–	–	65	1	4	–
5.0126	Italian studies	–	–	–	67	6	1	–
5.0127	Japanese studies	–	–	–	61	5	–	–
5.0128	Korean studies	–	–	–	–	4	–	–
5.0130	Spanish and Iberian studies	–	–	–	28	–	–	–
5.0199	Area studies, other	23	1	–	631	86	2	–
5.02	**Ethnic, cultural minority, and gender studies**	**154**	**72**	**116**	**4,059**	**475**	**71**	**–**
5.0201	African-American/Black studies	14	12	–	1,004	90	30	–
5.0202	American Indian/Native American studies	2	8	57	173	44	4	
5.0203	Hispanic-American, Puerto Rican and Mexican-American/Chicano studies	–	–	–	473	42	4	–
5.0206	Asian-American studies	–	3	–	203	8	–	–
5.0207	Women's studies	117	40	10	1,623	200	21	–
5.0208	Gay/lesbian studies	–	5	–	1	–	–	–
5.0299	Ethnic, cultural minority, and gender studies, other	21	4	49	582	91	12	–
5.99	**Area, ethnic, cultural, and gender studies, other**	**–**	**5**	**5**	**565**	**345**	**20**	**–**
9.	**Communication, journalism, and related programs**	**975**	**757**	**2,689**	**77,264**	**7,387**	**502**	**–**
9.01	Communication and media studies	127	18	874	42,538	3,490	399	–
9.0101	Communication studies/speech communication and rhetoric	25	17	760	32,953	2,347	292	–
9.0102	Mass communication/media studies	102	1	105	8,510	731	89	–
9.0199	Communication and media studies, other	–	–	9	1,075	412	18	–
9.04	Journalism	37	40	356	14,498	1,685	48	–
9.0401	Journalism	23	26	236	12,451	1,495	48	–
9.0402	Broadcast journalism	14	13	86	1,013	43	–	–
9.0404	Photojournalism	–	–	28	164	–	–	–
9.0499	Journalism, other	–	1	6	870	147	–	–
9.07	Radio, television, and digital communication	655	448	861	7,242	541	36	–
9.0701	Radio and television	533	266	486	6,134	381	16	–
9.0702	Digital communication and media/multimedia	122	176	354	923	157	20	–
9.0799	Radio, television, and digital communication, other	–	6	21	185	3	–	–
9.09	Public relations, advertising, and applied communication	45	155	494	10,307	715	1	–
9.0901	Organizational communication, general	15	–	2	867	118	–	–
9.0902	Public relations/image management	16	–	43	4,144	227	–	–
9.0903	Advertising	14	155	392	4,847	259	1	–

- None reported

Table VI–1. Earned awards and degrees, by field of study, 2005–06 — Continued

2000 Classification of Instructional Program (CIP) code and title		Awards of less than 1 academic year	1- to 4- year awards	Associate degrees	Bachelor's degrees	Master's degrees or post-baccalaureate certificates	Doctoral degrees or post-master's certificates	First professional degrees or certificates
9.0904	Political communication	–	–	–	65	–	–	–
9.0905	Health communication	–	–	–	15	30	–	–
9.0999	Public relations, advertising, and applied communication, other	–	–	57	369	81	–	–
9.10	Publishing	18	–	–	–	82	–	–
9.99	Communication, journalism, and related programs, other	93	96	104	2,679	874	18	–
10.	**Communications technologies/ technicians and support services**	**1,420**	**1,938**	**4,008**	**3,095**	**513**	**4**	**–**
10.01	Communications technology/ technician	135	70	753	145	81	–	–
10.02	Audiovisual communications technologies/technicians	899	462	1,370	987	176	4	–
10.0201	Photographic and film/video technology/technician and assistant	44	41	290	27	–	–	–
10.0202	Radio and television broadcasting technology/ technician	781	158	821	632	174	4	–
10.0203	Recording arts technology/ technician	71	190	223	195	2	–	–
10.0299	Audiovisual communications technologies/technicians, other	3	73	36	133	–	–	–
10.03	Graphic communications	368	708	1,736	1,751	207	–	–
10.0301	Graphic communications, general	57	60	191	160	–	–	–
10.0302	Printing management	–	–	4	93	6	–	–
10.0303	Prepress/desktop publishing and digital imaging design	142	115	249	28	–	–	–
10.0304	Animation, interactive technology, video graphics, and special effects	42	101	690	1,320	201	–	–
10.0305	Graphic and printing equipment operator, general production	108	327	458	115	–	–	–
10.0306	Platemaker/imager	1	4	26	–	–	–	–
10.0307	Printing press operator	15	67	11	6	–	–	–
10.0308	Computer typography and composition equipment operator	1	6	10	–	–	–	–
10.0399	Graphic communications, other	2	28	97	29	–	–	–
10.99	Communications technologies/ technicians and support services, other	18	698	149	212	49	–	–
11.	**Computer and information sciences and support services**	**13,331**	**9,273**	**32,935**	**48,889**	**17,891**	**1,650**	**–**
11.01	Computer and information sciences, general	2,979	1,444	6,568	22,401	7,231	669	–
11.0101	Computer and information sciences, general	2,455	789	4,958	15,451	6,441	642	–
11.0102	Artificial intelligence and robotics	–	4	–	–	56	18	–
11.0103	Information technology	429	531	1,545	6,849	702	9	–
11.0199	Computer and information sciences, other	95	120	65	101	32	–	–
11.02	Computer programming	1,211	1,091	3,237	870	141	–	–
11.0201	Computer programming/ programmer, general	678	899	2,316	617	89	–	–
11.0202	Computer programming, specific applications	490	176	851	26	52	–	–

- None reported

Table VI–1. Earned awards and degrees, by field of study, 2005–06 — Continued

2000 Classification of Instructional Program (CIP) code and title		Awards of less than 1 academic year	1- to 4- year awards	Associate degrees	Bachelor's degrees	Master's degrees or post-baccalaureate certificates	Doctoral degrees or post-master's certificates	First professional degrees or certificates
11.0203	Computer programming, vendor/product certification	35	12	49	–	–	–	–
11.0299	Computer programming, other	8	4	21	227	–	–	–
11.03	Data processing	817	685	1,208	217	9	–	–
11.04	Information science/studies	235	240	2,532	6,317	3,017	108	–
11.05	Computer systems analysis	224	304	830	1,570	271	6	–
11.06	Data entry/microcomputer applications	1,696	863	361	–	–	–	–
11.0601	Data entry/microcomputer applications, general	1,417	469	333	–	–	–	–
11.0602	Word processing	129	225	5	–	–	–	–
11.0699	Data entry/microcomputer applications, other	150	169	23	–	–	–	–
11.07	Computer science	47	134	926	10,289	4,512	656	–
11.08	Computer software and media applications	987	972	3,657	1,214	176	7	–
11.0801	Web page, digital/multimedia, and information resources design	715	747	2,555	718	50	1	–
11.0802	Data modeling/warehousing and database administration	59	18	88	77	22	–	–
11.0803	Computer graphics	143	148	557	305	58	6	–
11.0899	Computer software and media applications, other	70	59	457	114	46	–	–
11.09	Computer systems networking and telecommunications	2,205	1,537	7,977	3,497	536	4	–
11.10	Computer/information technology administration and management	1,164	1,263	3,142	1,333	792	5	–
11.1001	System administration/ administrator	245	198	743	73	4	–	–
11.1002	System, networking, and LAN/ WAN management/manager	476	95	861	124	–	–	–
11.1003	Computer and information systems security	122	760	498	715	225	3	–
11.1004	Web/multimedia management and webmaster	97	66	322	69	–	–	–
11.1099	Computer/information technology services administration and management, other	224	144	718	352	563	2	–
11.99	Computer and information sciences and support services, other	1,766	740	2,497	1,181	1,206	195	–
12.	**Personal and culinary services**	**30,003**	**64,630**	**17,253**	**658**	**22**	**–**	**–**
12.03	Funeral service and mortuary science	54	416	1,297	162	–	–	–
12.0301	Funeral service and mortuary science, general	44	375	1,141	162	–	–	–
12.0302	Funeral direction/service	10	36	19	–	–	–	–
12.0303	Mortuary science and embalming/embalmer	–	–	137	–	–	–	–
12.0399	Funeral service and mortuary science, other	–	5	–	–	–	–	–
12.04	Cosmetology and related personal grooming services	24,468	58,496	591	–	–	–	–
12.0401	Cosmetology/cosmetologist, general	6,511	51,440	455	–	–	–	–
12.0402	Barbering/barber	623	3,191	–	–	–	–	–
12.0404	Electrolysis/electrology and electrolysis technician	70	5	–	–	–	–	–
12.0406	Make-up artist/specialist	943	48	–	–	–	–	–

- None reported

Table VI–1. Earned awards and degrees, by field of study, 2005–06 — Continued

2000 Classification of Instructional Program (CIP) code and title		Awards of less than 1 academic year	1- to 4- year awards	Associate degrees	Bachelor's degrees	Master's degrees or post-baccalaureate certificates	Doctoral degrees or post-master's certificates	First professional degrees or certificates
12.0407	Hair styling/stylist and hair design	329	766	–	–	–	–	–
12.0408	Facial treatment specialist/ facialist	609	166	–	–	–	–	–
12.0409	Aesthetician/esthetician and skin care specialist	6,466	962	91	–	–	–	–
12.0410	Nail technician/specialist and manicurist	6,095	486	–	–	–	–	–
12.0411	Permanent cosmetics/makeup and tattooing	164	–	–	–	–	–	–
12.0412	Salon/beauty salon management/manager	24	34	39	–	–	–	–
12.0413	Cosmetology, barber/styling, and nail instructor	623	302	4	–	–	–	–
12.0499	Cosmetology and related personal grooming arts, other	2,011	1,096	2	–	–	–	–
12.05	Culinary arts and related services	4,676	5,661	15,361	496	22	–	–
12.0500	Cooking and related culinary arts, general	601	568	460	–	1	–	–
12.0501	Baking and pastry arts/baker/ pastry chef	883	962	1,127	57	1	–	–
12.0502	Bartending/bartender	391	37	–	–	2	–	–
12.0503	Culinary arts/chef training	1,831	3,220	12,787	322	12	–	–
12.0504	Restaurant, culinary, and catering management/manager	245	155	751	97	–	–	–
12.0505	Food preparation/professional cooking/kitchen assistant	463	186	22	–	–	–	–
12.0506	Meat cutting/meat cutter	43	9	2	–	–	–	–
12.0507	Food service, waiter/waitress, and dining room management/ manager	54	155	20	–	–	–	–
12.0508	Institutional food workers	35	39	73	–	–	–	–
12.0599	Culinary arts and related services, other	130	330	119	20	6	–	–
12.99	Personal and culinary services, other	805	57	4	–	–	–	–
13.	**Education**	**4,222**	**3,132**	**16,295**	**115,104**	**189,560**	**17,249**	**–**
13.01	Education, general	20	131	2,994	2,736	27,523	1,799	–
13.02	Bilingual, multilingual, and multicultural education	–	27	11	164	2,202	37	–
13.0201	Bilingual and multilingual education	–	19	11	163	2,169	25	–
13.0202	Multicultural education	–	8	–	–	18	12	–
13.0203	Indian/Native American education	–	–	–	1	13	–	–
13.0299	Bilingual, multilingual, and multicultural education, other	–	–	–	–	2	–	–
13.03	Curriculum and instruction	–	–	–	1	17,168	1,741	–
13.04	Educational administration and supervision	20	20	213	136	24,954	9,502	–
13.0401	Educational leadership and administration, general	17	–	–	21	18,003	5,670	–
13.0402	Administration of special education	2	–	–	–	43	29	–
13.0403	Adult and continuing education administration	–	–	–	8	216	75	–
13.0404	Educational, instructional, and curriculum supervision	–	–	–	59	1,253	1,034	–
13.0406	Higher education/higher education administration	–	20	–	–	1,078	301	–
13.0407	Community college education	–	–	–	–	51	12	–

- None reported

Table VI–1. Earned awards and degrees, by field of study, 2005–06 — Continued

2000 Classification of Instructional Program (CIP) code and title		Awards of less than 1 academic year	1- to 4- year awards	Associate degrees	Bachelor's degrees	Master's degrees or post-baccalaureate certificates	Doctoral degrees or post-master's certificates	First professional degrees or certificates
13.0408	Elementary and middle school administration/principalship	–	–	–	–	1,635	748	–
13.0409	Secondary school administration/principalship	–	–	–	–	379	98	–
13.0410	Urban education and leadership	–	–	–	46	263	27	–
13.0411	Superintendency and educational system administration.....	–	–	–	–	253	146	–
13.0499	Educational administration and supervision, other.....	1	–	213	2	1,780	1,362	–
13.05	Educational/instructional media design	35	23	122	51	4,292	189	–
13.06	Educational assessment, evaluation, and research	–	–	–	–	164	97	–
13.0601	Educational evaluation and research.....	–	–	–	–	37	45	–
13.0603	Educational statistics and research methods.....	–	–	–	–	36	20	–
13.0604	Educational assessment, testing, and measurement	–	–	–	–	66	27	–
13.0699	Educational assessment, evaluation, and research, other	–	–	–	–	25	5	–
13.07	International and comparative education	–	–	–	–	139	14	–
13.09	Social and philosophical foundations of education.....	–	–	–	2	1,712	153	–
13.10	Special education and teaching .	179	202	552	8,627	17,230	483	–
13.1001	Special education and teaching, general	99	13	181	6,925	13,428	344	–
13.1003	Education/teaching of individuals with hearing impairments, including deafness	–	18	42	161	179	3	–
13.1004	Education/teaching of the gifted and talented	–	–	–	–	273	67	–
13.1005	Education/teaching of individuals with emotional disturbances.....	–	–	–	102	169	14	–
13.1006	Education/teaching of individuals with mental retardation.....	–	–	–	225	151	7	–
13.1007	Education/teaching of individuals with multiple disabilities	–	–	–	83	384	17	–
13.1008	Education/teaching of individuals with orthopedic and other physical health impairments	–	–	3	15	28	–	–
13.1009	Education/teaching of individuals with vision impairments/ blindness	–	–	–	32	76	–	–
13.1011	Education/teaching of individuals with specific learning disabilities	–	–	–	292	993	12	–
13.1012	Education/teaching of individuals with speech or language impairments	–	5	8	307	135	–	–
13.1013	Education/teaching of individuals with autism	4	–	–	–	119	–	–
13.1014	Education/teaching of individuals who are developmentally delayed	–	–	–	–	2	–	–
13.1015	Education/teaching of individuals in early childhood special education programs.....	76	13	31	96	470	7	–

- None reported

Table VI–1. Earned awards and degrees, by field of study, 2005–06 — Continued

2000 Classification of Instructional Program (CIP) code and title		Awards of less than 1 academic year	1- to 4- year awards	Associate degrees	Bachelor's degrees	Master's degrees or post-baccalaureate certificates	Doctoral degrees or post-master's certificates	First professional degrees or certificates
13.1016	Education/teaching of individuals with traumatic brain injuries	–	–	–	–	6	–	–
13.1099	Special education and teaching, other	–	153	287	389	817	12	–
13.11	Student counseling and personnel services	4	14	5	36	13,803	885	–
13.1101	Counselor education/school counseling and guidance services	4	14	–	34	12,821	852	–
13.1102	College student counseling and personnel services	–	–	–	–	714	24	–
13.1199	Student counseling and personnel services, other	–	–	5	2	268	9	–
13.12	Teacher education and professional development, specific levels and methods	1,809	1,305	8,555	68,114	48,201	829	–
13.1201	Adult and continuing education and teaching	6	2	9	49	1,685	157	–
13.1202	Elementary education and teaching	30	66	2,778	47,440	22,384	356	–
13.1203	Junior high/intermediate/middle school education and teaching	–	2	122	2,705	1,846	67	–
13.1205	Secondary education and teaching	–	49	690	5,074	9,169	80	–
13.1206	Teacher education, multiple levels	–	–	559	1,328	5,403	35	–
13.1207	Montessori teacher education	10	9	–	1	199	–	–
13.1209	Kindergarten/preschool education and teaching	18	94	1,188	2,184	526	7	–
13.1210	Early childhood education and teaching	1,336	1,081	3,104	9,029	2,357	48	–
13.1299	Teacher education and professional development, specific levels and methods, other	409	2	105	304	4,632	79	–
13.13	Teacher education and professional development, specific subject areas	287	457	928	32,752	23,681	1,076	–
13.1301	Agricultural teacher education	–	–	26	559	461	40	–
13.1302	Art teacher education	–	–	27	1,682	1,016	44	–
13.1303	Business teacher education	–	–	7	608	355	9	–
13.1304	Driver and safety teacher education	–	–	–	–	17	–	–
13.1305	English/language arts teacher education	3	1	45	3,045	1,415	94	–
13.1306	Foreign language teacher education	–	–	3	161	181	17	–
13.1307	Health teacher education	78	–	61	1,659	668	56	–
13.1308	Family and consumer sciences/ home economics teacher education	–	–	3	376	70	9	–
13.1309	Technology teacher education/ industrial arts teacher education	–	–	27	859	498	24	–
13.1310	Sales and marketing operations/marketing and distribution teacher education	–	–	–	55	91	2	–
13.1311	Mathematics teacher education	–	–	27	2,059	1,636	70	–
13.1312	Music teacher education	–	3	35	3,313	1,059	83	–
13.1314	Physical education teaching and coaching	27	15	399	9,575	2,300	146	–
13.1315	Reading teacher education	–	–	–	156	7,526	168	–

- None reported

Table VI–1. Earned awards and degrees, by field of study, 2005–06 — Continued

2000 Classification of Instructional Program (CIP) code and title		Awards of less than 1 academic year	1- to 4- year awards	Associate degrees	Bachelor's degrees	Master's degrees or post-baccalaureate certificates	Doctoral degrees or post-master's certificates	First professional degrees or certificates
13.1316	Science teacher education/ general science teacher education	–	–	5	833	968	85	–
13.1317	Social science teacher education	–	–	–	685	283	26	–
13.1318	Social studies teacher education	–	–	38	2,326	864	17	–
13.1319	Technical teacher education	118	3	167	242	207	65	–
13.1320	Trade and industrial teacher education	21	23	9	1,351	383	37	–
13.1321	Computer teacher education	–	–	–	94	1,199	6	–
13.1322	Biology teacher education	–	2	–	411	304	14	–
13.1323	Chemistry teacher education	–	–	1	92	69	1	–
13.1324	Drama and dance teacher education	2	1	–	162	55	–	–
13.1325	French language teacher education	–	–	1	72	24	–	–
13.1326	German language teacher education	–	–	–	21	2	–	–
13.1327	Health occupations teacher education	–	–	–	22	39	1	–
13.1328	History teacher education	–	–	23	937	104	–	–
13.1329	Physics teacher education	–	–	–	52	26	–	–
13.1330	Spanish language teacher education	–	1	2	516	116	–	–
13.1331	Speech teacher education	–	–	1	189	7	–	–
13.1332	Geography teacher education	–	–	–	25	5	–	–
13.1333	Latin teacher education	–	–	–	6	8	–	–
13.1334	School librarian/school library media specialist	–	–	–	9	172	2	–
13.1335	Psychology teacher education	–	–	–	21	6	–	–
13.1399	Teacher education and professional development, specific subject areas, other	38	408	21	579	1,547	60	–
13.14	Teaching English or French as a second or foreign language	1,308	207	17	280	2,601	58	–
13.1401	Teaching English as second/ foreign language/ESL language instructor	1,301	207	17	280	2,600	58	–
13.1402	Teaching French as a second or foreign language	–	–	–	–	1	–	–
13.1499	Teaching English or French as a second or foreign language, other	7	–	–	–	–	–	–
13.15	Teaching assistants/aides	231	607	1,123	–	55	1	–
13.1501	Teacher assistant/aide	225	590	1,118	–	–	–	–
13.1502	Adult literacy tutor/instructor	–	17	4	–	55	1	–
13.1599	Teaching assistants/aides, other	6	–	1	–	–	–	–
13.99	Education, other	329	139	1,775	2,205	5,835	385	–
14.	**Engineering**	**114**	**93**	**2,224**	**68,821**	**32,264**	**7,722**	**–**
14.01	Engineering, general	6	16	1,364	2,058	1,625	251	–
14.02	Aerospace, aeronautical, and astronautical engineering	–	–	2	2,803	1,082	228	–
14.03	Agricultural/biological engineering and bioengineering	–	–	2	705	190	74	–
14.04	Architectural engineering	–	–	5	639	111	2	–
14.05	Biomedical/medical engineering	–	–	–	3,035	1,191	509	–
14.06	Ceramic sciences and engineering	–	–	–	61	15	16	–
14.07	Chemical engineering	–	–	6	4,481	1,128	837	–

- None reported

Table VI–1. Earned awards and degrees, by field of study, 2005–06 — Continued

2000 Classification of Instructional Program (CIP) code and title		Awards of less than 1 academic year	1- to 4- year awards	Associate degrees	Bachelor's degrees	Master's degrees or post-baccalaureate certificates	Doctoral degrees or post-master's certificates	First professional degrees or certificates
14.08	Civil engineering	4	–	27	9,334	3,820	789	–
14.0801	Civil engineering, general	–	–	27	9,134	3,518	729	–
14.0802	Geotechnical engineering	4	–	–	–	6	–	–
14.0803	Structural engineering	–	–	–	145	86	25	–
14.0804	Transportation and highway engineering	–	–	–	–	95	3	–
14.0805	Water resources engineering	–	–	–	6	53	25	–
14.0899	Civil engineering, other	–	–	–	49	62	7	–
14.09	Computer engineering, general	27	42	300	5,786	2,370	270	–
14.0901	Computer engineering, general	27	42	279	5,457	1,560	242	–
14.0903	Computer software engineering	–	–	12	160	600	2	–
14.0999	Computer engineering, other	–	–	9	169	210	26	–
14.10	Electrical, electronics, and communications engineering	–	8	235	14,417	8,289	1,930	–
14.11	Engineering mechanics	59	–	4	116	89	43	–
14.12	Engineering physics	–	–	–	355	90	34	–
14.13	Engineering science	–	1	94	296	294	90	–
14.14	Environmental/environmental health engineering	14	–	10	439	616	114	–
14.18	Materials engineering	–	–	2	618	542	409	–
14.19	Mechanical engineering	–	–	64	16,143	4,499	1,124	–
14.20	Metallurgical engineering	–	–	–	132	67	36	–
14.21	Mining and mineral engineering	–	–	–	117	53	13	–
14.22	Naval architecture and marine engineering	–	14	–	319	33	5	–
14.23	Nuclear engineering	–	–	–	369	223	80	–
14.24	Ocean engineering	–	–	–	125	63	9	–
14.25	Petroleum engineering	–	–	1	353	253	45	–
14.27	Systems engineering	2	–	18	656	1,365	95	–
14.28	Textile sciences and engineering	–	–	–	108	47	17	–
14.31	Materials science	–	–	8	218	154	154	–
14.32	Polymer/plastics engineering	–	–	–	49	55	44	–
14.33	Construction engineering	–	–	1	273	12	–	–
14.34	Forest engineering	–	–	–	9	5	1	–
14.35	Industrial engineering	–	1	23	3,193	1,869	241	–
14.36	Manufacturing engineering	–	2	28	289	273	19	–
14.37	Operations research	–	–	–	396	352	60	–
14.38	Surveying engineering	–	–	6	21	4	1	–
14.39	Geological/geophysical engineering	–	–	–	103	28	7	–
14.99	Engineering, other	2	9	24	805	1,457	175	–
15.	**Engineering technologies/ technicians**	**8,752**	**11,627**	**33,290**	**14,583**	**2,745**	**77**	**–**
15.00	Engineering technology, general	460	43	3,173	1,106	149	–	–
15.01	Architectural engineering technologies/technicians	221	82	1,066	528	–	–	–
15.02	Civil engineering technologies/ technicians	69	56	1,089	422	2	–	–
15.03	Electrical engineering technologies/technicians	775	2,207	7,579	2,572	110	–	–
15.0303	Electrical, electronic, and communications engineering technology/technician	500	1,002	6,483	2,158	23	–	–
15.0304	Laser and optical technology/ technician	2	19	99	1	–	–	–
15.0305	Telecommunications technology/technician	140	41	206	104	87	–	–
15.0399	Electrical/electronic engineering technologies/technicians, other	133	1,145	791	309	–	–	–

- None reported

Table VI–1. Earned awards and degrees, by field of study, 2005–06 — Continued

2000 Classification of Instructional Program (CIP) code and title		Awards of less than 1 academic year	1- to 4- year awards	Associate degrees	Bachelor's degrees	Master's degrees or post-baccalaureate certificates	Doctoral degrees or post-master's certificates	First professional degrees or certificates
15.04	Electromechanical instrumentation and maintenance technologies/ technicians	366	985	1,670	132	14	10	–
15.0401	Biomedical technology/ technician	12	25	371	24	14	10	–
15.0403	Electromechanical technology/ electromechanical engineering tech	92	725	498	49	–	–	–
15.0404	Instrumentation technology/ technician	106	169	557	17	–	–	–
15.0405	Robotics technology/technician	12	48	146	26	–	–	–
15.0499	Electromechanical instrumentation/maintenance techs, other	144	18	98	16	–	–	–
15.05	Environmental control technologies/technicians	1,651	2,434	1,820	177	123	–	–
15.0501	Heating, air conditioning, and refrigeration technology/ technician	1,179	2,159	1,002	16	–	–	–
15.0503	Energy management and systems technology/technician	–	4	54	35	25	–	–
15.0505	Solar energy technology/ technician	1	8	27	–	–	–	–
15.0506	Water quality and wastewater treatment management and recycling technology	175	115	207	31	–	–	–
15.0507	Environmental engineering technology/environmental technology	62	31	102	85	58	–	–
15.0508	Hazardous materials management and waste technology/technician	214	30	28	–	2	–	–
15.0599	Environmental control technologies/technicians, other	20	87	400	10	38	–	–
15.06	Industrial production technologies/technicians	391	548	2,560	2,753	349	14	–
15.0607	Plastics engineering technology/technician	24	13	78	75	3	–	–
15.0611	Metallurgical technology/ technician	–	7	70	3	–	–	–
15.0612	Industrial technology/technician	166	71	901	1,772	279	14	–
15.0613	Manufacturing technology/ technician	127	148	406	537	42	–	–
15.0699	Industrial production technologies/technicians, other	74	309	1,105	366	25	–	–
15.07	Quality control and safety technologies/technicians	226	196	426	497	177	–	–
15.0701	Occupational safety and health technology/technician	95	61	228	420	83	–	–
15.0702	Quality control technology/ technician	124	43	175	14	86	–	–
15.0703	Industrial safety technology/ technician	6	7	7	41	3	–	–
15.0704	Hazardous materials information systems technology/technician	–	–	2	–	–	–	–
15.0799	Quality control and safety technologies/technicians, other	1	85	14	22	5	–	–
15.08	Mechanical engineering related technologies/technicians	328	539	2,671	1,807	–	–	–
15.0801	Aeronautical/aerospace engineering technology/ technician	–	98	334	112	–	–	–

- None reported

Table VI–1. Earned awards and degrees, by field of study, 2005–06 — Continued

2000 Classification of Instructional Program (CIP) code and title		Awards of less than 1 academic year	1- to 4- year awards	Associate degrees	Bachelor's degrees	Master's degrees or post-baccalaureate certificates	Doctoral degrees or post-master's certificates	First professional degrees or certificates
15.0803	Automotive engineering technology/technician	165	231	826	316	–	–	–
15.0805	Mechanical engineering/ mechanical technology/ technician	149	117	1,052	1,069	–	–	–
15.0899	Mechanical engineering related technologies/technicians, other	14	93	459	310	–	–	–
15.09	Mining and petroleum technologies/technicians	111	5	44	14	3	–	–
15.0901	Mining technology/technician	98	5	6	2	–	–	–
15.0903	Petroleum technology/ technician	13	–	29	9	–	–	–
15.0999	Mining and petroleum technologies/technicians, other	–	–	9	3	3	–	–
15.10	Construction engineering technologies	145	103	917	1,569	93	–	–
15.11	Engineering related technologies	139	169	322	196	8	3	–
15.1102	Surveying technology/ surveying	132	112	280	196	8	3	–
15.1103	Hydraulics and fluid power technology/technician	7	32	24	–	–	–	–
15.1199	Engineering-related technologies, other	–	25	18	–	–	–	–
15.12	Computer engineering technologies/technicians	1,202	1,436	2,755	1,229	3	–	–
15.1201	Computer engineering technology/technician	350	140	780	938	3	–	–
15.1202	Computer technology/computer systems technology	805	1,032	1,833	211	–	–	–
15.1203	Computer hardware technology/technician	28	251	56	–	–	–	–
15.1204	Computer software technology/ technician	6	13	54	80	–	–	–
15.1299	Computer engineering technologies/technicians, other	13	–	32	–	–	–	–
15.13	Drafting/design engineering technologies/technicians	2,612	2,767	6,550	229	32	–	–
15.1301	Drafting and design technology/ technician, general	1,590	1,519	3,618	25	–	–	–
15.1302	CAD/CADD drafting and/or design technology/technician	449	432	645	57	8	–	–
15.1303	Architectural drafting and architectural CAD/CADD	204	491	1,265	–	–	–	–
15.1304	Civil drafting and civil engineering CAD/CADD	15	28	59	–	–	–	–
15.1305	Electrical/electronics drafting and electrical/electronics CAD/ CADD	46	9	47	–	–	–	–
15.1306	Mechanical drafting and mechanical drafting CAD/ CADD	284	181	794	139	–	–	–
15.1399	Drafting/design engineering technologies/technicians, other	24	107	122	8	24	–	–
15.14	Nuclear engineering technologies/technicians	–	7	20	–	–	–	–
15.15	Engineering related fields	2	–	49	458	1,531	50	–
15.99	Engineering technologies/ technicians, other	54	50	579	894	151	–	–
16.	**Foreign languages, literatures, and linguistics**	**835**	**455**	**1,163**	**26,546**	**3,625**	**1,230**	–

- None reported

Table VI–1. Earned awards and degrees, by field of study, 2005–06 — Continued

2000 Classification of Instructional Program (CIP) code and title		Awards of less than 1 academic year	1- to 4- year awards	Associate degrees	Bachelor's degrees	Master's degrees or post-baccalaureate certificates	Doctoral degrees or post-master's certificates	First professional degrees or certificates
16.01	Linguistics, comparative, and related language studies and services	131	11	181	4,072	1,225	427	–
16.0101	Foreign languages and literatures, general	19	4	156	1,741	252	35	–
16.0102	Linguistics	17	–	1	1,328	611	217	–
16.0103	Language interpretation and translation	84	7	24	60	133	–	–
16.0104	Comparative literature	11	–	–	887	202	166	–
16.0199	Linguistic/comparative/related language studies and services, other	–	–	–	56	27	9	–
16.02	African languages, literatures, and linguistics	–	–	–	2	5	–	–
16.03	East Asian languages, literatures, and linguistics	78	–	20	1,201	144	78	–
16.0300	East Asian languages, literatures, and linguistics, general	–	–	–	134	67	34	–
16.0301	Chinese language and literature	30	–	4	330	20	10	–
16.0302	Japanese language and literature	48	–	16	593	29	10	–
16.0303	Korean language and literature	–	–	–	19	4	3	–
16.0399	East Asian languages, literatures, and linguistics, other	–	–	–	125	24	21	–
16.04	Slavic, Baltic and Albanian languages, literatures, and linguistics	3	–	2	527	77	42	–
16.0400	Slavic languages, literatures, and linguistics, general	–	–	–	78	46	33	–
16.0402	Russian language and literature	3	–	2	435	28	8	–
16.0406	Czech language and literature	–	–	–	4	–	–	–
16.0407	Polish language and literature	–	–	–	6	–	–	–
16.0499	Slavic/Baltic/Albanian languages, literatures, and linguistics, other	–	–	–	4	3	1	–
16.05	Germanic languages, literatures, and linguistics	26	–	10	1,783	214	81	–
16.0500	Germanic languages, literatures, and linguistics, general	–	–	–	164	39	28	–
16.0501	German language and literature	26	–	10	1,587	173	49	–
16.0502	Scandinavian languages, literatures, and linguistics	–	–	–	18	2	4	–
16.0503	Danish language and literature	–	–	–	1	–	–	–
16.0505	Norwegian language and literature	–	–	–	7	–	–	–
16.0506	Swedish language and literature	–	–	–	5	–	–	–
16.0599	Germanic languages, literatures, and linguistics, other	–	–	–	1	–	–	–
16.06	Modern Greek language and literature	–	–	–	5	–	–	–
16.07	South Asian languages, literatures, and linguistics	–	–	–	10	4	4	–
16.0700	South Asian languages, literatures, and linguistics	–	–	–	5	4	3	–

- None reported

Table VI–1. Earned awards and degrees, by field of study, 2005–06 — Continued

2000 Classification of Instructional Program (CIP) code and title		Awards of less than 1 academic year	1- to 4- year awards	Associate degrees	Bachelor's degrees	Master's degrees or post-baccalaureate certificates	Doctoral degrees or post-master's certificates	First professional degrees or certificates
16.0702	Sanskrit/classical Indian languages, literatures, and linguistics	–	–	–	5	–	1	–
16.08	Iranian/Persian languages, literatures, and linguistics	–	–	–	–	1	–	–
16.09	Romance languages, literatures, and linguistics	364	11	250	16,781	1,616	434	–
16.0900	Romance languages, literatures, and linguistics, general	–	–	–	143	55	28	–
16.0901	French language and literature	35	1	26	3,540	397	107	–
16.0902	Italian language and literature	12	–	3	484	94	28	–
16.0904	Portuguese language and literature	1	–	–	46	10	3	–
16.0905	Spanish language and literature	316	10	219	12,343	998	213	–
16.0906	Romanian language and literature	–	–	–	2	–	–	–
16.0999	Romance languages, literatures, and linguistics, other	–	–	–	223	62	55	–
16.1001	American Indian/Native American languages, literatures, and linguistics	–	–	2	–	–	–	–
16.11	Middle/Near Eastern and Semitic languages, literatures, and linguistics	6	–	2	211	112	44	–
16.1100	Middle/Near Eastern and Semitic languages, literatures, and linguistics, general	–	–	–	5	2	9	–
16.1101	Arabic language and literature	6	–	2	35	4	2	–
16.1102	Hebrew language and literature	–	–	–	55	12	6	–
16.1103	Ancient Near Eastern/Biblical languages, literature, and linguistics	–	–	–	37	23	1	–
16.1199	Middle/Near Eastern/Semitic languages, literature, and linguistics, other	–	–	–	79	71	26	–
16.12	Classics and classical languages, literatures, and linguistics	16	–	–	1,524	187	95	–
16.1200	Classics and classical languages, literatures, and linguistics, general	1	–	–	1,314	165	91	–
16.1202	Ancient/classical Greek language and literature	–	–	–	48	1	–	–
16.1203	Latin language and literature	15	–	–	140	20	–	–
16.1299	Classics/classical languages, literature, and linguistics, other	–	–	–	22	1	4	–
16.13	Celtic languages, literatures, and linguistics	–	–	–	3	2	3	–
16.16	American sign language (ASL)	210	433	694	251	18	–	–
16.1601	American sign language (ASL)	54	91	72	59	–	–	–
16.1602	Linguistics of ASL and other sign languages	–	–	–	1	–	–	–
16.1603	Sign language interpretation and translation	143	342	620	191	8	–	–
16.1699	American sign language, other	13	–	2	–	10	–	–
16.99	Foreign languages, literatures, and linguistics, other	1	–	4	176	20	22	–
19.	**Family and consumer sciences/ human sciences**	**13,128**	**5,023**	**9,514**	**21,099**	**2,030**	**348**	**–**
19.00	Work and family studies	311	–	–	62	24	–	–

- None reported

Table VI–1. Earned awards and degrees, by field of study, 2005–06 — Continued

2000 Classification of Instructional Program (CIP) code and title		Awards of less than 1 academic year	1- to 4- year awards	Associate degrees	Bachelor's degrees	Master's degrees or post-baccalaureate certificates	Doctoral degrees or post-master's certificates	First professional degrees or certificates
19.01	Family and consumer sciences/ human sciences, general	–	1	154	4,542	451	66	–
19.02	Family and consumer sciences/ human sciences business services	–	4	–	373	11	2	–
19.0201	Business family and consumer sciences/human sciences	–	–	–	203	5	2	–
19.0202	Family and consumer sciences/human sciences communication	–	–	–	56	3	–	–
19.0203	Consumer merchandising/ retailing management	–	4	–	114	3	–	–
19.04	Family and consumer economics and related studies	–	–	–	1,343	67	10	–
19.0401	Family resource management studies, general	–	–	–	532	50	5	–
19.0402	Consumer economics	–	–	–	489	12	–	–
19.0403	Consumer services and advocacy	–	–	–	7	–	–	–
19.0499	Family and consumer economics and related services, other	–	–	–	315	5	5	–
19.05	Foods, nutrition, and related services	1,454	217	285	2,673	497	49	–
19.0501	Foods, nutrition, and wellness studies, general	17	97	25	1,704	327	28	–
19.0504	Human nutrition	4	1	5	235	128	21	–
19.0505	Food service systems administration/management	1,433	108	194	676	21	–	–
19.0599	Foods, nutrition, and related services, other	–	11	61	58	21	–	–
19.06	Housing and human environments	1,008	264	89	426	25	5	–
19.0601	Housing and human environments, general	–	27	–	377	22	5	–
19.0604	Facilities planning and management	–	–	11	20	3	–	–
19.0605	Home furnishings and equipment installers	55	24	53	–	–	–	–
19.0699	Housing and human environments, other	953	213	25	29	–	–	–
19.07	Human development, family studies, and related services	10,160	4,280	8,589	9,119	857	198	–
19.0701	Human development and family studies, general	170	14	123	6,152	524	111	–
19.0702	Adult development and aging	66	44	56	33	60	4	–
19.0704	Family systems	13	1	8	474	35	10	–
19.0706	Child development	5,538	1,612	3,130	1,382	124	58	–
19.0707	Family and community services	4	6	148	697	55	3	–
19.0708	Child care and support services management	1,118	662	2,866	171	36	–	–
19.0709	Child care provider/assistant	3,158	1,652	2,163	6	–	–	–
19.0799	Human development, family studies, and related services, other	93	289	95	204	23	12	–
19.09	Apparel and textiles	186	238	394	2,523	74	11	–
19.0901	Apparel and textiles, general	18	13	70	2,251	61	10	–
19.0902	Apparel and textile manufacture	34	124	33	23	–	–	–
19.0904	Textile science	–	–	–	–	–	1	–
19.0905	Apparel and textile marketing management	68	53	102	249	13	–	–
19.0906	Fashion and fabric consultant	7	4	32	–	–	–	–
19.0999	Apparel and textiles, other	59	44	157	–	–	–	–

- None reported

Table VI–1. Earned awards and degrees, by field of study, 2005–06 — Continued

2000 Classification of Instructional Program (CIP) code and title		Awards of less than 1 academic year	1- to 4- year awards	Associate degrees	Bachelor's degrees	Master's degrees or post-baccalaureate certificates	Doctoral degrees or post-master's certificates	First professional degrees or certificates
19.99	Family and consumer sciences/ human sciences, other	9	19	3	38	24	7	–
22.	**Legal professions and studies**	**2,425**	**3,755**	**10,611**	**3,600**	**4,985**	**158**	**44,335**
22.00	Legal studies, general	1	25	191	1,680	69	–	–
22.0000	Legal studies, general	1	9	51	1,349	69	–	–
22.0001	Pre-law studies	–	16	140	331	–	–	–
22.01	Law (LLB, JD)	–	–	–	–	–	–	44,147
22.02	Legal research and advanced professional studies (Post-LLB/ JD)	2	5	1	68	3,384	141	188
22.0201	Advanced legal research/ studies, general (LLM, MCL, MLI, MSL, JSD/SJD)	–	–	–	–	532	94	159
22.0202	Programs for foreign lawyers (LLM, MCL)	–	–	–	–	592	–	2
22.0203	American/US law/legal studies/ jurisprudence (LLM, MCJ, JSD/SJD)	–	–	1	55	169	9	8
22.0205	Banking, corporate, finance, and securities law (LLM, JSD/ SJD)	1	–	–	–	94	–	–
22.0206	Comparative law (LLM, MCL, JSD/SJD)	–	–	–	–	145	2	–
22.0207	Energy, environment, and natural resources law (LLM, MS, JSD/SJD)	–	4	–	–	13	10	9
22.0208	Health law (LLM, MJ, JSD/SJD)	1	–	–	–	75	1	–
22.0209	International law and legal studies (LLM, JSD/SJD)	–	–	–	–	225	1	–
22.0210	International business, trade, and tax law (LLM, JSD/SJD)	–	–	–	–	84	–	10
22.0211	Tax law/taxation (LLM, JSD/ SJD)	–	–	–	–	440	1	–
22.0299	Legal research and advanced professional studies, other	–	1	–	13	1,015	23	–
22.03	Legal support services	2,333	3,703	10,350	1,361	501	–	–
22.0301	Legal administrative assistant/ secretary	479	698	788	11	–	–	–
22.0302	Legal assistant/paralegal	1,807	2,713	9,318	1,334	493	–	–
22.0303	Court reporting/court reporter	46	286	242	16	–	–	–
22.0399	Legal support services, other	1	6	2	–	8	–	–
22.99	Legal professions and studies, other	89	22	69	491	1,031	17	–
23.	**English language and literature/ letters**	**1,111**	**280**	**1,105**	**58,736**	**8,933**	**1,354**	**–**
23.01	English language and literature, general	554	237	553	44,781	5,443	1,095	–
23.04	English composition	–	–	17	585	97	11	–
23.05	Creative writing	30	17	15	2,243	2,245	16	–
23.07	American literature (United States and Canadian)	–	–	–	116	10	4	–
23.08	English literature	–	–	12	992	106	63	–
23.10	Speech and rhetorical studies	333	–	280	8,361	516	110	–
23.11	Technical and business writing	42	7	33	473	298	3	–
23.99	English language and literature/ letters, other	152	19	195	1,185	218	52	–
24.	**Liberal arts and sciences, general studies, and humanities**	**390**	**3,493**	**245,101**	**45,869**	**3,920**	**88**	**–**

- None reported

Table VI–1. Earned awards and degrees, by field of study, 2005–06 — Continued

2000 Classification of Instructional Program (CIP) code and title		Awards of less than 1 academic year	1- to 4- year awards	Associate degrees	Bachelor's degrees	Master's degrees or post-baccalaureate certificates	Doctoral degrees or post-master's certificates	First professional degrees or certificates
24.01	Liberal arts and sciences, general studies, and humanities	390	3,493	245,101	45,869	3,920	88	–
24.0101	Liberal arts and sciences/liberal studies	353	2,635	186,620	28,642	2,626	8	–
24.0102	General studies	32	761	37,425	11,194	125	1	–
24.0103	Humanities/humanistic studies.	–	7	6,096	3,251	721	61	–
24.0199	Liberal arts and sciences, general studies and humanities, other	5	90	14,960	2,782	448	18	–
25.	**Library science**	**179**	**89**	**136**	**80**	**6,572**	**99**	**–**
25.01	Library science/librarianship	15	5	11	80	6,398	94	–
25.03	Library assistant	162	84	125	–	–	–	–
25.99	Library science, other	2	–	–	–	174	5	–
26.	**Biological and biomedical sciences**	**104**	**34**	**1,862**	**72,196**	**9,095**	**6,104**	**–**
26.01	Biology, general	40	1	1,605	52,041	3,094	1,027	–
26.0101	Biology/biological sciences, general	40	1	1,605	50,672	2,776	826	–
26.0102	Biomedical sciences, general	–	–	–	1,369	318	201	–
26.02	Biochemistry, biophysics and molecular biology	–	10	1	6,371	621	1,068	–
26.0202	Biochemistry	–	–	–	4,861	274	537	–
26.0203	Biophysics	–	–	1	51	57	106	–
26.0204	Molecular biology	–	–	–	644	122	223	–
26.0205	Molecular biochemistry	–	–	–	260	31	53	–
26.0206	Molecular biophysics	–	–	–	–	2	15	–
26.0207	Structural biology	–	–	–	–	5	5	–
26.0209	Radiation biology/radiobiology	–	10	–	1	21	8	–
26.0210	Biochemistry/biophysics and molecular biology	–	–	–	492	105	114	–
26.0299	Biochemistry, biophysics and molecular biology, other	–	–	–	62	4	7	–
26.03	Botany/plant biology	–	–	1	253	196	236	–
26.0301	Botany/plant biology	–	–	1	227	117	135	–
26.0305	Plant pathology/phytopathology	–	–	–	13	61	69	–
26.0307	Plant physiology	–	–	–	–	1	16	–
26.0308	Plant molecular biology	–	–	–	–	2	5	–
26.0399	Botany/plant biology, other	–	–	–	13	15	11	–
26.04	Cell/cellular biology and anatomical sciences	–	–	–	2,581	330	713	–
26.0401	Cell/cellular biology and histology	–	–	–	468	31	155	–
26.0403	Anatomy	–	–	–	201	81	67	–
26.0404	Developmental biology and embryology	–	–	–	–	23	21	–
26.0405	Neuroanatomy	–	–	–	–	4	9	–
26.0406	Cell/cellular and molecular biology	–	–	–	1,610	101	337	–
26.0407	Cell biology and anatomy	–	–	–	2	10	23	–
26.0499	Cell/cellular biology and anatomical sciences, other	–	–	–	300	80	101	–
26.05	Microbiological sciences and immunology	6	–	1	2,461	380	637	–
26.0502	Microbiology, general	6	–	1	1,559	199	177	–
26.0503	Medical microbiology and bacteriology	–	–	–	757	93	197	–
26.0504	Virology	–	–	–	–	3	14	–
26.0505	Parasitology	–	–	–	–	1	–	–

- None reported

Table VI–1. Earned awards and degrees, by field of study, 2005–06 — Continued

2000 Classification of Instructional Program (CIP) code and title		Awards of less than 1 academic year	1- to 4- year awards	Associate degrees	Bachelor's degrees	Master's degrees or post-baccalaureate certificates	Doctoral degrees or post-master's certificates	First professional degrees or certificates
26.0507	Immunology	–	–	–	–	26	144	–
26.0599	Microbiological sciences and immunology, other	–	–	–	145	58	105	–
26.07	Zoology/animal biology	–	–	5	2,222	387	254	–
26.0701	Zoology/animal biology	–	–	–	1,803	137	93	–
26.0702	Entomology	–	–	–	91	158	104	–
26.0707	Animal physiology	–	–	–	177	71	54	–
26.0708	Animal behavior and ethology	–	–	–	18	3	3	–
26.0709	Wildlife biology	–	–	5	133	14	–	–
26.0799	Zoology/animal biology, other	–	–	–	–	4	–	–
26.08	Genetics	–	–	–	406	181	297	–
26.0801	Genetics, general	–	–	–	254	49	128	–
26.0802	Molecular genetics	–	–	–	92	25	57	–
26.0804	Animal genetics	–	–	–	60	21	46	–
26.0805	Plant genetics	–	–	–	–	5	12	–
26.0806	Human/medical genetics	–	–	–	–	77	49	–
26.0899	Genetics, other	–	–	–	–	4	5	–
26.09	Physiology, pathology, and related sciences	16	–	54	1,438	598	505	–
26.0901	Physiology, general	14	–	15	704	381	142	–
26.0902	Molecular physiology	–	–	–	–	7	19	–
26.0903	Cell physiology	–	–	–	–	4	12	–
26.0904	Endocrinology	–	–	–	–	2	2	–
26.0905	Reproductive biology	–	–	–	–	4	2	–
26.0906	Neurobiology and neurophysiology	2	–	–	282	15	92	–
26.0907	Cardiovascular science	–	–	–	–	6	5	–
26.0908	Exercise physiology	–	–	13	344	45	3	–
26.0909	Vision science/physiological optics	–	–	–	57	10	9	–
26.0910	Pathology/experimental pathology	–	–	–	15	106	159	–
26.0911	Oncology and cancer biology	–	–	–	–	10	51	–
26.0999	Physiology, pathology, and related sciences, other	–	–	26	36	8	9	–
26.10	Pharmacology and toxicology	–	–	2	179	210	423	–
26.1001	Pharmacology	–	–	–	49	118	247	–
26.1002	Molecular pharmacology	–	–	–	36	4	31	–
26.1003	Neuropharmacology	–	–	–	–	6	–	–
26.1004	Toxicology	–	–	2	40	47	84	–
26.1005	Molecular toxicology	–	–	–	–	–	5	–
26.1006	Environmental toxicology	–	–	–	19	8	22	–
26.1007	Pharmacology and toxicology	–	–	–	35	27	34	–
26.11	Biomathematics and bioinformatics	–	–	–	132	525	142	–
26.1101	Biometry/biometrics	–	–	–	19	11	15	–
26.1102	Biostatistics	–	–	–	14	286	90	–
26.1103	Bioinformatics	–	–	–	97	223	36	–
26.1199	Biomathematics and bioinformatics, other	–	–	–	2	5	1	–
26.12	Biotechnology	6	18	79	436	502	8	–
26.13	Ecology, evolution, systematics and population biology	3	1	23	2,176	1,061	475	–
26.1301	Ecology	–	1	1	568	206	156	–
26.1302	Marine biology and biological oceanography	3	–	19	822	183	47	–
26.1303	Evolutionary biology	–	–	–	4	14	25	–
26.1304	Aquatic biology/limnology	–	–	–	65	3	–	–
26.1305	Environmental biology	–	–	3	238	37	2	–

- None reported

Table VI–1. Earned awards and degrees, by field of study, 2005–06 — Continued

2000 Classification of Instructional Program (CIP) code and title		Awards of less than 1 academic year	1- to 4- year awards	Associate degrees	Bachelor's degrees	Master's degrees or post-baccalaureate certificates	Doctoral degrees or post-master's certificates	First professional degrees or certificates
26.1306	Population biology	–	–	–	–	3	7	–
26.1307	Conservation biology	–	–	–	163	36	4	–
26.1309	Epidemiology	–	–	–	–	535	186	–
26.1399	Ecology, evolution, systematics and population biology, other	–	–	–	316	44	48	–
26.99	Biological and biomedical sciences, other	33	4	91	1,500	1,010	319	–
27.	**Mathematics and statistics**	**60**	**12**	**753**	**16,797**	**4,835**	**1,390**	**–**
27.01	Mathematics	47	11	750	14,812	2,736	887	–
27.0101	Mathematics, general	47	11	750	14,619	2,735	883	–
27.0199	Mathematics, other	–	–	–	193	1	4	–
27.03	Applied mathematics	–	1	–	1,273	629	214	–
27.0301	Applied mathematics	–	1	–	1,058	532	196	–
27.0303	Computational mathematics	–	–	–	77	27	10	–
27.0399	Applied mathematics, other	–	–	–	138	70	8	–
27.05	Statistics	12	–	–	606	1,351	283	–
27.0501	Statistics, general	12	–	–	594	1,334	277	–
27.0502	Mathematical statistics and probability	–	–	–	6	6	4	–
27.0599	Statistics, other	–	–	–	6	11	2	–
27.99	Mathematics and statistics, other	1	–	3	106	119	6	–
29.	**Military technologies**	**62**	**–**	**1,758**	**33**	**328**	**2**	**–**
29.01	Military technologies	62	–	1,758	33	328	2	–
30.	**Multi/interdisciplinary studies**	**482**	**525**	**14,516**	**33,658**	**5,011**	**1,236**	**–**
30.01	Biological and physical sciences	1	–	8,432	1,733	265	32	–
30.05	Peace studies and conflict resolution	6	38	–	261	402	14	–
30.06	Systems science and theory	–	–	–	103	237	13	–
30.08	Mathematics and computer science	–	–	–	214	33	15	–
30.10	Biopsychology	–	–	–	85	1	9	–
30.11	Gerontology	63	50	29	205	367	22	–
30.12	Historic preservation and conservation	12	–	1	122	181	4	–
30.1201	Historic preservation and conservation	12	–	1	122	175	4	–
30.1202	Cultural resource management and policy analysis	–	–	–	–	6	–	–
30.13	Medieval and renaissance studies	9	–	–	56	24	11	–
30.14	Museology/museum studies	–	–	–	23	311	4	–
30.15	Science, technology, and society	18	–	3	370	93	12	–
30.16	Accounting and computer science	56	34	14	13	–	–	–
30.17	Behavioral sciences	2	–	33	1,090	164	21	–
30.18	Natural sciences	–	–	102	729	95	–	–
30.19	Nutrition sciences	1	–	2	656	410	116	–
30.20	International/global studies	3	11	20	2,555	184	3	–
30.21	Holocaust and related studies	–	–	–	–	8	–	–
30.22	Classical and ancient studies	–	–	–	247	11	12	–
30.2201	Ancient studies/civilization	–	–	–	120	4	6	–
30.2202	Classical/ancient Mediterranean/Near Eastern studies and archaeology	–	–	–	127	7	6	–
30.23	Intercultural/multicultural and diversity studies	–	–	–	190	88	–	–
30.24	Neuroscience	–	–	–	1,518	101	394	–

- None reported

Table VI–1. Earned awards and degrees, by field of study, 2005–06 — Continued

2000 Classification of Instructional Program (CIP) code and title		Awards of less than 1 academic year	1- to 4- year awards	Associate degrees	Bachelor's degrees	Master's degrees or post-baccalaureate certificates	Doctoral degrees or post-master's certificates	First professional degrees or certificates
30.25	Cognitive science	–	–	–	391	7	28	–
30.99	Multi/interdisciplinary studies, other	311	392	5,880	23,097	2,029	526	–
31.	**Parks, recreation, leisure, and fitness studies**	**327**	**271**	**1,384**	**25,999**	**4,024**	**201**	**–**
31.01	Parks, recreation, and leisure studies	63	5	90	2,613	264	13	–
31.03	Parks, recreation, and leisure facilities management	14	41	171	2,928	285	17	–
31.05	Health and physical education/fitness	249	207	798	20,299	3,461	167	–
31.0501	Health and physical education, general	68	41	340	8,611	1,131	26	–
31.0504	Sport and fitness administration/management	107	16	262	4,041	1,242	13	–
31.0505	Kinesiology and exercise science	23	35	100	6,781	976	118	–
31.0599	Health and physical education/fitness, other	51	115	96	866	112	10	–
31.99	Parks, recreation, leisure, and fitness studies, other	1	18	325	159	14	4	–
38.	**Philosophy and religious studies**	**10**	**71**	**390**	**14,724**	**1,827**	**655**	**–**
38.01	Philosophy	1	–	61	8,555	782	396	–
38.0101	Philosophy	1	–	61	8,382	772	393	–
38.0102	Logic	–	–	–	1	2	3	–
38.0103	Ethics	–	–	–	44	8	–	–
38.0199	Philosophy, other	–	–	–	128	–	–	–
38.02	Religion/religious studies	9	71	329	5,634	816	230	–
38.0201	Religion/religious studies	–	63	51	4,978	571	209	–
38.0202	Buddhist studies	–	–	–	1	6	–	–
38.0203	Christian studies	7	8	29	286	76	8	–
38.0205	Islamic studies	–	–	–	2	2	3	–
38.0206	Jewish/Judaic studies	2	–	249	313	123	9	–
38.0299	Religion/religious studies, other	–	–	–	54	38	1	–
38.99	Philosophy and religious studies, other	–	–	–	535	229	29	–
39.	**Theology and religious vocations**	**211**	**1,110**	**664**	**10,132**	**7,058**	**2,275**	**6,434**
39.02	Bible/biblical studies	36	737	416	3,329	556	52	–
39.03	Missions/missionary studies and missiology	–	1	7	455	359	86	–
39.04	Religious education	–	29	53	1,163	672	238	–
39.05	Religious/sacred music	5	15	9	207	104	13	–
39.06	Theological and ministerial studies	129	217	127	3,104	3,989	1,507	6,423
39.0601	Theology/theological studies	18	47	66	1,546	2,986	1,170	–
39.0602	Divinity/ministry (BD, MDiv)	–	–	–	–	–	–	6,230
39.0604	Pre-theology/pre-ministerial studies	–	18	15	234	30	–	–
39.0605	Rabbinical studies (MHL/Rav)	–	–	–	–	–	–	188
39.0606	Talmudic studies	–	12	–	867	357	26	–
39.0699	Theological and ministerial studies, other	111	140	46	457	616	311	5
39.07	Pastoral counseling and specialized ministries	10	68	16	1,311	957	196	11
39.0701	Pastoral studies/counseling	10	67	15	561	818	187	11
39.0702	Youth ministry	–	–	1	572	33	–	–

- None reported

Table VI–1. Earned awards and degrees, by field of study, 2005–06 — Continued

2000 Classification of Instructional Program (CIP) code and title		Awards of less than 1 academic year	1- to 4- year awards	Associate degrees	Bachelor's degrees	Master's degrees or post-baccalaureate certificates	Doctoral degrees or post-master's certificates	First professional degrees or certificates
39.0799	Pastoral counseling and specialized ministries, other	–	1	–	178	106	9	–
39.99	Theology and religious vocations, other	31	43	36	563	421	183	–
40.	**Physical sciences**	**370**	**13**	**1,887**	**21,694**	**6,045**	**4,668**	**–**
40.01	Physical sciences	–	–	1,078	305	37	6	–
40.02	Astronomy and astrophysics	–	–	4	401	146	120	–
40.0201	Astronomy	–	–	4	216	94	80	–
40.0202	Astrophysics	–	–	–	136	35	25	–
40.0203	Planetary astronomy and science	–	–	–	2	7	6	–
40.0299	Astronomy and astrophysics, other	–	–	–	47	10	9	–
40.04	Atmospheric sciences and meteorology	–	1	154	670	239	102	–
40.0401	Atmospheric sciences and meteorology, general	–	1	147	489	198	90	–
40.0403	Atmospheric physics and dynamics	–	–	–	9	–	–	–
40.0404	Meteorology	–		7	157	41	12	–
40.0499	Atmospheric sciences and meteorology, other	–	–	–	15	–	–	–
40.05	Chemistry	156	8	300	11,481	2,074	2,475	–
40.0501	Chemistry, general	156	8	300	11,002	2,013	2,342	–
40.0502	Analytical chemistry	–	–	–	15	12	16	–
40.0503	Inorganic chemistry	–	–	–	–	4	2	–
40.0504	Organic chemistry	–	–	–	2	2	7	–
40.0506	Physical and theoretical chemistry	–	–	–	1	–	11	–
40.0507	Polymer chemistry	–	–	–	1	18	55	–
40.0508	Chemical physics	–	–	–	7	1	8	–
40.0599	Chemistry, other	–	–	–	453	24	34	–
40.06	Geological and earth sciences/ geosciences	211	–	61	3,470	1,510	529	–
40.0601	Geology/earth science, general	–	–	37	2,949	1,143	343	–
40.0602	Geochemistry	–	–	–	7	12	5	–
40.0603	Geophysics and seismology	–	–	–	66	79	50	–
40.0604	Paleontology	–	–	–	2	1	–	–
40.0605	Hydrology and water resources science	–	–	4	37	20	5	–
40.0607	Oceanography, chemical and physical	208	–	20	109	138	75	–
40.0699	Geological and earth sciences/ geosciences, other	3	–	–	300	117	51	–
40.08	Physics, general	2	4	143	5,060	1,894	1,411	–
40.0801	Physics, general	–	4	138	4,813	1,625	1,256	–
40.0802	Atomic/molecular physics	–	–	–	20	19	8	–
40.0806	Nuclear physics	–	–	–	–	3	12	–
40.0807	Optics/optical sciences	2	–	5	46	90	35	–
40.0809	Acoustics	–	–	–	17	24	8	–
40.0810	Theoretical and mathematical physics	–	–	–	13	–	–	–
40.0899	Physics, other	–	–	–	151	133	92	–
40.99	Physical sciences, other	1	–	147	307	145	25	–
41.	**Science technologies/ technicians**	**286**	**297**	**1,252**	**278**	**22**	**2**	**–**
41.01	Biology technician/biotechnology laboratory technician	191	73	270	37	–	2	–

- None reported

Table VI–1. Earned awards and degrees, by field of study, 2005–06 — Continued

2000 Classification of Instructional Program (CIP) code and title		Awards of less than 1 academic year	1- to 4- year awards	Associate degrees	Bachelor's degrees	Master's degrees or post-baccalaureate certificates	Doctoral degrees or post-master's certificates	First professional degrees or certificates
41.02	Nuclear and industrial radiologic technologies/technicians..........	1	32	38	31	5	–	–
41.0204	Industrial radiologic technology/ technician................................	–	32	25	–	–	–	–
41.0205	Nuclear/nuclear power technology/technician	1	–	10	31	5	–	–
41.0299	Nuclear and industrial radiologic technologies/ technicians, other....................	–	–	3	–	–	–	–
41.03	Physical science technologies/ technicians..............................	87	115	536	18	–	–	–
41.0301	Chemical technology/technician	87	115	536	13	–	–	–
41.0399	Physical science technologies/ technicians, other....................	–	–	–	5	–	–	–
41.99	Science technologies/ technicians, other....................	7	77	408	192	17	–	–
42.	**Psychology ....**	**90**	**31**	**1,953**	**93,830**	**20,444**	**6,140**	**–**
42.01	Psychology, general	33	20	1,800	88,473	5,209	1,601	–
42.02	Clinical psychology.....................	–	–	–	138	2,268	2,132	–
42.03	Cognitive psychology and psycholinguistics	–	–	–	58	25	7	–
42.04	Community psychology	–	–	24	237	302	4	–
42.05	Comparative psychology...........	–	–	–	–	4	–	–
42.06	Counseling psychology	6	3	1	432	7,317	367	–
42.07	Developmental and child psychology..............................	2	–	–	592	72	65	–
42.08	Experimental psychology	–	–	–	308	54	64	–
42.09	Industrial and organizational psychology..............................	4	1	–	313	768	142	–
42.10	Personality psychology	–	–	–	41	–	–	–
42.11	Physiological psychology/ psychobiology	–	–	–	458	4	23	–
42.16	Social psychology	–	4	3	1,165	52	24	–
42.17	School psychology	–	–	–	6	1,530	913	–
42.18	Educational psychology	–	–	–	201	1,316	421	–
42.19	Psychometrics and quantitative psychology.............................	–	–	–	1	51	4	–
42.20	Clinical child psychology	–	–	–	–	18	30	–
42.21	Environmental psychology	–	–	–	21	9	5	–
42.22	Geropsychology	–	–	–	–	–	4	–
42.23	Health psychology.....................	–	–	–	12	35	15	–
42.24	Psychopharmacology................	–	–	–	–	35	–	–
42.25	Family psychology.....................	3	3	1	35	19	23	–
42.26	Forensic psychology	–	–	–	436	477	20	–
42.99	Psychology, other......................	42	–	124	903	879	276	–
43.	**Security and protective services ....**	**22,009**	**6,113**	**27,707**	**37,000**	**4,625**	**88**	**–**
43.01	Criminal justice and corrections .	15,821	4,412	23,449	36,415	4,191	87	–
43.0102	Corrections..............................	3,845	215	891	525	7	–	–
43.0103	Criminal justice/law enforcement administration	351	292	5,471	9,463	1,453	28	–
43.0104	Criminal justice/safety studies..	529	703	6,866	21,885	1,847	55	–
43.0106	Forensic science and technology..............................	460	88	278	460	478	1	–
43.0107	Criminal justice/police science .	9,244	2,963	9,115	1,657	86	2	–
43.0109	Security and loss prevention services..................................	700	23	118	76	32	–	–
43.0110	Juvenile corrections	–	15	4	2	–	–	–

- None reported

Table VI–1. Earned awards and degrees, by field of study, 2005–06 — Continued

2000 Classification of Instructional Program (CIP) code and title		Awards of less than 1 academic year	1- to 4- year awards	Associate degrees	Bachelor's degrees	Master's degrees or post-baccalaureate certificates	Doctoral degrees or post-master's certificates	First professional degrees or certificates
43.0111	Criminalistics and criminal science	447	14	42	305	–	–	–
43.0112	Securities services administration/management	88	9	62	6	18	–	–
43.0113	Corrections administration	–	–	11	64	7	–	–
43.0199	Corrections and criminal justice, other	157	90	591	1,972	263	1	–
43.02	Fire protection	5,871	1,458	3,738	464	58	1	–
43.0201	Fire protection and safety technology/technician	810	53	1,145	177	3	–	–
43.0202	Fire services administration	162	28	180	206	9	–	–
43.0203	Fire science/fire-fighting	4,850	1,371	2,394	46	8	–	–
43.0299	Fire protection, other	49	6	19	35	38	1	–
43.99	Security and protective services, other	317	243	520	121	376	–	–
44.	**Public administration and social services professions**	**823**	**520**	**4,522**	**23,097**	**31,059**	**768**	**–**
44.00	Human services, general	406	267	1,299	2,076	568	25	–
44.02	Community organization and advocacy	78	110	1,233	2,114	692	3	–
44.04	Public administration and social services professions	54	67	111	2,680	9,301	180	–
44.05	Public policy analysis	–	–	13	942	1,858	162	–
44.07	Social work	194	49	1,778	14,321	17,623	369	–
44.0701	Social work	177	33	1,733	14,260	17,550	369	–
44.0702	Youth services/administration	–	4	–	34	8	–	–
44.0799	Social work, other	17	12	45	27	65	–	–
44.99	Public administration and social services professions, other	91	21	88	964	1,017	29	–
45.	**Social sciences**	**377**	**226**	**6,353**	**142,456**	**14,903**	**3,411**	**–**
45.01	Social sciences, general	3	19	4,964	8,532	706	25	–
45.02	Anthropology	11	4	99	8,579	1,138	526	–
45.0201	Anthropology	11	4	99	8,533	1,118	521	–
45.0202	Physical anthropology	–	–	–	–	10	–	–
45.0299	Anthropology, other	–	–	–	46	10	5	–
45.03	Archaeology	79	5	15	202	32	7	–
45.04	Criminology	–	–	26	6,049	577	25	–
45.05	Demography and population studies	–	–	–	–	28	14	–
45.06	Economics	6	1	293	26,787	2,973	1,060	–
45.0601	Economics, general	6	1	293	25,595	2,278	1,017	–
45.0602	Applied economics	–	–	–	181	163	24	–
45.0603	Econometrics and quantitative economics	–	–	–	143	8	2	–
45.0604	Development economics and international development	–	–	–	189	326	5	–
45.0605	International economics	–	–	–	207	142	10	–
45.0699	Economics, other	–	–	–	472	56	2	–
45.07	Geography and cartography	151	170	147	4,613	1,014	259	–
45.0701	Geography	49	21	45	4,403	904	256	–
45.0702	Cartography	63	61	73	101	49	2	–
45.0799	Geography, other	39	88	29	109	61	1	–
45.09	International relations and affairs	25	8	28	8,763	3,656	73	–
45.10	Political science and government	33	11	211	44,292	2,108	725	–
45.1001	Political science and government, general	23	6	201	43,191	1,925	703	–
45.1002	American government and politics (United States)	–	–	10	145	147	–	–

- None reported

Table VI–1. Earned awards and degrees, by field of study, 2005–06 — Continued

2000 Classification of Instructional Program (CIP) code and title		Awards of less than 1 academic year	1- to 4- year awards	Associate degrees	Bachelor's degrees	Master's degrees or post-baccalaureate certificates	Doctoral degrees or post-master's certificates	First professional degrees or certificates
45.1099	Political science and government, other	10	5	–	956	36	22	–
45.11	Sociology	47	8	476	31,482	1,549	608	–
45.12	Urban studies/affairs	–	–	2	958	453	52	–
45.99	Social sciences, other	22	–	92	2,199	669	37	–
46.	**Construction trades**	**11,145**	**10,840**	**3,860**	**147**	**–**	**–**	**–**
46.00	Construction trades, general	309	492	224	–	–	–	–
46.01	Mason/masonry	456	248	38	–	–	–	–
46.02	Carpentry/carpenter	1,693	1,711	524	2	–	–	–
46.03	Electrical and power transmission installers	4,247	5,773	1,895	1	–	–	–
46.0301	Electrical and power transmission installation/installer, general	140	170	181	–	–	–	–
46.0302	Electrician	4,052	5,085	1,553	1	–	–	–
46.0303	Lineworker	53	452	108	–	–	–	–
46.0399	Electrical and power transmission installers, other	2	66	53	–	–	–	–
46.04	Building/construction finishing, management, and inspection	1,226	1,357	615	93	–	–	–
46.0401	Building/property maintenance and management	705	881	114	–	–	–	–
46.0402	Concrete finishing/concrete finisher	9	–	–	–	–	–	–
46.0403	Building/home/construction inspection/inspector	226	204	114	11	–	–	–
46.0404	Drywall installation/drywaller	1	–	–	–	–	–	–
46.0406	Glazier	11	–	–	–	–	–	–
46.0408	Painting/painter and wall coverer	24	3	1	–	–	–	–
46.0410	Roofer	4	–	–	–	–	–	–
46.0411	Metal building assembly/assembler	31	11	–	–	–	–	–
46.0412	Building/construction site management/manager	37	84	106	6	–	–	–
46.0499	Building/construction finishing, management, and inspection, other	178	174	280	76	–	–	–
46.05	Plumbing and related water supply services	984	979	300	–	–	–	–
46.0502	Pipefitting/pipefitter and sprinkler fitter	141	126	242	–	–	–	–
46.0503	Plumbing technology/plumber	793	849	55	–	–	–	–
46.0504	Well drilling/driller	–	–	2	–	–	–	–
46.0599	Plumbing and related water supply services, other	50	4	1	–	–	–	–
46.99	Construction trades, other	2,230	280	264	51	–	–	–
47.	**Mechanic and repair technologies/technicians**	**20,735**	**47,128**	**17,949**	**305**	**–**	**–**	**–**
47.00	Mechanics and repairers, general	–	17	232	–	–	–	–
47.01	Electrical/electronics maintenance and repair technology	3,029	2,885	1,973	95	–	–	–
47.0101	Electrical/electronics equipment installation and repair, general	871	1,187	592	–	–	–	–
47.0102	Business machine repair	–	9	2	–	–	–	–
47.0103	Communications systems installation and repair technology	130	120	224	44	–	–	–

- None reported

Table VI–1. Earned awards and degrees, by field of study, 2005–06 — Continued

2000 Classification of Instructional Program (CIP) code and title		Awards of less than 1 academic year	1- to 4- year awards	Associate degrees	Bachelor's degrees	Master's degrees or post-baccalaureate certificates	Doctoral degrees or post-master's certificates	First professional degrees or certificates
47.0104	Computer installation and repair technology/technician	972	680	360	51	–	–	–
47.0105	Industrial electronics technology/technician	857	570	718	–	–	–	–
47.0106	Appliance installation and repair technology/technician	10	77	4	–	–	–	–
47.0110	Security system installation, repair, and inspection technology/technician	–	26	–	–	–	–	–
47.0199	Electrical/electronics maintenance and repair technology, other	189	216	73	–	–	–	–
47.02	Heating, air conditioning, ventilation, and refrigeration maintenance	4,315	5,960	1,224	–	–	–	–
47.03	Heavy/industrial equipment maintenance technologies	1,357	1,365	619	12	–	–	–
47.0302	Heavy equipment maintenance technology/technician	86	272	214	11	–	–	–
47.0303	Industrial mechanics and maintenance technology	1,164	922	327	1	–	–	–
47.0399	Heavy/industrial equipment maintenance technologies, other	107	171	78	–	–	–	–
47.04	Precision systems maintenance and repair technologies	251	1,622	184	–	–	–	–
47.0402	Gunsmithing/gunsmith	38	47	101	–	–	–	–
47.0403	Locksmithing and safe repair	37	12	–	–	–	–	–
47.0404	Musical instrument fabrication and repair	78	94	10	–	–	–	–
47.0408	Watchmaking and jewelrymaking	76	139	63	–	–	–	–
47.0409	Parts and warehousing operations/maintenance technology/technician	–	10	–	–	–	–	–
47.0499	Precision systems maintenance and repair technologies, other	22	1,320	10	–	–	–	–
47.06	Vehicle maintenance and repair technologies	11,554	34,563	13,353	198	–	–	–
47.0603	Autobody/collision and repair technology/technician	1,481	4,535	1,209	1	–	–	–
47.0604	Automobile/automotive mechanics technology/ technician	7,524	20,624	6,270	23	–	–	–
47.0605	Diesel mechanics technology/ technician	1,100	2,673	1,591	22	–	–	–
47.0606	Small engine mechanics and repair technology/technician	213	334	9	–	–	–	–
47.0607	Airframe mechanics and aircraft maintenance technology/ technician	159	2,098	456	66	–	–	–
47.0608	Aircraft powerplant technology/ technician	265	975	2,306	–	–	–	–
47.0609	Avionics maintenance technology/technician	19	201	1,042	86	–	–	–
47.0611	Motorcycle maintenance and repair technology/technician	588	2,390	29	–	–	–	–
47.0612	Vehicle emissions inspection/ maintenance technology/ technician	14	–	–	–	–	–	–
47.0613	Medium/heavy vehicle and truck technology/technician	23	68	28	–	–	–	–
47.0615	Engine machinist	5	18	1	–	–	–	–

- None reported

Table VI–1. Earned awards and degrees, by field of study, 2005–06 — Continued

2000 Classification of Instructional Program (CIP) code and title		Awards of less than 1 academic year	1- to 4- year awards	Associate degrees	Bachelor's degrees	Master's degrees or post-baccalaureate certificates	Doctoral degrees or post-master's certificates	First professional degrees or certificates
47.0616	Marine maintenance/fitter and ship repair technology/ technician	74	255	78	–	–	–	–
47.0699	Vehicle maintenance and repair technologies, other	89	392	334	–	–	–	–
47.99	Mechanic and repair technologies/technicians, other	229	716	364	–	–	–	–
48.	**Precision production**	**6,954**	**7,378**	**1,994**	**56**	**9**	**–**	**–**
48.03	Leatherworking and upholstery	153	133	7	–	–	–	–
48.0303	Upholstery/upholsterer	153	123	1	–	–	–	–
48.0304	Shoe, boot, and leather repair	–	10	–	–	–	–	–
48.0399	Leatherworking and upholstery, other	–	–	6	–	–	–	–
48.05	Precision metal working	6,591	6,796	1,840	17	–	–	–
48.0501	Machine tool technology/ machinist	1,346	771	575	–	–	–	–
48.0503	Machine shop technology/ assistant	615	859	236	–	–	–	–
48.0506	Sheet metal technology/ sheetworking	170	203	64	–	–	–	–
48.0507	Tool and die technology/ technician	51	257	227	2	–	–	–
48.0508	Welding technology/welder	4,317	4,639	687	15	–	–	–
48.0509	Ironworking/ironworker	48	37	29	–	–	–	–
48.0599	Precision metal working, other	44	30	22	–	–	–	–
48.07	Woodworking	167	317	69	39	9	–	–
48.0701	Woodworking, general	2	11	3	–	–	–	–
48.0702	Furniture design and manufacturing	33	39	3	39	9	–	–
48.0703	Cabinetmaking and millwork/ millwright	132	239	60	–	–	–	–
48.0799	Woodworking, other	–	28	3	–	–	–	–
48.08	Boilermaking/boilermaker	–	–	3	–	–	–	–
48.99	Precision production, other	43	132	75	–	–	–	–
49.	**Transportation and materials moving**	**20,939**	**1,761**	**2,185**	**5,450**	**784**	**1**	**–**
49.01	Air transportation	1,383	62	1,675	5,127	764	–	–
49.0101	Aeronautics/aviation/aerospace science and technology, general	–	5	609	2,752	10	–	–
49.0102	Airline/commercial/professional pilot and flight crew	170	26	489	1,364	666	–	–
49.0104	Aviation/airway management and operations	869	16	332	807	41	–	–
49.0105	Air traffic controller	28	1	231	187	–	–	–
49.0106	Airline flight attendant	46	14	12	–	–	–	–
49.0108	Flight instructor	1	–	–	7	–	–	–
49.0199	Air transportation, other	269	–	2	10	47	–	–
49.02	Ground transportation	19,063	880	54	–	–	–	–
49.0202	Construction/heavy equipment/ earthmoving equipment operation	204	260	7	–	–	–	–
49.0205	Truck and bus driver/ commercial vehicle operation	17,969	598	4	–	–	–	–
49.0299	Ground transportation, other	890	22	43	–	–	–	–
49.03	Marine transportation	318	570	23	304	–	–	–
49.0304	Diver, professional and instructor	312	542	7	–	–	–	–

- None reported

Table VI–1. Earned awards and degrees, by field of study, 2005–06 — Continued

2000 Classification of Instructional Program (CIP) code and title		Awards of less than 1 academic year	1- to 4- year awards	Associate degrees	Bachelor's degrees	Master's degrees or post-baccalaureate certificates	Doctoral degrees or post-master's certificates	First professional degrees or certificates
49.0309	Marine science/merchant marine officer	5	28	16	304	–	–	–
49.0399	Marine transportation, other	1	–	–	–	–	–	–
49.99	Transportation and materials moving, other	175	249	433	19	20	1	–
50.	**Visual and performing arts**	**5,930**	**6,942**	**21,943**	**87,070**	**14,044**	**1,698**	**–**
50.01	Visual and performing arts, general	10	91	520	2,108	115	18	–
50.02	Crafts/craft design, folk art and artisanry	8	3	5	173	11	–	–
50.03	Dance, general	33	37	79	1,763	209	2	–
50.0301	Dance, general	32	35	79	1,697	204	–	–
50.0302	Ballet	–	–	–	27	5	–	–
50.0399	Dance, other	1	2	–	39	–	2	–
50.04	Design and applied arts	1,208	2,690	13,998	18,433	1,319	17	–
50.0401	Design and visual communications, general	72	154	1,715	3,637	187	4	–
50.0402	Commercial and advertising art	434	858	4,069	3,094	330	9	–
50.0404	Industrial design	4	–	47	1,202	85	–	–
50.0406	Commercial photography	203	213	553	1	13	–	–
50.0407	Fashion/apparel design	76	206	2,161	1,689	48	–	–
50.0408	Interior design	250	760	2,549	3,375	228	–	–
50.0409	Graphic design	154	406	2,343	3,821	170	4	–
50.0410	Illustration	10	9	25	866	50	–	–
50.0499	Design and applied arts, othe	5	84	536	748	208	–	–
50.05	Drama/theatre arts and stagecraft	139	773	781	10,463	1,687	98	–
50.0501	Drama and dramatics/theatre arts, general	44	124	378	9,259	1,222	91	–
50.0502	Technical theatre/theatre design and technology	13	14	286	257	82	–	–
50.0504	Playwriting and screenwriting	–	10	8	103	101	3	–
50.0505	Theatre literature, history, and criticism	–	2	–	18	2	2	–
50.0506	Acting	82	78	107	527	137	–	–
50.0507	Directing and theatrical production	–	2	–	31	45	1	–
50.0508	Theatre/theatre arts management	–	–	–	34	10	–	–
50.0599	Dramatic/theatre arts and stagecraft, other	–	543	2	234	88	1	–
50.06	Film/video and photographic arts	302	689	2,322	7,669	1,076	22	–
50.0601	Film/cinema studies	33	5	16	2,350	321	20	–
50.0602	Cinematography and film/video production	146	129	1,467	2,526	516	2	–
50.0605	Photography	123	326	669	1,869	195	–	–
50.0699	Film/video and photographic arts, other	–	229	170	924	44	–	–
50.07	Fine and studio art	3,166	1,235	1,653	31,393	3,907	276	–
50.0701	Art/art studies, general	24	1,047	1,103	13,849	731	7	–
50.0702	Fine/studio arts, general	3	41	274	9,145	1,407	13	–
50.0703	Art history, criticism, and conservation	–	–	2	3,688	649	255	–
50.0704	Arts management	3	5	13	515	321	1	–
50.0705	Drawing	7	8	39	279	40	–	–
50.0706	Intermedia/multimedia	7	4	50	798	71	–	–
50.0708	Painting	–	32	–	793	198	–	–
50.0709	Sculpture	6	15	10	284	58	–	–
50.0710	Printmaking	4	2	3	158	58	–	–

- None reported

Table VI–1. Earned awards and degrees, by field of study, 2005–06 — Continued

2000 Classification of Instructional Program (CIP) code and title		Awards of less than 1 academic year	1- to 4- year awards	Associate degrees	Bachelor's degrees	Master's degrees or post-baccalaureate certificates	Doctoral degrees or post-master's certificates	First professional degrees or certificates
50.0711	Ceramic arts and ceramics	7	2	5	198	49	–	–
50.0712	Fiber, textile, and weaving arts.	–	2	2	129	32	–	–
50.0713	Metal and jewelry arts	3,104	73	17	106	33	–	–
50.0799	Fine arts and art studies, other	1	4	135	1,451	260	–	–
50.08	Music	1,016	1,423	2,486	14,595	5,279	1,233	–
50.0901	Music, general	63	90	595	7,429	1,585	453	–
50.0902	Music history, literature, and theory	1	–	1	104	50	15	–
50.0903	Music performance, general.....	–	399	143	4,028	2,288	483	–
50.0904	Music theory and composition..	–	33	5	473	234	59	–
50.0905	Musicology and ethnomusicology	–	–	–	23	55	48	–
50.0906	Conducting	–	–	–	–	121	41	–
50.0907	Piano and organ	–	1	2	125	195	52	–
50.0908	Voice and opera	–	2	2	250	204	26	–
50.0909	Music management and merchandising	90	137	147	1,031	7	–	–
50.0910	Jazz/jazz studies	–	1	2	213	80	12	–
50.0911	Violin, viola, guitar, and other stringed instruments	–	4	–	135	145	21	–
50.0912	Music pedagogy	–	2	–	64	48	2	–
50.0999	Music, other	862	754	1,589	720	267	21	–
50.99	Visual and performing arts, other	48	1	99	473	441	32	–
51.	**Health professions and related clinical sciences ....**	**166,164**	**148,978**	**138,496**	**94,084**	**53,794**	**8,052**	**39,894**
51.00	Health services/allied health/ health sciences, general	215	423	624	2,307	156	10	–
51.01	Chiropractic (DC)	–	–	–	–	–	–	2,564
51.02	Communication disorder sciences and services	30	14	140	6,349	5,508	1,013	–
51.0201	Communication disorders, general	1	–	11	1,805	1,136	33	–
51.0202	Audiology/audiologist and hearing sciences	2	–	5	106	127	847	–
51.0203	Speech-language pathology/ pathologist	17	–	67	906	1,889	32	–
51.0204	Audiology/audiologist and speech-language pathology/ pathologist	9	14	38	3,451	2,302	80	–
51.0299	Communication disorders sciences and services, other ...	1	–	19	81	54	21	–
51.04	Dentistry (DDS, DMD)	–	–	–	–	–	–	4,465
51.05	Advanced/graduate dentistry and oral sciences (Cert, MS, PhD) .	–	–	–	–	483	106	503
51.0501	Dental clinical sciences, general (MS, PhD)	–	–	–	–	246	66	48
51.0502	Advanced general dentistry (Cert, MS, PhD)	–	–	–	–	9	–	173
51.0503	Oral biology and oral pathology (MS, PhD)	–	–	–	–	40	8	–
51.0504	Dental public health and education (Cert, MS/MPH, PhD/DPH)	–	–	–	–	6	–	1
51.0505	Dental materials (MS, PhD)	–	–	–	–	1	–	–
51.0506	Endodontics/endodontology (Cert, MS, PhD)	–	–	–	–	13	5	61
51.0507	Oral/maxillofacial surgery (Cert, MS, PhD)	–	–	–	–	2	–	20
51.0508	Orthodontics/orthodontology (Cert, MS, PhD)	–	–	–	–	59	13	56

- None reported

Table VI–1. Earned awards and degrees, by field of study, 2005–06 — Continued

2000 Classification of Instructional Program (CIP) code and title		Awards of less than 1 academic year	1- to 4- year awards	Associate degrees	Bachelor's degrees	Master's degrees or post-baccalaureate certificates	Doctoral degrees or post-master's certificates	First professional degrees or certificates
51.0509	Pediatric dentistry/pedodontics (Cert, MS, PhD)	–	–	–	–	12	–	52
51.0510	Periodontics/periodontology (Cert, MS, PhD)	–	–	–	–	25	3	40
51.0511	Prosthodontics/ prosthodontology (Cert, MS, PhD)	–	–	–	–	17	–	29
51.0599	Advanced/graduate dentistry and oral sciences, other	–	–	–	–	53	11	23
51.06	Dental support services and allied professions	7,768	7,610	6,369	1,435	45	–	–
51.0601	Dental assisting/assistant	7,433	7,181	1,171	–	–	–	–
51.0602	Dental hygiene/hygienist	121	205	4,986	1,410	34	–	–
51.0603	Dental laboratory technology/ technician	104	209	189	10	5	–	–
51.0699	Dental services and allied professions, other	110	15	23	15	6	–	–
51.07	Health and medical administrative services	26,246	19,258	9,436	5,089	6,194	113	–
51.0701	Health/health care administration/management	48	94	249	3,518	5,192	86	–
51.0702	Hospital and health care facilities administration/ management	25	18	3	540	619	11	–
51.0703	Health unit coordinator/ward clerk	852	56	5	–	–	–	–
51.0704	Health unit manager/ward supervisor	–	–	6	–	8	–	–
51.0705	Medical office management/ administration	2,466	1,094	1,175	2	7	–	–
51.0706	Health information/medical records administration/ administrator	670	828	207	588	27	–	–
51.0707	Health information/medical records technology/technician	1,179	1,900	2,424	–	8	6	–
51.0708	Medical transcription/ transcriptionist	1,100	1,135	146	–	–	–	–
51.0709	Medical office computer specialist/assistant	320	65	78	–	–	–	–
51.0710	Medical office assistant/ specialist	2,663	2,742	669	1	–	–	–
51.0711	Medical/health management and clinical assistant/specialist	313	161	162	14	8	–	–
51.0712	Medical reception/receptionist	444	154	15	–	–	–	–
51.0713	Medical insurance coding specialist/coder	5,065	2,760	357	–	–	–	–
51.0714	Medical insurance specialist/ medical biller	4,273	1,862	734	–	–	–	–
51.0715	Health/medical claims examiner	73	–	–	–	–	–	–
51.0716	Medical administrative/ executive assistant and medical secretary	3,931	5,543	2,725	–	–	–	–
51.0717	Medical staff services technology/technician	61	–	29	2	–	–	–
51.0799	Health and medical administrative services, other	2,763	846	452	424	325	10	–
51.08	Allied health and medical assisting services	47,913	37,958	22,694	346	71	32	–
51.0801	Medical/clinical assistant	34,311	30,301	12,383	6	–	–	–
51.0802	Clinical/medical laboratory assistant	673	134	97	–	–	–	–
51.0803	Occupational therapist assistant	4	25	1,620	–	–	–	–

- None reported

Table VI–1. Earned awards and degrees, by field of study, 2005–06 — Continued

2000 Classification of Instructional Program (CIP) code and title		Awards of less than 1 academic year	1- to 4- year awards	Associate degrees	Bachelor's degrees	Master's degrees or post-baccalaureate certificates	Doctoral degrees or post-master's certificates	First professional degrees or certificates
51.0805	Pharmacy technician/assistant.	7,570	4,478	1,342	–	–	–	–
51.0806	Physical therapist assistant......	536	204	3,209	32	–	32	–
51.0808	Veterinary/animal health technology/technician/ veterinary assistant..................	794	384	2,822	221	1	–	–
51.0809	Anesthesiologist assistant........	–	–	31	–	31	–	–
51.0810	Emergency care attendant (EMT ambulance)	766	2	–	–	–	–	–
51.0811	Pathology/pathologist assistant	–	–	–	2	4	–	–
51.0812	Respiratory therapy technician/ assistant..................................	–	88	165	3	–	–	–
51.0813	Chiropractic assistant/ technician................................	–	1	8	–	–	–	–
51.0899	Allied health and medical assisting services, other...........	3,259	2,341	1,017	82	35	–	–
51.09	Allied health diagnostic, intervention, and treatment professions..............................	17,266	16,418	22,234	6,287	4,030	3	–
51.0901	Cardiovascular technology/ technologist.............................	765	907	416	53	4	–	–
51.0902	Electrocardiograph technology/ technician................................	156	50	19	1	–	–	–
51.0903	Electro-neurodiagnostic/ electro-encephalographic technology/technician	36	27	36	–	–	–	–
51.0904	Emergency medical technology/technician (EMT paramedic)..............................	14,149	3,694	2,001	87	26	–	–
51.0905	Nuclear medical technology/ technologist.............................	35	273	422	305	–	–	–
51.0906	Perfusion technology/ perfusionist.............................	–	–	–	13	34	–	–
51.0907	Medical radiologic technology/ science—radiation therapist	709	1,953	6,384	953	7	–	–
51.0908	Respiratory care therapy/ therapist	102	568	5,310	506	–	–	–
51.0909	Surgical technology/ technologist.............................	426	5,520	2,340	2	–	–	–
51.0910	Diagnostic medical sonography/sonographer and ultrasound technician..............	260	1,930	1,183	278	4	–	–
51.0911	Radiologic technology/ science—radiographer............	296	1,132	3,783	566	13	3	–
51.0912	Physician assistant..................	28	141	118	1,231	3,738	–	–
51.0913	Athletic training/trainer.............	54	17	32	2,080	170	–	–
51.0914	Gene/genetic therapy..............	–	–	–	21	–	–	–
51.0916	Radiation protection/health physics technician....................	7	–	1	14	5	–	–
51.0999	Allied health diagnostic/ intervention/treatment professions, other	243	206	189	177	29	–	–
51.10	Clinical/medical laboratory science and allied professions.	5,192	1,153	2,250	2,136	420	8	–
51.1001	Blood bank technology specialist.................................	477	25	–	–	–	–	–
51.1002	Cytotechnology/ cytotechnologist.......................	5	28	1	97	25	–	–
51.1003	Hematology technology/ technician................................	131	–	–	–	6	–	–
51.1004	Clinical/medical laboratory technician................................	192	558	2,114	48	–	–	–
51.1005	Clinical laboratory science/ medical technology/ technologist.............................	70	52	19	1,890	299	1	–

- None reported

2000 Classification of Instructional Program (CIP) code and title		Awards of less than 1 academic year	1- to 4- year awards	Associate degrees	Bachelor's degrees	Master's degrees or post-baccalaureate certificates	Doctoral degrees or post-master's certificates	First professional degrees or certificates
51.1006	Ophthalmic laboratory technology/technician	16	20	–	–	–	–	–
51.1007	Histologic technology/ histotechnologist	–	12	28	–	–	–	–
51.1008	Histologic technician	17	66	26	–	–	–	–
51.1009	Phlebotomy/phlebotomist	3,799	253	7	–	–	–	–
51.1010	Cytogenetics/genetics/ clinical genetics technology/ technologist	–	1	–	11	–	–	–
51.1011	Renal/dialysis technologist/ technician	81	43	2	–	–	–	–
51.1099	Clinical/medical laboratory science and allied professions, other	404	95	53	90	90	7	–
51.11	Health/medical preparatory programs	43	36	1,032	1,752	284	–	–
51.1101	Pre-dentistry studies	–	–	33	66	17	–	–
51.1102	Pre-medicine/pre-medical studies	2	–	233	748	175	–	–
51.1103	Pre-pharmacy studies	–	–	112	117	–	–	–
51.1104	Pre-veterinary studies	–	8	55	116	–	–	–
51.1105	Pre-nursing studies	37	20	244	8	–	–	–
51.1199	Health/medical preparatory programs, other	4	8	355	697	92	–	–
51.12	Medicine (MD)	–	–	–	–	–	–	15,969
51.14	Medical clinical sciences/ graduate medical studies	–	–	–	–	191	56	–
51.15	Mental and social health services and allied professions	3,140	1,659	2,896	1,767	3,104	242	–
51.1501	Substance abuse/addiction counseling	456	923	941	192	151	40	–
51.1502	Psychiatric/mental health services technician	242	561	1,061	109	19	–	–
51.1503	Clinical/medical social work	12	1	134	135	308	11	–
51.1504	Community health services/ liaison/counseling	113	16	87	892	182	7	–
51.1505	Marriage and family therapy/ counseling	–	4	–	4	1,425	104	–
51.1506	Clinical pastoral counseling/ patient counseling	–	–	–	4	88	13	–
51.1507	Psychoanalysis and psychotherapy	–	–	–	–	4	10	–
51.1508	Mental health counseling/ counselor	–	–	21	1	471	37	–
51.1509	Genetic counseling/counselor	–	–	–	2	59	–	–
51.1599	Mental and social health services and allied professions, other	2,317	154	652	428	397	20	–
51.16	Nursing	36,429	52,109	64,852	54,645	14,863	975	–
51.1601	Nursing/registered nurse (RN, ASN, BSN, MSN)	1,397	5,253	62,421	52,082	5,731	212	–
51.1602	Nursing administration (MSN, MS, PhD)	–	3	4	193	827	97	–
51.1603	Adult health nurse/nursing	–	–	100	9	407	20	–
51.1604	Nurse anesthetist	–	–	–	–	1,260	9	–
51.1605	Family practice nurse/nurse practitioner	–	6	2	–	1,399	66	–
51.1606	Maternal/child health and neonatal nurse/nursing	–	–	6	–	192	21	–
51.1607	Nurse midwife/nursing midwifery	–	–	–	–	88	1	–
51.1608	Nursing science (MS, PhD)	–	1	–	729	2,379	255	–

- None reported

Table VI–1. Earned awards and degrees, by field of study, 2005–06 — Continued

2000 Classification of Instructional Program (CIP) code and title		Awards of less than 1 academic year	1- to 4- year awards	Associate degrees	Bachelor's degrees	Master's degrees or post-baccalaureate certificates	Doctoral degrees or post-master's certificates	First professional degrees or certificates
51.1609	Pediatric nurse/nursing	–	–	–	–	146	4	–
51.1610	Psychiatric/mental health nurse/nursing	–	–	–	–	128	42	–
51.1611	Public health/community nurse/ nursing	–	–	–	–	229	–	–
51.1612	Perioperative/operating room and surgical nurse/nursing	61	–	–	–	25	–	–
51.1613	Licensed practical/vocational nurse training	4,883	43,409	1,713	9	–	–	–
51.1614	Nurse/nursing assistant/aide and patient care assistant	28,711	1,072	101	–	–	–	–
51.1616	Clinical nurse specialist	–	–	–	2	99	–	–
51.1617	Critical care nursing	–	–	–	–	103	1	–
51.1618	Occupational and environmental health nursing	–	–	–	–	5	–	–
51.1699	Nursing, other	1,377	2,365	505	1,621	1,845	247	–
51.17	Optometry (OD)	–	–	–	–	–	–	1,227
51.18	Ophthalmic and optometric support services and allied professions	370	115	397	38	61	1	–
51.1801	Opticianry/ophthalmic dispensing optician	258	22	250	–	–	–	–
51.1802	Optometric technician/assistant	81	57	99	–	–	–	–
51.1803	Ophthalmic technician/ technologist	20	29	44	7	–	–	–
51.1899	Ophthalmic/optometric support services and allied professions, other	11	7	4	31	61	1	–
51.19	Osteopathic medicine/ osteopathy (DO)	–	–	–	–	–	–	2,718
51.20	Pharmacy, pharmaceutical sciences, and administration	87	56	1	639	568	495	9,461
51.2001	Pharmacy (PharmD [USA], PharmD or BS/BPharm [Canada])	–	–	–	244	–	–	9,461
51.2002	Pharmacy administration/policy/ regulatory affairs (MS, PhD)	–	–	–	–	144	13	–
51.2003	Pharmaceutics and drug design (MS, PhD)	–	–	–	152	100	199	–
51.2004	Medicinal and pharmaceutical chemistry (MS, PhD)	–	–	–	18	25	87	–
51.2005	Natural products chemistry and pharmacognosy (MS, PhD)	–	–	–	–	1	11	–
51.2006	Clinical and industrial drug development (MS, PhD)	–	–	–	10	177	2	–
51.2007	Pharmacoeconomics/ pharmaceutical economics (MS, PhD)	–	–	–	–	–	2	–
51.2008	Clinical, hospital, and managed care pharmacy (MS, PhD)	–	–	–	–	3	32	–
51.2009	Industrial and physical pharmacy and cosmetic sciences (MS, PhD)	–	–	–	–	9	–	–
51.2099	Pharmacy, pharmaceutical sciences, and administration, other	87	56	1	215	109	149	–
51.21	Podiatric medicine/podiatry (DPM)	–	–	–	–	–	–	354
51.22	Public health	50	68	329	2,205	7,024	528	–
51.2201	Public health, general (MPH, DPH)	15	22	6	447	4,486	283	–
51.2202	Environmental health	1	2	17	213	344	50	–
51.2205	Health/medical physics	3	28	–	15	36	2	–

- None reported

Table VI–1. Earned awards and degrees, by field of study, 2005–06 — Continued

2000 Classification of Instructional Program (CIP) code and title		Awards of less than 1 academic year	1- to 4- year awards	Associate degrees	Bachelor's degrees	Master's degrees or post-baccalaureate certificates	Doctoral degrees or post-master's certificates	First professional degrees or certificates
51.2206	Occupational health and industrial hygiene	–	1	89	66	85	11	–
51.2207	Public health education and promotion	3	6	–	686	502	37	–
51.2208	Community health and preventive medicine	2	2	7	353	76	28	–
51.2209	Maternal and child health	–	–	–	–	102	6	–
51.2210	International public health/ international health	–	–	–	1	100	–	–
51.2211	Health services administration	26	2	132	217	439	10	–
51.2299	Public health, other	–	5	78	207	854	101	–
51.23	Rehabilitation and therapeutic professions	297	50	666	3,843	7,203	4,045	47
51.2301	Art therapy/therapist	4	–	2	93	247	9	–
51.2302	Dance therapy/therapist	–	–	–	–	18	–	–
51.2305	Music therapy/therapist	–	3	–	244	54	1	–
51.2306	Occupational therapy/therapist	–	–	95	1,288	2,484	76	–
51.2307	Orthotist/prosthetist	7	30	64	20	26	55	–
51.2308	Physical therapy/therapist	–	–	165	780	3,144	3,842	47
51.2309	Therapeutic recreation/ recreational therapy	49	8	50	384	33	3	–
51.2310	Vocational rehabilitation counseling/counselor	–	–	16	220	863	12	–
51.2311	Kinesiotherapy/kinesiotherapist	47	2	–	21	3	1	–
51.2312	Assistive/augmentative technology and rehabilitation engineering	–	–	–	–	–	1	–
51.2399	Rehabilitation and therapeutic professions, other	190	7	274	793	331	45	–
51.24	Veterinary medicine (DVM)	–	–	–	–	–	–	2,370
51.25	Veterinary biomedical and clinical sciences (Cert, MS, PhD)	–	14	–	61	236	120	–
51.2501	Veterinary sciences/veterinary clinical sciences, general (Cert, MS, PhD)	–	14	–	61	196	99	–
51.2502	Veterinary anatomy (Cert, MS, PhD)	–	–	–	–	1	3	–
51.2503	Veterinary physiology (Cert, MS, PhD)	–	–	–	–	2	6	–
51.2504	Veterinary microbiology and immunobiology (Cert, MS, PhD)	–	–	–	–	5	3	–
51.2505	Veterinary pathology and pathobiology (Cert, MS, PhD)	–	–	–	–	3	4	–
51.2506	Veterinary toxicology and pharmacology (Cert, MS, PhD)	–	–	–	–	1	2	–
51.2507	Large animal/food animal and equine surgery/medicine (Cert, MS, PhD)	–	–	–	–	2	1	–
51.2508	Small/companion animal surgery and medicine (Cert, MS, PhD)	–	–	–	–	2	–	–
51.2509	Comparative and laboratory animal medicine (Cert, MS, PhD)	–	–	–	–	14	–	–
51.2510	Veterinary preventive medicine epidemiology and public health (Cert, MS, PhD)	–	–	–	–	1	–	–
51.2511	Veterinary infectious diseases (Cert, MS, PhD)	–	–	–	–	5	2	–

- None reported

Table VI–1. Earned awards and degrees, by field of study, 2005–06 — Continued

2000 Classification of Instructional Program (CIP) code and title	Awards of less than 1 academic year	1- to 4- year awards	Associate degrees	Bachelor's degrees	Master's degrees or post-baccalaureate certificates	Doctoral degrees or post-master's certificates	First professional degrees or certificates
51.2599 Veterinary biomedical and clinical sciences, other (Cert, MS, PhD)	–	–	–	–	4	–	–
51.26 Health aides/attendants/orderlies	3,182	288	50	–	–	–	–
51.2601 Health aide	1,220	218	14	–	–	–	–
51.2602 Home health aide/home attendant	1,576	40	–	–	–	–	–
51.2603 Medication aide	310	–	–	–	–	–	–
51.2699 Health aides/attendants/orderlies, other	76	30	36	–	–	–	–
51.27 Medical illustration and informatics	–	3	1	44	130	13	–
51.2703 Medical illustration/medical illustrator	–	3	–	36	25	–	–
51.2706 Medical informatics	–	–	1	8	105	13	–
51.31 Dietetics and clinical nutrition services	223	47	362	1,719	468	16	–
51.3101 Dietetics/dietitian (RD)	82	1	61	1,660	359	15	–
51.3102 Clinical nutrition/nutritionist	–	–	–	14	72	1	–
51.3103 Dietetic technician (DTR)	13	26	108	–	–	–	–
51.3104 Dietitian assistant	90	18	166	–	–	–	–
51.3199 Dietetics and clinical nutrition services, other	38	2	27	45	37	–	–
51.32 Bioethics/medical ethics	–	–	–	8	114	23	–
51.33 Alternative and complementary medicine and medical systems	18	146	2	140	1,747	58	216
51.3301 Acupuncture	–	120	–	63	1,195	19	–
51.3302 Traditional Chinese/Asian medicine and Chinese herbology	–	–	–	41	552	21	–
51.3303 Naturopathic medicine/naturopathy (ND)	–	–	–	–	–	18	216
51.3304 Homeopathic medicine/homeopathy	–	24	–	–	–	–	–
51.3399 Alternative and complementary medicine and medical systems, other	18	2	2	36	–	–	–
51.34 Alternative and complementary medical support services	–	28	38	11	–	1	–
51.3401 Direct entry midwifery (LM, CPM)	–	24	–	1	–	1	–
51.3499 Alternative and complementary medical support services, other	–	4	38	10	–	–	–
51.35 Somatic bodywork and related therapeutical services	16,779	10,831	3,049	1	–	–	–
51.3501 Massage therapy/therapeutic massage	16,759	10,831	3,049	1	–	–	–
51.3502 Asian bodywork therapy	12	–	–	–	–	–	–
51.3599 Somatic bodywork and related therapeutic services, other	8	–	–	–	–	–	–
51.36 Movement and mind-body therapies and education	65	175	–	23	19	9	–
51.3601 Movement therapy and movement education	–	–	–	18	19	9	–
51.3602 Yoga teacher training/yoga therapy	37	–	–	–	–	–	–
51.3603 Hypnotherapy/hypnotherapist	28	175	–	–	–	–	–
51.3699 Movement and mind-body therapies and education, other	–	–	–	5	–	–	–
51.37 Energy and biologically based therapies	18	–	–	17	13	–	–
51.3702 Herbalism/herbalist	2	–	–	17	13	–	–

- None reported

Table VI–1. Earned awards and degrees, by field of study, 2005–06 — Continued

2000 Classification of Instructional Program (CIP) code and title		Awards of less than 1 academic year	1- to 4- year awards	Associate degrees	Bachelor's degrees	Master's degrees or post-baccalaureate certificates	Doctoral degrees or post-master's certificates	First professional degrees or certificates
51.3703	Polarity therapy	16	–	–	–	–	–	–
51.99	Health professions and related clinical sciences, other	833	519	1,074	3,222	862	185	–
52.	**Business, management, marketing, and related support services**	**40,932**	**23,592**	**101,612**	**339,217**	**154,456**	**2,135**	**–**
52.01	Business/commerce, general	1,342	1,100	13,366	23,851	9,683	242	–
52.02	Business administration, management, and operations	6,848	3,628	46,116	142,454	92,675	957	–
52.0201	Business administration and management, general	4,533	2,870	39,724	129,998	86,305	877	–
52.0202	Purchasing, procurement/ acquisitions, and contracts management	52	3	178	329	224	–	–
52.0203	Logistics and materials management	240	64	891	1,254	477	–	–
52.0204	Office management and supervision	690	362	1,806	825	20	–	–
52.0205	Operations management and supervision	585	141	935	2,265	978	11	–
52.0206	Non-profit/public/organizational management	11	20	11	482	621	11	–
52.0207	Customer service management	281	1	3	40	3	–	–
52.0208	E-commerce/electronic commerce	45	38	90	334	474	10	–
52.0209	Transportation/transportation management	–	1	2	88	31	1	–
52.0299	Business administration, management, and operations, other	411	128	2,476	6,839	3,542	47	–
52.03	Accounting and related services	5,227	4,589	14,047	43,656	11,372	99	–
52.0301	Accounting	2,437	1,701	7,610	42,132	10,276	96	–
52.0302	Accounting technology/ technician and bookkeeping	2,304	2,546	5,920	95	2	–	–
52.0303	Auditing	–	–	–	25	46	–	–
52.0304	Accounting and finance	40	13	15	705	733	–	–
52.0305	Accounting and business/ management	16	21	320	336	55	–	–
52.0399	Accounting and related services, other	430	308	182	363	260	3	–
52.04	Business operations support and assistant services	12,349	9,557	10,511	737	73	–	–
52.0401	Administrative assistant and secretarial science, general	4,469	5,582	7,181	363	4	–	–
52.0402	Executive assistant/executive secretary	1,807	555	1,729	49	–	–	–
52.0406	Receptionist	80	100	–	–	–	–	–
52.0407	Business/office automation/ technology/data entry	1,643	1,428	1,049	198	–	–	–
52.0408	General office occupations and clerical services	1,883	1,125	294	47	–	–	–
52.0411	Customer service support/call center/teleservice operation	1,852	22	20	–	–	–	–
52.0499	Business operations support and secretarial services, other	615	745	238	80	69	–	–
52.05	Business/corporate communications	18	6	40	486	113	–	–
52.06	Business/managerial economics	12	14	11	4,738	357	51	–
52.07	Entrepreneurial and small business operations	1,048	266	442	1,451	524	–	–
52.0701	Entrepreneurship/ entrepreneurial studies	669	80	227	1,250	417	–	–

- None reported

Table VI–1. Earned awards and degrees, by field of study, 2005–06 — Continued

2000 Classification of Instructional Program (CIP) code and title		Awards of less than 1 academic year	1- to 4- year awards	Associate degrees	Bachelor's degrees	Master's degrees or post-baccalaureate certificates	Doctoral degrees or post-master's certificates	First professional degrees or certificates
52.0702	Franchising and franchise operations	1	–	–	–	1	–	–
52.0703	Small business administration/ management	320	178	196	176	78	–	–
52.0799	Entrepreneurial and small business operations, other	58	8	19	25	28	–	–
52.08	Finance and financial management services	773	819	724	32,600	6,557	106	–
52.0801	Finance, general	10	28	227	30,846	5,203	88	–
52.0803	Banking and financial support services	686	749	447	582	178	2	–
52.0804	Financial planning and services	5	29	6	208	306	–	–
52.0806	International finance	1	–	–	11	169	1	–
52.0807	Investments and securities	22	1	–	623	255	–	–
52.0808	Public finance	–	–	–	–	–	13	–
52.0809	Credit management	–	–	16	–	–	–	–
52.0899	Finance and financial management services, other	49	12	28	330	446	2	–
52.09	Hospitality administration/ management	1,129	690	3,223	7,304	679	27	–
52.0901	Hospitality administration/ management, general	186	129	971	4,025	274	15	–
52.0903	Tourism and travel services management	286	162	547	489	172	–	–
52.0904	Hotel/motel administration/ management	377	270	1,171	1,844	161	9	–
52.0905	Restaurant/food services management	19	107	188	340	34	–	–
52.0906	Resort management	6	1	22	45	–	–	–
52.0999	Hospitality administration/ management, other	255	21	324	561	38	3	–
52.10	Human resources management and services	931	329	2,073	11,055	10,313	296	–
52.1001	Human resources management/personnel administration, general	739	116	1,717	5,931	4,683	71	–
52.1002	Labor and industrial relations	21	189	301	1,051	703	9	–
52.1003	Organizational behavior studies	80	1	39	3,209	2,883	207	–
52.1004	Labor studies	–	12	13	99	1	1	–
52.1005	Human resources development	87	–	–	313	711	8	–
52.1099	Human resources management and services, other	4	11	3	452	1,332	–	–
52.11	International business	193	127	317	5,913	3,504	38	–
52.12	Management information systems and services	639	793	2,228	11,348	7,387	36	–
52.1201	Management information systems, general	561	430	1,898	10,860	7,020	17	–
52.1206	Information resources management/CIO training	11	16	3	139	261	19	–
52.1207	Knowledge management	–	–	–	11	57	–	–
52.1299	Management information systems and services, other	67	347	327	338	49	–	–
52.13	Management sciences and quantitative methods	7	7	105	5,839	2,766	24	–
52.1301	Management science, general	7	7	105	4,960	2,144	10	–
52.1302	Business statistics	–	–	–	47	27	5	–
52.1304	Actuarial science	–	–	–	480	112	–	–
52.1399	Management sciences and quantitative methods, other	–	–	–	352	483	9	–
52.14	Marketing	321	237	2,064	36,550	3,509	51	–

- None reported

Table VI–1. Earned awards and degrees, by field of study, 2005–06 — Continued

2000 Classification of Instructional Program (CIP) code and title		Awards of less than 1 academic year	1- to 4- year awards	Associate degrees	Bachelor's degrees	Master's degrees or post-baccalaureate certificates	Doctoral degrees or post-master's certificates	First professional degrees or certificates
52.1401	Marketing/marketing management, general	284	215	1,988	35,149	3,256	43	–
52.1402	Marketing research	–	–	–	69	85	–	–
52.1403	International marketing	10	16	24	22	77	–	–
52.1499	Marketing, other	27	6	52	1,310	91	8	–
52.15	Real estate	3,184	268	362	1,207	531	86	–
52.16	Taxation	59	29	15	–	1,273	23	–
52.17	Insurance	247	26	3	820	86	8	–
52.18	General sales, merchandising, and related marketing operations	4,328	415	2,052	2,593	416	3	–
52.1801	Sales, distribution, and marketing operations, general	347	251	821	1,588	394	3	–
52.1802	Merchandising and buying operations	1	–	16	151	8	–	–
52.1803	Retailing and retail operations	207	94	238	189	7	–	–
52.1804	Selling skills and sales operations	3,714	33	684	283	2	–	–
52.1899	General merchandising/sales/related marketing operations, other	59	37	293	302	5	–	–
52.19	Specialized sales, merchandising, and marketing operations	1,870	529	2,604	2,634	93	–	–
52.1901	Auctioneering	16	–	–	–	–	–	–
52.1902	Fashion merchandising	11	51	1,957	1,767	1	–	–
52.1903	Fashion modeling	8	–	–	–	–	–	–
52.1904	Apparel and accessories marketing operations	20	7	80	115	6	–	–
52.1905	Tourism and travel services marketing operations	263	101	181	32	1	–	–
52.1906	Tourism promotion operations	7	205	162	75	–	–	–
52.1907	Vehicle and vehicle parts and accessories marketing operations	73	57	108	264	–	–	–
52.1908	Business and personal/financial services marketing operations	1,412	1	43	14	–	–	–
52.1909	Special products marketing operations	54	92	12	136	17	–	–
52.1910	Hospitality and recreation marketing operations	2	11	53	83	–	–	–
52.1999	Specialized merchandising, sales, and marketing operations, other	4	4	8	148	68	–	–
52.20	Construction management	63	15	85	1,258	118	–	–
52.99	Business, management, marketing, and related support services, other	344	148	1,224	2,723	2,427	88	–
54.	**History**	**4**	**7**	**430**	**36,629**	**3,061**	**1,020**	**–**
54.01	History	4	7	430	36,629	3,061	1,020	–
54.0101	History, general	3	7	403	35,854	2,923	928	–
54.0102	American history (United States)	–	–	7	79	20	8	–
54.0103	European history	–	–	–	32	–	1	–
54.0104	History and philosophy of science and technology	–	–	–	126	41	34	–
54.0105	Public/applied history and archival administration	1	–	8	29	45	30	–
54.0106	Asian history	–	–	–	1	–	3	–
54.0199	History, other	–	–	12	508	32	16	–

- None reported

Appendix. Sources of State and Local Labor Market and Career Information

State employment security agencies develop detailed information about local labor markets, such as information on current and projected employment by occupation and industry, characteristics of the workforce, and changes in State and local area economic activity. Listed in this appendix are the Internet addresses of these agencies and addresses and telephone numbers of their directors of research and analysis. State occupational projections also are available on the Internet at **http://www.projectionscentral.com.**

Alabama
Labor Market Information Division, Alabama Department of Industrial Relations, 649 Monroe St., Room 422, Montgomery, AL 36131. Telephone: (334) 242-8859. Internet: **http://dir.alabama.gov**

Alaska
Research and Analysis Section, Department of Labor and Workforce Development, P.O. Box 25501, Juneau, AK 99802-5501. Telephone: (907) 465-4500. Internet: **http://www.jobs.state.ak.us**

Arizona
Arizona Department of Economic Security, P.O. Box 6123 SC 733A, Phoenix, AZ 85005-6123. Telephone: (602) 542-5984. Internet: **http://www.workforce.az.gov**

Arkansas
Labor Market Information, Department of Workforce Services, #2 Capital Mall, Little Rock, AR 72201. Telephone: (501) 682-3198. Internet: **http://www.arkansas.gov/esd**

California
State of California Employment Development Department, Labor Market Information Division, P.O. Box 826880, Sacramento, CA 94280-0001. Telephone: (916) 262-2162. Internet: **http://www.labormarketinfo.edd.ca.gov**

Colorado
Labor Market Information, Colorado Department of Labor and Employment, 633 17th St., Suite 201, Denver, CO 80202-3660.Telephone: (303) 318-8000.Internet: **http://www.coworkforce.com/lmi**

Connecticut
Office of Research, Connecticut Department of Labor, 200 Folly Brook Blvd., Wethersfield, CT 06109-1114.Telephone: (860) 263-6275.Internet: **http://www.ctdol.state.ct.us/lmi**

Delaware
Office of Occupational and Labor Market Information, Department of Labor, 19 West Lea Blvd., Wilmington, DE 19802-. Telephone: (302) 761-8069.
Internet: **http://www.delawareworks.com/oolmi/welcome.shtml**

District of Columbia
DC Department of Employment Services, 609 H St. NE., Washington, D.C. 20002. Telephone: (202) 724-7000.
Internet: **http://www.does.dc.gov/does**

Florida
Labor Market Statistics, Agency for Workforce Innovation, MSC G-020, 107 E. Madison St., Tallahassee, FL 32399-4111.Telephone: (850) 245-7205.Internet: **http://www.labormarketinfo.com**

Georgia
Workforce Information and Analysis, Room 300, Department of Labor, 223 Courtland St., CWC Building, Atlanta, GA 30303. Telephone: (404) 232-3875. Internet:
http://www.dol.state.ga.us/em/get_labor_market_information.htm

Guam
Guam Department of Labor, 504 D St., Tiyan, Guam 96910.
Telephone: (671) 475-0101.

Hawaii
Research and Statistics Office, Department of Labor and Industrial Relations, 830 Punchbowl St., Room 304, Honolulu, HI 96813.
Telephone: (808) 586-8999. Internet: **http://www.hiwi.org**

Idaho
Research and Analysis Bureau, Department of Commerce and Labor, 317 West Main St., Boise, ID 83735-0670. Telephone: (208) 332-3570. Internet: **http://lmi.idaho.gov**

Illinois
Illinois Department of Employment Security, Economic Information and Analysis Division, 33 S. State St., 9th Floor , Chicago, IL 60603. Telephone: (312) 793-2316. Internet: **http://lmi.ides.state.il.us**

Indiana
Research and Analysis—Indiana Workforce Development, Indiana Government Center South, 10 North Senate Ave., Indianapolis, IN 46204. Telephone: (800) 891-6499. Internet: **http://www.in.gov/dwd**

Iowa
Policy and Information Division, Iowa Workforce Development, 1000 East Grand Ave., Des Moines, IA 50319-0209. Telephone: (515) 281-5116 Internet: **http://www.iowaworkforce.org/lmi**

Kansas
Kansas Department of Labor, Labor Market Information Services, 401 SW Topeka Blvd., Topeka, KS 66603-3182. Telephone: (785) 296-5000. Internet: **http://laborstats.dol.ks.gov**

Kentucky
Research and Statistics Branch, Office of Employment and Training, 275 East Main St., Frankfort, KY 40621.Telephone: (502) 564-7976. Internet: **http://www.workforcekentucky.ky.gov**

Louisiana
Research and Statistics Division, Department of Labor, 1001 North 23rd St., Baton Rouge, LA 70802-3338. Telephone: (225) 342-3111. Internet: **http://www.laworks.net**

Maine
Labor Market Information Services Division, Maine Department of Labor, State House Station 54, P.O. Box 259 45 Commerce Dr., Augusta, ME 04330.Telephone: (207) 621-5182.
Internet: **http://www.state.me.us/labor/lmis/index.html**

Maryland
Maryland Department of Labor Licensing and Regulation, Office of Labor Market Analysis and Information, Room 316, 1100 N. Eutaw, Baltimore, MD 21201.Telephone: (410) 767-2250. Internet: **http://www.dllr.state.md.us/lmi/index.htm**

Massachusetts
Executive Office of Labor and Workforce Development, Division of Career Services, 19 Staniford St., Boston, MA 02114.Telephone: (617) 626-5300.Internet: **http://www.detma.org/LMIdataprog.htm**

Michigan
Bureau of Labor Market Information and Strategic Initiatives, Department of Labor and Economic Growth, 3032 West Grand Blvd., Suite 9-100, Detroit, MI 48202.Telephone: (313) 456-3090. Internet: **http://www.milmi.org**

Minnesota
Department of Employment and Economic Development, Labor Market Information Office, 1st National Bank Building, 332 Minnesota St., Suite E200, St. Paul, MN 55101-1351. Telephone: (888) 234-1114.Internet: **http://www.deed.state.mn.us/lmi**

Mississippi
Labor Market Information Division, Mississippi Department of Employment Security , 1235 Echelon Pkwy., P.O. Box 1699, Jackson, MS 39215. Telephone: (601) 321-6000. Internet: **http://mdes.ms.gov**

Missouri
Missouri Economic Research and Information Center, P.O. Box 3150, Jefferson City, MO 65102-3150. Telephone: (866) 225-8113. Internet. **http://www.missourieconomy.org**

Montana
Research and Analysis Bureau, P.O. Box 1728, Helena, MT 59624. Telephone: (800) 541-3904. Internet: **http://www.ourfactsyourfuture.org**

Nebraska
Nebraska Workforce Development—Labor Market Information, Nebraska Department of Labor, 550 South 16tth St., P.O. Box 94600, Lincoln, NE 68509. Telephone: (402) 471-2600. Internet: **http://www.dol.state.ne.us/nelmi.htm**

Nevada
Research and Analysis, Department of Employment Training and Rehabilitation, 500 East Third St., Carson City, NV 89713. Telephone: (775) 684-0450. Internet: **http://www.nevadaworkforce.com**

New Hampshire
Economic and Labor Market Information Bureau, New Hampshire Employment Security, 32 South Main St., Concord, NH 03301-4857. Telephone: (603) 228-4124. Internet: **http://www.nhes.state.nh.us/elmi**

New Jersey
Division of Labor Market and Demographic Research, Department of Labor and Workforce Development, P.O. Box 388, Trenton, NJ 08625-0388. Telephone: (609) 984-2593.Internet: **http://www.wnjpin.net**

New Mexico
New Mexico Department of Labor, Economic Research and Analysis, 401 Broadway NE., Albuquerque, NM 87102. Telephone: (505) 222-4683. Internet: **http://www.dws.state.nm.us/dws-lmi.html**

New York
Research and Statistics, New York State Department of Labor, State Office Campus, Room 490, Albany, NY 12240. Telephone: (518) 457-2919. Internet: **http://www.labor.state.ny.us/workforceindustrydata/index.asp**

North Carolina
Labor Market Information Division, Employment Security Commission, 700 Wade Ave., Raleigh, NC 27605. Telephone: (919) 733-4329. Internet: **http://www.ncesc.com**

North Dakota
Labor Market Information Manager, Job Service North Dakota, 1000 East Divide Ave., Bismarck, ND 58506. Telephone: (800) 732-9787. Internet: **http://www.ndworkforceintelligence.com**

Ohio
Bureau of Labor Market Information, Office of Workforce Development, Ohio Department of Job and Family Services, P.O. Box 1618, Columbus, OH 43216-1618.Telephone: (614) 752-9494.
Internet: **http://www.ohioworkforceinformer.org**

Oklahoma
Labor Market Information, Oklahoma Employment Security Commission, 2401 N. Lincoln Blvd., Oklahoma City, OK 73105. Telephone: (405) 557-7100. Internet:
http://www.oesc.state.ok.us/lmi/default.htm

Oregon
Oregon Employment Department, Research Division, 875 Union St. NE., Salem, OR 97311.Telephone: (503) 947-1200. Internet: **http://www.qualityinfo.org/olmisj/OlmisZine**

Pennsylvania
Center for Workforce Information & Analysis, Pennsylvania Department of Labor and Industry, 220 Labor and Industry Building, Seventh and Forster Sts., Harrisburg, PA 17121. Telephone: (877) 493-3282. Internet: **http://www.paworkstats.state.pa.us**

Puerto Rico
Labor Market Information Office, P.O. Box 195540, San Juan, Puerto Rico 00919-5540.Telephone: (787) 281-5760. Internet:
http://www.dtrh.gobierno.pr/oficina_procurador_del_trabajo.asp

Rhode Island
Labor Market Information, Rhode Island Department of Labor and Training, 1511 Pontiac Ave., Cranston, RI 02920. Telephone: (401) 462-8740. Internet: **http://www.dlt.ri.gov/lmi**

South Carolina
Labor Market Information Department, South Carolina Employment Security Commission, 631 Hampton St., Columbia, SC 29202. Telephone: (803) 737-2660. Internet: **http://www.sces.org/lmi/index.asp**

South Dakota
Labor Market Information Center, Department of Labor, P.O. Box 4730, Aberdeen, SD 57402-4730. Telephone: (605) 626-2314. Internet: **http://www.state.sd.us/dol/lmic/index.htm**

Tennessee
Research and Statistics Division, Department of Labor and Workforce Development, 710 James Robertson Pkwy., Nashville, TN 37243. Telephone: (615) 741-6642. Internet:
http://www.state.tn.us/labor-wfd/lmi.htm

Texas
Labor Market Information, Texas Workforce Commission, 9001 North IH-35, Suite 103A, Austin, TX 75753. Telephone: (866) 938-4444. Internet: **http://www.tracer2.com**

Utah
Director of Workforce Information, Utah Department of Workforce Services, P.O. Box 45249, Salt Lake City, UT 84145-0249. Telephone: (801) 526-9675. Internet: **http://jobs.utah.gov/opencms/wi**

Vermont
Research and Analysis, Vermont Department of Labor, P.O. Box 488, Montpelier, VT 05601-0488. Telephone: (802) 828-4000. Internet: **http://www.labor.vermont.gov**

Virgin Islands
Bureau of Labor Statistics, Department of Labor, P.O. Box 302608, St Thomas, VI 00803-2608.Telephone: (340) 776-3700. Internet: **http://www.vidol.gov**

Virginia
Economic Information Services, Virginia Employment Commission, P.O. Box 1358, Richmond, VA 23218-1358. Telephone: (804) 786-8223. Internet: **http://velma.virtuallmi.com**

Washington
Labor Market and Economic Analysis, Washington Employment Security Department, PO Box 9046, Olympia, WA 98507-9046. Telephone: (800) 215-1617. Internet: **http://www.workforceexplorer.com**

West Virginia
WORKFORCE West Virginia, Research, Information and Analysis Division, 112 California Ave., Charleston, WV 25303-0112.Telephone: (304) 558-2660.Internet: **http://www.wvbep.org/bep/lmi**

Wisconsin
Bureau of Workforce Information, Department of Workforce Development, P.O.Box 7944, Madison, WI 53707-7944. Telephone: (608) 266-8212. Internet: **http://worknet.wisconsin.gov/worknet**

Wyoming
Research and Planning, Wyoming Department of Employment, 246 S. Center St., Casper, WY 82602. Telephone: (307) 473-3807. Internet: **http://doe.state.wy.us/lmi**